John Addington Symonds

Renaissance in Italy - Italian literature

John Addington Symonds

Renaissance in Italy - Italian literature

ISBN/EAN: 9783742858054

Manufactured in Europe, USA, Canada, Australia, Japa

Cover: Foto ©Thomas Meinert / pixelio.de

Manufactured and distributed by brebook publishing software
(www.brebook.com)

John Addington Symonds

Renaissance in Italy - Italian literature

ITALIAN LITERATURE

In Two Parts

BY

JOHN ADDINGTON SYMONDS

AUTHOR OF

'STUDIES OF THE GREEK POETS' 'SKETCHES IN ITALY AND GREECE' ETC.

' Italia, sepoltura
De' lumi suoi, d' esterni candeliere'

CAMPANELLA : *Poesie Filosofiche*

PART II.

LONDON

SMITH, ELDER, & CO., 15 WATERLOO PLACE

1881

RENAISSANCE IN ITALY

CONTENTS

OF

THE SECOND PART

———◆◇◆———

CHAPTER IX.

THE ORLANDO FURIOSO.

CHAPTER X.

THE NOVELLIERI.

CHAPTER XI.

THE DRAMA.

CHAPTER XV.

PIETRO ARETINO.

CHAPTER XVI.

HISTORY AND PHILOSOPHY.

CHAPTER XVII.

CONCLUSION.

APPENDICES.

RENAISSANCE IN ITALY.

CHAPTER IX.

THE ORLANDO FURIOSO.

Orlando Furioso and *Divina Commedia*—Ariosto expresses the Renaissance as Dante the Middle Ages—Definition of Romantic, Heroic, Burlesque, Heroic-comic, and Satiric Poems—Ariosto's Bias toward Romance—Sense of Beauty in the *Cinque Cento*—Choice of Boiardo's unfinished Theme—The Propriety of this Choice—Ariosto's Irony and Humour—The Subject of the *Furioso*—Siege of Paris—Orlando's Madness—Loves of Ruggiero and Bradamante—Flattery of the House of Este—The World of Chivalry—Ariosto's Delight in the Creatures of his Fancy—Close Structure of the Poem—Exaggeration of Motives—Power of Picture-painting—Faculty of Vision—Minute Description—Rhetorical Amplification—Rapidity of Movement—Solidity—Nicety of Ethical Analysis—The Introductions to the Cantos—Episodes and *Novelle*—Imitations of the Classics—Power of Appropriation and Transmutation—Irony—Astolfo's Journey to the Moon—Ariosto's Portrait—S. Michael in the Monastery—The Cave of Sleep—Humour - Pathos and Sublimity—Olimpia and Bireno—Conception of Female Character—The Heroines—Passion and Love—Ariosto's Morality—His Style—The Epithet of Divine—Exquisite Finish—Ariosto and Tasso—Little Landscape-Painting—Similes—Realism—Adaptation of Homeric Images—Ariosto's Relation to his Age.

ARIOSTO'S Satires make us know the man *intus et in cute*—to the very core. The lyrics have a breadth and amplitude of style that mark no common master of the poet's craft. Yet neither the Satires nor the Lyrics reveal the author of the *Furioso*. The artist in Ariosto was greater than the man; and the *Furioso* conceived and executed with no reference to the poet's personal experience, enthroned him as the Orpheus of his age. The *Orlando Furioso* gave full and final expression to the *cinque cento*, just as the *Divina Commedia* uttered the last word of the middle ages. The two supreme Italian singers stood in the same relation to their several epochs. Dante immortalised medieval thoughts and aspirations at the moment when they were already losing their reality for the Italian people. Separated from him by a short interval of time, came Petrarch, who substituted the art of poetry for the prophetic inspiration ; and while Petrarch was yet singing, Boccaccio anticipated in his multifarious literature the age of the Renaissance. Then the evolution of Italian literature was interrupted by the classical revival ; and when Ariosto appeared, it was his duty to close the epoch which Petrarch had inaugurated and Boccaccio had determined, by a poem investing Boccaccio's world, the sensuous world of the Renaissance, with the refined artistic form of Petrarch. This he accomplished. But even while he was at work, Italy underwent those political and mental changes, in the wars of invasion, in the sack of Rome, in the siege of Florence, in the Spanish occupation, in the reconstruction of the Papacy beneath the pressure of Luther's schism, which ended the Renaissance and opened a new age with Tasso for its poet. Those, therefore, who would comprehend the spirit of Italy upon the point of transition from the middle ages, must study the Divine Comedy. Those who would contemplate the genius of the Renaissance, consummated and conscious of its aim, upon the very verge of trasmutation and eventual ruin, must turn to the *Orlando Furioso*. It seems to be a law of intellectual development that the highest works of art can only be achieved when the forces which produced them are already doomed and in the act of disappearance.[1]

Italian critics have classified their narrative poems, of which the name is legion, into Romantic, Heroic, Burlesque, Heroic-comic, and Satiric.[2] The romantic poet is one who having formed a purely imaginary world, deals with the figments of his fancy as though they were realities. His object is to astonish, fascinate, amuse and interest his readers. Nothing comes amiss to him, whether the nature of the material be comic or tragic, pathetic or satiric, miraculous or commonplace, impossible or natural, so long as it contributes grace and charm to the picture of adventurous existence he desires to paint. His aim is not instruction; nor does he seek to promote laughter. Putting all serious purposes aside, he creates a wonderland, wherein the actions and passions of mankind shall be displayed, with truth to nature, under the strongly coloured light of the artistic phantasy. The burlesque poet enters the same enchanted region; but he deliberately degrades it below the level of common life, parodies the fanciful extravagances of romance, and seeks to raise a laugh at the expense of its most delicate illusions. The heroic poet has nothing to do

---

[1] Students who care to trace the thoughts and characters of this great poem to their sources, should read Pio Rajna's exhaustive essay, *Le Fonti dell' Orlando Furioso*, Firenze, Sansoni, 1876. The details of the *Orlando* are here investigated and referred with scientific patience to Greek, Latin, French, Italian, and other originals. If anything, Signor Rajna may seem to have overstrained the point of critical sagacity. It is hardly probable that Ariosto, reader of few books as Virginio says he was, should have drawn on stores so multifarious of erudition.

[2] See Ugo Foscolo's essay on the Narrative and Romantic Poems of Italy in the *Quarterly Review* for April 1819.

with pure romance and pleasurable fiction. He deals with the truths of history, resolving to embellish them by art, to extract lessons of utility, to magnify the virtues and the valour of the noblest men, and to in-flame his audience with the fire of lofty aspiration. His object, unlike that of the romancer, is essentially serious. He is less anxious to produce a work of pure beauty than to raise a monument of ideal and moralised sublimity. The heroic-comic poet adopts the tone, style, conduct and machinery of the heroic manner; but he employs his art on some trivial or absurd subject, making his ridicule of baseness and pettiness the more pungent by the mock-gravity of his treatment. Unlike the burlesque writer, he does not aim at mere scurrility. There is always method in his buffoonery, and a satiric purpose in his parody. The satirist strikes more directly ; he either attacks manners, customs, institutions, and persons without disguise, or he does so under a thin veil of parable. He differs from the heroic-comic poet chiefly in this, that he does not array himself in the epical panoply. Within the range of Italian literature we find ready examples of these several styles. Boiardo and Ariosto are romantic poets. The *Morgante Maggiore* is a romance with considerable elements of burlesque and satire mingled.[1] Tasso's *Gerusalemme Liberata* is a fair specimen of the heroic, and Tassoni's *Secchia Rapita* of the heroic-comic species. The *Ricciardetto* of Fortiguerri and Folengo's *Orlandino* represent burlesque, while Casti's *Animali Parlanti* is a narrative satire.

It may seem at first sight strange that Ariosto

[1] Especially in Morgante and Margutte.

should have preferred the romantic to the heroic style of poetry, and that/the epic of the Italian Renaissance should be a pure play of the fancy. Yet this was no less natural to the man revealed in his Epistles, than to the spirit of his century as we have learned to know it. The passions and convictions that give force to patriotism, to religion, and to morality, were extinct in Italy ; nor was Ariosto an exception to the general temper of his age. Yet the heroic style demands some spiritual motive analogous to the enthusiasm for Rome which inspired Virgil, or to the faith that touched the lips of Milton with coals from the altar. An indolent and tranquil epicurean, indifferent to the world around him, desiring nothing better than a life among his books, with leisure for his loves and day-dreams, had not the fibre of a true heroic poet ; and where in Italy could Ariosto have found a proper theme ? Before he settled to the great work of his life, he began a poem in *terza rima* on the glories of the House of Este. That was meant to be heroic ; but the fragment which remains, proves how frigid, how all unsuited to his genius and his times, this insincere and literary epic would have been.[1] Italy offered elements of greatness only to a prophet or a satirist. She found her prophet in Michelangelo. But what remained for a poet like Ariosto, without Danté's anger or Swift's indignation, without the humour of Cervantes or the fire of Juvenal, without Tasso's piety or Shakspere's England, yet equal as an artist to the greatest singers whom the world has known ? The answer to this question is not far to seek. What really survived of noble and enthu-

[1] See *Capitolo* iii.

siastic in the *cinque cento* was the sense of beauty, the adoration of form, the worship of art. The supreme artist of his age obeyed a right instinct when he undertook a work which required no sublime motive, and which left him free for the production of a master-piece of beauty. In this sphere the defects of his nature were not felt, and he became the mouthpiece of his age in all that still remained of greatness to his country.

In like manner we can explain to ourselves Ariosto's choice of Boiardo's unfinished theme. He was not a poet with something irresistible to say, but an artist seeking a fit theatre for the exercise of his omnipotent skill. He did not feel impelled to create, but to embellish. Boiardo had constructed a vast hall in the style of the Renaissance, when it first usurped on Gothic; he had sketched a series of frescoes for the adornment of its walls and roof, and then had died, leaving his work incomplete. To enrich the remaining panels with pictures conceived in the same spirit, but executed in a freer and a grander manner, to adorn them with all that the most wealthy and fertile fancy could conceive, and to bestow upon them perfect finish, was a task for which Ariosto was eminently suited. Nor did he vary from the practice of the greatest masters in the other arts, who willingly lent their own genius to the continuation of designs begun by pre-decessors. Few craftsmen of the Renaissance thought as much of the purpose of their work or of its main motive as of execution in detail and richness of effect. They lacked the classic sense of unity, the medieval sincerity and spontaneity of inspiration. Therefore Ariosto was contented to receive from Boiardo a theme he could embroider and make beautiful, with full employment of his rare inventive gifts upon a multitude of episodical inventions. It is vain to regret that a poet of his calibre should not have bent his faculties to the task of a truly original epic—to the re-awakening of prostrate Italy, to the scourging of her feebleness and folly, or even to the celebration of her former glories. Had he done either of these things, his poem would not have been so truly national, and we should have lacked the final product of a most brilliant though defective period of civilisation.

Ariosto's own temperament and the conditions of his age alike condemned him to the completion of a romance longer than the *Iliad* and the *Odyssey* together, which has for its sole serious aim, if serious aim it has of any sort, the glorification of an obscure family, and which, while it abounds in pathos, wisdom, wit, and poetry of dazzling brilliance, may at the same time be accused of levity, adulation, and licentiousness. To arraign Ariosto for these faults is tantamount to arraigning his whole century and nation. The greatest artist of the sixteenth century found no task worthier of his genius then to flatter the House of Este with false pedigrees and fulsome praises. He had no faith that could prevent him from laughing at all things human and divine, not, indeed, with the Titanic play of Aristophanes, whose merriment is but the obverse of profound seriousness, but with the indulgent nonchalance of an epicurean. No sentiment of sublimity raised him above the grosser atmosphere in which love is tainted with lust, luxurious images are sought for their own sake,

and passion dwindles in the languor of voluptuousness. The decay of liberty, the relaxation of morals
and the corruption of the Church had brought the
Italians to this point, that their representative Renaissance poem is stained with flattery, contaminated
with licentiousness, enfeebled with levity. Poetic
beauty of the highest order it cannot claim. That
implies more earnestness of purpose and an ideal of
sublimer purity. Still, though the *Furioso* misses the
supreme beauty of the *Iliad*, the *Antigone* and the
Paradise Lost, it has in superfluity that secondary
beauty which expressed itself less perfectly in Italian
painting. In one respect it stands almost alone. The
form reveals no inequalities or flaws. This artist's
hand has never for a moment lost its cunning ; this
Homer never nods.

Pulci approached the romance of Charlemagne
from a *bourgeois* point of view. He felt no sincere
sympathy with the knightly or the religious sentiment
of his originals. Boiardo treated similar material in a
chivalrous spirit. The novelty of his poem consisted
in the fusion of the Carolingian and Arthurian Cycles ;
for while he handled an episode of the former group,
he felt sincere admiration for errant knighthood as
figured in the tales of Lancelot and Tristram.
Throughout the *Orlando Innamorato* we trace the
vivid influence of feudal ideals. Ariosto differed in
his attitude from both of his predecessors. The irony
that gives a special quality to his romance, is equally
removed from the humour of Pulci and the frank enthusiasm of Boiardo. Ariosto was neither the citizen
of a free burgh playing with the legends of a bygone

age, nor yet the highborn noble in whose eyes the adventures of Orlando and his comrades formed a picture of existence as it ought to be. / He was a courtier and a man of letters, and his poem is a masterpiece of courtly and literary art. / Boiardo never flattered the princes of the House of Este. Ariosto took every occasion to interweave their panegyric with his verse. For Boiardo the days of chivalry were a glorious irrecoverable golden age. / Ariosto contemplated this mythical past less with the regret of a man who had fallen upon worse days, than with the satisfaction of an artist who perceives the rare opportunities for poetic handling it afforded. He does not really believe in chivalry, where Boiardo is in earnest, Ariosto jests. It is not that, like Cervantes, he sought to satirise the absurdities of romance, or that he set himself, like Folengo, to burlesque the poems of his predecessors; but his philosophy inclined him to watch the doings of humanity with a genial half-smile, an all-pervasive irony that had no sting in it. / A poet who stands thus aside and contemplates the comedy of the world with the dry light of a kindly and indulgent intellect, could not treat the tales of Paladins and giants seriously. He uses them as the machinery of a great work on human life, painting mankind, not as he thinks it ought to be, but as he finds it. This treatment of romance from the standpoint of good sense and quiet humour produces an apparent discrepancy between his practical knowledge of the world and his fanciful extravagance. In the artistic harmony effected by Ariosto between these opposite elements lies the secret of his irony. His worldly wisdom has the solidity of prose

and embraces every circumstance of life. The creatures of his imagination belong to fairyland and exceed
the wildest dreams in waywardness. He smiles to see
them play their pranks; yet he never loses sight of
reality, and moves his puppets by impulses and passions worthy of real men and women. Having
granted the romantic elements of wonder and exaggeration for a basis, we find the superstructure to be
natural. Never was sagacity of insight combined
more perfectly with exuberance of fancy and a joyous
lightheartedness than in this poem. Nowhere else
have sound lessons in worldly wisdom been conveyed
upon a stage of so much palpable impossibility.

We may here ask what is the main subject of the
Orlando Furioso. The poem has three chief sources
of interest—the siege of Paris and the final rout of the
Saracen army, the insanity of Orlando, and the loves
of Ruggiero and Bradamante. The first serves merely
as a groundwork for embroidery, a background for relieving more attractive incidents. Orlando's madness,
though it gives its name to the romance, is subordinate to the principal action. It forms a proper development of the situation in the *Orlando Innamorato*;
and Ariosto intends it to be important, because he
frequently laments that the Paladin's absence from the
field injured the cause of Christendom. But Charlemagne, by help of Rinaldo, Bradamante, and Marfisa,
conquers without Orlando's aid. Thus the hero's insanity is only operative in neutralising an influence
that was not needed; and when he regains his wits, he
performs no critical prodigies of valour. Finding the
Saracens expelled from France, and Charlemagne at

peace, Orlando fights a duel with a crownless king upon a desert island more for show than for real service. Far different is the remaining motive of the poem. If the *Furioso* can be said to have constructive unity, the central subject is the love and marriage of Ruggiero. Ariosto found this solution of the plot foreshadowed in the *Innamorato.* The pomp and ceremony with which the fourth book opens, the value attached to the co-operation of Ruggiero in the war with Charlemagne, and the romantic beginning of his love for Bradamante, make it clear that Boiardo would have crowned his poem, as Ariosto has done, with the union of the ancestors of Casa d' Este. Flattery, moreover, was Ariosto's serious purpose. Consequently, the love of Ruggiero and Bradamante, whose protracted disappointments furnished the occasion for renewed prophecies and promises of future glory for their descendants, formed the artistic centre of his romance. The growing importance of all that concerns this pair of characters, the accumulation of difficulties which interfere with their union, and the final honour reserved for Ruggiero of killing the dreadful Rodomonte in single combat, are so disposed and graduated as to make the marriage of the august couple the right and natural climax to an epic of 100,000 lines. The fascinations of Angelica, the achievements of Orlando and Rinaldo, the barbaric chivalry of Rodomonte and Marfisa, even the shock of Christian and Pagan armies, sink into insignificance before the interest that environs Bradamante toward the poem's ending. Victorious art was needed for the achievement of this success. Like a pyramid, upon the top of which a sculptor places a gilded statue, up grows this voluminous romance, covering acres of the plain at first, but narrowing to a point whereon the poet sets his heroes of the House of Este.[1]

Though the marriage of Ruggiero and Brada-mante forms the consummation of the *Furioso*, it would show want of sympathy with 'Ariosto's intention to imagine that he wrote his poem for this incident alone. The opening lines of the first canto are explicit:

> Le donne, i cavalier, l' arme, gli amori,
> Le cortesie, l' audaci imprese io canto
> Che furo al tempo che passaro i Mori
> D' Africa il mare, e in Francia nocquer tanto. . . .

'The ladies, the knights, the feats of arms, the loves, the courtesies, the bold adventures are my theme.' In one word, his purpose was to paint the world of chivalry. Agramante's expedition into France gives him the time; Orlando's madness is an episode; Ruggiero's marriage forms a fitting climax. But his

---

[1] Ariosto's method of introducing flattery is simple. He makes Merlin utter predictions from his tomb, Melissa prophesy to Bradamante and Atlante to Ruggiero; or he displays magic frescoes, statues, and embroideries, where the future splendours of the Este family are figured; or, again, in the exordia of his cantos he directly addresses his patrons. Omitting lesser passages, we may reckon fifteen principal panegyrics of the Este house : canto iii. 16 to end, the fabulous pedigree; viii. 62, 63, praise of Ippolito; xiii. 57 and on, praises of the women of the family; xiv. beginning, the battle of Ravenna and Alfonso; xv. 2, 29, Alfonso's defeat of the Venetians; xviii. 1, 2, Alfonso's justice; xxxv. 4–9, prophecy of Ippolito; xxxvi. 1–9, Ippolito and the Venetians; xl. 1–5, defeat of the Venetians again; xli. 1–3, general adulation; xli. 62–67, pedigree again; xlii. 3, Alfonso wounded; xlii. 83–92, women of the family again; xliii. 54–62, praises of Ferrara; xlvii. 85–97, life of Ippolito. The most extravagant flatteries are lavished upon Ippolito and Lucrezia Borgia. When we remember who and what these Este princes were—how brutal in his cruelty Alfonso, how coarse and selfish and sensual Ippolito, how doubtful in her life Lucrezia—we cannot but feel these panegyrics to be sickening in their impudence.

true subject-matter is chivalry—the dream-world of love, honour, magic, marvel, courtesy, adventure, that afforded to his fancy scope for its most brilliant imaginings. In Ariosto's age chivalry was a thing of the past, even among the nations of the North. It is true that Francis I. was kneeling on the battlefield before Bayard to receive the honour of knighthood in the names of Oliver and Roland. It is true that Henry VIII. was challenging his Most Christian cousin to a kingly settlement of their disputed claims in a pitched field. But the spirit of the times was not in these picturesque incidents. Charles V., who incarnated modern diplomacy, dynastic despotism, and autocratic statecraft, was deciding the destinies of Europe. Gunpowder had already revolutionised the art of feudal war.[1] The order of the Golden Fleece, monarchical and pompous, had eclipsed the orders of the Temple and S. John. What remained of chivalry formed a splendid adjunct to Court-equipage ; and the knight errant, if he ever existed, was merged in the modern gentleman. Far less of real vitality had chivalry among the cities of the South, in the land of Popes like Sixtus, adventurers like Cesare Borgia, princes like Lodovico Sforza, commercial aristocracies like the Republic of S. Mark. A certain ideal of life, summed up in the word *cortesia*, existed in Italy ; where numerous petty Courts had become the school of refined sentiment and manners. But this was not what we mean by chivalry, and even this was daily falsified by the cynicism and corruption of the princes and their

---

[1] See the ending of the ninth and the beginning of the eleventh cantos of the *Furioso*.

servants.[1] Castiglione's *Cortegiano*, the handbook of
that new ideal, must be read by the light of the Roman
diaries and Machiavelli's speculative essays. The
Renaissance was rapidly destroying the feudal fabric
of ideas throughout Europe. Those ideas were always
weak in Italy, and it was in Italy that the modern
intellect first attained to self-consciousness. Therefore
the magic and marvels of romance, the restless movement of knight-errantry, the love of peril and adventure for their own sake, the insane appetite for combat,
the unpractical virtues no less than the capricious
wilfulness of Paladins and Saracens, presented to the
age and race of men like Guicciardini nothing but a
mad unprofitable medley. *Dove avete trovato, messer
Lodovico, tante minchionerie?-* was no unpardonable
question for a Cardinal to make, when he opened the
Furioso in the pontificate of Clement VII. Of all this
Ariosto was doubtless well aware. Yet he recognised
in the *Orlando* a fit framework for the exercise of his
unrivalled painter's power. He knew that the magic
world he had evoked was but a plaything of the fancy,
a glittering bubble blown by the imagination. This
did not suggest an afterthought of hesitation or regret :
for he could make the plaything beautiful. The serious
problem of his life was to construct a miracle of art,
organically complete, harmonious as a whole and lovely
in the slightest details. Yet he never forgot that

---

[1] What Ariosto thought about contemporary Italy may be gathered
from these lines (xvii. 76) :

  O d' ogni vizio fetida sentina,
  Dormi, Italia imbriaca, e non ti pesa
  Ch' ora di questa gente, ora di quella,
  Che già serva ti fu, sei fatta ancella ?

chivalry was a dream; and thus there is an airy un-substantiality in his romantic world. His characters, though they are so much closer to us in time and sympathy, lack the real humanity of Achilles in the *Iliad* or of Penelope in the *Odyssey*. They do not live for us, because they were not living for the poet, but painted with perfection from an image in his brain. He stood aloof from the work of his own hands, and turned it round for his recreation, viewing it with a smile of conscious and delighted irony. Nowhere did he suffer himself to be immersed in his own visionary universe. That wonderland of love and laughter, magic and adventure, which so amused his fancy that once he walked from Carpi to Ferrara in slippers dreaming of it, was to him no more solid than the shapes of clouds we form, no more durable than the rime that melts before the sun to nothing. The smile with which he contemplates this fleeting image, is both tender and ironical. Sarcasm and pathos mingle on his lips and in his eyes; for while he knows it to be but a vision, he has used it as the form of all his thought and feeling, making of this dream a mirror for the world in which his days were spent.

Notwithstanding the difficulty of precisely ascertaining the main subject of the *Orlando Furioso*, the unity of the poem is close, subtle, serried. But it is the unity of a vast piece of tapestry rather than of architecture. There is nothing massive in its structure, no simple and yet colossal design like that which forms the strength of the *Iliad* or the *Divine Comedy*. The delicacy of its connecting links, and the perpetual shifting of its scene distinguish it as a romantic

poem from the true epic. The threads by which the
scheme is held together, are slight as gossamer ; the
principal figures are confounded with a multitude of
subordinate characters ; the interest is divided between
a succession of episodical narratives. At no point are
we aroused by the shock of a supreme sensation, such
as that which the death of Patroclus in the *Iliad*
communicates. The rage of Rodomonte inside the
walls of Paris has been cited as an instance of heroic
grandeur. But the effect is exaggerated. Ariosto is
too much amused with the extravagant situation for
the blustering of his Pagan to arouse either terror or
surprise. When we compare this episode with the
appearance of Achilles in the trench, the elaborate
similes and prolonged description of the Italian poet
are as nothing side by side with the terrific shout of
the Greek hero stung at last into activity. And what
is true of Rodomonte may be said of all the studied
situations in the *Furioso*. Ariosto pushes every motive
to the verge of the burlesque, heightening the passion
of love till it becomes insanity, and the sense of honour
till it passes over into whimsical punctiliousness, and
the marvellous until the utmost bounds of credibility are
passed. This is not done without profound artistic
purpose. The finest comic effects in the poem are due
to such exaggerations of the motives, and the ironic
laughter of the poet is heard at moments when, if he
preserved his gravity, we should accuse him of unpardonable childishness. Our chief difficulty in appre-
ciating the *Furioso* is to take the author's point of view,
to comprehend the expenditure of so much genius and
wisdom upon paradoxes, and to sympathise with the

spirit of a masterpiece which, while it verges on the burlesque, is never meant to pass the limit.

In putting this dream-world of his phantasy upon the canvas, Ariosto showed the power of an accomplished painter. This is the secret of the *Furioso's* greatness. This makes it in a deep sense the representative poem of the Italian Renaissance. All the affinities of its style are with the ruling art of Italy, rather than with sculpture or with architecture ; and the poet is less a singer uttering his soul forth to the world in song, than an artist painting a multitude of images with words instead of colours. His power of delineation never fails him. Through the lucid medium of exquisitely chosen language we see the object as clearly as he saw it. We scarcely seem to see it with his eyes so much as with our own, for the poet stands aloof from his handiwork and is a spectator of his pictures like ourselves. So authentic is the vision that, while he is obliged by his subject to treat the same situations—in duels, battles, storms, love-passages —he never repeats himself. A fresh image has passed across the camera obscura of his brain, and has been copied in its salient features. For the whole of this pictured world is in movement and the master has the art to seize those details which convey the very truth of life and motion. We sit in a dim theatre of thought, and watch the motley crowd of his fantastic personages glide across the stage. They group themselves for a moment ere they flit away ; and then the scene is shifted, and a new procession enters ; fresh *tableaux vivants* are arranged, and when we have enjoyed their melodies of form and colour, the spell is once more broken and new actors enter. The stage is never empty ; scene melts into scene without breathing-space or interruption ; but lest the show should weary by its continuity, the curtain is let down upon each canto's closing, and the wizard who evokes these phantoms for our pleasure, stands before it for a moment and discourses wit and wisdom to his audience.

It is this all-embracing universally illuminating faculty of vision that justifies Galileo's epithet of the DIVINE for Ariosto. This renders his title of the Italian Homer intelligible. But we must remember that these high-sounding compliments are paid him by a nation in whose genius the art of painting holds the highest rank ; and it may well happen that critics less finely sensitive to pictorial delineation shall contest them both. As in Italian painting, so in Ariosto's poetry, deep thought and poignant passion are not suffered to interrupt the calm unfolding of a world where plastic beauty reigns supreme.   No thrilling cry from the heart of humanity is heard ; no dreadful insight into mortal woe disturbs the rhythmic dance. Tragedy is drowned and swallowed in a sea of images ; and if the deeper chords of pathos are touched here and there, they are so finely modulated and blent with the pervading melody that a harsh note never jars upon our ears. A nation in whom the dramatic instinct is paramount, an audience attuned to *Hamlet* or *King Lear*, will feel that something essential to the highest poetry has been omitted. The same imperious pictorial faculty compels Ariosto to describe what more dramatic poets are contented to suggest.   Where

Dante conveys an image in one pregnant line, he employs an octave for the exhibition of a finished picture.[1] Thus our attention is withdrawn from the main object to a multitude of minor illustrations, each of which is offered to us with the same lucidity. The dædal labyrinth of exquisitely modelled forms begins to cloy, and in our tired ingratitude we wish the artist had left something to our own imagination. It is too much to be forced to contemplate a countless number of highly-wrought compositions. We long for something half-seen, indicated, shyly revealed by lightning flashes and withdrawn before it has been fully shown. When Lessing in *Laocoon* censured the famous portrait of Alcina, this was, in part at least, the truth of his complaint. She wearies us by the minuteness of the touches that present her to our gaze ; and the elaboration of each detail prevents us from forming a complete conception of her beauty. But the Italians of the sixteenth century, accustomed to painted forms in fresco and in oils, and educated in the descriptive traditions of Boccaccio's school, would not have recognised the soundness of this criticism. For them each studied phrase of Ariosto was the index to an image, summoned by memory from the works of their own masters, or from life. His method of delineation was analogous to that of figurative art. In a word, the defect pointed out by the German critic is the defect of

Those who are curious may compare the three lines in which Dante likens Piero delle Vigne's voice issuing from his tree of torment to the hissing of sap in a green log upon the fire (*Inf.* xiii. 40) with the eight lines used by Ariosto to expand the same simile (*Orl. Fur.* vi. 27) ; or, again, Dante's picture of the sick woman on her bed of fever (*Purg.* vi. 149) with Ariosto's copy (*Orl. Fur.* xxviii. 90).

Ariosto's greatest quality, the quality belonging to an age and race in which painting was supreme.

Closely allied to this pictorial method in the representation of all objects to our mental vision, was Ariosto's rhetorical amplification.   He rarely allows a situation to be briefly indicated or a sentiment to be divined.   The emotions of his characters are analysed at length; and their utterances, even at the fever-heat of passion, are expanded with a dazzling wealth of illustration.   Many of the episodes in the *Furioso* are eminently dramatic, and the impression left upon the memory is forcible enough. But they are not wrought out as a dramatist would handle them.   The persons do not act before us, or express themselves by direct speech.   The artist has seen them in motion, has understood what they are feeling; and by his manner of describing them he makes us see them also.   But it is always a picture, always an image, that presents itself.   Soul rarely speaks to soul without the intervention of interpretative art.   This does not prevent Ariosto from being a master of the story-teller's craft.   No poet of any nation knew better what to say and what to leave unsaid in managing a fable. The facility of his narration is perfect ; and though the incidents of his tales are extremely complicated, there is no confusion.   Each story is as limpid as each picture he invents.   Nor, again, is there any languor in his poem.   Its extraordinary swiftness can only be compared to the rush of a shining river, flowing so smoothly that we have to measure its speed by objects on the surface.   The *Furioso*, in spite of its accumulated images, in spite of its elaborated rhetoric, is in rapid onward movement from the first line to the last.   It has an elasticity which is lacking to the monumental architecture of the *Divine Comedy.* It is free from the stationary digressions that impede a student of *Paradise Lost.*

The fairy-like fantastic structure of the *Furioso* has a groundwork of philosophical solidity. ¡ Externally a child's story-book, it is internally a mine of deep world-wisdom, the product of a sane and vigorous intellect., Not that we have any right to seek for allegory in the substance of the poem. When Spenser fancied that Ariosto had 'ensampled a good governour and vertuous man' in Orlando—in the Orlando who went mad, neglected his liege-lord, and exposed Christendom to peril for Angelica's fair face—he was clearly on the wrong tack. For a man of Ariosto's temperament, in an age of violent contrast between moral corruption and mental activity, it was enough to observe human nature without creating ideals. His knowledge of the actions, motives, passions and characters of men is concrete ; and his readings in the lessons of humanity, are literal. The excellence of his delineation consists precisely in the nicety of *nuances*, the blending of vice and virtue, the correct analysis of motives. He paints men and women as he finds them, not without the irony of one who stands aloof from life and takes malicious pleasure in pointing out its misery and weakness. If I wished to indicate a single passage that displays this knowledge of the heart, I should not select the too transparent allegory of Logistilla [1]— though even here the contrast between Alcina's seductive charms and the permanent beauty of her sister is

[1] Canto x. 52 *et seq.*

wrought with a magnificence of detail worthy of Spenser. I would rather point to the reflections which conclude the tale of Marganorre and his wicked sons.[1] In lucid exposition of fact lay the strength of Ariosto; and here it may be said that he proved his affinity to the profoundest spirits of his age in Italy—to Machiavelli and Guicciardini, the founders of analytical science for modern Europe. This intimate study of the laws which govern human action when it seems most wayward, is displayed in Grifone's subjection to the faithless Orrigille, in the conflict of passions which agitate the heroes of Agramante's camp, in the agony of Orlando when he finds Medoro's name coupled with Angelica's, in Bradamante's jealousy, in the conflict of courtesy between Leone and Ruggiero, in the delusive visions of Atlante's castle, in the pride of Rodomonte, and in the comic termination of Angelica's coquetries. The difference between Ariosto and Machiavelli is, that while the latter seems to have dissected human nature with a scalpel, the former has gained this wisdom by sympathy. The one exhibits his anatomical preparations with grim scientific gravity ; the other makes his puppets move before us, and smiles sarcastically at their antics.

Sometimes he condenses his philosophy of life in short essays that form the prefaces to cantos, introducing us as through a shapely vestibule into the enchanted palace of his narrative. Among these the finest are the exordia on Love and Honour, on Jealousy, on Loyalty, on Avarice, on the fickleness of Fortune, on

---

[1] Canto xxxvii. 104 et seq.

Hypocrisy in Courts, and on the pains of Love.[1] The merit of these discourses does not consist in their profundity so much as in their truth. They have been deeply felt and are of universal applicability. What all men have experienced, what every age and race of men have known, the supreme poet expresses with his transparent style, his tender and caressing melody of phrase, his graceful blending of sympathy and satire. Tasso in the preface to *Rinaldo* rebukes Ariosto for the introduction of these *I*digressions. He says they are below the dignity of the heroic manner, and that a true poet should be able by example and the action of his characters to point the moral without disquisition. This may be true. Yet Ariosto was writing a romance, and we welcome these personal utterances as a relief from the perpetual movement of his figures. In like manner we should be loth to lose the lyrical inter-breathings of Euripidean chorusses, or Portia's descant upon mercy, or Fielding's interpolated reflections, all of which are halting-places for the mind to rest on in the rapid course of dramatic or narrative evolution. Still it is not in these detached passages that Ariosto shows his greatest wealth of observation. The *novelle*, scattered with a lavish hand through all his cantos, combine the same sagacity with energy of action and pictorial effect. Whatever men are wont to do, feel, hope for, fear—what moves their wrath—what yields them pleasure, or inflicts upon them pain—that is the material of Ariosto's tales. He does not use this matter either as a satirist or a moralist, as a tragic poet to effect a purification of the passions, or, again, as a didactic

[1] Cantos xxxviii. xxxi. xxi. xliii. xlv. xliv. xvi.

poet to inculcate lessons. Like Plautus, he seems
to say : ' Whatever be the hues of life, my words shall
paint them.' Following the course of events without
comment, his page reflects the masque of human joys
and griefs which is played out before him. In the tale
of Polinesso and Ginevra, all the elements of pathos
that can be extracted from the love of women and the
treachery of men, are accumulated. The desertion of
Olimpia by Bireno after the sacrifices she has made
for him, invests the myth of Ariadne with a wild romantic charm. Isabella's devotion to Zerbino through
captivity and danger ; the friendship of Cloridano for
the beautiful Medoro, and their piety toward Dardin-
ello's corpse ; Angelica's doting on Medoro, and the
idyll of their happiness among the shepherd folk ; the
death of Brandimarte, and Fiordeligi's agony of grief;
Fiordespina's vain love for Bradamante, and her con-
solation in the arms of Ricciardetto ; the wild legend
of the Amazons, who suffered no male stranger to
approach their city ; Norandino's loyalty to Lucina in
the cave of Orco ; Lidia's cruel treatment of Alceste ;
the arts whereby Tanacro and Olindo, sons of Marganorre, work their wicked will in love; Gabrina's
treachery toward husband and paramour ; Giocondo's
adventures with the king Astolfo ; the ruse by which
Argia justifies her infidelity to Anselmo ; the sublime
courtesies of Leone ; the artful machinations of Melissa—these are the rubrics of tales and situations, so
varied, so fertile in resource, that a hundred comedies
and tragedies might be wrought from them. Ariosto,
in his conduct of these stories, attempts no poetical
justice. Virtue in distress, vice triumphant, one pas-

sion expelling another, nobler motives conquered by baser, loyalty undermined by avarice, feminine frailty made strong to suffer by the force of love ; so runs the world, and so the poet paints it.

New and old, false and real, he mixes all together, and by the alchemy of his imagination makes the fusion true. The classics and the Italian poets, writers of history and romance, geographers and chroniclers, have been laid under contribution. But though the poem is composed of imitations, it is invariably original, because Ariosto has seen and felt whatever he described. Angelica on the horse going out to sea recalls Europa. The battle with the Orc is borrowed from the tale of Perseus. Astolfo in the myrtle grove comes straight from Virgil. Cloridano and Medoro are Nisus and Euryalus in modern dress. The shield of Atlante suggests Medusa's head. Pegasus was the parent of the Hippogriff, and Polyphemus of Orco. Rodomonte rages like Mezentius and dies like Turnus. Grifone on the bridge is a Renaissance study from Horatius Cocles. Senapo repeats the myth of Phineus and the Harpies. Yet throughout these plagiarisms Ariosto remains himself. He has assimilated his originals to his own genius, and has given every incident new life by the vividness of his humanity. If it were needful to cite an instance of his playful, practical, ironic treatment of old material, we might point to Lucinda's feminine delicacy in the cave of Orco. She refuses to smear herself with the old goat's fat, and fails to escape with Norandino and his comrades from the hands of this new Polyphemus. So comprehensive is the poet's fancy that it embraces the classic no

less than the medieval past. Both are blent in a third
substance which takes life from his own experience
and observation. In this respect the art of Ariosto
corresponds to Raphael's—to the Stanza of the Seg-
natura or the Antinous-Jonah of the Chigi Chapel.
It is the first emancipation of the modern spirit in a
work of catholic beauty, preluding to the final emancipation of the reason in the sphere of criticism, thought,
and science.

The quality which gives salt and savour to
Ariosto's philosophy of life is irony, sometimes bordering on satire, sometimes running over into drollery
and humour. Irony is implicit in the very substance
of the *Furioso*. The choice of a *mad* Orlando for
hero reveals the poet's intention ; and the recovery of
his lost wits from the moon parodies the medieval
doctrine that only in the other world shall we find our
true selves. The fate of Angelica, again, is supremely
ironical. After flouting kings and Paladins, the noblest knights of the whole world, her lovers, she dotes
upon a handsome country-lad and marries him in a
shepherd's hut. Medoro plucks the rose for which
both Christendom and Paynimry had fought in furious
rivalry ; and wayward Love requites their insults with
a by-blow from his dart. Such, smiles the poet, is
the end of pride, ambition, passion, and the coquetries
that placed the kingdoms of the East and West in
peril. Angelica is the embodiment of mortal frailty.
The vanity of human wishes, the vicissitudes which
blind desire prepares for haughtiest souls, the paradoxes
held in store by destiny, are symbolised and imaged in
her fate.

Astolfo's journey to the moon, related in the thirty-fourth and thirty-fifth cantos, presents the Ariostean irony with all its gradations of satire, parody, and comic humour. This Duke of England in the Italian romances played the part of an adventurous vain-glorious cavalier, eminent for courtesy and courage, who carried the wandering impulse of knight-errantry to the extreme verge of the ridiculous. We find him at the opening of the thirty-fourth canto in possession of Atlante's Hippogriff and Logistilla's marvellous horn. Mounting his winged horse, he flies through space, visits the sources of the Nile, and traverses the realm of Ethiopia. There he delivers King Senapo from a brood of Harpies, whom he pursues to the mouth of a cavern whence issues dense smoke. This is the entrance into Hell :

> L' orecchie attente allo spiraglio tenne,
> E l' aria ne sentì percossa e rotta
> Da pianti e d' urli, e da lamento eterno ;
> Segno evidente quivi esser lo 'nferno.

The paladin's curiosity is roused, and he determines to advance :

> Di che debbo temer, dicea, s' io v' entro ?
> Chè mi posso aiutar sempre col corno.
> Farò fuggir Plutone e Satanasso,
> E 'l can trifauce leverò dal passo.

This light-hearted reliance in a perfectly practical spirit upon his magic horn is wholly in keeping with Ariosto's genius. The terrible situation, the good sense of the adventurer, and the enchantment which protects him are so combined as to be prosaically natural. Astolfo gropes his way into the cavern and is immediately suffocated by dense smoke. In the midst of it above his head he sees a body hanging and swinging to and fro like a corpse on a gibbet. He cuts at this object with his sword, and wakes the melancholy voice of Lidia, who tells him that in the smoke are punished obdurate and faithless lovers. The tale of her falseness to Alceste is very beautiful, and shows great knowledge of the heart. But it leads to nothing in the action of the poem, and Astolfo goes out of Hell as he came in—except that the smoke has befouled both face and armour, and he has to scrub himself in a fountain before he can get clean again. Meanwhile Ariosto has parodied the opening of Dante's *Inferno* with its sublime :

> Mi mise dentro alle segrete cose.

Lidia is the inversion of Francesca ; for her sin was, not compliance with the impulses of nature, but unkindness to her lover. This travesty is wrought with no deliberate purpose, but by a mere caprice of fancy, to entertain his audience with a novel while he flouts the faiths and fears of a more earnest age. For Ariosto, the child of the Renaissance, there remained nothing to affirm or to deny about the future of the soul. The Inferno of the middle ages had become a plaything of romance. Astolfo now pursues his journey, looks in on Prester John, and scales the mountain of the Earthly Paradise. There he finds a palace wrought of precious stones, and in the vestibule an ancient man with venerable beard and snowy hair. This is no other than S. John the Evangelist, who hastens to feed the knight's horse with good corn, and sets before him a table spread with fruits which make the sin of Adam seem excusable :

Con accoglienza grata il cavaliero
Fu dai santi alloggiato in una stanza :
Fu provvisto in un' altra al suo destriero
Di buona biada, che gli fu abbastanza.
De' frutti a lui del paradiso diero,
Di tal sapor, ch' a suo giudicio, sanza
Scusa non sono i duo primi parenti,
Se per quei fur sì poco ubbidienti !

S. John, delighted with his courteous guest, discourses many things about Orlando, his lost wits, and the moon where they have been stored with other rubbish. At the close of their conversation, he remarks that it is a fine night for a journey to the moon ; and orders out the fiery chariot which erewhile took Elijah up to heaven. It holds two passengers with comfort; and after a short voyage through the air, Astolfo and the Evangelist land upon the lunar shores. The stanzas which describe the valley of vain things and useless lumber lost to earth, are justly famous for their satire and their pathos.[1] There are found the presents made to kings in hope of rich reward, the flatteries of poets, shameful loves, the services of courtiers, the false beauties of women, and bottles filled with the lost sense of men. The list is long; nor was Milton unmindful of it when he wrote his lines upon the Paradise of Fools.[2] The passage illustrates certain qualities in Ariosto's imagination. He has no dread of the prosaic and the simple. Inexhaustibly various alike in thought, in rhythm, in imagery, and in melody of phrase, he yet keeps close to reality, and passes without modulation from seriousness to extravagant fun, returning again to the sadness of profound reflection. His poetry is like the picture of his own face—a large

[1] Canto xxxiv. 76-85.   [2] *Par. Lost,* iii. 440.

and handsome man with sleepy eyes and epicurean mouth, over whose broad forehead and open features, ploughed by no wrinkles of old age or care, float subtle smiles and misty multitudes of thoughts half lost in dreams. Human life to Ariosto was a comedy such as Menander put upon the Attic stage; and the critic may ask of him, too, whether he or nature were the plagiarist.

Meanwhile S. John is waiting at Astolfo's elbow to point out the Fates, spinning their web of human destinies, and Time carrying the records of history to the river of oblivion. It is a sad picture, did not Ariosto enliven the most sombre matter with his incorrigible humour. By the river bank of Lethe wait cormorants and swans. The former aid Time in his labour of destruction. The latter, who symbolize great poets, save chosen names from undeserved neglect. This leads to a discourse on the services rendered by writers to their patrons, which is marked by Ariosto's levity. He has just been penning praises for Ippolito.[1] Yet here he frankly confesses that the eulogies of poets are distortions of the truth, that history is a lie, and that the whole pageant of humanity conceals a sorry sham. S. John is even made to hint that his good place in Paradise is the guerdon of a panegyric written on his Master:

> Gli scrittori amo, e fo il debito mio ;
> Ch' al vostro mondo fui scrittore anch' io :
>   E sopra tutti gli altri io feci acquisto
> Che non mi può levar tempo nè morte ;
> E ben convenne al mio lodato Cristo
> Rendermi guidardon di sì gran sorte.

[1] Canto xxxv. 4-9.

The episode of Astolfo's journey to the moon abounds in satire upon human weakness in general. Another celebrated passage has satire of a more direct kind, and is, moreover, valuable for illustrating Ariosto's conduct of his poem. Paris is besieged by the assembled forces of the Saracens. The chief Paladins are absent, and Charlemagne in his sore need addresses a prayer to Heaven.[1] It is just such a prayer as the Israelites offer up in Rossini's *Mosè in Egitto*—very resonant, very rhetorical, but without sincerity of feeling. Ariosto selects a number of decorous phrases redolent of Renaissance humanism, *tolte agl' inimici stigi, al maggior tempio, gli occhi al ciel supini*, and combines them with melodramatic effect. God accepts the Emperor's prayer, and sends Michael down to earth to find Discord and Silence, in order that the former may sow strife in the Saracen camp, and the latter lead reinforcements into Paris. Michael starts upon his errand :

Dovunque drizza Michelangel l' ale,
Fuggon le nubi, e torna il ciel sereno ;
Gli gira intorno un aureo cerchio, quale
Veggiam di notte lampeggiar baleno.

He flies straight to a monastery, expecting to find Silence there. The choir, the parlour, the dormitory, the refectory are searched. Wherever he goes, he sees *Silenzio* written up ; but Silence cannot be found. Instead of him, Discord presents herself, and is recognised by her robe of many-coloured fluttering ribbons, dishevelled hair, and armful of law-papers. Fraud, too, accosts the angel with a gentle face like Gabriel's

---

[1] Canto xiv. 68–73.

when he said *Ave!* To Michael's question after Silence,
Fraud replies: he used to live in convents and the
cells of sages; but now he goes by night with thieves,
false coiners and lovers, and you may find him in the
houses of treason and homicide. Yet if you are very
anxious to lay hands on him at once, haste to the haunt
of Sleep. This cavern is described in stanzas that undoubtedly suggested Spenser's; but Ariosto has nothing
so delicate as:

> A trickling stream from high rock tumbling down,
> And ever drizzling rain upon the loft,
> Mixed with a murmuring wind much like the sown
> Of swarming bees.

Instead, he paints in his peculiar style of realistic
imagery the corpulent form of Ease, Sloth that cannot walk and scarce can stand, Forgetfulness who bars
the door to messengers, and Silence walking round the
cave with slippers of felt. Silence, summoned by the
archangel, sets forth to meet Rinaldo. Discord also
quits the convent with her comrade Pride, leaving
Fraud and Hypocrisy to keep their places warm till
they return. But Discord does her work inadequately;
and the cries of Rodomonte's victims rise to heaven.
This rouses Michael from his slumber of beatitude.
He blushes, plumes his pinions, and shoots down again
to earth in search of Discord among the monks. He
finds her sitting in a chapter convened for the election
of officers, and makes her in a moment feel his
presence: [1]

> Le man le pose l' Angelo nel crine,
> E pugna e calci le diè senza fine.
> Indi le roppe un manico di croce

[1] Canto xxvii. 37.

Per la testa, pel dosso e per le braccia.
Mercè grida la misera a gran voce,
E le ginocchia al divin nunzio abbraccia.

This is a good specimen both of Ariosto's peculiar levity and of the romantic style which in the most serious portion of his poem permitted such extravagance. The robust archangel tearing Discord's dishevelled hair, kicking her, pounding her with his fists, breaking a cross upon her back, and sending her about her business with a bee in her bonnet, presents a picture of drollery which is exceedingly absurd. Nor is there any impropriety in the picture from the poet's point of view. Michael and the Evangelist are scarcely serious beings. They both form part of his machinery and help to make the action move.

Broad fun, untinctured by irony, seasons the *Furioso*—as when Astolfo creates a fleet by throwing leaves into the sea, and mounts his Ethiopian cavalry on horses made of stone, and catches the wind in a bladder; all of which burlesque miracles are told with that keen relish of their practical utility which formed an element of Ariosto's sprightliness.[1] Ruggiero's pleasure-trip on Rabicane; Orlando's achievement of spitting six fat Dutchmen like frogs upon one spear; the index to Astolfo's magic book; the conceit of the knights who jousted with the golden lance and ascribed its success to their own valour; Orlando's feats of prowess with the table in the robber's den; are other instances of Ariosto's light-heartedness, when he banters with his subject and takes his readers into

[1] Canto xxxviii. 30, 33, 26.

confidence with his own sense of drollery.[1] The donkey race in armour between Marfisa and Zerbino for a cantankerous old hag, with its courteous ceremonies and chivalrous conclusion, might be cited as an example of more sustained humour.[2] And such, too, though in another region, is the novel of Jocondo.

Ariosto's irony, no less than his romantic method, deprived the *Furioso* of that sublimity which only belongs to works of greater seriousness and deeper conviction. Yet he sometimes touches the sublime by force of dramatic description or by pathetic intensity. The climax of Orlando's madness has commonly been cited as an instance of poetic grandeur. Yet I should be inclined to prefer the gathering of the storm of discord in Agramante's camp.[3] The whole of this elaborate scene, where the fiery characters and tempestuous passions of the Moslem chiefs, of Ruggiero, Rodomonte, Gradasso, Mandricardo, and Marfisa, are brought successively into play by impulses and motives natural to each and powerful to produce a clash of adverse claims and interests, is not only conceived and excuted in a truly dramatic spirit, but is eminently important for the action of the poem. The thunderclouds which had been mustering to break in ruin upon Christendom, rush together and spend their fury in mid air. Thus the moment is decisive, and nothing has been spared to dignify the passions that provoke the final crash. They go on accumulating in complexity, like a fugue of discords, till at last the hyperbole of this sonorous stanza seems justified [1] :

---

[1] Canto x. 72 ; ix. 68 ; xxii. 16 ; xlv. 65 ; xiii. 36.
[2] Canto xx. 122.   [3] Canto xxvii.   [1] *Ibid.* 101.

Tremò Parigi, e turbidossi Senna
All' alta voce, a quell' orribil grido ;
Rimbombò il suon fin alla selva Ardenna
Sì che lasciâr tutte le fiere il nido.
Udiron l' Alpi e il monte di Gebenna,
Di Blaia e d' Arli e di Roano il lido ;
Rodano e Sonna udì, Garonna e il Reno :
Si strinsero le madri i figli al seno.

His pathos also has its own sublimity. Imogen
stretched lifeless on the corpse of Cloten ; the Duchess
of Malfi telling Cariola to see that her daughter says
her prayers ; Bellario describing his own sacrifice as a
mere piece of boyhood flung away—these are instances
from our own drama, in which the pathetic is sublime.
Ariosto's method is different, and the effect is more
rhetorical. Yet he can produce passages of almost
equal poignancy, prolonged situations of overmastering
emotion, worthy to be set side by side with the Euripidean pictures of Polyxena, Alcestis, or Iphigenia.[1]
The death of Zerbino ; the death of Brandimarte with
half of Fiordeligi's name upon his lips ; the constancy
of Isabella offering her neck to Rodomonte's sword ;
the anguish of Olimpia upon the desert island ; are
instances of sublime poetry wrung from pathos by
the force of highly-wrought impassioned oratory. Zerbino is one of the most sympathetic creations of the
poet's fancy. Of him Ariosto wrote the famous line [2] :

Natura il fece, e poi ruppe la stampa.

[1] The comparison of Ariosto and Euripides is not wholly fanciful.
Both were supreme artists in an age of incipient decadence, lacking the
convictions of their predecessors, and depending for effect upon rhetorical
devices. Both were τραγικώτατοι in Aristotle's sense of the phrase, and
both were romantic rather than heroic poets.
[2] Canto x. 84.

He is killed by the Tartar Mandricardo before his
lady Isabella's eyes [1] :

> A questo la mestissima Isabella,
> Declinando la faccia lacrimosa,
> E congiungendo la sua bocca a quella
> Di Zerbin, languidetta come rosa,
> Rosa non colta in sua stagion, sì ch' ella
> Impallidisca in su la siepe ombrosa,
> Disse : Non vi pensate già, mia vita,
> Far senza me quest' ultima partita.

With stanzas like this the poet cheats the sorrow
he has stirred in us.   Their imagery is too beautiful to
admit of painful feeling while we read ; and thus,
though the passion of the scene is tragic, its anguish is
brought by touches of pure art into harmony with the
romantic tone of the whole poem.   So also when Isabella, kneeling before Rodomonte's sword, like S.
Catherine in Luini's fresco at Milan, has met her own
death, Ariosto heals the wound he has inflicted on our
sensibility by lines of exquisitely cadenced melody [2] :

> Vattene in pace, alma beata e bella.
> Così i miei versi avesson forza, come
> Ben m' affaticherei con tutta quella
> Arte che tanto il parlar orna e come,
> Perchè mille e mill' anni, e più, novella
> Sentisse il mondo del tuo chiaro nome.
> Vattene in pace alla superna sede,
> E lascia all' altre esempio di tua fede.

But it is in the situations, the elegiac lamentations,
the unexpected vicissitudes, and the strong pictorial
beauties of Olimpia's novel, that Ariosto strains his

---

[1] The whole scene, with all its gradations of emotion, is too long to
quote.   But see xxiv. 74–87.

[2] Canto xxix. 27.

power over pathos to the utmost. Olimpia has lost her kingdom and spent her substance for her husband, Bireno. Orlando aids her in her sore distress, and frees Bireno from his prison. Bireno proves faithless, and deserts her on an island. She is taken by corsairs, exposed like Andromeda on a rock to a sea-monster, and is finally rescued by Orlando. Each of these touching incidents is developed with consummate skill; and the pathos reaches its height when Olimpia, who had risked all for her husband, wakes at dawn to find herself abandoned by him on a desolate sea-beach.[1] In this passage Ariosto comes into competition with two poets of a different stamp—with Catullus, who thus describes Ariadne :

Saxea ut effigies Bacchantis prospicit :

and with Fletcher, who makes Aspatia in the *Maid's Tragedy* dramatise the situation. Catullus in a single felicitous simile, Fletcher by the agony of passionate declamation, surpass Ariosto's detailed picture. The one is more restrained, the other more tragic. But Ariosto goes straight to our heart by the natural touch of Olimpia feeling for Bireno in the darkness, and by the suggestion of pallid moonlight and a shivering dawn. The numerous prosaic details with which he has charged his picture, add to its reality, and enhance the Euripidean quality we admire in it.

In the case of a poet whose imagination was invariably balanced by practical sound sense, the personal experience he acquired of the female sex could not fail to influence his delineation of women. He was

[1] Canto x. 20-34.

not a man to cherish illusion or to romance in verse
about perfection he had never found in fact. He did
not place a Beatrice or Laura on the pedestal of his
heart ; nor was it till he reached the age of forty-seven,
when the *Furioso* had lain for six years finished on his
desk, that he married Alessandra Strozzi. His great
poem, completed in 1515, must have been written
under the influence of those more volatile amours he
celebrated in his Latin verses. Therefore we are not
surprised to find that the female characters of the
Orlando illustrate his epistle on the choice of a wife.[1]
His highest ideal of woman is presented to us in
Bradamante, whose virtues are a loyal attachment to
Ruggiero and a modest submission to the will of her
parents. Yet even in Bradamante he has painted a
virago from whom the more delicate humanity of
Skakspere would have recoiled. The scene in which
she quarrels with Marfisa about Ruggiero degrades
her in our eyes, and makes us feel that such a terma-
gant might prove a sorry wife.[2] It was almost impossible to combine true feminine qualities with the blood-
thirst of an Amazon. Consequently when, just before
her marriage, she snuffs the carnage of the Saracens
from afar, and regrets that she must withold her hand
from ' such rich spoil of slaughter in a spacious field,'
a painful sense of incongruity is left upon our mind.[3]
Marfisa, who remains a warrior to the last, and who
in her first girlhood had preserved her virginity by
slaughtering a palace-full of Pagans,[4] is artistically
justified as a romantic heroine. But Bradamante,

---

[1] See above, Part i. p. 510.   [2] Canto xxxvi., especially stanza 50.
[3] Canto xxxix. 10–15 ; cp. *ib.* 67–72.   [4] Canto xxxvii. 15.

destined to become a mother, gentle in her hom
affections, obedient to her father's wishes, tremulous i.
her attachment to Ruggiero, cannot with any propriety
be compared to a leopard loosed from the leash upon
defenceless gazelles.[1] Between the Amazonian virgin
and the mother of a race of kings to be, the outline of
her character wavers.

After the more finished portrait of Bradamante,
we find in Isabella and Fiordeligi, the lovers of
Zerbino and Brandimarte, Ariosto's purest types of
feminine affection. The cardinal virtue of woman in his
eyes was self-devotion—loyalty to the death, unhesitat-
ing sacrifice of wealth, ease, reputation, life, to the
one object of passionate attachment. And this self-
devotion he has painted in Olimpia no less romantically than in Isabella and Fiordeligi. Still it must
be remembered that Isabella had eloped with Zerbino
from her father's palace, that Fiordeligi was only a
wife in name, and that Olimpia murdered her first
husband and consoled herself very rapidly for Bireno's
loss in the arms of Oberto. The poet has not cared
to interweave with either portrait such threads of
piety and purity as harmonise the self-abandonment
of Juliet. Fiordespina's ready credence of the absurd
story by which Ricciardetto persuades her that he
is Bradamante metamorphosed by a water-fairy to a
man, and her love-longings, so frankly confessed, so
unblushingly indulged, illustrate the passion Ariosto
delighted to describe. He feels a tender sympathy
for feminine frailty, and in more than one exquisitely
written passage claims for women a similar licence in

[1] Canto xxxix. 69.

love to that of men.' Indeed, he never judges a woman severely, unless she adds to her want of chastity the spitefulness of Gabrina or the treachery of Orrigille or the cupidity of Argia or the heartlessness of Angelica. Angelica, who in the *Innamorato* touches our feelings by her tenderness for Rinaldo, in the *Furioso* becomes a mere coquette, and is well punished by her insane passion for the first pretty fellow that takes her fancy. The common faults for which Ariosto taxes women are cupidity, infidelity, and fraud.[2] The indulgence due to them from men is almost cynically illustrated by the story of Adonio and the magic virtues of Merlin's goblet.[3] In the preface to the fifth canto he condemns the brutality of husbands, and in the tenth he recommends ladies to be free of their favours to none but middle-aged lovers.[4]

Ariosto's morality was clearly on a level with that of the novelists from Boccaccio to Bandello ; and his apology is that he was not inferior to the standard of his age. Still it is not much to his credit to plead that his cantos are less impure than the *Capitoli* of Monsignore La Casa or the prurient comedies of Aretino. Even allowing for the laxity of Renaissance manners, it must be conceded that he combined vulgar emotions and a coarse-fibred nature with the most refined artistic genius.[5] Our Elizabethan drama, in spite of

---

' See especially iv. 63-67.

" Introductions to cantos xliii. xxviii. xxix. xxii. xxvi.; cp. xxvii. 123.

' Canto xlii.   ⁴ Stanzas 6–9.

⁵ If this seems over-stated, I might refer the reader to the prologue of the *Suppositi*, where the worst vice of the Renaissance is treated with a flippant relish ; or, again, to the prologue of the *Lena*, where the *double entendre* is worthy of the grossest *Capitolo*. The plots of all Ariosto's comedies are of a vulgar, obscene, *bourgeois* type.

moral crudity, contains nothing so cynical as Ariosto's novel of Jocondo. The beauty of its style, the absence of tragedy in its situations or of passion in its characters, and the humorous smile with which the poet acts as showman to the secrets of the alcove, render this tale one of the most licentious in literature. Nor is this licentiousness balanced by any sublimer spiritual quality. His ideal of manliness is physical force and animal courage. Cruelty and bloodshed for the sake of slaughter stain his heroes.[1] The noblest conflict of emotion he portrays is the struggle between love and honour in Ruggiero,[2] and the contest of courtesy between Ruggiero and Leone.[3] In the few passages where he celebrates the chivalrous ideal, he dwells chiefly on the scorn of gain and the contempt for ease which characterised the errant knighthood.[4]

The style of the *Furioso* is said to have taught Galileo how to write Italian. This style won from him for Ariosto the title of *divine*. As the luminous and flowing octave stanzas pass before us, we are almost tempted to forget that they are products of deliberate art. The beauty of their form consists in its limpidity and naturalness. Ariosto has no mannerism. He always finds exactly the expression needed to give clearness to the object he presents. Whether the mood be elegiac or satiric, humorous or

---

[1] See xxxix. 10-72, xx. 113, xlvi. 137, and *passim*, for the carnage wrought by knights cased in enchanted armour with invulnerable bodies upon defenceless Saracens or unarmed peasants. It was partly this that made Shelley shrink with loathing from the *Furioso*.

[2] Cantos xxi. 1-3, xx. 143, xxxviii. introduction, xlv. 57, xxv. introduction. [3] Cantos xlv. xlv.

[4] Canto vi. 80, vii. 41-44. The sentiments, though superficial, are exquisitely uttered.

heroic, idyllic or rhetorical, this absolute sincerity and directness of language maintains him at an even level. In each case he has given the right, the best, the natural investiture to thought, and his phrases have the self-evidence of crystals. Just as he collected the materials of his poem from all sources, so he appropriated every word that seemed to serve his need. The vocabulary of Dante, Petrarch, and Boccaccio, the racy terms of popular poetry, together with Latinisms and Lombardisms, were alike laid under contribution. Yet these diverse elements were so fused together and brought into a common toning by his taste that, though the language of his poem was new, it was at once accepted as classical. When we remember the difficulties which in his days beset Italian composition, when we call to mind the frigid experiments of Bembo in Tuscan diction, the meticulous proprieties of critics like Speron Speroni, and the warfare waged around the *Gerusalemme Liberata*, we know not whether to wonder at Ariosto's happy audacities in language or at their still happier success. His triumph was not won without severe labour. He spent ten years in the composition of the *Furioso* and sixteen in its polishing. The autograph at Ferrara shows page upon page of alteration, transposition, and refinement on the first draught, proving that the Homeric limpidity and ease we now admire, were gained by assiduous self-criticism. The result of this long toil is that there cannot be found a rough or languid or inharmonious passage in an epic of 50,000 lines. If we do not discern in Ariosto the inexhaustible freshness of Homer, the sublime music of Milton, the sculpturesque brevity of Dante, the purity of Petrarch, or the majestic sweetness of Virgilian cadences, it can fairly be said that no other poet is so varied. None mingles strength, sweetness, subtlety, rapidity, rhetoric, breadth of effect and delicacy of suggestion, in a harmony so perfect. None combines workmanship so artistic with a facility that precludes all weariness. Whether we read him simply to enjoy his story or to taste the most exquisite flavours of poetic diction, we shall be equally satisfied. Language in his hands is like a soft and yielding paste, which takes all forms beneath the moulder's hand, and then, when it has hardened, stays for ever sharp in outline, glittering as adamant.

While following the romantic method of Boiardo and borrowing the polished numbers of Poliziano, Ariosto refined the stanzas of the former poet without losing rapidity, and avoided the stationary pomp of the latter without sacrificing richness. He thus effected a combination of the two chief currents of Italian versification, and brought the octave to its final perfection. When we study the passage which describes the entrance of Ruggiero into the island home of Alcina, we feel the advance in melody and movement that he made. We are reminded of the gardens of Morgana and Venus ; but both are surpassed in their own qualities of beauty, while the fluidity that springs from complete command of the material, is added. Such touches as the following [1] :

> Pensier canuto nè molto nè poco
> Si può quivi albergare in alcun core :

· Canto vi. 73

are wholly beyond the scope of Boiardo's style. Again, this stanza, without the brocaded splendour of Poliziano, contains all that he derived from Claudian [1] :

> Per le cime dei pini e degli allori,
> Degli alti faggi e degli irsuti abeti,
> Volan scherzando i pargoletti Amori ;
> Di lor vittorie altri godendo lieti,
> Altri pigliando a saettare i cori
> La mira quindi, altri tendendo reti :
> Chi tempra dardi ad un ruscel più basso,
> E chi gli aguzza ad un volubil sasso.

Raphael, Correggio and Titian have succeeded to Botticelli and Mantegna ; and as those supreme painters fused the several excellences of their predecessors in a fully-developed work of art, so has Ariosto passed beyond his masters in the art of poetry. Nor was the process one of mere eclecticism. Intent upon similar aims, the final artists of the early sixteenth century brought the same profound sentiment for reality, the same firm grasp on truth, the same vivid imagination as their precursors to the task. But they possessed surer hands and a more accomplished method. They stood above their subject and surveyed it from the height of conscious power.

After the island of Alcina, it only remained for Tasso to produce novelty in his description of Armida's gardens by pushing one of Ariosto's qualities to exaggeration. The *dolcezza*, which in Tasso is too sugared, has in Ariosto the fine flavour of wild honeycombs. In the tropical magnificence of Tasso's stanzas there is a sultry stupor which the fresh sunlight

[1] Canto vi. 75.

of the *Furioso* never sheds. This wilding grace of
the Ferrarese Homer is due to the lightness of his
touch—to the blending of humorous with luxurious
images in a style that passes swiftly over all it paints.[1]
After a like fashion, the idyll of Angelica among the
shepherds surpasses the celebrated episode of Erminia
in the *Gerusalemme.* It is not that Tasso has not invented a new music and wrung a novel effect from the
situation by the impassioned fervour of his sympathy
and by the majestic languor of his cadences. But we
feel that what Tasso relies on for his main effect,
Ariosto had already suggested in combination with
other and still subtler qualities. The one has the
overpowering perfume of a hothouse jasmine; the
other has the mingled scents of a garden where roses
and carnations are in bloom.

Ariosto's pictorial faculty has already formed the
topic of a paragraph, nor is it necessary to adduce
instances of what determines the whole character of
the *Orlando Furioso.* Otherwise it would be easy to
form a gallery of portraits and landscapes; to compare
the double treatment of Andromeda exposed to the
sea monster in the tenth and eleventh cantos,[2] to set a
pageant in the style of Mantegna by the side of a
Correggiesque vignette,[3] or to enlarge upon the beauty
of those magical Renaissance buildings which the poet
dreamed of in the midst of verdant lawns and flowery
wildernesses.[4] True to the spirit of Italian art, he had

---

[1] Notice, for example, the irony of the seventh line in vi. 71, and of
the third and fourth in the next stanza.
[2] Canto x. 95, 96, xi. 65, 66. The one is Angelica, the other Olimpia.
[3] Canto vi. 62, 63, 75.
[4] Canto vi. 71, xxxiv. 51–53.

no strong sentiment for nature except in connection with humanity. Therefore we find but little of landscape-painting for its own sake and small sympathy with the wilder and úncultivated beauties of the world. His scenery recalls the backgrounds to Carpaccio's pictures or the idyllic gardens of the Giorgionesque school. Sometimes there is a magnificent drawing in the style of Titian's purple mountain ranges, and here and there we come upon minutely finished studies that imply deep feeling for the moods of nature. Of this sort is the description of autumn [1] :

> Tra il fin d' ottobre e il capo di novembre,
> Nella stagion che la frondosa vesta
> Vede levarsi, e discoprir le membre,
> Trepida pianta, finchè nuda resta,
> E van gli augelli a strette schiere insembre.

The illuminative force of his similes is quite extra-ordinary. He uses them not only as occasions for painting cabinet pictures of exquisite richness, but also for casting strong imaginative light upon the object under treatment. In the earlier part of the *Furioso* he describes two battles with a huge sea monster. The Orc is a kind of romantic whale, such as Piero di Cosimo painted in his tale of Andromeda ; and Ruggiero has to fight it first, while riding on the Hippo-griff. It is therefore necessary for Ariosto to image forth a battle between behemoth and a mighty bird. He does so by elaborately painting the more familiar struggles of an eagle who has caught a snake, and of a mastiff snapping at a fly.[2] At the same time he adds realistic touches like the following :

[1] Canto ix. 7.   [2] Canto x. 102–106.

L' orca, che vede sotto le grandi ale
L' ombra di qua e di là correr su l' onda,
Lascia la preda certa littorale,
E quella vana segue furibonda.

Or, again, when Ruggiero is afraid of wetting his
aërial courser's wings :

Chè se lo sprazzo in tal modo ha a durare,
Teme sì l' ale innaffi all' Ippogrifo,
Che brami invano avere o zucca o schifo.

The mixture of imagery with prosaic detail brings
the whole scene distinctly before our eyes. When
Orlando engages the same monster, he is in a boat, and
the conditions of the contest are altered. Accordingly
we have a different set of similes. A cloud that fills a
valley, rolling to and fro between the mountain sides,
describes the movement of the Orc upon the waters ;
and when Orlando thrusts his anchor in between its
jaws to keep them open, he is compared to miners
propping up their galleries with beams in order that
they may pursue their work in safety.[1]   In this way we
realise the formidable nature of the beast, and comprehend the stratagem that tames it to Orlando's will.

The same nice adaptation of images may be noticed
in the similes showered on Rodomonte. The giant is
alone inside the walls of Paris, and the poet is bound
to make us feel that a whole city may have cause to
tremble before a single man. Therefore he never
leaves our fancy for a moment in repose. At one time
it is a castle shaken by a storm ; at another a lion re-
treating before the hunters ; again, a tigress deprived of
her cubs, or a bull that has broken from the baiting-

[1] Canto xi. 34–38.

pole, or the whelps of a lioness attacking a fierce young steer.[1] Image succeeds image with dazzling rapidity, all tending to render a strained situation possible.

Some of Ariosto's illustrations—like the ploughman and the thunderbolt, the two dogs fighting, the powder magazine struck by lightning, the house on fire at night, the leaves of autumn, the pine that braves a tempest, the forest bending beneath mighty winds, the April avalanche of suddenly dissolving snow—though wrought with energy and spirit, have not more than the usual excellences of carefully developed Homeric imitation.[2] Framed in single octave stanzas, they are pictures for the mind to rest on. Others illuminate the matter they are used to illustrate, with the radiance of subtle and remote fancy. Of this sort is the brief image by which the Paladins in Charlemagne's army are likened to jewels in a cloth of gold[3] :

> Ed hanno i paladin sparsi tra loro,
> Come le gemme in un ricamo d' oro.

A common metaphor takes new beauty by its handling in this simile[4] :

> Pallido come colto al mattutino
> E da sera il ligustro o il molle acanto.

Homer had compared the wound of Menelaus to ivory stained by a Mæonian woman with crimson.[5] Ariosto refines on this conceit[6] :

> Così talora un bel purpureo nastro
> Ho veduto partir tela d' argento

---

[1] Canto xviii. 11, 14, 19, 22, 35.
[2] Canto i. 65, ii. 5, ix. 78, xx. 89, xxi. 15, 16, xxiv. 63, xxxvi. 40.
[3] Canto xxxix. 17.   [4] Canto xliii. 169.   [5] *Iliad*, iv. 140.
[6] Canto xxiv. 66.

> Da quella bianca man più ch' alabastro,
> Da cui partire il cor spesso mi sento.

Both Homer and Virgil likened their dying heroes to flowers cut down by the tempest or the plough. The following passage will bear comparison even with the death of Euphorbus : [1]

> Come purpureo fior languendo muore,
> Che 'l vomere al passar tagliato lassa,
> O come carco di superchio umore
> Il papaver nell' orto il capo abbassa :
> Così, giù della faccia ogni colore
> Cadendo, Dardinel di vita passa ;
> Passa di vita, e fa passar con lui
> L' ardire e la virtù di tutti i sui.

One more example may be chosen where Ariosto has borrowed nothing from any model. He uses the perfume that clings to the hair or dress of youth or maiden, as a metaphor for the aroma of noble ancestry [2] :

> L' odor ch' è sparso in ben notrita e bella
> O chioma o barba o delicata vesta
> Di giovene leggiadro o di donzella,
> Ch' amor sovente sospirando desta ;
> Se spira, e fa sentir di sè novella,
> E dopo molti giorni ancora resta,
> Mostra con chiaro ed evidente effetto,
> Come a principio buono era e perfetto.

The unique importance of Ariosto in the history of Renaissance poetry justifies a lengthy examination of his masterpiece. In him the chief artistic forces of the age were so combined that he remains its best interpreter. Painting, the cardinal art of Italy, determined his method ; and the tide of his narrative car-

---

[1] Canto xviii. 153.   [2] Canto xli. 1.

ried with it the idyll, the elegy, and the *novella*. In these forms the genius of the Renaissance found fittest literary expression ; for the epic and the drama lay beyond the scope of the Italians at this period. The defect of deep passion and serious thought, the absence of enthusiasm, combined with rare analytic powers and an acute insight into human nature, placed Ariosto in close relation to his age. [1] Free from illusions, struggling after no high-set ideal, accepting the world as he found it, without the impulse to affirm or to deny, without hate, scorn, indignation or revolt, he represented the spirit of the sixteenth century in those qualities which were the source of moral and political decay to the Italians.   But he also embodied the strong points of his epoch—especially that sustained pursuit of beauty in form, that width of intellectual sympathy, that urbanity of tone and delicacy of perception, which rendered Italy the mistress of the arts, the propagator of culture for the rest of Europe.

CHAPTER X.

THE NOVELLIERI.

Boccaccio's Legacy—Social Conditions of Literature in Italy—Importance of the *Novella*—Definition of the *Novella*—Method of the Novelists—Their Style—Materials used—Large Numbers of *Novelle* in Print—Lombard and Tuscan Species—Introductions to Il Lasca's *Cene*, Parabosco's *Diporti*—Bandello's Dedications—Life of Bandello—His Moral Attitude—Bandello as an Artist—Comparison of Bandello and Fletcher—The Tale of *Gerardo and Elena—Romeo and Juliet*—The Tale of *Nicuola*—The *Countess of Salisbury*—Bandello's Apology for his Morals and his Style—Il Lasca—Mixture of Cruelty and Lust—Extravagant Situations—Treatment of the *Parisina* Motive—The Florentine *Burla*—Apology for Il Lasca's Repulsiveness—Firenzuola—His Life—His Satires on the Clergy—His Dialogue on Beauty—Novelettes and Poems—Doni's Career—His Bizarre Humour—Bohemian Life at Venice—The Pellegrini—His *Novelle*—Miscellaneous Works—The *Marmi*—The Novelists of Siena—Their Specific Character—Sermini—Fortini—Bargagli's Description of the Siege of Siena—Illicini's Novel of *Angelica*—The *Proverbi* of Cornazano—The *Notti Piacevoli* of Straparola—The Novel of *Belphegor*—Straparola and Machiavelli—Giraldi Cinthio's *Hecatommithi*—Description of the Sack of Rome—Plan of the Collection—The Legend of the Borgias—Comparison of Italian Novels and English Plays.

OF Boccaccio's legacy the most considerable portion, and the one that bore the richest fruit, was the Decameron. During the sixteenth century the *Novella*, as he shaped it, continued to be a popular and widely practised form of literature. In Italy the keynote of the Renaissance was struck by the *Novella*, as in England by the Drama. Nor is this predominance of what must be reckoned a subordinate branch of fiction, altogether singular; for the *Novella* was in a special

sense adapted to the public which during the Age of
the Despots grew up in Italy. Since the fourteenth
century the conditions of social life had undergone a
thorough revolution. Under the influence of dynastic
rulers stationed in great cities, merchants and manu-
facturers were confounded with the old nobility ; and
in commonwealths like Florence the *bourgeoisie* gave
their tone to society. At the same time the community thus formed was separated from the people by
the bar of humanistic culture. Literature felt this
social transformation. Its products were shaped to
suit the taste of the middle classes, and at the same
time to amuse the leisure of the aristocracy. The
Novella was the natural outcome of these circumstances.
Its qualities and its defects alike betray the ascendancy
of the *bourgeois* element.

When a whole nation is addressed in drama or
epic, it is necessary for the poet to strike a lofty and
noble note. He appeals to collective humanity, and
there is no room for aught that savours of the trivial
and base. Homer and Sophocles, Dante and Shakspere, owed their grandeur in no slight measure to the
audience for whom they laboured. The case is altered
when a nation comes to be divided into orders, each of
which has its own peculiar virtues and its own beset-
ting sins. Limitations are of necessity introduced, and
deflections from the canon of universality are welcomed. If the poet, for example, writes for the
lowest classes of society, he can afford to be coarse,
but he must be natural. An aristocracy, taken by
itself, is apt, on the contrary, to demand from literature
the refinements of fashionable vice and the subtleties

of artificial sentiment. Under such influence we obtain the Arthurian legends of the later middle ages, which contrast unfavourably, in all points of simplicity and directness, with the earlier Niebelungen and Carolingian Cycles. The middle classes, for their part, delight in pictures of daily life, presented with realism, and flavoured with satire that touches on the points of their experience. Literature produced to please the *bourgeois*, must be sensible and positive ; and its success will greatly depend upon the piquancy of its appeal to ordinary unidealised appetites. The Italians lacked such means of addressing the aggregated masses of the nation as the panhellenic festivals of Greece afforded. The public which gave its scale of grandeur and sincerity to the Attic and Elizabethan drama, was wanting. The literature of the *cinque cento*, though it owed much to the justice of perception and simple taste of the true people, was composed for the most part by men of middle rank for the amusement of citizens and nobles. It partook of those qualities which characterise the upper and middle classes. It was deficient in the breadth, the magnitude, the purity, which an audience composed of the whole nation can alone communicate. We find it cynical, satirical, ingenious in sly appeals to appetite, and oftentimes superfluously naughty. Above all it was emphatically the literature of a society confined to cities.

It may be difficult to decide what special quality of the Italian temperament was satisfied with the *Novella*. Yet the fact remains that this species of composition largely governed their production, not only in the field of narrative, but also in the associated region of poetry and in the plastic arts. So powerful was the attraction it possessed, that even the legends of the saints assumed this character. A notable portion of the *Sacre Rappresentazioni* were dramatised *Novelle.* The romantic poets interwove *Novelle* with their main theme, and the charm of the *Orlando Furioso* is due in no small measure to such episodes. Popular poems of the type represented by *Ginevra degli Almieri* were versified *Novelle.* Celebrated trials, like that of the Countess of Cellant, Vittoria Accoramboni, or the Cenci, were offered to the people in the form of *Novelle.* The humanists—Pontano, Poggio, Æneas Sylvius—wrote *Novelle* in Latin. The best serial pictures of the secondary painters—whether we select Benozzo Gozzoli's legend of S. Augustine at San Gemignano, or Carpaccio's legend of S. Ursula at Venice, or Sodoma's legend of S. Benedict at Monte Oliveto, or Lippo Lippi's legend of S. John at Prato— are executed in the spirit of the novelists. They are *Novelle* painted in their salient incidents for the laity to study on the walls of church and oratory.

The term *Novella* requires definition, lest the thing in question should be confounded with our modern novel. Although they bear the same name, these species have less in common than might be supposed. Both, indeed, are narratives ; but while the novel is a history extending over a considerable space of time, embracing a complicated tissue of events, and necessitating a study of character, the *Novella* is invariably brief and sketchy. It does not aim at presenting a detailed picture of human life within certain artistically chosen limitations, but confines itself to a striking situation, or tells an anecdote illustrative of some moral quality. This is shown by the headings of the sections into which Italian *Novellieri* divided their collections. We read such rubrics as the following : ' On the magnanimity of princes ; ' ' Concerning those who have been fortunate in love ; ' ' Of sudden changes from prosperity to evil fortune ; ' ' The guiles of women practised on their husbands.' A theme is proposed, and the *Novelle* are intended to exemplify it. The *Novelle* were descended in a direct line from the anecdotes embedded in medieval Treasuries, Bestiaries, and similar collections. The novel, on the other hand, as Cervantes, Richardson, and Fielding formed it for the modern nations, is an expansion and prose digest of the drama. It implies the drama as a previous condition of its being, and flourishes among races gifted with the dramatic faculty.

Furthermore, the *Novelle* were composed for the amusement of mixed companies, who met together and passed their time in conversation. All the *Novellieri* pretend that their stories were originally recited and then written down, nor is there the least doubt that in a large majority of cases they were really read aloud or improvised upon occasions similar to those invented by their authors. These circumstances determined the length and ruled the mechanism of the *Novella*. It was impossible within the short space of a spoken tale to attempt any minute analysis of character, or to weave the meshes of a complicated plot. The narrator went straight to his object, which was to arrest the attention, stimulate the curiosity, gratify the sensual instincts, excite the laughter, or stir the tender emotions

of his audience by some fantastic, extraordinary, voluptuous, comic, or pathetic incident. He sketched his
personages with a few swift touches, set forth their
circumstances with pungent brevity, and expended his
force upon the painting of the central motive. Sometimes he contented himself with a bare narrative,
leaving its details to the fancy. Many *Novelle* are the
mere skeletons of stories, short notes, and epitomes of
tales. At another time he indulged in descriptive
passages of great verbal beauty, when it was his
purpose to delight the ideal audience with pictures, or
to arouse their sympathy for his characters in a situation of peculiar vividness. Or he introduced digressions upon moral themes suggested by the passion of
the moment, discoursing with the easy flow of one who
raises points of casuistry in a drawing-room. Again,
he heightened the effects of his anecdote by elaborate
rhetorical development of the main emotions, placing
carefully-studied speeches into the mouth of heroine or
hero, and using every artifice for appealing directly to
the feelings of his hearers. Thus, while the several
Novellieri pursue different methods at different times
according to their purpose, their styles are all determined by the fact that recitation was essential to the
species. All of them, moreover, have a common
object in amusement. Though the *Novellieri* profess to
teach morality by precept, and though some of them
prefix prayers to their most impudent debauches of
the fancy,[1] it is clear that entertainment was their one

---

[1] See Bandello's Introduction to *Nov.* xxxv. of Part i., where a most
disgusting story is ushered in with ethical reflections ; and take this passage from the opening of one of Il Lasca's least presentable novels :
‘ Prima che al novellare di questa sera si dia principio, mi rivolgo a te, Dio

sole end in view. For their success they relied on the novelty and strangeness of their incidents ; on obscenity, sometimes veiled beneath the innuendoes and suggestive metaphors of Italian convention, but more often unabashed and naked to the view ; on startling horrors, acts of insane passion, or the ingenuities of diabolical cruelty. The humour of *beffe* and *burle*, jests played by rogues on simpletons, practical jokes, and the various devices whereby wives and lovers fooled confiding husbands, supplied abundant material for relieving the more tragic stories. Lastly, the wide realm of pathos, the spectacle of beauty in distress, young lovers overwhelmed by undeserved calamity, sudden reverses of fortune, and accidents of travel upon land and sea, provided the narrator with plentiful matter for working on the sympathy of his readers. Of moral purpose in any strict sense of the phrase the *Novelle* have none. This does not mean that they are invariably immoral ; on the contrary, the theme of a considerable number is such that the tale can be agreeably told without violence to the most sensitive taste. But the novelist had no ethical intention ; therefore he brought every motive into use that might amuse or stimulate, with business-like indifference. He felt no qualm of conscience at provoking the cruder animal instincts, at dragging the sanctities of domestic life in the mire of his buffoonery, or at playing on the appetite for monstrous vice, the

ottimo e grandissimo, che solo tutto sai e tutto puoi, pregandoti divotamente e di cuore, che per la tua infinita bontà e clemenza mi conceda, e a tutti questi altri che dopo me diranno, tanto del tuo ajuto e della tua grazia, che la mia lingua e la loro non dica cosa niuna, se non a tua lode e a nostra consolazione.'—*Le Cene* (Firenze, Lemonnier, 1857), p. 7.

thirst for abnormal sensations, in his audience. So long as he could excite attention, he was satisfied. We cannot but wonder at the customs of a society which derived its entertainment from these tales, when we know that noble ladies listened to them without blushing, and that bishops composed them as a graceful compliment to the daughter of a reigning duke.[1]

In style the *Novelle* are, as might be expected, very unequal. Everybody tried his hand at them : some wrote sparkling Tuscan, others a dense Lombard dialect; some were witty, others dull. Yet all affected to be following Boccaccio. His artificial periods and rhetorical amplifications, ill-managed by men of imperfect literary training, who could not free themselves from local jargons, produced an awkward mixture of discordant faults. Yet the public expected little from the novelist in diction. What they required was movement, stimulus, excitement of their passions. So long as the tale-maker kept curiosity awake, it was a matter of comparative indifference what sort of words he used. The *Novella* was a literary no-man's-land, where the critic exercised a feeble sway, and amateurs or artists did what each found suited to his powers. It held its ground under conditions similar to those which determined the supply of plays among us in the seventeenth century, or of magazine novels in this.

---

[1] It may be mentioned that not *all* stories were recited before women. Bandello introduces one of his tales with the remark that in the absence of the ladies men may be less careful in their choice of themes (*Nov.* xxx. pt. i.). The exception is singular, as illustrating what was thought unfit for female ears. The *Novella* itself consists of a few jokes upon a disgusting subject ; but it is less immodest than many which he dedicated to noble women.

In their material the *Novelle* embraced the whole
of Italian society, furnishing pictures of its life and
manners from the palaces of princes to the cottages of
contadini. Every class is represented—the man of
books, the soldier, the parish priest, the cardinal, the
counter-jumper, the confessor, the peasant, the duke,
the merchant, the noble lady, the village maiden, the
serving-man, the artisan, the actor, the beggar, the
courtesan, the cut-throat, the astrologer, the lawyer,
the physician, the midwife, the thief, the preacher, the
nun, the pander, the fop, the witch, the saint, the
galley-slave, the friar—they move before us in a motley
multitude like the masquerade figures of carnival time,
jostling each other in a whirl of merriment and passion,
mixing together in the frank democracy of vice.
Though these pictures of life are brightly coloured and
various beyond description, they are superficial. It is
only the surface of existence that the *Novelliere* touches.
He leaves its depths unanalysed, except when he
plunges a sinister glance into some horrible abyss of
cruelty or lust, or, stirred by gentler feeling, paints an
innocent unhappy youthful love. The student of contemporary Italian customs will glean abundant information from these pages ; the student of human nature
gathers little except reflections on the morals of sixteenth-century society. It was perhaps this prodigal
superfluity of striking incident, in combination with
poverty of intellectual content, which made the *Novelle*
so precious to our playwrights. The tales of Cinthio
and Bandello supplied them with the outlines of tragedies, leaving the poet free to exercise his analytic and
imaginative powers upon the creation of character and

the elaboration of motive. But that in spite of all their faults, the *Novelle* fascinate the fancy and stimulate the mental energies, will be admitted by all who have made them the subject of careful study.

To render an adequate account of the *Novellieri* and their works is very difficult.[1] The printing-press poured novels forth in every town in Italy, and authors of all districts vied with one another in their composition. At Florence Firenzuola penned stories with the golden fluency and dazzling wealth of phrase peculiar to him. Il Lasca's *Cene* rank among the most considerable literary products of the age. At Florence, again, Machiavelli wrote *Belphegor*, and Scipione Bargagli printed his *Trattenimenti*. Gentile Sermini, Pietro Fortini and Giustiniano Nelli were the novelists of Siena; Masuccio and Antonio Mariconda, of Naples. At Rome the Modenese Francesco Maria Molza rivalled the purity of Tuscan in his *Decamerone*. But it was chiefly in the North of Italy that novelists abounded. Giraldi's hundred tales, entitled *Hecatommithi*, issued from Ferrara. They were heavy in style, and prosaic; yet their matter made them widely popular. Sabadino wrote his *Porretane* at Bologna, and Francesco Straparola of Caravaggio published his *Tredici piacevoli Notti* at Venice. There also appeared the *Diporti* of Girolamo Parabosco, the *Sei Giornate* of Sebastiano Erizzo, Celio Malespini's *Ducento Novelle*, and the *Proverbi* of Antonio Cornazano. Cademosto of Lodi, Monsignor Brevio of Venice, Ascanio de' Mori of Mantua, Luigi da Porto

---

[1] *I Novellieri in Prosa*, by Giambattista Passano (Milano, Schiepatti, 1864), will be found an excellent dictionary of reference.

of Vicenza, and, last not least, the illustrious Matteo
Bandello, proved how rich in this species of literature
were the northern provinces. The Lombards displayed a special faculty for tales in which romance
predominated. Venice, notorious for her pleasure-
marts of luxury, became the emporium of publications which supplied her courtesans and rufflers with
appropriate mental food. The Tuscans showed more
comic humour, and, of course, a purer style. But in
point of matter, intellectual and moral, there is not
much to choose between the works of Florentine and
Lombard authors.

Following the precedent of Boccaccio, it was usual
for the *Novellieri* to invent a framework for their
stories, making it appear that a polite society of men
and women (called in Italy a *lieta brigata*) had by some
chance accident been thrown upon their own resources
in circumstances of piquant novelty. One of the
party suggests that they should spend their time in
telling tales, and a captain is chosen who sets the
theme and determines the order of the story-tellers.
These introductions are not unfrequently the most
carefully written portion of the collection, and abound
in charming sketches of Italian life. Thus Il Lasca
at the opening of *Le Cene* feigns that a company of
young men and women went in winter time to visit at
a friend's house in Florence. It was snowing, and the
youths amused themselves by a snow-ball match in the
inner courtyard of the palace. The ladies watched
them from a *loggia*, till it came into their heads to join
the game. Snow was brought them from the roofs,
and they began to pelt the young men from their bal-

cony.[1] The fire was returned; and when the *brigata*
had enough of this fun, they entered the house together, dried their clothes, and, sitting round a blazing
hearth, formed a plan for telling stories at supper.
Girolamo Parabosco places the scene of his *Diporti* on
the Venetian lagoons. A party of gentlemen have
left the city to live in huts of wood and straw
upon the islands, with the intention of fowling and
fishing. The weather proves too bad for sport, and
they while away the hours of idleness with anecdotes.
Bandello follows a different method, which had been
suggested by Masuccio. He dedicates his *Novelle* to
the distinguished people of his acquaintance, in prefaces not devoid of flattery, but highly interesting to a
student of those times. Princes, poets, warriors, men
of state, illustrious women, and humanists pass before
us in these dedications, proving that polite society in
Italy, the society of the learned and the noble, was a
republic of wit and culture. Alessandro Bentivoglio
and Ippolita Sforza, the leaders of fashion and Bandello's special patrons, take the first rank.[2] Then we
have the Gonzaga family of Mantua, Lancinus Cur-
tius, Aldus Manutius, Machiavelli, Molsa, Guicciardini,
Castiglione, the Duchess of Urbino, Giovanni de'
Medici, Julius Cæsar Scaliger, Bernardo Tasso, Pro-
spero Colonna, Julius II., Porcellio, Pontano, Berni, the
Milanese Visconti, the Neapolitan Sanseverini, the
Adorni of Genoa, the Foscari of Venice, the Estensi

---

[1] This motive may have been suggested by Folgore da S. Gemignano's sonnet on the month of January.

[2] These are the pair so nobly painted by Luini above the high-altar of
S. Maurizio at Milan. See my *Sketches and Studies in Italy.*

of Ferrara. Either directly addressed in prefaces or mentioned with familiar allusion in the course of the narratives, these historic names remind us that the author lived at the centre of civilisation, and that his *Novelle* were intended for the entertainment of the great world. What Castiglione presents abstractedly and in theory as a critique of noble society, is set before us by Bandello in the concrete form of every-day occurrence. Nor does the author forget that he is speaking to th   company. His words are framed to suit their prejudices; his allusions have reference to their sentiments and predilections. The whole work of art breathes the air of good manners and is tuned to a certain pitch-note of fashionable tone. We may be astounded that ladies and gentlemen of the highest birth and breeding could tolerate the licences of language and suggestion furnished by Bandello for their delectation. We may draw conclusions as to their corruption and essential coarseness in the midst of re-fined living and external gallantries.[1] Yet the fact remains that these *Novelle* were a customary adjunct to the courtly pleasures of the sixteenth century; and it was only through the printing-press that they passed into the taverns and the brothels, where perhaps they found their fittest audience.

Matteo Bandello was a member of the petty Lombard nobility, born at Castelnuovo in Tortona. His uncle was General of the Dominicans, and this circum-

---

[1] What we know about manners at the Courts of our Elizabeth and James, and the gossip of the French Court in Brantome's *Dames Galantes*, remind us that this blending of grossness and luxury was not peculiar to Italy.

stance determined Matteo's career. After spending
some years of his youth at Rome, he entered the
order of the Predicatori in the Convent delle Grazie at
Milan. He was not, however, destined to the seclusion of a convent; for he attended his uncle, in the
character apparently of a companion or familiar secretary, when the General visited the chief Dominican
establishments of Italy, Spain, France and Germany.
A considerable portion of Bandello's manhood was
passed at Mantua, where he became the tutor and the
platonic lover of Lucrezia Gonzaga. Before the date
1525, when French and Spaniards contested the
Duchy of Milan, he had already formed a collection of
Novelle in manuscript—the fruits of all that he had
heard and seen upon his frequent travels. These
were dispersed when the Spaniards entered Milan and
pillaged the house of the Bandello family.[1] Matteo,
after numerous adventures as an exile, succeeded in
recovering a portion of his papers, and retired with
Cesare Fregoso to the Court of France. He now set
himself seriously to the task of preparing his *Novelle*
for the press ; nor was this occupation interrupted by
the duties of the see of Agen, conferred upon him in
1550 by Henry II. The new bishop allowed his
colleague of Grasse to administer the see, drawing
enough of its emoluments for his private needs, and
attending till his death, about the year 1560, to study
and composition.

Bandello's life was itself a *novella*. The scion of a
noble house, early dedicated to the order of S. Dominic,
but with the General of that order for his uncle, he

---

[1] *See Dedication to Nov.* xi. *of second part.*

enjoyed rare opportunities of studying men and manners in all parts of Europe. His good abilities and active mind enabled him to master the essentials of scholarship, and introduced him as tutor to one of the most fascinating learned women of his age. These privileges he put to use by carrying on a courtly flirtation with his interesting pupil, at the same time that he penned his celebrated novels. The disasters of the Milanese Duchy deprived him of his literary collections and probably injured his fortune. But he found advancement on a foreign soil, and died a bishop at the moment when Europe was ringing with the scandals of his too licentious tales. These tales furnished the Reformers with a weapon in their war against the Church ; nor would it have been easy to devise one better to their purpose. Even now it moves astonishment to think that a monk should have written, and a bishop should have published, the *facetiæ* with which Bandello's books are filled.

Bandello paints a society in dissolution, bound together by no monarchical or feudal principles, without patriotism, without piety, united by none of the common spiritual enthusiasms that make a people powerful. The word honour is on everybody's lips ; but the thing is nowhere : and when the story-teller seeks to present its ideal image to his audience, he proves by the absurdity of his exaggeration that he has no clear conception of its meaning.[1] The virtues which inspired

---

[1] Read, for example, the *Novella* of Zilia, who imposed silence on her lover because he kissed her, and the whole sequel to his preposterous obedience (iii. 17) ; or the tale of Don Giovanni Emmanuel in the lion's den (iii. 39) ; or the rambling story of Don Diego and Ginevra la Bionda (i. 27). The two latter have a touch of Spanish extravagance, but without

an earlier and less corrupt civility, have become occasions for insipid rhetoric. The vice that formerly
stirred indignation, is now the subject of mirth. There
is no satire, because there is no moral sense. Bandello's revelations of clerical and monastic immorality
supplied the enemies of Rome with a full brief; but it
is obvious that Bandello and his audience regarded
the monstrous tale of profligacy with amusement. His
frankness upon the very eve of the Council of Trent
has something at once cynical and sinister. It makes
us feel that the hypocrisy engendered by the German
Reformation, the *si non caste tamen caute* of the new
ecclesiastical *régime*, was the last resort of a system so
debased that vital regeneration had become impossible.
This does not necessarily mean that the Italian Church
had no worthy ministers in the sixteenth century. But
when her dealing with the people ended in a humorous acceptance of such sin, we perceive that the
rottenness had reached the core. To present the
details of Bandello's clerical stories would be impossible
in pages meant for modern readers. It is enough to
say that he spares no rank or order of the Roman
priesthood. The prelate, the parish curate, the abbot
and the prioress, the monk and nun, are made the
subject of impartial ribaldry.[1] The secrets of convents
abandoned to debauchery are revealed with good-
humoured candour, as though the scandal was too
common to need special comment.[2] Sometimes Ban-

the glowing Spanish passion. In quoting Bandello, I shall refer to *Part*
and *Novel* by two numerals. References are made to the Milanese edition,
Novellieri Italiani, 1813–1816.

[1] For instance, Parte ii. *Nov.* 14 ; ii. xlv. ; iii. 2, 3, 4, 7, 20.
[2] See the description in ii. 36 (vol. v. p. 270) ; and again, iii. 61, ii. 45.

dello extracts comedy from the contrast between the hypocritical pretensions of his clerical ruffians and their lawless conduct, as in the story of the priest who for his own ends persuaded his parishioners that the village was haunted by a griffin.[1] Sometimes he succeeds in drawing a satirical portrait, like that of the Franciscan friar who domesticated himself as chaplain in the castle of a noble Norman family.[2] But the majority of these tales are simply obscene, with no point but a coarse picture or a shockingly painful climax.[3]

The same judgment may be passed upon a large portion of the *Novelle* which deal with secular characters. They are indecent anecdotes, and do not illustrate any specific quality in the author or in the temper of his times.[4] The seasoning of horror only serves to render their licentiousness more loathsome. As Bandello lacked the indignation of Masuccio, so he failed to touch Masuccio's tragic chord. When he attempted it, as in the ghastly story of Violante, who revenged herself upon a faithless lover by tearing him to pieces with pincers, or in the disgusting novel of Pandora, or again in the tale of the husband who forced his wife to strangle her lover with her own hands, he only rouses physical repulsion.[5] He makes our flesh creep, and produces literature analogous to that of the *Police Times.* Nor does he succeed better with subjects that require the handling of a profound psychologist. His

---

[1] ii. 2. [2] ii. 24.

[3] See, for instance, ii. 20 ; ii. 7.

[4] I need not give any references to the *Novelle* of this grovelling type. But I may call attention to i. 35 ; ii. 11 ; iv. 34, 35. These tales are not exceptionally obscene ; they illustrate to what extent mere filth of the Swiftian sort passed for fun in the Italy of Bembo and Castiglione.

[5] i. 42 ; iii. 21 ; iii. 52 ; ii. 12.

Rosmunda and Tarquin, his Faustina and Seleucus, leave an impression of failure through defect of imaginative force[1]; while the incestuous theme of one tale, treated as it is with frigid levity, can claim no justification on the score of dramatic handling or high-wrought spiritual agony.[2]

It was not in this region of tragic terror that Bandello's genius moved with freedom. In describing the luxury of Milan or the manners of the Venetian courtesans, in bringing before us scenes from the *demi-monde* of Rome or painting the life of a *grisette*, he shows acute knowledge of society, studied under its more superficial aspects, and produces pictures that are valuable for the antiquarian.[3] The same merit of freshness belongs to many minor anecdotes, like the romance of the girl who drowned herself in the Oglio to save her honour, or the pretty episode of Costantino Boccali who swam the Adige in winter at a thoughtless lady's behest.[4] Yet in Bandello's versions of contemporary histories which taxed the imaginative powers or demanded deeper insight into human passions, we miss the true dramatic ring. It was only when it fell into the hands of Webster, that his dull narrative of the Duchess of Amalfi revealed its capacities for artistic treatment.[5] Nor is the story of the Countess of

[1] iii. 18 ; ii. 21 ; i. 36 ; iii. 55.   [2] ii. 35 ; cp. i. 37.

[3] The pictures of Milanese luxury before the Spanish occupation are particularly interesting. See i. 9, and the beginning of ii. 8. It seems that then, as now, Milan was famous for her equipages and horses. The tale of the two fops who always dressed in white (iii. 11) brings that life before us. For the Venetian and Roman *demi-monde*, iii. 31 ; i. 19 ; i. 42 ; ii. 51, may be consulted. These passages have the value of authentic studies from contemporary life, and are told about persons whom the author knew at least by name.

[4] 1. 8 ; i. 47.   [5] i. 26.

Cellant, though full of striking details, so presented as to leave the impression of tragedy upon our minds.[1] We only feel what Webster, dealing with it as he dealt with Vittoria Corombona's crime, might have made out of this poor material.

It may be asked, if this is all, why anyone should take the pains to read through the two hundred and fourteen *Novelle* of Bandello, and, having done so,' should think it worth his while to write about them. Ought they not rather to be left among the things the world would willingly let die? The answer to this question is twofold. In the first place they fairly represent the whole class of novels which were produced so abundantly in Italy that the historian of Renaissance literature cannot pass them by in silence. Secondly, Bandello at his best is a great artist in the story-teller's craft. The conditions under which he displayed his powers to true advantage, require some definition. Once only did he successfully handle a really comic situation. That was in his tale of the monkey who dressed himself up in a dead woman's clothes, and frightened her family when they returned from the funeral, by mimicking her movement.[2] He was never truly tragic. But in the intermediate region between tragedy and comedy, where situations of romantic beauty offer themselves to the sympathetic imagination —in that realm of pathos and adventure, where pictures of eventful living can be painted, and the conflicts of tender emotion have to be described, Bandello proved himself a master. It would make the orthodox Italian critics shudder in their graves to hear that he had been

[1] i. 108.   [2] iii. 65.

compared to Ariosto. Yet a foreigner, gifted with obtuser sensibility to the refinements of Italian diction, may venture the remark that Bandello was a kind of prose Ariosto—in the same sense as Heywood seemed a prose Shakspere to Charles Lamb. Judged by the high standard of Athenian or Elizabethan art, neither Ariosto nor Bandello was a first-rate dramatist. But both commanded the material of which romantic tragedies can be constructed. Bandello's best *Novelle* abound in the situations which delighted our playwrights of the Jacobean age—in the thrilling incidents and scenes of high-wrought passion we are wont to deem the special property of Fletcher. He puts them before us with a force of realistic colouring, and develops them with a warmth of feeling, that leave no doubt of his artistic skill. Composition and style may fail him, but his sympathy with the poetic situation, and his power to express it are unmistakeable. In support of this opinion I might point to his vigorous but repulsive presentation of Parisina's legend, where the gradual yielding of a sensitive young man to the seductions of a sensual woman, is painted with touches of terrible veracity.[1] Or the tale of the Venetian lovers might be chosen.[2] Gerardo and Elena were secretly married; but in his absence on a voyage, she was plighted by her father to another husband. Before the consummation of this second marriage, Elena fell through misery into a death-like trance, and was taken by her kindred to be buried at Castello on the shores of the lagoons. At the moment when the funeral procession was crossing the waters by the light of many torches, the ship of Gerardo

---

[1] i. 44.   [2] ii. 41.

cast anchor in the port of Venice, and the young man heard that his wife was dead. Attended by a single friend, he went under cover of the night to where she had been laid in a sarcophagus outside the church. This he opened, and, frantic between grief and joy, bore the corpse of his beloved to his boat. He kissed her lips, and laid himself beside her lifeless body, wildly refusing to listen to his friend's expostulations. Then while the gondola rocked on the waves of the lagoons and the sea-wind freshened before daybreak, Elena awoke. It is needless to add that the story ends in happiness. This brief sketch conveys no notion of the picturesque beauty of the incidents described, or of the intimate acquaintance with Venetian customs displayed in the *Novella*. To one who knows Venice, it is full of delicate suggestions, and the reader illuminates the margin with illustrations in the manner of Carpaccio.

There is a point of Romeo and Juliet in the tale of Gerardo and Elena. Bandello's own treatment of the Veronese romance deserves comparison with Shakspere's.[1] The evolution of the tragedy is nearly the same in all its leading incidents ; for we hear of Romeo's earlier love, and the friar who dealt in simples is there, and so are the nurse and apothecary. Bandello has anticipated Shakspere even in Juliet's soliloquy before she drinks the potion, when the dreadful thought occurs to her that she may wake too soon, and find herself alone among the dry bones of her ancestors, with Tybalt festering in his shroud. But the prose version exhibits one motive which Shakspere

[1] ii. 37. It is clear that both followed the earlier version of Da Porto.

missed. When Romeo opens the tomb, he rouses Juliet from her slumber, and in his joy forgets that he has drunk the poison. For a while the lovers are in paradise together in that region of the dead ; and it is only when the chill of coming death assails him, that Romeo remembers what he has done. He dies, and Juliet stabs herself with his sword. Had Shakspere chosen to develop this catastrophe, instead of making Romeo perish before the waking of Juliet, he might have wrought the most pathetically tragic scene in poetry. Reading the climax in Bandello, where it is overpoweringly affecting, we feel what we have lost.

Another *Novella* which provokes comparison with our dramatic literature—with the *Twelfth Night* or with Fletcher's *Philaster*—is the tale of Nicuola.[1] She and her brother Paolo were twins, so like in height and form and feature that it was difficult even for friends to know them apart. They were living with their father at Rome, when the siege of 1527 dispersed the family. Paolo was taken prisoner by Spaniards, and Nicuola went to dwell at Jesi. The *Novella* goes on to relate how she fell in love with a nobleman of Jesi, and entering his service disguised as a page, was sent by him to woo the lady of his heart ; and how this lady loved her in her page's

---

[1] ii. 36. This tale was fashionable in Italy. It forms the basis of that rare comedy, *Gli Ingannati*, performed by the Academy degli Intronati at Siena, and printed in 1538. The scene in this play is laid at Modena ; the main plot is interwoven with two intrigues—between Isabella's father and Lelia, the heroine ; and between Isabella's maid and a Spaniard. In spite of these complications the action is lucid, and the comedy is one of the best we possess. There is an excellent humorous scene of two innkeepers touting against each other for travellers (Act iii. 2). That Shakespere knew the *Novella* or the comedy before he wrote his *Twelfth Night* is more than probable.

dress. Then her brother, Paolo, returned, attired like her in white, and recognitions were made, and both couples, Paolo and the lady, Nicuola and the nobleman, were happily married in the end. It will be seen that these situations, involving confusions of identity and sex, unexpected discoveries, and cross-play of passions, offered opportunities for rhetorical and picturesque development in the style of a modern Euripides ; nor did Bandello fail to utilise them.

Of a higher type is the *Novella* which narrates the love of Edward III. for the virtuous Alice of Salisbury.[1] Here the interest centres in four characters— the King, Alice, and her father and mother, the Earl and Countess of Salisbury. There is no action beyond the conflict of motives and emotions caused by Edward's passion, and its successive phases. But that conflict is so vigorously presented that attention never flags ; and, though the tale is long, we are drawn without weariness by finely-modulated transitions to the point where a felicitous catastrophe is not only natural but necessary. What is at first a mere desire in Edward, passes through graduated moods of confident, despairing, soul-absorbing love. The ordinary artifices of a seducer are replaced by the powerful compulsion of a monarch, who strives to corrupt the daughter by working on her father's ambition and her mother's weakness. Thwarted by the girl's constancy at every turn, he sinks into love-melancholy, then rouses himself with the furious resolve to attempt force, and lastly, yielding to his nobler nature, offers

---

[1] ii. 37. Historians will not look for accuracy in what is an Italian love-tale founded on an English legend.

his crown to Alice. These several moments in the King's passion are exhibited with a descriptive wealth and exuberance of resource that remind us forcibly of our own stage. The contrasts between the girl's invincible honour and her lover's ungovernable impulse, between her firmness and her mother's feebler nature, and again between the sovereign's overbearing wilfulness and the Earl's stubborn but respectful resistance, suggest a series of high-wrought situations, which only need to be versified and divided into acts to make a drama. Fletcher himself might have proudly owned the scene in which Edward discovers his love to the Earl, begs him to plead with his daughter, and has to hear his reproaches, so courteously and yet unflinchingly expressed. What follows is equally dramatic. The Earl explains to Alice his own ideal of honour ; still he fairly sets before her the King's lawless offer, and then receives the assurance of her unconquerable chastity. Her mother, moved to feebler issues by the same pressure, attempts to break her daughter's resolve, and at last extorts a reluctant consent by her own physical agony. Finally, the girl, when left alone with her royal lover, demands from him or death or honour, and wins her cause by the nobility of her carriage in this hour of trial. The whole *Novella* in its choice of motives, method of treatment, and ethical tone, challenges comparison with Beaumont and Fletcher's serious plays. Nor is the style unlike theirs ; for the situations are worked out in copious and coloured language, hasty and diffuse, but charged and surcharged with the passion of the thing to be portrayed. Bandello, like Fletcher, strikes out images at every turn, enlarges in rhetorical digressions, and pours forth floods of voluble eloquence.[1] The morality, though romantic, is above his usual level ; for while he paints a dissolute and wilful prince in Edward, he contrives to make us feel that the very force of passion, when purified to true love by the constancy of Alice, has brought the monarch to a knowledge of his better self. Nor is the type of honour in Alice and the Earl exaggerated. They act and speak as subjects, conscious of their duty to the King, but resolved to preserve their self-respect at any cost, should speak and act. The compliance of the Countess, who is willing to sacrifice her daughter's honour under the impulse of blind terror, cannot be called unnatural. The consequent struggle between a mother's frailty and a daughter's firmness, though painful enough, is not so disagreeably presented as in Tourneur's *Revenger's Tragedy*. If all Bandello's novels had been conceived in the same spirit as this, he would have ranked among the best romantic writers of the modern age. As it is, we English may perhaps take credit to ourselves for the superior inspiration of the legend he here handled. The moral fibre of the tale is rather English than Italian.

Bandello was not unaware that his *Novelle* lay under

---

[1] Take the description of the King's love-sickness (*Nov. It.* vol. v. p. 352), the incident of the King's offer to the Earl (pp. 353, 354), Edward's musings (p. 364), Alice alone in London (p. 376), the King's defiance of opinion (p. 379), the people's verdict against Alice (p. 380), Alice arming herself with the dagger (p. 398), the garden scene upon the Thames (p. 399). Then the discourses upon love and temperament (p. 325), on discreet conduct in love affairs (pp. 334–338), on real and false courtiers (pp. 382–388). Compare the descriptive passages on pp. 352, 354, 369, 393, 395, 398, with similar passages in Beaumont and Fletcher.

censure for licentiousness. His apology deserves to be considered, since it places the Italian conscience on this point in a clear light. In the preface to the eleventh *Novella* of the second part, he attacks the question boldly.[1] 'They say that my stories are not honest. In this I am with them, if they rightly apprehend honesty. I do not deny that some are not only not honest, but I affirm and confess that they are most dishonest; for if I write that a maiden grants favours to a lover, I cannot pretend that the fact is not in the highest sense immoral. So also of many things I have narrated. No sane person will fail to blame incest, theft, homicide, and other vicious actions; and I concede that my *Novelle* set forth these and similar enormous crimes. But I do not admit that I deserve to be therefore blamed. The world ought to blame and stigmatise those who commit such crimes, and not the man who writes about them.' He then affirms that he has written his stories down as he heard them from the lips of the narrators, that he has clothed them in decent language, and that he has always been careful to condemn vice and to praise virtue. In the twenty-fourth novel of the same part he returns to the charge.[2] Hypocrites, he argues, complain that the Decameron and similar collections corrupt the morality of women and teach vice; 'but I was always of opinion that to commit crimes rather than to know about them was vicious. Ignorance is never good, and it is better to be instructed in the wickedness of

---

[1] *Nov. It.* vol. iv. p. 226. Compare the peroration of his Preface to the third part (vol. vii. p. 13).

[2] Vol. v. p. 38.

the world than to fall into error through defect of knowledge.' This apology, when read by the light of Bandello's own *Novelle*, is an impudent evasion of the accusation. They are a school of profligacy; and the author was at pains to make his pictures of sensuality attractive. That he should plume himself upon the decorum of his language, is simply comic. Such simulation of a conscience was all that remained at an epoch when the sense of shame had been extinguished, while acquiescence in the doctrines of a corrupt Church had not ceased to be fashionable.

Bandello is more sensitive to strictures on his literary style, and makes a better defence. ' They say that I have no style. I grant it; nor do I profess to be a master of prose, believing that if those only wrote who were consummate in their art, very few would write at all. But I maintain that any history, composed in however rough and uncouth a language, will not fail to delight the reader; and these novels of mine (unless I am deceived by their narrators) are not fables but true histories.'[1] In another place he confesses that his manner is and always has been 'light and low and deficient in intellectual quality.'[2] Again, he meets the objection that his diction is not modelled on the purest Tuscan masterpieces, by arguing that even Petrarch wrote Italian and not Tuscan, and that if Livy smacked of Patavinity, he, a Lombard, does not shrink from Lombardisms in his style.[3] The line of defence is good; but, what is more, Bandello knew that he was popular. He cared to be read by all

---

[1] Vol. iv. p. 226. Cp. vol. ix. p. 339.
[2] Vol. vi. p. 254.　　　　　　　[3] Vol. vii. p. 11.

classes of the people rather than to be praised by
pedants for the purity of his language. Therefore he
snapped his fingers at Speron Sperone and Trifone,
the so-called Socrates of his century. The *Novella*
was not a branch of scholarly but of vulgar literature ;
and Bandello had far better right to class himself
among Italian authors than Straparola or Giraldi,
whose novels were none the less sought after with
avidity and read with pleasure by thousands. It is
true that he was not a master of the best Italian prose,
and that his *Novelle* do not rank among the *Testi di
Lingua.* He is at one and the same time prolix and
involved, ornate and vulgar, coarse in phraseology and
ambitious in rhetoric. He uses metaphors borrowed
from the slang of the fashionable world to express
gross thoughts or actions. He indulges in pompous
digressions and overloads his narrative with illustrations. But, in spite of these defects, he is rarely dull.
His energy and copiousness of diction never fail him.
His style is penetrated with the passion of the subject, and he delights our imagination with wonderfully
varied pictures drawn from life. It is probable that
foreigners can render better justice to the merits of
Bandello as a writer, than Italians, who are trained to
criticise language from a highly refined and technical
point of view. We recognise his vividness and force
without being disgusted by his Lombardisms or the
coarseness of his phrases. Yet even some Italian
critics of no mean standing have been found to say a
good word for his style. Among these may be reckoned the judicious Mazzuchelli.[1]

[1] In the biography of Bandello he says, 'Lo stile è piuttosto colto e

The author of *Le Cene* presents a marked contrast to Bandello. Antonfrancesco Grazzini belonged to an ancient and honourable family of Staggia in Valdelsa.[1] Some of his ancestors held office in the Florentine republic, and many were registered in the Art of the Notaries. Born at Florence in 1503, he was matriculated into the Speziali, and followed the profession of a druggist. His literary career was closely connected with the academies of Gli Umidi and La Crusca.[2] The sobriquet Il Lasca, or The Roach, assumed by him as a member of the Umidi, is the name by which he is best known. Besides *Novelle*, he wrote comedies and poems, and made the renowned collection of *Canti Carnascialeschi*. He died in 1583 and was buried in S. Pier Maggiore. Thus while Bandello might claim to be a citizen of the great world, reared in the ecclesiastical purple and conversant with the noblest society of Northern Italy, Il Lasca began life and ended it as a Florentine burgher. For aught we know, he may not have travelled beyond the bounds of the republic. His stories are written in the raciest Tuscan idiom, and are redolent of the humour peculiar to Florence. If Bandello appropriated the romantic element in Boccaccio, Il Lasca chose his comic side for imitation. Nearly all his novels turn on *beffe* and *burle*, similar to those sketched in Sacchetti's anecdotes, or developed with greater detail by Pulci and the author of *Il Grasso, Legnaiuolo*.[3] Three boon companions, Lo

studiato, che che taluno n' abbia detto in contrario, non però in guisa che possa mettersi a confronto di quello del Boccaccio.'

[1] See Sonnet 79, *Rime* (ed. 1741).

[2] Founded respectively in 1540 and 1583. Grazzini quarrelled with them both.

[3] *Cena* i. *Nov.* 3, is in its main motive modelled on that novel.

Scheggia, Il Monaco, and Il Pilucca are the heroes of his comedy ; and the pranks they play, are described with farcical humour of the broadest and most powerful sort. Still the specific note of Il Lasca's novels is not pure fun. He combines obscenity with fierce carnal cruelty and inhuman jesting, in a mixture that speaks but ill for the taste of his time.[1] Neither Boccaccio nor the author of *Il Grasso* struck a chord so vicious, though the latter carried his buffoonery to the utmost stretch of heartlessness. It needed the depravity of the sixteenth century to relish the lust, seasoned with physical torture and spiritual agony, which was so cunningly revealed, so coldly revelled in by Il Lasca.[2] A practical joke or an act of refined vengeance had peculiar attraction for the Florentines. But the men must have been blunted in moral sensibility and surfeited with strange experiences, who could enjoy Pilucca's brutal tricks, or derive pleasure from the climax of a tale so ghastly as the fifth *Novella* of the second series.

This is a story of incest and a husband's vengeance. Substantially the same as Parisina's tragedy, Il Lasca has invented for it his own whimsically horrible conclusion. The husband surprises his wife and son. Then, having cut off their hands, feet, eyes and

---

[1] The contrast between the amiable manners of the young men and women described in the introduction to *Le Cene*, and the stories put into their mouths ; between the profound immorality, frigid and repellent, of the tales and Ghiacinto's prayer at the beginning ; need not be insisted on.

[2] As I shall not dilate upon these novels further in the text, I may support the above censure by reference to the practical joke played upon the pedagogue (i. 2), to the inhuman novel of *Il Berna* (ii. 2), to the cruel vengeance of a brother (ii. 7), and to the story of the priest (ii. 8).

tongues, he leaves them to die together on the bed where he had found them. The rhetoric with which this catastrophe is embellished, and the purring sympathy expressed for the guilty couple, only serve to make its inhumanity more glaring. Incapable of understanding tragedy, these writers of a vitiated age sought excitement in monstrous situations. The work produced is a proper pendent to the filth of the burlesque *Capitoli.* Literature of this sort might have amused Caligula and his gladiators. Prefaced by an unctuous prayer to God, it realises the very superfluity of naughtiness.[1]

In favour of the Florentines, we might plead that these *Novelle* were accepted as pure fictions—debauches of the fancy, escapades of inventive wit. The ideal world they represented, claimed no contact with realities of life. The pranks of Lo Scheggia and Il Pilucca, which drove one man into exile, another to the hospital, and a third to his death, had no more actuality than the tricks of clown and pantaloon. A plea of this sort was advanced by Charles Lamb for the dramatists of the Restoration ; and it carries, undoubtedly, its measure of conviction. Literature of convention, which begins by stimulating curiosity, must find novel combinations and fresh seasonings, to pique the palate of the public. Thus the abominations of Il Lasca's stories would have to be regarded as the last desperate bids for popularity, as final hyperboles of exhausted rhetoric. Yet, after all, books remain the mirror of a people's taste. Whatever their quality may be, they are produced to satisfy some demand. And the wonderful

[1] See above, p. 56, note.

vivacity of Il Lasca's colouring, the veracity of his
art, preclude him from the benefit of a defence which
presupposes that he stood in some unnatural relation
to his age. While we read his tales, we cannot but
remember the faces painted by Bronzino, or modelled
by Cellini. The sixteenth-century Florentines were
hard and cold as steel. Their temper had been brutal-
ised by servitude, superficially polished by humanism,
blunted by the extraordinary intellectual activity of
three centuries. Compared with the voluptuous but
sympathetic mood of the Lombard novelists, this
cruelty means something special to the race.

Some of Il Lasca's stories, fortunately, need no
such strained apology or explanation. The tale of
Lisabetta's dream, though it lacks point, is free from his
worse faults[1]; while the novel of Zoroaster is not only
innocent, but highly humorous and charged with
playful sarcasm.[2] It contains a portrait of a knavish
astrologer, worthy to be set beside the *Negromante* of
Ariosto or Ben Jonson's *Alchemist*. When Jerome
Cardan was coquetting with chiromancy and magic,
when Cellini was raising fiends with the Sicilian necromancer in the Coliseum, a novelist found sufficient
stuff for comedy and satire in the foibles of ghost-
seekers and the tricks of philtre-mongers. The companion portrait of the dissolute monk, who sets his
hand to any dirty work that has the spice of fun in it,
is also executed with no little spirit.

Among the most graceful of the Tuscan novelists
may be mentioned Agnolo Firenzuola. His family
derived its name from a village at the foot of the

---

[1] *Cena* ii. 3.   [2] *Cena* ii. 4.

Pistojan Apennines, and his father was a citizen of Florence. Agnolo spent his youth at Siena and Perugia, where he made the friendship of Pietro Aretino, leading the wild student life described in their correspondence.[1] That he subsequently entered the Vallombrosan order seems to be certain ; but it is somewhat doubtful whether he attained the dignity of Abbot which his biographers ascribe to him.[2] Tiraboschi, unwilling to admit so great a scandal to the Church, has adduced reasons why we should suspend our judgment.[3] Yet the tradition rests on substantial authority. A monument erected by Firenzuola to his uncle Alessandro Braccio in the church of S. Prassede at Rome, describes him as *ædis hujus Abbas*. S. Maria di Spoleti and S. Salvator di Vaiano are supposed to have been his benefices. Some further collateral proof might be drawn from the opening of the dialogue *Sopra le Bellezze delle Donne*. The scene of it is laid in the convent grounds of Grignano, and Celso is undoubtedly Firenzuola. A portion of his manhood was spent at Rome in friendship with Molza, Berni, and other brilliant literary men. While resident in Rome, he contracted a severe and tedious illness, which obliged him to retire to Prato, where he spent some of the happiest years of his life.[4] Nearly all his works contain frequent and affectionate recollections of

---

[1] See the Letters of Aretino, vol. ii. p. 239.
[2] All my references are made to the *Opere di Messer Agnolo Firenzuola*, 5 vols. Milan, 1802.
[3] *Storia della Lett. It.* lib. iii. cap. 3, sect. 27.
[4] In a letter to Aretino, dated Prato, Oct. 5, 1541, he says he had been ill for eleven years. It seems probable that his illness was of the kind alluded to in his *Capitolo* 'In Lode del Legno Santo' (*Op. Volg.* iv. p. 204).

this sunny little town, the beauty of whose women is enthusiastically celebrated by him. Firenzuola died before the middle of the sixteenth century at the age of about fifty. Neither his life nor his friendships nor yet his writings were consistent with his monastic profession and the dignity of Abbot. The charm of Firenzuola's *Novelle* is due in a large measure to his style, which has a wonderful transparency and ease, a wealth of the rarest Tuscan phrases, and a freshness of humour that renders them delightful reading. The storm at sea in the first tale, and the night scene in the streets of Florence in the third, are described with Ariostean brilliancy.[1]   In point of subject-matter they do not greatly differ from the ordinary novels of the day, and some of the tales reappear in the collections of other novelists.[2] Most of them turn upon the foibles and the vices of the clergy. The fourth *Novella*, which is perhaps the best of all in style and humour, presents a truly comic picture of the parish priest, while the fifth describes the interior of a dissolute convent at Perugia, and the tenth exposes the arts whereby confessors induced silly women to make wills in the favour of their convents. Don Giovanni, Suor Appellagia, and Fra Cherubino, the chief actors in these stories, might be selected as typical characters in the Italian comedy of clerical dissoluteness.

Firenzuola prefaced his novels with an elaborate introduction, describing the meeting of some friends at Celso's villa near Pazolatico, and their discourse on

---

[1] *Op.* ii. pp. 94, 130.
[2] For example, *Nov.* iv. is the same as Bandello's II. xx. ; *Nov.* vii. is the same as Il Lasca's ii. 10, and Fortini's xiv.

love.[1] From discussion they pass to telling amorous stories under the guidance of a Queen selected by the company.[2] The introductory conversation is full of a dreamy, sensualised, disintegrated Platonism. It parades conventional distinctions between earthly and heavenly love, between the beauty of the soul and the beauty of the body ; and then we pass without modulation into the region of what is here called *accidenti amorosi*. The same insincere Platonism gives colour to Firenzuola's discourse on the Beauty of Women— one of the most important productions of the sixteenth century in illustration of popular and artistic taste.[3] The author imagines himself to have interrupted a bevy of fair ladies from Prato in the midst of a dispute about the beauty of Mona Amelia della Torre Nuova. Mona Amelia herself was present; and so were Mona Lampiada, Mona Amorrorisca, Mona Selvaggia, and Mona Verdespina.' Under these names it is clear that living persons of the town of Prato are designated ; and all the examples of beauty given in the dialogue are chosen from well-known women of the district. The composition must therefore be reckoned as an

---

[1] Vol. ii. p. 28. The poem put into Celso's mouth, p. 39, is clearly autobiographical.

[2] There is the usual reference to Boccaccio, at p. 32. I may take this occasion for citing an allusion to Boccaccio from the Introduction to *Le Cene*, which shows how truly he was recognised as the patron saint of novelists. See *Le Cene* (Firenze, Lemonnier, 1857), p. 4.

[3] Vol. i. pp. 1–97. I may here allude to a still more copious and detailed treatise on the same theme by Federigo Luigino of Udine : *Il Libro della Bella Donna*, Milano, Daelli, 1863 ; a reprint from the Venetian edition of 1554. This book is a symphony of graceful images and delicately chosen phrases ; it is a dithyramb in praise of feminine beauty, which owes its charm to the intense sympathy, sensual and æsthetic, of the author for his subject.

[4] Selvaggia was the lady of Firenzuola's *Rime*.

elaborate compliment from Firenzuola to the fair sex of Prato.[1] Celso begins his exposition of beauty by declaring that 'it is God's highest gift to human nature, inasmuch as by its virtue we direct our soul to contemplation, and through contemplation to the desire of heavenly things.'[2] He then proceeds to define beauty as 'an ordered concord, or, as it were, a harmony inscrutably resulting from the composition, union, and commission of divers members, each of which shall in itself be well proportioned and in a certain sense beautiful, but which, before they combine to make one body, shall be different and discrepant among themselves.'[3] Having explained each clause of this definition, he passes to the appetite for beauty, and tells the myth invented for Aristophanes in Plato's *Symposium.* This leads by natural transitions to the real business of the dialogue, which consists in analysing and defining every kind of loveliness in women, and minutely describing the proportions, qualities, and colours of each portion of the female body. The whole is carried through with the method of a philosopher, the enthusiasm of an artist, and the refinement of a well-bred gentleman. The articles upon *Leggiadria, Grazia, Vaghezza, Venustà, Aria, Maestà,* may even now be read with profit by those who desire to comprehend the nice gradations of meaning implied by these terms.[4] The discourses on the form and colour of the ear, and on the proper way of wearing ornamental flowers, bring incomparably graceful images

---

[1] See the *Elegia alle Donne Pratesi,* vol. iv. p. 41.

[2] Vol. i. p. 16. Compare the extraordinary paragraph about female beauty being an earnest of the beauties of Paradise (pp. 31, 32).

[3] *Ibid.* p. 21.   [4] *Ibid.* pp. 51–62.

before us [1]; and this, indeed, can be said about the whole dialogue, for there is hardly a sentence that does not reveal the delicate perceptions of an artistic nature.

Firenzuola's adaptation of the *Golden Ass* may be reckoned among the triumphs of his style, and the fables contained in his *Discorsi degli Animali* are so many minutely finished novelettes.[2] Both of these works belong to the proper subject of the present chapter. His comedies and his burlesque poems must be left for discussion under different headings. With regard to his serious verses, addressed to Mona Selvaggia, it will be enough to say that they are modelled upon Petrarch. Though limpid in style and musical, as all Firenzuola's writing never failed to be, they ring hollow. The true note of the man's feeling was sensual. The highest point it reached was the admiration for plastic beauty expressed in his dialogue on women. It had nothing in common with Petrarch's melancholy. Of these minor poems I admire the little ballad beginning *O rozza pastorella*, and the wonderfully lucid version of Poliziano's *Violæ—O viole formose, o dolci viole*—more than any others.[3]

Except for the long illness which brought him to Prato, Firenzuola appears to have spent a happy and mirthful life; and if we may trust his introduction to the Novels, he was fairly wealthy. What we know about the biography of Antonfrancesco Doni, who also deserves a place among the Tuscan novelists, presents

[1] Vol. i. pp. 75–80.
[2] Vol. iii. The *Golden Ass* begins with an autobiography (vol. i. p. 103).
[3] Vol. iv. pp. 19, 76.

a striking contrast to this luxurious and amorous existence.[1] He was a Florentine, and, like Firenzuola, dedicated to religion. Born in 1513, he entered the Servite order in the cloister of the Annunziata. He began by teaching the boys entrusted to the monks for education. But about 1540 he was obliged to fly the monastery under the cloud of some grave charge connected with his pupils.[2] Doni turned his back on Florence; and after wandering from town to town in Northern Italy, settled at last in 1542 at Piacenza, where he seems for a short while to have applied himself with an unwilling mind to law-studies. At Piacenza he made the acquaintance of Lodovico Domenichi, who introduced him into the Accademia Ortolana. This was a semi-literary club of profligates with the Priapic emblems for its ensign. Doni's wild and capricious humour made him a chief orna-ment of the society; but the members so misconducted themselves in word and deed that it was soon found necessary to suppress their meetings. While amusing himself with poetry and music among his boon com-panions, Doni was on the look-out for a place at Court or in the household of a wealthy nobleman. His letters at this period show that he was willing to become anything from poet or musician down to fool or something worse. Failing in all his applications, he at last resolved to make what gains he could by literature. His friend Domenichi had already settled at Venice, when Doni joined him there in 1544. But

---

[1] My principal authority is Doni's Life by S. Bongi prefixed to an edi-tion of the *Novelle*, 1851, and reprinted in Fanfani's edition of *I Marmi*, Florence, 1863.

[2] See Zilioli, quoted by Bongi, *I Marmi*, vol. i. p. xiv.

his stay was of brief duration. We find him again at Piacenza, next at Rome, and then at Florence, where he established a printing-press. The principal event of this Florentine residence was a definite rupture with Domenichi. We do not know the causes of their quarrel ; but both of them were such scamps that it is probable they took good care, while abusing one another in general terms, to guard the secrets of their respective crimes. During the rest of Doni's life he pursued his old friend with relentless animosity. His invectives deserve to be compared with those of the humanists in the preceding century ; while Domenichi, who had succeeded in securing a position for himself at Florence, replied with no less hostility in the tone of injured virtue.

In 1547 Doni settled finally at Venice. The city of the lagoons was the only safe resort for a man who had offended the Church by abandoning his vows, and whose life and writings were a scandal even in that age of licence. Everywhere else he would have been exposed to peril from the Inquisition. Though he had dropped the cowl, he could not throw aside the cassock, and his condition as priest proved not only irksome but perilous.[1] At Venice he lived a singular Bohemian existence, inhabiting a garret which overlooked one of the noisiest of the small canals, and scribbling for his daily bread. He was a rapid and prolific writer,

---

[1] How Doni hated his orders may be gathered from these extracts :
'La bestial cosa che sia sopportare quattro corna in capo senza belare unquanco. Io ho un capriccio di farmi scomunicare per non cantare più *Domine labia*, e spretarmi per non essere a noia a tutte le persone.'
'L' esser colla chierica puzza a tutti.' His chief grievance was that he had made no money out of the Church.

sending his copy to the press before it was dry, and never caring for revision. To gain money was the sole object of his labours. The versatility of his mind and his peculiar humour made his miscellanies popular ; and like Aretino he wheedled or menaced ducats out of patrons. Indeed, Doni's life at Venice is the proper pendent to Aretino's, who was once his friend and afterwards his bitter foe. But while Aretino contrived to live like a prince, Doni, for many years at any rate, endured the miseries of Grub Street. They quarrelled about a present which the Duke of Urbino had promised Doni through his secretary. Aretino thought that this meant poaching on his manors. Accordingly he threatened his comrade with a thorough literary scourging. Doni replied by a pamphlet with this singular title : ' Terremoto del Doni fiorentino, con la rovina d' un gran Colosso bestiale Antichristo della nostra età.' His capricious nature and bizarre passions made Doni a bad friend ; but he was an incomparably amusing companion. Accordingly we find that his society was sought by the literary circles of all cities where he lived. At Florence he had been appointed secretary to the Umidi. At Venice he became a member of the Pellegrini. This academy was founded before the League of Cambrai in a deserted villa near the lagoons.[1] Mystery hung over its origin and continued to involve its objects. Several wealthy noblemen of Venice supplied the club with ample funds. They had a good library, and employed two presses

---

[1] The greater part of what we know about the Pellegrini occurs in Doni's *I Marmi*. See also a memoir by Giaxich, and the notices in Mutinelli's *Diari Urbani*.

for the printing of their works. The members formed a kind of masonic body, bound together by strict mutual obligations, and sworn to maintain each other in peril or in want. They also exercised generosity toward needy men of letters, dowered poor girls, and practised many charities of a similar description. Their meetings took place in certain gardens at Murano or on the island of S. Giorgio Maggiore. The two Sansovini, Nardi, Titian, Dolce, and other eminent men belonged to the society; but Doni appears to have been its moving spirit on all occasions of convivial intercourse.

The last years of this Bohemian life were spent beneath the Euganean hills in a square castle, which, picturesquely draped with ivy, may still be seen towering above Monselice. That Doni had accumulated some capital by his incessant scribbling, is proved by the fact that he laid out the grounds about his fortress with considerable luxury. A passage quoted from the Venetian Zilioli serves to bring the man more vividly before us : ' At the summit of the hill above Monselice stands the house where Antonfrancesco Doni indulged his leisure with philosophy and poetry. He was a man of bizarre humour, who had but little patience with his neighbours. Retiring from society, he chose this abode in order to give full scope in his own way and without regard for anyone to his caprices, which were often very ludicrous. Who could have refrained from laughter, when he saw a man of mature age, with a beard down to his breast, going abroad at night barefooted and in his shirt, careering among the fields, singing his own songs and those of other poets ; or else in daytime playing on a lute and dancing like a little boy ?' Doni died at Venice in the autumn of 1574.

Doni's *Novelle* are rather detached scenes of life than stories with a plot or theme. Glowing and picturesque in style, sharply outlined, and smartly told, they have the point of epigrams. The fourth of the series might be chosen to illustrate the extravagant efforts after effect made by the Italian novelist with a view to stimulating the attention of his audience. It is a tale of two mortal enemies, one of whom kills the father and the brother of his foe. The injured man challenges and conquers him in single combat, when, having the ruffian at his mercy, he raises him from the ground, pardons him, and makes him his bosom friend. Likelihood and moral propriety are sacrificed in order that the *Novella* may end with a surprise.

Doni's *Novelle*, taken by themselves, would scarcely have justified the space allotted to him in this chapter. His biography has, however, the importance attaching to the history of a representative man, for much of the literature of amusement in the sixteenth century was supplied by Bohemians of Doni's type. To give a complete account of his miscellaneous works would be out of the question. Besides treatises on music and the arts of design and a catalogue of Italian books, which might be valuable if the author had not used it as a vehicle for his literary animosities, he published letters and poems, collections of proverbs and short tales under the title of *La Zucca*, dialogues and dissertations on various topics with the name of *I Mondi*, an essay on moral philosophy, an edition of Burchiello's poems illustrated by notes more difficult to understand than the text, an explanation of the Apocalypse proving Luther to be Antichrist, a libel upon Aretino, two commonplace books of sentences and maxims styled *I Cancellieri*, a work on villa-building, a series of imaginary pictures, a comedy called *Lo Stufaiuolo*, and many others which it would be tedious to catalogue. It is not probable that anyone has made a thorough study of Doni's writings ; but those who know them best, report that they are all marked by the same sallies of capricious humour and wild fancy.[1]

A glance at the *Marmi* will suffice to illustrate Doni's method in these miscellanies.[2] In his preface to the reader he says it often happens that, awaked from sleep, he spends the night-hours in thinking of himself and of his neighbours—' not, however, as the common folk do, nor like men of learning, but following the whimsies of a teeming brain. I am at home, you see. I fly aloft into the air, above some city, and believe myself to be a huge bird, monstrous, monstrous, piercing with keen sight to everything that's going on below ; and in the twinkling of an eye, the roofs fly off, and I behold each man, each woman at their several affairs. One is at home and weeping, another laughing ; one giving birth to children, one begetting ; this man reading, that man writing ; one eating, another praying. One is scolding his household, another playing ; and see, yon fellow has fallen starved to earth, while that one vomits his superfluous

---

[1] Those I am acquainted with are *I Marmi, I Mondi, Lo Stufaiuolo,* the *Novelle*, and two little burlesque caprices in prose, *La Mula* and *La Chiave.*

[2] *I Marmi*, per Fanfani e Bongi, Firenze, Barbèra, 1863, 2 vols.

food! What contrasts are there in one single city, at one single moment! Then I pass from land to land, and notice divers customs, with variety of speech and converse. In Naples, for example, the gentry are wont to ride abroad and take the evening freshness. In Rome they haunt cool vineyards, or seek their pleasure by artificial fountains. In Venice they roam the canals in dainty gondolas, or sweep the salt lagoons, with music, women, and such delights, putting to flight the day's annoyances and heat. But above all other pleasures in the cool, methinks the Florentines do best. Their way is this. They have the square of Santa Liberata, midway between the ancient shrine of Mars, now San Giovanni, and the marvellous modern Duomo. They have, I say, certain stairs of marble, and the topmost stair leads to a large space, where the young men come to rest in those great heats, seeing that a most refreshing wind is always blowing there, and a delicious breeze, and, besides, the fair white marbles for the most part keep their freshness. It is there I find my best amusements; for, as I sail through the air, invisibly I settle, soaring over them; and hear and see their talk and doings. And forasmuch as they are all fine wits and comely, they have a thousand lovely things to say—novels, stratagems and fables; they tell of intrigues, stories, jokes, tricks played off on men and women—all things sprightly, noble, noteworthy and fit for gentle ears.' Such is the exordium. What follows, consists of conversations, held at night upon these marble slabs by citizens of Florence. The dialogue is lively; the pictures tersely etched; the language racy; the matter almost always worthy of attention. One sustained dialogue on printing is particularly interesting, since it involves a review of contemporary literature from the standpoint of one who was himself exclusively employed in hack production for the press.[1] The whole book, however, abounds in excellent criticism and clever hints. 'See what the world is coming to,' says one of the speakers, 'when no one can read anything, full though it be of learning and goodness, without flinging it away at the end of three words! More artifice than patience goes nowadays to the writing of a book; more racking the brains to invent some whimsical title, which makes one take it up and read a word or two, than the composition of the whole book demands. Just try and tell people to touch a volume labelled *Doctrine of Good Living* or *The Spiritual Life*! God preserve you! Put upon the title page *An Invective against an Honest Man*, or *New Pasquinade*, or *Pimps Expounded*, or *The Whore Lost*, and all the world will grab at it. If our Gelli, when he wanted to teach a thousand fine things, full of philosophy and useful to a Christian, had not called them *The Cobbler's Caprices*, there's not a soul would have so much as touched them. Had he christened his book *Instructions in Civil Conduct* or *Divine Discourses*, it must have fallen stillborn; but that *Cobbler*, those *Caprices* make everyone cry out: "I'll see what sort of balderdash it is!"'

One might fancy that this passage had been written to satirise our own times rather than the sixteenth century. More than enough, however, re-

[1] Parte ii. 'Della Stampa.'

mains from the popular literature of Doni's days to illustrate his observation. We have already seen how ingeniously he titillated public curiosity in the title of his invective against Aretino. '*The Earthquake of Doni, the Florentine, with the Ruin of a Great Bestial Colossus, the Antichrist of our Age,*' is worthy to take rank among the most capricious pamphlets of the English Commonwealth. Meanwhile the Venetian press kept pouring out stores of miscellaneous information under bizarre titles ; such as the *Piazza*, which described all sorts of trades, including the most infamous, and *Il Perchè*, which was a kind of vulgar cyclopædia, with special reference to physiology. Manuals of domestic medicine or directions for the toilette, like the curious *Comare* on obstetrics, and Marinello's interesting *Ornamenti delle Donne*; eccentricities in the style of the *Hospidale de' Pazzi* or the *Sinagoga degli Ignoranti*; might be cited through a dozen pages. It is impossible to do justice to this undergrowth of literature, which testifies to the extent of the plebeian reading public in Italy.

The Novelists of Siena form a separate group, and are distinguished by a certain air of delicate voluptuous grace.[1] Siena, though it wears so pensive

---

[1] *Novelle di Autori Senesi*, edited by Gaetano Poggiali, Londra (Livorno). 1796. This collection, reprinted in the *Raccolta di Novellieri Italiani*, Milano, 1815, vols. xiv. and xv., contains Bernardo Illicini, Giustiniano Nelli, Scipione Bargagli, Gentile Sermini, Pietro Fortini, and others. Of Sermini's *Novelle* a complete edition appeared in 1874 at Livorno, from the press of Francesco Vigo ; and to this the student should now go. Romagnoli of Bologna in 1877 published three hitherto inedited novels of Fortini, together with the rubrics of all those which have not yet been printed. Their titles enable us to comprehend the scruples which prevented Poggiali from issuing the whole series.

an aspect now, was famous in the middle ages for the refinements of sensuality. It was here that the *godereccia brigata,* condemned to Hell by Dante, spent their substance in gay living. Folgore da San Gemignano's pleasure-seeking Company was Sienese. Beccadelli called the city *molles Senæ,* and Æneas Sylvius dedicated her groves and palaces to Venus—the Venus who appeared in dreams to Gentile Sermini.[1] The impress of luxury is stamped upon the works of her best novelists. They blend the *morbidezza* of the senses with a rare feeling for natural and artistic beauty. Descriptions of banquets and gardens, fountains and wayside thickets, form a delightful background to the never-ending festival of love. We wander through pleasant bypaths of Tuscan country, abloom in spring with acacia trees and resonant with song-birds. Though indescribably licentious, these novelists are rarely coarse or vulgar. There is no Florentine blackguardism, no acerbity of scorn or stain of blood-lust on their pages. They are humorous; but they do not season humour with cruelty. Their tales, for the most part, are the lunes of wanton love, day-dreams of erotic fancy, a free debauch of images, now laughable, now lewd, but all provocative of sensual desire. At the same time, their delight in landscape-painting, combined with a certain refinement of æsthetic taste, saves them from the brutalities of lust.

The foregoing remarks apply in their fullest extension to Sermini and Fortini. The best passages from the *Ars Amandi* of these authors admit of no quotation. Attention may, however, be called to the graphic de-

[1] *Imbasciata di Venere,* Sermini, ed. cit. p. 117.

scription by Sermini of the Sienese boxing-matches.[1] It is a masterpiece of vigorous dialogue and lively movement—a little drama in epitome or profile, bringing the excitement of the champions and their backers vividly before us by a series of exclamations and ejaculated sentences. Fortini does not offer the same advantage to a modest critic; yet his handling of a very comic situation in the fourteenth *Novella* may be conveniently compared with Firenzuola's and Il Lasca's treatment of the same theme.[2] Those, too, who are curious in such matters, may trace the correspondences between his twelfth *Novella* and many similar subjects in the *Cent nouvelles Nouvelles.* The common material of a *fabliau* is here Italianised with an exquisite sense of plastic and landscape beauty; and the crude obscenity of the *motif* craves pardon for the sake of its rare setting.

Bargagli's tales are less offensive to modern notions of propriety than either Sermini's or Fortini's. They do not detach themselves from the average of such compositions by any peculiarly Sienese quality. But his *Trattenimenti* are valuable for their introduction, which consists of a minute and pathetically simple narrative of the sufferings sustained by the Sienese during the siege of 1553. Boccaccio's description of the Plague at Florence was in Bargagli's mind, when he made this unaffected record of a city's agony the frontispiece to tales of mirth and passion. Though somewhat out of place, it has the interest which belongs to the faithful history of an eyewitness.

---

[1] *Il Giuoco della pugna,* Sermini, ed. cit. p. 105.
[2] See *Le Cene,* pt. ii. *Nov.* 10, and Firenzuola's seventh *Novella.*

One beautiful story, borrowed from the annals of their own city, was treated by the two Sienese novelists, Illicini and Sermini. The palm of excellence, however, must be awarded to the elder of these authors. Of Bernardo Lapini, surnamed Illicini or Ollicino, very little is known, except that he served both Gian Galeazzo Visconti and Borso da Este in the capacity of physician, and composed a commentary on the *Trionfi* of Petrarch. His *Novella* opens with a conversation between certain noble ladies of Siena, who agreed that the three most eminent virtues of a generous nature are courtesy, gratitude, and liberality. An ancient dame, who kept them company on that occasion, offered to relate a tale, which should illustrate these qualities and raise certain fine questions concerning their exercise in actual life. The two Sienese families De' Salimbeni and De' Montanini had long been on terms of coldness; and though their ancient feuds were passing into oblivion, no treaty of peace had yet been ratified between their houses, when Anselmo Salimbeni fell deeply in love with Angelica the only sister of Carlo Montanini. Anselmo was wealthy; but to Carlo and his sister there only remained, of their vast ancestral possessions, one small estate, where they lived together in retirement. Delicacy thus prevented the rich Anselmo from declaring his affection, until an event happened which placed it in his power to be of signal service to the Montanini. A prosperous member of the Sienese government desired to purchase Carlo's house at the price of one thousand ducats. Carlo refused to sell this estate, seeing it was his sister's only support and future source of dowry. Thereupon the powerful man of state accused him falsely of treason to the commonwealth. He was cast into prison and condemned to death or the forfeit of one thousand ducats. Anselmo, the very night before Carlo's threatened execution, paid this fine, and sent the deed of release by the hands of a servant to the prison. When Carlo was once more at liberty, he made enquiries which proved beyond doubt that Anselmo, a man unknown to him, the member of a house at ancient feud with his, had done him this great courtesy. It then rushed across his mind that certain acts and gestures of Anselmo betrayed a secret liking for Angelica. This decided him upon the course he had to take. Having communicated the plan to his sister, he went alone with her at night to Salimbeni's castle, and, when he had expressed his gratitude, there left her in her lover's power, as the most precious thing he could bestow upon the saviour of his life. Carlo, not to be surpassed in this exchange of courtesies, delivered Angelica to the women of his household, and afterwards, attended by the train of his retainers, sought Anselmo in his home. There he made a public statement of what had passed between them, wedded Angelica with three rings, dowered her with the half of his estates, and by a formal deed of gift assigned the residue of his fortune to Carlo. This is a bare outline of the story, which Illicini has adorned in all its details with subtle analyses of feeling and reflections on the several situations. The problem proposed to the gentlewomen is to decide which of the two men, Anselmo and Carlo, showed the more perfect courtesy in their several circumstances. How they settled this knotty point, may be left to the readers of *Novelle* to discover.

Bandello more than adequately represents the Lombard group of novelists; and since his works have been already discussed, it will suffice to allude briefly to three collections which in their day were highly popular. These are *I Proverbi* of Antonio Cornazano, *Le Piacevoli Notti* of Straparola, and Giraldi's *Hecatommithi.*[1] Cornazano was a copious writer both in Latin and Italian. He passed his life at the Courts of Francesco Sforza, Bartolommeo Colleoni, and Ercole I. of Ferrara. One of his earliest compositions was a Life of Christ. This fact is not insignificant, as a sign of the conditions under which literature was produced in the Renaissance. A man who had gained reputation by a learned or religious treatise, ventured to extend it by jests of the broadest humour. The *Proverbi*, by which alone Cornazano's name is now distinguished, are sixteen carefully-wrought stories, very droll but very dirty. Each illustrates a common proverb, and pretends to relate the circumstances which gave it currency. The author opens one tale with a simple statement: 'From the deserts of the Thebaid came to us that trite and much used saying, *Better late than never*; and this was how it happened.' Having stated the theme, he enters on his narrative, diverts attention by a series of ab-

---

[1] None of them are included in the Milanese *Novellieri Italiani.* The editions I shall use are *Proverbii di Messer Antonio Cornazano in Facetie*, Bologna, Romagnoli, 1865 ; *Le Piacevoli Notti*, in Vinegia per Comin da Trino di Monferrato, MDLI. ; *Gli Hecatommithi di M. Giovanbattista Giraldi Cinthio, Nobile Ferrarese*, in Vinegia, MDLXVI., Girolamo Scotto, 2 vols.

surdities which lead to an unexpected climax. He concludes it thus : 'The abbot answered : " It is not this
which makes me weep, but to think of my misfortune,
who have been so long without discovering and com-
mending so excellent an usage." " Father," said the
monk, " *Better late than never.*" ' There is considerable
comic vigour in the working of this motive. Our sense
of the ridiculous is stimulated by a studied dispropor-
tion between the universality of the proverb and the
strangeness of the incidents invented to account for it.

Straparola breaks ground in a different direction.
The majority of his novels bear traces of their origin
in fairy stories or *Volksmärchen.* Much interest attaches to the *Notti Piacevoli,* as the literary reproduction of a popular species which the Venetian Gozzi
afterwards rendered famous. Students of folk-lore may
compare them with the Sicilian fables recently committed to the press by Signor Pitrè.[1] The element
of bizarre fancy is remarkable in all these tales ; but
the marvellous has been so mingled with the facts of
common life as to give each narrative the true air of the
conventional *Novella.* One in particular may be mentioned, since it is written on the same motive as Machiavelli's *Belphegor.* The rubric runs as follows : ' The
Devil, hearing the complaints of husbands against their
wives, marries Silvia Ballastro, and takes Gasparino
Boncio for gossip of the ring, and forasmuch as he finds
it impossible to live with his wife, enters into the body

---

[1] *Fiabe, Novelle, Racconti,* Palermo, Lauriel, 1875, 4 vols. I may
here take occasion to notice that one *Novella* by the Conte Lorenzo
Magalotti (*Nov. It.* vol. xiii. p. 362), is the story of Whittington and his
Cat, told of a certain Florentine, Ansaldo degli Ormanni, and the King of
the Canary Islands.

of the Duke of Melphi, and Gasparino, his gossip, expels him thence.' Between Straparola's and Machiavelli's treatment of this subject, the resemblance is so close as to justify the opinion that the former tale was simply modelled on the latter, or that both were drawn from an original source. In each case it is the wife's pride which renders life unendurable to her demon husband, and in both he is expelled from the possessed person by mistaking a brass band in full play for the approach of his tumultuous consort. But Straparola's loose and careless style of narrative bears no comparison with the caustic satire of Machiavelli's meditated art.[1] The same theme was treated in Italian by Giovanni Brevio; and since Machiavelli's novel first appeared in print in the year 1549, Straparola's seeing the light in 1550, and Brevio's in 1545, we may reasonably conclude that each version was an adaptation of some primitive monastic story.[2]

On the score of style alone, it would be difficult to explain the widespread popularity of Giraldi Cinthio's one hundred and ten tales.[3] The *Hecatommithi* are written in a lumbering manner, and the stories are often lifeless. Compared with the brilliancy of the Tuscan *Novelle*, the point and sparkle of *Le Cene*, the

[1] John Wilson's play of *Belphegor*, Dekker's *If it be not good the Divel is in it*, and Ben Jonson's *The Devil is an Ass*, were more or less founded on Machiavelli's and Straparola's novels.

[2] Dunlop in his *History of Fiction*, vol. ii. p. 411, speaks of a Latin MS. preserved in the library of S. Martin at Tours which contained the tale, but he also says that it was lost at 'the period of the civil wars in France.'

[3] The title leads us to expect one hundred tales; but counting the ten of the Introduction, there are one hundred and ten. When the book first circulated, it contained but seventy. The first edition is that of Monte Regale in Sicily, 1565. My copy of the Venetian edition of 1566 is complete.

grace and gusto of Sermini, or Firenzuola's golden
fluency, the diction of this noble Ferrarese is dull.
Yet the *Hecatommithi* were reprinted again and again,
and translated into several languages. In England,
through Painter's *Palace of Pleasure*, they obtained
wide circulation and supplied our best dramatists, including Shakspere and Fletcher, with hints for plays.
It is probable that they owed their fame in no small
measure to what we reckon their defects. Giraldi's
language was more intelligible to ordinary readers of
Italian than the racy Tuscan of the Sienese authors.
His stories had less of a purely local flavour than
those of the Florentines. They enjoyed, moreover,
the singular advantage of diffusion through the press
of Venice, which then commanded the book-market of
Europe. But, if we put this point of style aside, the
vogue of Cinthio in Italy and Europe becomes at once
intelligible. There is a massive force and volume in his
matter, which proclaims him an author to be reckoned
with. The variety of scenes he represents, the tragic
gravity of many of his motives, his intimate acquaintance with the manners and customs of a class that
never fails to interest the vulgar, combined with great
sagacity in selecting and multiplying instances of
striking crime, stood him in the stead of finer art
with the special public for whom *Novelle* were composed.[1] Compared even with Boccaccio, the prince of
story-tellers, Cinthio holds his own, not as a great
dramatic or descriptive writer, but as one who has

---

[1] The ten novels of the Introduction deal exclusively with the manners
of Italian prostitutes. Placed as a frontispiece to the whole repertory,
they seem intended to attract the vulgar reader.

studied, analysed, dissected, and digested the material
of human action and passion in a vast variety of
modes. His work is more solid and reflective than
Bandello's; more moralised than Il Lasca's. The
ethical tendency both of the tales and the discussions
they occasion, is, for the most part, singularly wholesome. In spite, therefore, of the almost revolting
frankness with which impurity, fraud, cruelty, violence, and bestial lust are exposed to view, one rises
from the perusal of the *Hecatommithi* with an unim-
paired consciousness of good and evil. It is just the
negation of this conscience which renders the mass of
Italian *Novelle* worse than unprofitable.

The plan of the *Hecatommithi* deserves a passing
notice, if only because it illustrates the more than ordinary force of brain which Cinthio brought to bear
upon his light material. He begins with an elaborate
description of the Sack of Rome. A party of men
and women take refuge from its horrors of rape, pestilence and tortures in one of the Colonna palaces.
When affairs have been proved desperate, they set
sail from Cività Vecchia for Marseilles, and enliven
their voyage with story-telling. A man of mature
years opens the discussion with a long panegyric of
wedded love, serving as introduction to the tales
which treat of illicit passion. From this first day's
debate the women of the party are absent. They
intervene next day, and upon this and the following
nine days one hundred stories are related by different
members of the party upon subjects selected for illustration. Each novel is followed by a copious commentary in the form of dialogue, and songs are inter-

spersed. Cinthio thus adhered, as closely as possible, to the model furnished by Boccaccio. But his frame- work, though ingeniously put together, lacks the grace and sweetness of the Decameron. Not a few of the novels are founded upon facts of history. In the tenth tale of the ninth decade, for example, he repeats the legend of the Borgia family—the murder of the Duke of Gandia, Alexander's death by poison, and Cesare's escape. The names are changed; but the facts, as related by Guicciardini, can be clearly dis- cerned through the transparent veil of fiction.

In concluding this chapter on the *Novelle*, it may be repeated that the species of narrative in question was, in its ultimate development, a peculiar Italian product. Originally derived through the French *fabliaux* from medieval Latin stories, the *Novella* received in Italy more serious and more artistic treat- ment. It satisfied the craving of the race for such delineation of life and manners as a great literature demands; and it did this, for reasons which will be explained in the next chapter, with more originality, more adequacy to the special qualities of the Italian people, than even their comedies. What De Quincey wrote concerning our theatre in the age of Elizabeth and James, might almost be applied to the material which the *Novellieri* used : ' No literature, not excep- ting even that of Athens, has ever presented such a multiform theatre, such a carnival display, mask and antimask of impassioned life—breathing, moving, acting, suffering, laughing :

> Quicquid agunt homines—votum, timor, ira, voluptas,
> Gaudia, discursus.'

But, when we quit material to think of form, the parallel fails. De Quincey's further description of our dramas, 'scenically grouped, draped, and gorgeously coloured,' is highly inapplicable to the brief, careless, almost pedestrian prose of the *Novelle*. In spite of their indescribable wealth of subject-matter, in spite of those inexhaustible stores of plots and situations, characters and motives, which have made them a mine for playwrights in succeeding ages, they rarely rise to the height of poetry, nor are they ever dramas. The artistic limitations of the Italian *Novella* are among the most interesting phenomena presented by the history of literature.

CHAPTER XI.

THE DRAMA.

First attempts at Secular Drama—The *Orfeo* and *Timone*—General Character of Italian Plays—Court Pageants and Comedies borrowed from the Latin—Conditions under which a National Drama is formed—Their absence in Italy—Lack of Tragic Genius—Eminently Tragic Material in Italian History—The Use made of this by English Playwrights—The Ballad and the Drama—The Humanistic Bias in Italy—Parallels between Greek and Italian Life—Il Lasca's Critique of the Latinising Playwrights—The *Sofonisba* of Trissino—Rucellai's *Rosmunda*—Sperone's *Canace*—Giraldi's *Orbecche*—Dolce's *Marianna*—Transcripts from the Greek Tragedians and Seneca—General Character of Italian Tragedies—Sources of their Failure—Influence of Plautus and Terence over Comedy—Latin Comedies acted at Florence, Rome, Ferrara—Translations of Latin Comedies—Manner of Representation at Court—Want of Permanent Theatres—Bibbiena's *Calandra*—Leo X. and Comedy at Rome—Ariosto's Treatment of his Latin Models—The *Cassaria, Suppositi, Lena, Negromante, Scolastica*—Qualities of Ariosto's Comedies—Machiavelli's Plays—The *Commedia in Prosa*—Fra Alberigo and Margherita—The *Clizia*—Its Humour—The *Mandragola*—Its sinister Philosophy—Conditions under which it was Composed—Aretino disengages Comedy from Latin Rules—His Point of View—The *Cortegiana, Marescalco, Talanta*—Italy had innumerable Comedies, but no great Comic Art—General Character of the *Commedia Erudita*—Its fixed Personages—Gelli, Firenzuola, Cecchi, Ambra, Il Lasca—The Farsa—Conclusion on the Moral Aspects of Italian Comedy.

CONTEMPORANEOUSLY with the Romantic Epic, the Drama began to be a work of studied art in Italy. Boiardo by his *Timone* and Poliziano by his *Orfeo* gave the earliest specimens at Ferrara and Mantua of secular plays written in the vulgar tongue. The *Timone* must have been composed before 1494, the date of Boiardo's death; and we have already seen that the *Orfeo* was in all probability represented in 1472. It is significant that the two poets who were mainly instrumental in effecting a revival of Italian poetry, should have tried their hands at two species of composition for the stage. In the *Orfeo* we find a direct outgrowth from the *Sacre Rappresentazioni*. The form of the Florentine religious show is adapted with very little alteration to a pagan story. In substance the *Orfeo* is a pastoral melodrama with a tragic climax. Boiardo in the *Timone* followed a different direction. The subject is borrowed from Lucian, who speaks the prologue, as Gower prologises in the *Pericles* of Shakspere. The comedy aims at regularity of structure, and is written in *terza rima*. Yet the chief character leaves the stage before the end of the fifth act, and the conclusion is narrated by an allegorical personage, Lo Ausilio.[1]

These plays, though generally considered to have been the first attempts at secular Italian dramatic poetry, were by no means the earliest in date, if we admit the Latin plays of scholars.[2] Besides some

---

[1] 'Comedia de Timone per el Magnifico Conte Matheo Maria Boyardo Conte de Scandiano traducta de uno Dialogo de Luciano. Stampata in Venetia per Georgio di Rusconi Milanese, del MDXVIII. adì iii di Decembre.' From the play itself we learn that it must have been represented on a double stage, a lower one standing for earth and a higher one for heaven. The first three acts consist chiefly of soliloquies by Timon and conversations with celestial personages—Jove, Mercury, Wealth, Poverty. In the fourth act we are introduced to characters of Athenians—Gnatonide, Phylade, Demea, Trasycle, who serve to bring Timone's misanthropy into relief; and the fifth act brings two slaves, Syro and Parmeno, upon the scene, with a kind of underplot which is not solved at the close of the play. The whole piece must be regarded rather as a Morality than a Comedy, and the characters are allegories or types more than living persons.

[2] To determine the question of priority in such matters is neither easy

tragedies, which will afterwards be mentioned, it is
enough here to cite the *Philogenia* of Ugolino Pisani
(Parma, 1430), the *Philodoxius* of Alberti, the *Polis-
sena* of Leonardo Bruni, and the *Progne* of Gregorio
Corrado. It is therefore a fact that, in addition to
religious dramas in the mother tongue, the Italians
from an early period turned their attention to dramatic
composition. Still the drama never flourished at any
time in Italy as a form of poetry indigenous and
national. It did not succeed in freeing itself from
classical imitation on the one hand, or on the other
from the hampering adjuncts of Court-pageants and
costly entertainments. Why the Italians failed to
develop a national theatre, is a question easier to ask
than to answer. The attempt to solve this problem
will, however, serve to throw some light upon their
intellectual conditions at the height of the Renaissance.

Plays in Italy at this period were either religious
Feste of the kind peculiar to Florence, or Masques at
Court, or Comedies and Tragedies imitated by men of
learning from classical models, or, lastly, Pastorals combining the scenic attractions of the Masque with the
action of a regular drama. None of these five species
can be called in a true sense popular; nor were they
addressed by their authors to the masses of the people.
Performed in private by pious confraternities or erudite
academies, or exhibited on state occasions in the halls
of princely palaces, they were not an expression of the

nor important. Students who desire to follow the gradual steps in the
development of Italian play-writing before the date of Ariosto and Machiavelli may be referred to D' Ancona's work on the *Origini del Teatro.*

national genius but a highly-cultivated form of aristo-
cratic luxury. | When Heywood in his prologue to the
Challenge for Beauty wrote :

> Those [*i.e.* plays] that frequent are
> In Italy or France, *even in these days*,
> *Compared with ours*, are rather jigs than plays :

when Marlowe in the first scene of *Edward II.*,
made Gaveston, thinking how he may divert the
pleasure-loving king, exclaim :

> Therefore I'll have Italian masks by night,
> Sweet speeches, comedies, and pleasing shows :

both of these poets uttered a true criticism of the
Italian theatre. Marlowe accurately describes the
scenic exhibitions in vogue at the Courts of Ferrara,
Mantua, Urbino, and Rome, where the stage was
reckoned among the many instruments of wanton
amusement. Heywood, by his scornful phrase *jigs*,
indicates their mixed nature between comedies and
ballets, with interludes of pageantry and accompani-
ment of music. The words italicised show that the
English playwrights were conscious of having developed a nobler type of the drama than had been
produced in Italy. In order to complete the outline
sketched by Heywood and Marlowe, we must bear in
mind that comedies adapted from the Latin, like the
Suppositi of Ariosto, or constructed upon Latin principles, like Machiavelli's *Mandragola* or the *Calandra*
of Bibbiena, were highly relished by a society educated
in humanistic traditions. Such efforts of the scholarly
muse approved themselves even in England to the
taste of critics like Sir Philip Sidney, who shows in
his *Defence of Poesy* that he had failed to discern the

future greatness of the national drama.   But they had
the fatal defect of being imitations and exotics.   The
stage, however learnedly adorned by men of scholarship and fancy, remained within the narrow sphere of
courtly pastime.   What was a mere *hors d'œuvre* in
the Elizabethan age of England, formed the whole
dramatic art of the Italians.

If tragedy and comedy sprang by a natural process of evolution from the medieval Mystery, then the
Florentines should have had a drama.   We have seen
how rich in the elements of both species were the
Sacre Rappresentazioni; and how men of culture like
Lorenzo de' Medici, and Bernardo Pulci deigned to
compose them.   But the *Sacre Rappresentazioni* died
a natural death, and left no heritage.   They had
no vital relation to the people, either as a source of
amusement or as embodying the real thoughts and
passions of the race.   Designed for the edification
of youth, their piety was too often hypocritical, and
their extravagant monastic morality stood in glaring
opposition to the ethics of society.   We must go far
deeper in our analysis, if we wish to comprehend this
failure of the Italians to produce a drama.

Three conditions, enjoyed by Greece and England, but denied to Italy, seem necessary for the
poetry of a nation to reach this final stage of artistic
development.   The first is a free and sympathetic
public, not made up of courtiers and scholars, but of
men of all classes—a public representative of the
whole nation, with whom the playwright shall feel
himself in close *rapport*.   The second is, a centre of
social life : an Athens, Paris or London : where the

heart of the nation beats and where its brain is ever active. The third is a perturbation of the race in some great effort, like the Persian war or the struggle of the Reformation, which unites the people in a common consciousness of heroism. Taken in combination, these three conditions explain the appearance of a drama fitted to express the very life and soul of a puissant nation, with the temper of the times impressed upon it, but with a truth and breadth that renders it the heritage of every race and age. A national drama is the image created for itself in art by a people which has arrived at knowledge of its power, at the enjoyment of its faculties, after a period of successful action. Concentrated in a capital, gifted with a common instrument of self-expression, it projects itself in tragedies and comedies that bear the name of individual poets, but are in reality the spirit of the race made vocal.[1]

These conditions have only twice in the world's history existed—once in the Athens of Pericles, once in the London of Elizabeth. The measure of greatness to which the dramas of Paris and Madrid, though still not comparable with the Attic and the English, can lay claim, is due to the participation by the French and Spanish peoples in these privileges. But in Italy there was no public, no metropolis, no agitation of the people in successful combat with antagonistic force. The educated classes were, indeed, conscious of intellectual unity; but they had no meeting-point in any

---

[1] I have enlarged on these points in my Essay on Euripides (*Greek Poets*, Series i.). I may take occasion here to say that until Sept. 1879, after this chapter was written, I had not met with Professor Hillebrand's *Etudes Italiennes* (Paris, Franck, 1868).

city, where they might have developed the theatre upon the only principles then possible, the principles of erudition. And, what was worse, there existed no enthusiasms, moral, religious or political, from which a drama could arise. A society without depth of thought or seriousness of passion, highly cultured, but devoid of energy and aspiration, had not the seed of tragedy within its loins. In those polite Italian Courts and pleasure-seeking coteries, the idyll, the *Novella*, and the vision of a golden age might entertain men weary with public calamities, indulgent to the vice and crime around them. From this soil the forest-trees of a great drama could not spring. But it yielded an abundant crop of comedies, an undergrowth of rankly sprouting vegetation. It was, moreover, well adapted to the one original production of the Italian stage. Pastoral comedy, attaining perfection in Tasso's *Aminta* and Guarini's *Pastor Fido*, and bearing the germs of the Opera in its voluptuous scenes, formed the climax of dramatic art in Italy.

Independently of these external drawbacks, we find in the nature of the Italian genius a reason why the drama never reached perfection. Tragedy, which is the soul of great dramatic poetry, was almost uniformly wanting after Dante. Petrarch, Boccaccio, Poliziano, Boiardo, Ariosto, Tasso are pathetic, graceful, polished, elevated, touching, witty, humorous, reflective, radiant inventive, fanciful—everything but stern, impassioned, tragic in the true heroic sense. Even the Florentines, who dallied sometimes with the thoughts of Death and Judgment in bizarre pageants like the show of Hell recorded by Villani, or the Masque of Penitence designed by Piero di Cosimo, or the burlesque festivals recorded in the life of Rustici by Giorgio Vasari— even the Florentines shrank in literature from what is terrible and charged with anguish of the soul. The horrors of the *Novelle* are used by them to stimulate a jaded appetite, to point the pleasures of the sense by contrast with the shambles and the charnel-house. We are never invited to the spectacle of human energies ravaged by passion, at war with destiny, yet superior to fate and fortune and internal tempest in the strength of will and dignity of heroism. It is not possible to imagine those *liete brigate* of young men and maidens responding to the fierce appeal of Marston's prologue :

> Therefore we proclaim,
> If any spirit breathes within this round,
> Uncapable of weighty passion—
> As from his birth being huggéd in the arms
> And nuzzled twixt the breasts of happiness—
> Who winks, and shuts his apprehension up
> From common sense of what men were, and are,
> Who would not know what men must be ; let such
> Hurry amain from our black-visaged shows :
> We shall affright their eyes. But if a breast
> Nailed to the earth with grief, if any heart
> Pierced through with anguish pant within this ring,
> If there be any blood whose heat is choked
> And stifled with true sense of misery,
> If aught of these strains fill this consort up,
> They arrive most welcome.

Sterner, and it may be gloomier conditions of external life than those which the Italians enjoyed, were needed as a preparation of the public for such spectacles. It was not on these aspects of human existence that a race, accustomed to that genial climate and refined by the contemplation of all-golden art, loved to dwell in hours of recreation. The *Novella*, with its mixture of comedy and pathos, licence and satire, gave the tone, as we have seen, to literature. The same quality of the Italian temperament may be illustrated from the painting of the sixteenth century, which rarely rises to the height of tragedy. If we except Michelangelo and Tintoretto, we find no masters of sublime and fervid genius, able to conceive with intensity and to express with force the thrilling moods of human passion. Raphael marks the height of national achievement, and even the more serious work of Raphael found no adequate interpreters among his pupils.

The absence of the tragic element in Italian art and literature is all the more remarkable because the essence of Italian history, whether political or domestic, was eminently dramatic. When we consider what the nation suffered during the civil wars of the thirteenth and fourteenth centuries, under the tyranny of monsters like Ezzelino, from plagues that swept away the population of great cities, and beneath the scourge of sinister religious revivals, it may well cause wonder that the Italian spirit should not have assumed a stern and tragic tone instead of that serenity and cheerfulness which from the first distinguished it. The Italians lived their tragedies in the dynasties of the Visconti and the Sforzas, in the contests of the Baglioni and Manfredi, in the persons of Pandolfo Sigismondo Malatesta and Cesare Borgia, in the murders, poisonings, rapes and treasons that form the staple of the annals of their noble houses. But it was the English and not the Italian poets who seized upon this tragic matter and placed it with the light of poetry upon the stage.[1] Our Elizabethan playwrights dramatised the legends of Othello and Juliet, the loves of Bianca Capello and Vittoria Accoramboni, the tragedies of the Duchess of Amalfi and the Duke of Milan. There is something even appalling in the tenacity with which poets of the stamp of Marlowe, Webster, Ford, Massinger and Tourneur clung to the episodes of blood and treachery furnished by Italian stories. Their darkest delineations of villany, their subtlest analyses of evil motives, their most audacious pictures of vice, are all contained within the charmed circle of Italian history. A play could scarcely succeed in London unless the characters were furnished with Italian names.[2] Italy fascinated the Northern fancy, and the imagination of our dramatists found itself at home among her scenes of mingled splendour and atrocity. Nowhere, therefore, can a truer study of Italian Court-intrigue be found than in the plays of Webster. His portraits, it may be allowed, are painted without relief or due gradation of tone.

[1] Exception must be made in favour of some ancient quasi-tragedies, which seem to prove that before the influences of Boccaccio and the Renaissance had penetrated the nation, they were not deficient in the impulse to dramatise history. The *Eccerinis* of Albertino Mussato (*c.* 1300), half dialogue and half narration, upon the fate of Ezzellino da Romano, composed in the style of Seneca; the dialogue upon the destruction of Cesena (1377) falsely attributed to Petrarch; Giovanni Mangini della Motta's poem on the downfall of Antonio della Scala (1387), Lodovico da Vezzano's tragedy of Jacopo Piccinino; though far from popular in their character, and but partially dramatic, were such as under happier auspices might have fostered the beginnings of the tragic theatre. Later on we hear of the *Fall of Granada* being represented before Cardinal Riario at Rome, as well as the *Ferrandus Servatus* of Carlo Verradi (1492).

[2] See the first cast of Jonson's *Every Man in his Humour*.

Flamineo and Bosola seem made to justify the proverb—*Inglese Italianato è un diavolo incarnato.* Yet
after reading the secret history of the Borgias, or estimating the burden on Ferdinand's conscience when he
quaked before the French advance on Naples, who can
say that Webster has exaggerated the bare truth? He
has but intensified it by the incubation of his intellect.
Varchi's account of Lorenzino de' Medici, affecting
profligacy and effeminacy in order to deceive Duke
Alessandro, and forming to his purpose the ruffian
Scoronconcolo from the dregs of the prisons, furnishes
a complete justification for even Tourneur's plots. The
snare this traitor laid for Alessandro, when he offered
to bring his own aunt to the duke's lust, bears a close
resemblance to Vendice's scheme in the *Revenger's Tragedy*; while the inconsequence of his action after the
crime, tallies with the moral collapse of Duke Ferdinand
before his strangled sister's corpse in the last act of the
Duchess of Malfi.

The reality of these acted tragedies may have been
a bar to their mimic presentation on the stage in Italy.
When the Borgias were poisoning their victims in
Rome; when Lodovico Sforza was compassing his
nephew's death at Pavia; when the Venetians were de-
capitating Carmagnuola; when Sixtus was plotting the
murder of the Medici in church, and Grifonetto Baglioni was executing *il gran tradimento*; could an Italian
audience, in the Court or on the Piazza, have taken a
keen pleasure in witnessing the scenic presentment of
barbarities so close at hand? The sense of contrast
between the world of fact and the work of art, which
forms an essential element of æsthetic pleasure, would

have been wanting. The poets turned from these crimes to comedy and romance, though the politicians analysed their motives with impartial curiosity. At the same time, we may question whether the Despots would have welcomed tragic shows which dramatised their deeds of violence ; whether they would have suffered the patriotism of Brutus, the vengeance of Virginius, the plots of Catiline, or the downfall of Sejanus to be displayed with spirit-stirring pomp in theatres of Milan and Ferrara, when conspiracies like that of Olgiati were frequent. It was the freedom of the English public and the self-restraint of the English character, in combination with the profound appetite for tragic emotion inherent in our Northern blood, which rendered the Shaksperian drama possible and acceptable.

In connection with this inaptitude of the Italians for tragedy, it is worth noticing that their popular poetry exhibits but rare examples of the ballad. It abounds in love-ditties and lyrics of the inner life. But references to history and the tragedies of noble families are comparatively scarce.[1] In Great Britain, on the contrary, while our popular poetry can show but few songs of sentiment, the Border and Robin Hood ballads record events in national history or episodes from actual domestic dramas, blent with the memories of old mythology. These poems prove in the unknown minstrels who produced them, a genuine appreciation of dramatic incident ; and their manner is marked by vigorous objectivity. The minstrel loses himself in his subject and aims at creating in his

---

[1] See above, Part I, p. 276, where one ballad of the Border type is discussed.

audience a vivid sense of the action he has undertaken to set forth. The race which could produce such ballads, already contained the germs of Marlowe's tragedy. It would be interesting to pursue this subject further, and by examining the ballad-literature of the several European nations to trace how far the capacities which in a rude state of society were directed to this type of minstrelsy, found at a later period their true sphere of art in the drama.[1]

The deficiency of the tragic instinct among the Italians seems to be further exhibited by their failure to produce novels of the higher type.[2] Though Boccaccio is the prince of story-tellers, his *Novelle* are tales, more interesting for their grace of manner and beautifully described situations, than for analysis of character or strength of plot. Recent Italian *romanzi* are histories rather than works of free fiction ; and these novels were produced after the style of Sir Walter Scott had been acclimatised in every part of Europe. Meanwhile no Balzac or George Sand, no Thackeray or George Eliot, no Cervantes or Fielding, has appeared in Italy. The nearest approach to a great Italian novel of life and character is the autobiography

[1] It is certainly significant that the Spanish share with the English the chief honours both of the ballad and the drama. The Scandinavian nations, rich in ballads, have been, through Danish poets, successful in dramatic composition. The Niebelungen Lied and the Song of Roland would, in the case of Germany and France, have to be set against the English ballads of action. But these Epics are different in character from the minstrelsy which turned passing events into poetry and bequeathed them in the form of spirit-stirring narratives to posterity. Long after the epical impulse had ceased and the British epic of Arthur had passed into the sphere of literature, the ballad minstrels continued to work with dramatic energy upon the substance of contemporary incidents.

[2] See above, p. 54, for the distinction between the Italian *Novella* and the modern novel.

of Cellini.[1] As the Italians lived instead of playing
their tragedies, so they lived instead of imagining their
novels.

If a national drama could have been produced in
Italy, it might have appeared at Florence during the
reign of Lorenzo de' Medici. In no other place and at
no other period was the Italian genius more alive and
centralised. But a city is not a nation, and the Com-
pagnia di San Giovanni was not the Globe Theatre.
The desires of the Florentines, so studiously gratified
by their merchant prince, were bent on carnival shows
and dances. In this modern Athens the fine arts
failed to find their meeting-point and fulfilment on the
stage, because the people lacked the spirit and the
freedom necessary to the drama. Artists were satisfied with decorating masques and cars. Poets amused
their patrons with romantic stories. Scholars were absorbed in the fervent passion for antiquity. Michelangelo carved and Lionardo painted the wonders of
the modern world. Thus the Florentine genius found
channels that led far afield from tragedy. At a later
period, when culture had become more universally
Italian, it might have been imagined that the bright
spirit of Ariosto, the pregnant wit of Machiavelli, the
genial humour of Bibbiena would have given birth to
plays of fancy like Fletcher's or to original comedies of
manners like Jonson's and Massinger's. But such was
the respect of these Italian playwrights for their classic
models, that the scenes of even the best Florentine

---

[1] In the same way Alfieri's biography is a tragic and Goldoni's a comic
novel. The Memoirs of Casanova, which I incline to accept as genuine,
might rather be cited as a string of brilliantly written *Novelle.*

comedies are crowded with spendthrifts, misers, courtesans, lovers and slaves, borrowed from the Latin authors. Plautus and Terence, Ariosto and Machiavelli, not nature, were their source of inspiration.[1] Mistakes between two brothers, confusions of sex, discoveries that poor girls are the lost daughters of princely parents, form the staple of their plots. The framework of comedy being thus antique, the playwright was reduced to narrow limits for that exhibition of 'truth's image, the ensample of manners, the mirror of life,' which Il Lasca rightly designated as the proper object of the comic art.

The similarity of conditions between late Greek and modern Italian life facilitated this custom of leaning on antique models, and deceived the poets into thinking they might safely apply Græco-Roman plots to the facts of fifteenth-century romance. With the Turk at Otranto, with the Cardinals of Este and Medici opposing his advance in Hungary, with the episodes of French invasion, with the confusions of the Sack of Rome, there was enough of social anarchy and public peril to justify dramatic intrigues based on kidnapping and anagnorisis. The playwrights, when they adapted comedies of Plautus and Terence, were fully alive to the advantage of these correspondences. Claudio in Ariosto's *Suppositi* had his son stolen in the taking of

---

[1] Cantù quotes the prologue of a MS. play which goes so far as to apologise for the scene not being laid at Athens (*Lett. It.* p. 471) :

Benchè l' usanza sia
Che ogni commedia
Si soglia fare a Atene,
Non so donde si viene
Che questa non grecizza,
Anzi fiorentinizza.

Otranto. Bartolo in the *Scolastica* lost sight of his intended wife at the moment of Lodovico Sforza's expulsion from Milan. Callimaco in Machiavelli's *Mandragola* remained in Paris to avoid the troubles consequent on Charles VIII's. invasion. Lidio and Santilla in Bibbiena's *Calandra*, Blando's children in Aretino's *Talanta*, were taken by the Turks. Fabrizio in the *Ingannati* was lost in the Sack of Rome. Maestro Cornelio in Ambra's *Furto* was captured by the German Lanzi. In the *Cofanaria* of the same author there is a girl kidnapped in the Siege of Florence. Slavery itself was by no means obsolete in Italy upon the close of the middle ages ; and the slave-merchant of Ariosto's *Cassaria*, hardly distinguished from a common brothel-keeper, was not so anachronistic as to be impossible. The parasites of Latin comedy found their counterpart in the clients of rich families and the poorer courtiers of princes. The indispensable Davus was represented by the body servants of wealthy householders. The *miles gloriosus* reappeared in professional *bravi* and captains of mercenaries. Thus the personages of the Latin stage could easily be furnished with Italian masks. Still there remained an awkwardness in fitting these new masks to the old lay-figures ; and when we read the genuine Italian comedies of Aretino, especially the *Cortigiana* and the *Marescalco*, we feel how much was lost to the nation by the close adherence of its greater playwrights, Ariosto and Machiavelli, to the conventions of the *Commedia erudita*.

The example of Ariosto and Machiavelli led even the best Florentine playwrights—Cecchi, Ambra, and

Gelli—into a false path. The plays of these younger
authors abound in reminiscences of the *Suppositi* and
Clizia, adapted with incomparable skill and humour to
contemporary customs, but suffering from too close
adherence to models, which had been in their turn
copied from the antique. It was not until the middle
of the sixteenth century that criticism hit the vein of
common sense. Il Lasca, who deserves great credit for
his perspicacity, carried on an unremitting warfare
against the comedy of *anagnorisis*. In the prologue to his
Gelosia he says [1] : · All the comedies which have been
exhibited in Florence since the Siege, end in discoveries of lost relatives. This has become so irksome
to the audience that, when they hear in the argument
how at the taking of this city or the sack of that,
children have been lost or kidnapped, they know only
too well what is coming, and would fain leave the
room. . . . Authors of such comedies jumble up the
new and the old, antique and modern together, making
a hodge-podge and confusion, without rhyme or
reason, head or tail. They lay their scenes in modern
cities and depict the manners of to-day, but foist in
obsolete customs and habits of remote antiquity.
Then they excuse themselves by saying : Plautus did
thus, and this was Menander's way and Terence's ;
never perceiving that in Florence, Pisa and Lucca
people do not live as they used to do in Rome and
Athens. For heaven's sake let these fellows take to
translation, if they have no vein of invention, but leave
off cobbling and spoiling the property of others and

---

[1] *Commedie di Antonfrancesco Grazzini* (Firenze, Lemonnier, 1859),
p. 5.

their own.' The prologue to the *Spiritata* contains a similar polemic against 'quei ritrovamenti nei tempi nostri impossibili e sciocchi.'[1] In the prologue to the *Strega*, after once more condemning 'quelle recognizioni deboli e sgarbate,' he proceeds to attack the authority of ancient critics on whom the pedantic school relied[2] : 'Aristotle and Horace knew their own times. But ours are wholly different. We have other manners, another religion, another way of life ; and therefore our comedies ought to be composed after a different fashion. People do not live at Florence as they did in Rome and Athens. There are no slaves here ; it is not customary to adopt children ; our pimps do not put up girls for sale at auction ; nor do the soldiers of the present century carry long-clothes babies off in the sack of cities, to educate them as their own daughters and give them dowries ; nowadays they make as much booty as they can, and should girls or married women fall into their hands, they either look for a large ransom or rob them of their maidenhead and honour.'

This polemic of Il Lasca, and, indeed, all that he says about the art and aim of comedy, is very sensible. But at his date there was no hope for a great comedy of manners. What between the tyranny of the Medici and the pressure of the Inquisition, Spanish suspicion and Papal anxiety for a reform of manners, the liberty essential to a new development of the dramatic art had been extinguished. And even if external conditions had been favourable, the spirit of the race was spent. All intellectual energy was now losing itself in the quagmire of academical discussions and literary

[1] *Op. cit.* p. 109.　　　[2] *Ibid.* p. 173.

disputations upon verbal niceties. Attention was turned backward to the study of Petrarch and Boccaccio. Authors aiming above all things at correctness, slavishly observant of rules and absurdly fearful of each other's ferules, had not the stuff in them to create. What has been said of comedy, is still more true of tragedy. The tragic dramas of this period are stiff and lifeless, designed to illustrate critical principles rather than to stir and purify the passions. They have no relation to the spirit of the people or the times; and the blood spilt at their conclusion fails to distinguish them from moral lucubrations in the blankest verse.[1]

The first regular Italian tragedy was the *Sofonisba* of Gian Giorgio Trissino, finished in 1515, and six times printed before the date of its first representation at Vicenza in 1562. Trissino was a man of immense erudition and laborious intellect, who devoted himself to questions of grammatical and literary accuracy, studying the critics of antiquity with indefatigable diligence and seeking to establish canons for the regulation of correct Italian composition. He was by no means deficient in originality of aim, and professed himself the pioneer of novelties in poetry.[3] Thus, besides innovating in the minor matter of orthography, he set himself to supply the deficiencies of Italian literature by producing an epic in the heroic style and

[1] I have put into an Appendix some further notes upon the opinions recorded by the playwrights concerning the progress of the dramatic art.

[2] My references to Italian tragedies will be made to the *Teatro Italiano Antico*, 10 vols., Milano, 1809.

[3] This is shown by his device of a Golden Fleece, referring to the voyage of the Argonauts. To sail the ocean of antiquity as an explorer, and to bring back the spoils of their artistic method was his ambition.

a tragedy that should compete with those of Athens. He had made a profound study of the *Poetics* and believed that Aristotle's analyses of the epic and the drama might be used as recipes for manufacturing similar masterpieces in a modern tongue.[1] The *Italia Liberata* and the *Sofonisba*, meritorious but lifeless exercises which lacked nothing but the genius for poetry, were the results of these ambitious theories. Aristotle presided over both, while Homer served as the professed model for Trissino's heroic poem, and Sophocles was copied in his play. Of the *Italia Liberata* this is not the place to speak. The *Sofonisba* is founded on a famous episode in the Punic Wars, when the wife of Syphax was married by Massinissa contrary to the express will cf Lælius and Scipio. She takes poison at her new husband's orders, and her death forms the catastrophe. There is some attempt to mark character in Lelio, Scipione, and Massinissa ; but these persons do not act and react on one another, nor is there real dramatic movement in the play. Sofonisba passes through it automatically, giving her hand to Massinissa without remorse for Syphax, drinking the poison like an obedient girl, and dying with decorous but ineffective pathos. Massinissa plays the part of an idiot by sending her the poison

[1] Compare what Giraldi says in the dedication of his *Orbecche* to Duke Ercole II. : ' Ancora che Aristotele ci dia il modo di comporle.' In the same passage he dwells on the difficulties of producing tragedies in the absence of dramatic instinct, with an ingenuousness that moves our pity : ' Quando altri si dà a scrivere in quella maniera de' Poemi, che sono stati per tanti secoli tralasciati, che appena di loro vi resta una lieve ombra.' It never occurred to him that great poetry comes neither by observation nor by imitation of predecessors. The same dedication contains the monstrous critical assertion that the Latin poets, *i.e.* Seneca, improved upon Greek tragedy—*assai più grave la fecero.*

which he thinks, apparently, she will not take. His surprise and grief, no less than his previous impulse of passionate love, are stationary. In a word, Trissino selected a well-known story from Roman history, and forgot that, in order to dramatise it, he must present the circumstances, not as a narrated fable, but as a sequence of actions determined by powerful and convincing motives. The two essentials of dramatic art, action evolved before the eyes of the spectators, and what Goethe called the *motiviren* of each incident, are conspicuous by their absence. The would-be tragic poet was too mindful of rules—his unities, his diction, his connection of scenes that should occupy the stage without interruption, his employment of the Chorus in harmony with antique precedent—to conceive intensely or to express vividly. In form the *Sofonisba* is a fair imitation of Attic tragedy, and the good taste of its author secures a certain pale and frigid reflection of classical simplicity. Blank verse is judiciously mingled with lyric metres, which are only introduced at moments of high-wrought feeling. The Chorus plays an unobtrusive part in the dialogue, and utters appropriate odes in the right places. Consequently, the *Sofonisba* was hailed as a triumph of skill by the learned audience to whom alone the author appealed. Its merits of ingenuity and scholarship were such as they could appreciate. Its lack of vitality and imaginative vigour did not strike men who were accustomed to judge of poetry by rule and precedent.

Numerous scholars entered the lists in competition with Trissino. Among these the first place must be given to Giovanni Rucellai, whose *Rosmunda* was composed almost contemporaneously with the *Sofo-nisba* and was acted before Leo X. in the Rucellai Gardens upon the occasion of a Papal visit to Florence. The chief merit of *Rosmunda* is brevity. But it has the fatal fault of being a story told in scenes and dialogues, not an action moving and expanding through a series of connected incidents. Rosmunda's father, Comundo, has been slain in battle with the Lombards under Albuino. Like Antigone, the princess goes by night to bury his corpse; and when the tyrant threatens her, she replies in language borrowed from Sophocles. Albuino decapitates Comundo and makes a wine-cup of his skull, from which, after his marriage to Rosmunda, he forces her to drink. This determines the catastrophe. Almachilde appears upon the scene and slaughters Albuino in his tent. We are left to conjecture the murderer's future marriage with the heroine. That the old tale of the *Donna Lombarda* is eminently fitted for tragic handling, admits of no doubt. But it is equally certain that Rucellai failed to dramatise it. Almachilde is not introduced until the fourth act, and he assassinates Albuino without any previous communication with Rosmunda. The horrible banquet scene and the incident of the murder are described by messengers, while the chief actors rarely come to speech together face to face. The business of the play is narrated in dialogues with servants. This abuse of the Messenger and of subordinate characters, introduced for the sole purpose of describing and relating what ought to be enacted, is not peculiar to the *Rosmunda*. It weakens all the tragedies of the sixteenth century, reducing their scenes to vacant discussions, where one person tells another what the author has conceived but what he cannot bring before his audience. Afraid of straining his imaginative faculties by the display of characters in action, the poet studiously keeps the chief personages apart, supplying the hero and the heroine with a shadow or an echo, whose sympathetic utterances serve to elicit the plot without making any demand upon the dramatist's power of presentation. Unfortunately for the tragic poets, the precedent of Seneca seemed to justify this false method of dramatic composition. And Seneca's tragedies, we know, were written, not for action, but for recitation.

These defects culminate in Speron Sperone's *Canace.* The tale is horrible. Eolo, god of the winds, has two children, Canace and Macareo, born at one birth by his wife Deiopea. Under the malign influence of Venus this unlucky couple love ; and the fruit of their union is a baby, killed as soon as born. The brother and the sister commit suicide separately, after their father's anger has thrown the light of publicity upon their passion. In order to justify the exhibition of incest in this repulsive form, there should at least have been such scenes of self-abandonment to impulse as Ford has found for Giovanni and Annabella ; or the poet might have suggested the operation of agencies beyond human control by treading in the footsteps of Euripides ; or, again, he might have risen from the sordid facts of sin into the region of ideal passion by the presentation of commanding personality in his principal actors. Nothing of this kind redeems the dreary disgust of his plot. The first act

consists of a dialogue between Eolo and his Grand
Vizier; the second, of a dialogue between Canace and
her nurse; the third, of dialogues between Deiopea
and her servants; the fourth, of a Messenger's narrative;
the fifth, of Macareo's dialogues with his valet and his
father's henchman. This analysis of the situations
shows how little of dramatic genius Sperone brought
to bear upon the hideous theme he had selected. The
Canace is a succession of conversations referring to
events which happen off the stage, and which involve
no play of character in the chief personages. It is
written throughout in lyrical measures with an affected
diction, where rhetorical conceits produce the same
effect as artificial flowers and ribbons stuck upon a
skeleton.

Giraldi, the author of the *Hecatommithi*, fares little
better in his *Orbecche*.[1] It is a play founded on one
of the poet's own *Novelle*.[2] Orbecche, the innocent
child of Sulmone and Selina, has led her father to
detect his wife's adultery with his own eldest son.
Selina, killed together with her paramour, exercises a
baleful influence from the world of ghosts over this
daughter who unwittingly betrayed her sin. Orbecche
privately marries the low-born Oronte and has two
sons by her husband. Sulmone, when he discovers this
mésalliance, assassinates Oronte and his children in a
secret place, and makes a present of his head and

[1] This tragedy was acted at Ferrara in Giraldi's house before Ercole
II., Duke of Ferrara, and a brilliant company of noble persons, in 1541.
The music was composed by M. Alfonso dalla Viuola, the scenery by M.
Girolamo Carpi.

[2] Giraldi, a prolific writer of plays, dramatised three other of his novels
in the *Arrenopia*, the *Altile* and the *Antivalomeni*. He also composed
a *Didone* and a *Cleopatra*.

hands to his miserable daughter. Upon this, Orbecche stabs her father and then ends her own life. To horrors of extravagant passion and bloodshed we are accustomed in the works of our inferior playwrights. Nor would it perhaps be just to quarrel with Giraldi for having chosen a theme so morbid, if any excuse could have been pleaded on the score of stirring scenes or vivid incidents. Unluckily, the life of dramatic action and passion is wanting to his ponderous tragedy. Instead of it, we are treated to disquisitions in the style of Seneca, and to descriptions that would be harrowing but for their invincible frigidity. No amount of crime and bloodshed will atone for the stationary mechanism of this lucubration.

Lacking dramatic instinct, these Italian scholars might have redeemed their essential feebleness by acute analysis of character. Their tragedies might at least have contained versified studies of motives, metrical essays on the leading passions. But we look in vain for such compensations. Stock tyrants, conventional lovers, rhetorical pedants, form their *dramatis personæ*. The inherent vices of the *Novella*, expanded to excessive length and invested with the forms of antique art, neutralise the labours of the lamp and file that have been spent upon them.[1] If it were requisite

---

[1] It may here be remarked that though the scholarly playwrights of the Renaissance paid great attention to Aristotle's *Poetics*, and made a conscientious study of some Greek plays, especially the *Antigone*, the *Œdipus Tyrannus*, the *Phœnissæ*, and the *Iphigenia in Tauris*, they held the uncritical opinion, openly expressed by Giraldi, that Seneca had improved the form of the Greek drama. Their worst faults of construction, interminable monologues, dialogues between heroines and confidantes, dry choric dissertations, and rhetorical declamations are due to the preference for Seneca. The more we study Italian literature in the sixteenth century, the more we are compelled to acknowledge that

to select one play in which a glimmer of dramatic light is visible, we could point to the *Marianna* of Lodovico Dolce. Here the passion of love in a tyrant, dotingly affectionate but egotistic, roused to suspicion by the slightest hint, and jealous beyond Othello's lunacy, has been depicted with considerable skill. Herod is a fantastical Creon, who murders the fancied paramour of Marianna, and subsequently assassinates Marianna herself, his two sons by her, and her mother, in successive paroxysms of insane vindictiveness, waking up too late from his dream of self-injury into ignoble remorse. Though his conviction that Marianna meant to poison him, and his persuasion of her adultery with Soemo are so ill prepared by reasonable motives as to be ridiculous, the operation of these beliefs upon his wild-beast nature leads to more real movement than is common in Italian tragedies. The inevitable Chorus is employed for the utterance of sententious commonplaces ; and the part of the Messenger is abused for the detailed and disgusting description of executions that inspire no horror.

The tragedies hitherto discussed, though conforming to the type of the classical drama, were composed on original subjects. Yet the best plays of this pedantic school are those which closely follow some Attic model. Rucellai's *Oreste*, produced in imitation of the *Iphi-*

humanism and all its consequences were a revival of Latin culture, only slightly tinctured with the simpler and purer influences of the Greeks. Latin poetry had the fatal attraction of facility. It was, moreover, itself composite and derivatory, like the literature of the new age. We may profitably illustrate the attitude of the Italian critics by Sidney's eulogy of *Gorboduc* : ' full of stately speeches and well-sounding phrases, climbing to the height of Seneca his style, and as full of notable morality which it doth most delightfully teach and so obtain the very end of Poesy.'

genia in Tauris, far surpasses the *Rosmunda*, not only as a poem of action, but also for the richness and the beauty of its style. That Rucellai should spoil the plot of Euripides by his alterations, protracting the famous recognition-scene till we are forced to suppose that Orestes and Iphigenia kept up a game of mutual misunderstanding out of consideration for the poet, and spinning out the contest between Orestes and Pylades to absurdity, was to be expected. A scholar in his study can scarcely hope to improve upon the work of a poet whose very blemishes were the defects of a dramatic quality. He fancies that expansion of striking situations will fortify them, and that the addition of ingenious rhetoric will render a simple action more effective. The reverse of this is true ; and the best line open to such a poet is to produce a faithful version of his original. This was done by Luigi Alamanni, whose translation of the *Antigone*, though open to objections on the score of scholarship, is a brilliant and beautiful piece of Italian versification. Lodovico Dolce in his *Giocasta* attempted to remodel the *Phœnissæ* with very indifferent success ; while Giovanni Andrea dell' Anguillara defaced the *Œdipus Tyrannus* in his *Edippo*, by adding a final act and interweaving episodical matter borrowed from Seneca. A more repulsive tragi-comedy than this *pasticcio* of Sophocles and Seneca, can scarcely be imagined. Yet Quadrio and Tiraboschi mention it with cautious compliment, and it received the honour of public recitation at Vicenza in 1565, when Palladio erected a theatre for the purpose in the noble Palazzo della Ragione. We cannot contemplate these *rifacimenti* of standard-making masterpieces without mixed feelings of scorn and pity. Sprouting fungus-like upon the venerable limbs of august poetry, they lived their season of mildewy fame, and may now be reckoned among the things which the world would only too willingly let die. The ineptitude of such performance reached a climax in Lodovico Martelli's *Tullia*, where the Roman legend of Lucius Tarquinius is violently altered to suit the plot of Sophocles' *Electra*. Romulus appears at the conclusion of the play as a *deus ex machina*, and the insufferable tedium of the speeches may be imagined from the fact that one of them runs to the length of 211 lines.

These tragedies were the literary manufacture of scholars, writing in no relation of reciprocity with the world of action or the audience of busy cities. Applying rules of Aristotle and Horace, travestying Sophocles and Euripides, copying the worst faults of Seneca, patching, boggling, rehandling, misconceiving, devising petty traps instead of plots, mistaking bloodshed and brutality for terror, attending to niceties of diction, composing commonplace sentences for superfluous Choruses, intent on everything but the main points of passion, character, and action, they produced the dreariest *caput mortuum* of unintelligent industry which it is the melancholy duty of historians to chronicle. Their personages are shadows evoked in the camera obscura of a pedant's brain from figures that have crossed the orbit of his solitary studies. No breath or juice of life animates these formal marionettes. Their movements of passion are the spasms of machinery. No charm of poetry, no bursts of lyrical music, no resolutions of tragic solemnity into irony or sarcasm, afford relief from clumsy horrors and stale disquisitions, parcelled out by weight and measure in the leaden acts. An intolerable wordiness oppresses the reader, who wades through speeches reckoned by the hundred lines, wondering how any audience could endure the torment of their recitation. Each play is a flat and arid wilderness, piled with barrows of extinct sentences in Seneca's manner and with pyramids of reflection heaped up from the commonplace books of a pedagogue.

The failure of Italian tragedy was inseparable from its artificial origin. It was the conscious product of cultivated persons, who aimed at nothing nobler than the imitation of the ancients and the observance of inapplicable rules. The curse of intellectual barrenness weighed upon the starvelings of this system from the moment of their birth, and nothing better came of them than our own *Gorboduc*. That tragedy, built upon the false Italian method, is indeed a sign of what we English might have suffered, if Sidney and the Court had gained their way with the Elizabethan Drama.

The humanistic influences of the fifteenth century were scarcely less unpropitious to national comedy at its outset than they had been to tragedy. Although the *Sacre Rappresentazioni* contained the germ of vernacular farce, though interludes in dialect amused the folk of more than one Italian province, among which special reference may be made to the Neapolitan *Farse*, yet the playwrights of the Renaissance preferred Plautus and Terence to the indigenous growth of their own age and country.[1] We may note this fact with regret, since it helped to deprive the Italians of a national theatre. Still we must not forget that it was inevitable. Humanism embraced the several districts of Italy in a common culture, effacing the distinctions of dialect, and bringing the separate elements of the nation to a consciousness of intellectual unity. Divided as Venetians, as Florentines, as Neapolitans, as Lombards, and as Romans, the members of the Italian community recognised their identity in the spiritual city they had reconquered from the past. What the English translation of the Bible effected for us, the recovery of Latin and the humanistic education of the middle classes achieved for the Italians. For a Florentine scholar to have developed the comic elements existing in the *Feste*, for a Neapolitan to have refined the matter of the *Farse*, would have seemed the same in either case as self-restriction to the limits of a single province. But the whole nation possessed the Latin poets as a common heritage; and on the ground of Plautus, Florentines and Neapolitans could understand each other. It was therefore natural that the cultivated orders, brought into communion by the ancients, should look to these for models of an art they were intent on making national. Together with this imperious instinct, which impelled the Italians to create their literature in sympathy with the commanding spirit of the age, we must reckon the fashionable indifference toward vernacular and obscure forms of

---

[1] D' Ancona (*Origini del Teatro*, vol. ii. sec. xxxix.) may be consulted upon the attempts to secularise the *Sacre Rappresentazioni* which preceded the revival of classical comedy.

poetry. The princes and their courtiers strove alike to remodel modern customs in accordance with the classics. Illiterate mechanics might amuse themselves with farces.[1] Men who had once tasted the refined and pungent salt of Attic wit, could stomach nothing simpler than scenes from antique comedy.

We therefore find that, at the close of the fifteenth century, it was common to recite the plays of Plautus and Terence in their original language. Paolo Comparini at Florence in 1488 wrote a prologue to the *Menæchmi*, which his pupils represented, much to the disgust of the elder religious Companies, who felt that the ruin of their *Feste* was involved in this revival of antiquity.[2] Pomponius Lætus at Rome, about the same time, encouraged the members of his Academy to rehearse Terence and Plautus in the palaces of nobles and prelates.[3] The company of youthful actors formed by him were employed by the Cardinal Raffaello Riario in the magnificent spectacles he provided for the amusement of the Papal Court. During the pontificate of Sixtus IV. and Innocent VIII., the mausoleum of Hadrian, not then transformed into a fortress, or else the squares of Rome were temporarily

[1] Leo X., with a Medici's true sympathy for plebeian literature added to his own coarse sense of fun, patronised the farces of the Sienese Company called Rozzi. Had his influence lasted, had there been anyone to continue the traditions of his Court at Rome, it is not impossible that a more natural comedy, as distinguished from the *Commedia erudita*, might have been produced by this fashionable patronage of popular dramatic art.

[2] See D' Ancona, *Or. del Teatro*, vol. ii. p. 201.

[3] Sabellico, quoted by Tiraboschi, says of him : 'primorum antistitum atriis suo theatro usus, in quibus Plauti, Terentii, recentiorum etiam quædam agerentur fabulæ, quas ipse honestos adolescentes et docuit et agentibus præfuit.'

arranged as theatres for these exhibitions.[1] It was on
this stage that Tommaso Inghirami, by his brilliant
acting in the *Hippolytus* of Seneca, gained the sur-
name of Phædra which clung to him through life. In
the pontificate of Alexander we hear of similar shows,
as when, upon the occasion of Lucrezia Borgia's
espousal to the Duke of Ferrara in 1502, the *Menæchmi* was represented at the Vatican.[2]

The Court which accomplished most for the resuscitation of Latin Comedy was that of the Estensi at
Ferrara. Ercole I. had spent a delicate youth in humanistic studies, collecting manuscripts and encouraging
his courtiers to make Italian translations of ancient
authors. He took special interest in theatrical compositions, and spared no pains in putting Latin comedies with all the pomp of modern art upon the stage.
Thus the Ferrarese diaries mention a representation of
the *Menæchmi* in 1486, which cost above 1000 ducats.
In 1487 the courtyard of the castle was fitted up as a
theatre for the exhibition of Nicolò da Correggio's
Pastoral of *Cefalo*.[3] Again, upon the occasion of

[1] See the letter of Sulpizio da Veroli to Raffaello Riario, quoted by
Tiraboschi ; 'eamdemque, postquam in Hadriani mole Divo Innocentio
spectante est acta, rursus inter tuos penates, tamquam in media Circi
cavea, toto consessu umbraculis tecto, admisso populo, et pluribus tui
ordinis spectatoribus honorifice excepisti. Tu etiam primus picturatæ
scenæ faciem, quum Pomponiam comœdiam agerent, nostro sæculo
ostendisti.'
[2] See *Lucrezia Borgia*, by Gregorovius (Stuttgart, 1874), vol. i. p. 201.
[3] Nicolò was a descendant of the princely house of Correggio. He
married Cassandra, daughter of Bartolommeo Colleoni. His *Cefalo* was
a mixed composition resembling the *Sacre Rappresentazioni* in structure.
In the Prologue he says :

> Requiret autem nullus hic Comœdiæ
> Leges ut observentur, aut Tragœdiæ ;
> Agenda nempe est historia, non fabula.

See D' Ancona, *op. cit.* vol. 2, pp. 143-146, 155.

Annibale de' Bentivogli's betrothal to a princess of
the Este family, the *Amphitryon* was performed ; and
in 1491, when Anna Sforza gave her hand to Alfonso
d' Este, the same comedy was repeated.   In 1493
Lodovico Sforza, on a visit to Ferrara, witnessed a
representation of the *Menæchmi,* which so delighted
him that he begged Ercole to send his company to
Milan.   The Duke went thither in person, attended
by his son Alfonso and by gentle actors of his Court,
among whom Lodovico Ariosto played a part.   Later on,
in 1499, we again hear of Latin comedies at Ferrara.
Bembo in a letter of that year mentions the *Trinummus,*
Pœnulus and *Eunuchus.*[1]

It is probable that Latin comedies were recited at
Ferrara, as at Rome, in the original.   At the same
time we know that both Plautus and Terence were
being translated into Italian for the amusement of an
audience as yet but partially acquainted with ancient
languages.   Tiraboschi mentions the *Anfitrione* of
Pandolfo Collenuccio, the *Cassina* and *Mostellaria* versified in *terza rima* by Girolamo Berardo, and the
Menechmi of Duke Ercole, among the earliest of
these versions.   Guarini and Ariosto followed on their
path with translations from the Latin made for special
occasions.   It was thus that Italian comedy began to
disengage itself from Latin.   After the presentation of
the original plays, came translation ; and after translation, imitation.   The further transition from imitation
to freedom was never perfectly effected.   The comic
drama, determined in its form by the circumstances of
its origin, remained emphatically a *commedia erudita.*

---

[1] *Ep. Fam.* i. 18, quoted by Tiraboschi.

Adapted to the conditions of modern life, it never lost dependence upon Latin models; and its most ingenious representations of manners were defaced by reminiscences which condemn them to a place among artistic hybrids. Ariosto, who did so much to stamp Italian comedy with the mark of his own genius, was educated, as we have already seen, in the traditions of Duke Ercole's Latin theatre; and Ariosto gave the law to his most genial successor, Cecchi. The Pegasus of the Italian drama, if I may venture on a burlesque metaphor, was a mule begotten by the sturdy ass of Latin on the fleet mare of the Italian spirit; and it had the sterility of the mule.

The year 1502, when Lucrezia Borgia came as Alfonso d' Este's bride to Ferrara, marks the climax of these Latin spectacles.[1] Ercole had arranged a theatre in the Palace of the Podestà (now called the Palazzo della Ragione), which was connected with the castle by a private gallery. His troupe, recruited from Ferrara, Rome, Siena and Mantua, numbered one hundred and ten actors of both sexes. Accomplished singers, dancers, and scene-painters were summoned to add richness to the spectacle. We hear of musical interludes performed by six violins; while every comedy was diversified by morris-dances of Saracens, satyrs, gladiators, wild men, hunters, and allegorical personages.[2] The entertainment lasted over

---

[1] Gregorovius in his book on *Lucrezia Borgia* (pp. 228–239) has condensed the authorities. See, too, Dennistoun, *Dukes of Urbino*, vol. i. pp. 441–448.

[2] The minute descriptions furnished by Sanudo of these festivals read like the prose letterpress accompanying the Masques of our Ben Jonson.

five nights, a comedy of Plautus forming the principal piece on each occasion. On the first evening the *Epidicus* was given ; on the second, the *Bacchides* ; on the third, the *Miles Gloriosus* ; on the fourth, the *Asinaria* ; on the fifth, the *Casina*. From the reports of Cagnolo, Zambotto, and Isabella Gonzaga, we are led to believe that the unlettered audience judged the recitations of the Plautine comedies somewhat tedious. They were in the same position as unmusical people of the present day, condemned to listen to Bach's Passion Music, and afraid of expressing their dissatisfaction. Yet these more frivolous spectators found ample gratification in the ingenious ballets, accompanied with music, which relieved each act. The occasion was memorable. In those five evenings the Court of Ferrara presented to the fashionable world of Italy a carefully-studied picture of Latin comedy framed in a setting of luxuriant modern arabesques. The simplicity of Plautus, executed with the fidelity born of reverence for antique art, was thrown into relief by extravagances borrowed from medieval chivalry, tinctured with Oriental associations, enhanced by music and coloured with the glowing hues of Ferrarese imagination. The city of Boiardo, of Dossi, of Bello, of Ariosto, strained her resources to devise fantastic foils for the antique. It was as though Cellini had been called to mount an onyx of Augustus in labyrinths of gold-work and enamel for the stomacher of a Grand-Duchess.

We may without exaggeration affirm that the practice of the Ferrarese stage, culminating in the marriage shows of 1502, determined the future of

Italian comedy. The fashion of the Court of Ercole was followed by all patrons of dramatic art. When a play was written, the author planned it in connection with subordinate exhibitions of dancing and music.[1] He wrote a poem in five acts upon the model of Plautus or Terence, understanding that his scenes of classical simplicity would be embedded in the grotesques of *cinque cento* allegory. The whole performance lasted some six hours ; but the comedy itself was but a portion of the entertainment. For the majority of the audience the dances and the pageants formed the chief attraction.[2] It is therefore no marvel if the drama, considered as a branch of high poetic art, was suffocated by the growth of its mere accessories. Nor was this inconsistent with the ruling tendencies of the Renaissance. We have no reason to suppose that even Ariosto or Machiavelli grudged the participation of painters like Peruzzi, musicians like Dalla Viuola, architects like San Gallo, and dancers of ephemeral distinction, in the triumph of their plays.

The habit of regarding scenic exhibitions as the adjunct to extravagant Court luxury, prevented the development of a theatre in which the genius of poets

[1] Il Lasca in his prologue to the *Strega* (*ed. cit.* p. 171) says : ' Questa non è fatta da principi, nè da signori, nè in palazzi ducali e signorili ; e però non avrà quella pompa d' apparato, di prospettiva, e d' intermedj che ad alcune altre nei tempi nostri s' è veduto.'

[2] A fine example of the Italian Masque is furnished by *El Sacrificio*, played with great pomp by the Intronati of Siena in 1531 and printed in 1537. *El Sacrificio de gli Intronati Celebrato ne i giuochi del Carnovale in Siena l' Anno MDXXXI.* Full particulars regarding the music, *mise en scène*, and ballets on such ceremonial occasions, will be found in two curious pamphlets, *Descrizione dell' Apparato fatto nel Tempio di S. Giov. di Fiorenza*, etc. (Giunti, 1568), and *Descrizione dell' Entrata della Serenissima Reina Giovanna d' Austria*, etc. (Giunti, 1566). They refer to a later period, but they abound in the most curious details.

might have shone with undimmed intellectual lustre. The want of permanent buildings, devoted to acting, in any great Italian town, may again be reckoned among the causes which checked the expansion of the drama. When a play had to be acted, a stage was erected at a great expense for the occasion.[1] It is true that Alfonso I. built a theatre after Ariosto's designs at Ferrara in 1528 ; but it was burnt down in 1532. According to Gregorovius, Leo X. fitted one up at Rome upon the Capitol in 1513,[2] capable of holding the two thousand spectators who witnessed a performance of the *Suppositi*. This does not, however, seem to have been used continuously ; nor was it until the second half of the sixteenth century that theatres began to form a part of the palatial residences of princes. One precious relic of those more permanent stages remains to show the style they then assumed. This is the Teatro Farnese at Parma, erected in 1618 by Ranuzio I. after the design of Galeotti Aleotti of Ferrara. It could accommodate seven thousand spectators ; and, though now in ruins, it is still a stately and harmonious monument of architectural magnificence.[3] What, however, was always wanting in Italy was a theatre open to all classes and at all seasons of the year, where the people might have been the patrons of their playwrights.[4]

---

[1] See the details brought together by Campori, *Notizie per la vita di Lodovico Ariosto*, p. 74, Castiglione's letter on the *Calandra* at Urbino, the private representation of the *Rosmunda* in the Rucellai gardens, of the *Orbecche* in Giraldi's house, of the *Sofonisba* at Vicenza, of Gelli's *Errore* by the Fantastichi, etc.

[2] *Stadt Rom*, viii. 350.

[3] See the article 'Fornovo' in my *Sketches and Studies in Italy*.

[4] At this point, in illustration of what has been already stated, I take the opportunity of transcribing a passage which fairly represents the con-

The transition from Latin to Italian comedy was effected almost simultaneously by three poets, Bernardo Dovizio, Lodovico Ariosto, and Niccolò Machiavelli. Dovizio was born at Bibbiena in 1470. He attached himself to the Cardinal Giovanni de' Medici, and received the scarlet from his master in 1513. We need not concern ourselves with his ecclesiastical career. It is enough to say that the *Calandra*, which raised him to a foremost place among the literary men of Italy, was composed before his elevation to the dignity of Cardinal, and was first performed at Urbino some time between the dates 1504 and 1513, possibly in 1508. The reader will already have observed that the most popular Latin play, both at Ferrara and Rome, was the *Menæchmi* of Plautus. In Dovizio's *Calandra* the influence of this comedy is so noticeable that we may best describe it as an accommodation of the Latin form to Italian circumstance. The intrigue depends upon the close resemblance of a brother and sister, Lidio and Santilla, whose appearance by turns in male and female costume gives rise to a variety of farcical incidents. The name is derived from Calandro, a simpleton of Calandrino's type; and the interest of the plot is that of a *Novella*. The characters are very

ditions of play-going in the *cinque cento*. Doni, in the *Marmi*, gives this description of two comedies performed in the Sala del Papa of the Palazzo Vecchio at Florence.* 'By my faith, in Florence never was there any-. thing so fine : two stages, one at each end of the Hall : two wonderful scenes, the one by Francesco Salviati, the other by Bronzino : two most amusing comedies, and of the newest coinage ; the *Mandragola* and the *Assiuolo* : when the first act of the one was over, there followed the first act of the other, and so forth, each play taking up the other, without interludes, in such wise that the one comedy served as interlude for the other. The music began at the opening, and ended with the close.'

---

* Barbèra's edition, 1863, vol. i. p. 67.

slightly sketched; but the movement is continuous, and the dialogue is always lively. The *Calandra* achieved immediate success by reproducing both the humour of Boccaccio and the invention of Plautus in the wittiest vernacular.[1] A famous letter of Baldassare Castiglione, describing its representation at Urbino, enlarges upon the splendour of the scenery and dresses, the masques of Jason, Venus, Love, Neptune and Juno, accompanied by morris-dances and concerts of stringed instruments, which were introduced as interludes.[2] From Urbino the comedy passed through all the Courts of Italy, finding the highest favour at Rome, where Leo more than once decreed its representation. One of these occasions was memorable. Wishing to entertain the Marchioness Isabella of Mantua (1514), he put the *Calandra* with great pomp upon his private stage in the Vatican. Baldassare Peruzzi designed and painted the decorations, giving a new impulse to this species of art by the beauty of his inventions.[3]

Leo had an insatiable appetite for scenic shows. Comedies of the new Latinising style were his favourite recreation. But he also invited the Sienese Company of the Rozzi, who only played farces, every year to Rome; nor was he averse to even less artistic buffoonery, as may be gathered from many of the

---

[1] One of the chief merits of the *Calandra* in the eyes of contemporaries was the successful adaptation of Boccaccio's style to the stage. Though Italians alone have the right to pronounce judgment on such matters, I confess to preferring the limpid ease of Ariosto and the plebeian freshness of Gelli. The former has the merit of facile lucidity, the latter of native raciness. Bibbiena's somewhat pompous phraseology sits ill upon his farcical obscenities.

[2] See the translation in Dennistoun, vol. ii. p. 141.

[3] See Vasari, viii. 227.

stories told about him.[1] In 1513 Leo opened a theatre upon the Capitol, and here in 1519, surrounded with two thousand spectators, he witnessed an exhibition of Ariosto's *Suppositi*. We have a description of the scene from the pen of an eye-witness, who relates how the Pope sat at the entrance to the gallery leading into the theatre, and admitted with his benediction those whom he thought worthy of partaking in the night's amusements.[2] When the house was full, he took his throne in the orchestra, and sat, with eye-glass in hand, to watch the play. Raphael had painted the scenery, which is said to have been, and doubtless was, extremely beautiful. Leo's behaviour scandalised the foreign ambassadors, who thought it indecorous that a Pope should not only listen to the equivocal jests of the Prologue but also laugh immoderately at them.[3] As usual, the inter-acts consisted of vocal and instrumental concerts, with ballets on classical and allegorical subjects.

Enough has now been said concerning the mode of presenting comedies in vogue throughout Italy. The mention of Leo's entertainment in 1519 introduces the subject of Ariosto's plays. The *Suppositi*, originally written in prose and afterwards versified by its author, first appeared in 1509 at Ferrara. In the preceding

---

[1] See D' Ancona, *op. cit.* vol. ii. p. 250, for the special nature of the *Farsa*. See also *ib.* p. 211, the description by Paolucci of Leo's buffooneries in the Vatican.

[2] See Campori, *Notizie Inedite di Raffaello di Urbino*, Modena, 1863, quoted by D' Ancona, *op. cit.* p. 212. The entertainment cost Leo 1,000 ducats.

[3] No doubt Paolucci refers to the obscene play upon the word *Suppositi*, and to the ironical epithet of *Santa* applied to *Roma* in a passage which does no honour to Ariosto.

year Ariosto exhibited the *Cassaria*, which, like the *Suppositi*, was planned in prose and subsequently versified in *sdrucciolo* iambics.[1]

In Ariosto's comedies the form of Roman art becomes a lay-figure, dressed according to various modes of the Italian Renaissance. The wire-work, so to speak, of Plautus or of Terence can be everywhere detected; but this skeleton has been incarnated with modern flesh and blood, habited in Ferrarese costume, and taught the paces of contemporary fashion. Blent with the traditions of Plautine comedy, we find in each of the four plays an Italian *Novella*. The motive is invariably trivial. In the *Cassaria* two young men are in love with two girls kept by a slave-merchant. The intrigue turns upon the arts of their valets, who cheat the pander and procure the girls for nothing for their masters. In the *Suppositi* a young man of good family has assumed the part of servant, in order to seduce the daughter of his master. The devices by which he contrives to secure her hand in marriage, furnish the action of the play. The *Lena* has even a simpler plan. A young man needs a few quiet hours for corrupting his neighbour's daughter. Lena, the chief actress, will not serve as a go-between without a sum of ready money paid down by the hero. The move-

---

[1] For the dates of Ariosto's dramatic compositions, see above, Part 1, p. 499. The edition I shall refer to, is that of Giovanni Tortoli (Firenze, Barbèra, 1856), which gives both the prose and verse redactions of the *Cassaria* and *Suppositi*. It may here be incidentally remarked that there are few thoroughly good editions of Italian plays. Descriptions of the *dramatis personæ*, stage directions, and illustrative notes are almost uniformly wanting. The reader is left to puzzle out an intricate action without help. All the slang, the local customs, and the passing allusions which give life to comedy and present so many difficulties to the student, are for the most part unexplained.

ment of the piece depends on the expedients whereby this money is raised, and the farcical obstacles which interrupt the lovers at the point of their felicity. In the *Negromante* a young man has been secretly married to one woman, and openly to another. Cinthio loves his real wife, Lavinia, and feigns impotence in order to explain his want of affection for Emilia, who is the recognised mistress of his home. An astrologer, Iacchelino, holds the threads of the intrigue in his hands. Possessed of Cinthio's secret, paid by the parents of Emilia to restore Cinthio's virility, paid again by a lover of Emilia to advance his own suit, and seeking in the midst of these rival interests to make money out of the follies and ambitions of his clients, Iacchelino has the whole domestic company at his discretion. The comic point lies in the various passions which betray each dupe to the astrologer—Cinthio's wish to escape from Emilia, Camillo's eagerness to win her, the old folk's anxiety to cure Cinthio. Temolo, a servant, who is hoodwinked by no personal desire, sees that Iacchelino is an impostor; and the inordinate avarice of the astrologer undoes him. Thus the *Negromante* presents a really fine comic web of humours at cross purposes and appetites that overreach themselves.

There is considerable similarity in Ariosto's plots. In all of them, except the *Negromante*, we have a subplot which brings a tricksy valet into play. A sum of money is imperatively needed to effect the main scheme of the hero; and this has to be provided by the servant's ingenuity. Such direct satire as the poet thought fit to introduce, is common to them all.

It concerns the costs, delays and frauds of legal procedure, favouritism at Court, the Ferrarese game-laws, and the tyranny of custom-house officials.   But satire of an indirect, indulgent species—the Horatian satire of Ariosto's own epistles—adds a pleasant pungency to his pictures of contemporary manners no less than to his occasional discourses.   The prologue to the *Cassaria*, on its reappearance as a versified play, might be quoted for the perfection of genial sarcasm, playing about the foibles of society without inflicting a serious wound.   All the prologues, however, are not innocent. Those prefixed to the *Lena* and the *Suppositi* contain allusions so indecent, and veil obscenities under metaphors so flimsy, as to justify a belief in Ariosto's vulgarity of soul.   Here the satirist borders too much on the sympathiser with a vice he professes to condemn.

It remains to speak of the *Scolastica*, a comedy left incomplete at Ariosto's death, and finished by his brother Gabrielle, but bearing the unmistakeable stamp of his ripest genius impressed upon the style no less than on the structure of the plot.[1]   The scene is laid at Ferrara, where we find ourselves among the scholars of its famous university, and are made acquainted in the liveliest manner with their habits.   The heroes are two young students, Claudio and Eurialo, firm friends, who have passed some years at Pavia reading with Messer Lazzaro, a doctor of laws.   The disturbance of the country having driven both professors and pupils

---

[1] Gabrielle added the last two scenes of the fifth act. See his prologue. But whether he introduced any modifications into the body of the play, or filled up any gaps, does not appear.

from Pavia,[1] a variety of accidents brings all the actors
of the comedy to Ferrara, where Eurialo is living with
his father, Bartolo. Of course the two lads are in love
—Claudio with the daughter of his former tutor, and
Eurialo with a fatherless girl in the service of a noble
lady at Pavia. The intrigue is rather farcical than
comic. It turns upon the difficulties encountered by
Claudio and Eurialo in concealing their sweethearts
from their respective fathers, the absurd mistakes they
make in the hurry of the moment, and the misunder-
standings which ensue between themselves and the
old people. Ariosto has so cleverly complicated the
threads of his plot and has developed them with such
lucidity of method that any analysis would fall short
of the original in brevity and clearness. The *dé-
nouement* is effected by the device of a recognition at
the last moment. Eurialo's *innamorata* is found to be
the lost ward of his father, Bartolo ; and Claudio is
happily married to his love, Flaminia. The merit of
the play lies, however, less in the argument than the
characters, which are ably conceived and sustained
with more than even Ariosto's usual skill. The timid
and perplexed Eurialo, trembling before his terrible
father, seeking advice from every counseller, despairing, resigning himself to fate, is admirably contrasted
with the more passionate and impulsive Claudio, who
takes rash steps with inconsiderate boldness, relies on
his own address to extricate himself, and vibrates between the ecstasies of love and the suspicions of an angry

---

[1] Poichè a Pavia levato era il salario
Alli dottor, nè più si facea studio
Per le guerre che più ogni dì augumentano.

jealousy.[1] Bartolo, burdened in his conscience by an ancient act of broken faith, and punished in the disobedience of his son, forms an excellent pendent to the honest but pedantic Messer Lazzaro, who cannot bear to see his daughter suffer from an unrequited passion.[2] Each of the servants, too, has a well-marked physiognomy—the witty Accursio, picking up what learning he can from his master's books, and turning all he says to epigrams ; the easy-going, Bacchanalian duenna ; blunt Pistone ; garrulous Stanna. But the most original of all the *dramatis personæ* is Bonifazio, that excellent keeper of lodgings for Ferrarese students, who identifies himself with their interests, sympathises in their love-affairs, takes side with them against their fathers, and puts his conscience in his pocket when required to pull them out of scrapes.[3] Each of these characters has been copied from the life. The taint of Latin comedy has been purged out of them.[4] They

---

[1] Their opposite humours are admirably developed in the dialogues of act ii. sc. 5, act iii. sc. 5.

[2] Compare Bartolo's soliloquy in act iv. sc. 6, with Lazzaro's confidences to Bonifazio, whom he mistakes for Bartolo, in act v. sc. 3.

[3] His action in the comedy is admirably illustrated by the self-revelation of the following soliloquy (act iv. sc. 1) :

> Io vuò a ogni modo aiutar questo giovane,
> E dir dieci bugìe, perchè ad incorrere
> Non abbia con suo padre in rissa e in scandalo :
> E così ancor quest' altro mio, che all' ultima
> Disperazione è condotto da un credere
> Falso e da gelosia che a torto il stimola.
> Nè mi vergognerò d' ordire, o tessere
> Fallacie e giunti, *e far ciò ch' eran soliti*
> *Gli antichi servi già nelle commedie :*
> Chè veramente.l' aiutare un povero
> Innamorato, non mi pare uffizio
> Servil, ma di gentil qualsivoglia animo.

[4] The process is well indicated in the lines I have italicised in Boni-

move, speak, act like living beings, true to themselves in every circumstance, and justifying the minutest details of the argument by the operation of their several qualities of head and heart. Viewed as a work of pure dramatic art, the *Scolastica* is not only the most genial and sympathetic of Ariosto's comedies, but also the least fettered by his Latinising prepossessions, and the strongest in psychological analysis. Like the *Lena*, it has the rare merit of making us at home in the Ferrara which he knew so well; but it does not, like that play, disgust us by the spectacle of abject profligacy.[1] There is a sunny, jovial freshness in this latest product of Ariosto's genius, which invigorates while it amuses and instructs.

The *Scolastica* is not without an element of satire. I have said that Bartolo had a sin upon his conscience. In early manhood he promised to adopt a friend's daughter, and to marry her in due course to his own Eurialo. But he neglected this duty, lost sight of the girl, and appropriated her heritage. He has reason to think that she may still be found in Naples; and the parish priest, to whom he confided his secret in confession, will not absolve him, unless he take the journey and do all he can to rectify the error of his past. Bartolo is disinclined to this long pilgrimage, with the probable loss of a fortune at the end of it. In his difficulty he has recourse to a Frate Predicatore,

fazio's soliloquy. He is no longer a copy of the Latin slaves, but a free agent who emulates their qualities.

[1] With all admiration for the *Lena*, how can we appreciate the cynicism of the situation revealed in the first scene—the crudely exposed appetites of Flavio, the infamous conduct of Fazio, who places his daughter under the tutelage of his old mistress?

who professes to hold ample powers for dispensing
with troublesome vows and pious obligations [1] :

> Voi potete veder la bolla, e leggere
> Le facultadi mie, che sono amplissime ;
> E come, senza che pigliate, Bartolo,
> Questo pellegrinaggio, io posso assolvere
> E commutar i voti ; e maravigliomi
> Che essendo, com' io son, vostro amicissimo,
> Non m' abbiate richiesto ; perchè, dandomi
> Quel solamente che potreste spendere
> Voi col famiglio nel viaggio, assolvere
> Vi posso, e farvi schifar un grandissimo
> Disconcio, all' età vostra incomportabile :
> Oltra diversi infiniti pericoli,
> Che ponno a chi va per cammino occorrere.

The irony of this speech depends upon its plain and
business-like statement of a simoniacal bargain, which
will prove of mutual benefit to the parties concerned.
Bartolo confides his case of conscience to the Friar,
previously telling him that he has confessed it to the
parson :

> Ma non mi sa decidere
> Questo caso, chè, come voi, teologo
> Non è ; sa un poco di ragion canonica.

At the close of the communication, which is admirable
for its lucid exposition of a domestic romance adapted
to the circumstances of the sixteenth century, the Friar
asks his penitent once more whether he would not
willingly escape this pilgrimage. Who could doubt it?
answers Bartolo. Well then :

> Ben si potrà commutare in qualche opera
> Pia. Non si trova al mondo sì forte obbligo,
> Che non si possa scior con l' elemosine.

Here again the sarcasm consists in the hypocritical

---

[1] Act iii. sc. 6.

adaptation of the old axiom that everything in this world can be got for money. On both sides the transaction is commercial. Bartolo, like a good man of business, wishes to examine the Frate's title-deeds before he engages in the purchase of his spiritual privileges. In other words he must be permitted to examine the Bull of Indulgence [1] :

> Porterollavi,
> E ve la lascerò vedere e leggere.
> Siate pur certo che la bolla è amplissima,
> E che di tutti i casi, componendovi
> Meco, vi posso interamente assolvere,
> Non meno che potria 'l Papa medesimo.

Bartolo. Vi credo ; nondimeno, per iscarico
> Della mia coscienza, la desidero
> Veder, e farla anco vedere e leggere
> Al mio parrocchiano.

Frate.   Ora sia *in nomine*
> *Domini*, porterolla, e mostrerolla
> A chi vi pare.

We may further notice how the parish priest is here meant to play the part of solicitor in the bargain. He does not deal in these spiritual commodities ; but he can give advice upon the point of validity. The episode of Bartolo and the Dominican reminds us that we are on the eve of the Reformation. While Rome and Ferrara laughed at the hypocrisies, credulities, and religious frauds implied in such transactions, Northern Europe broke into flame, and Luther opened the great schism.[2]

---

[1] Act. iv. sc. 4. In the last line but one, ought we not to read *mostre-ratela* or else *mostrerollavi?*

[2] Room must be found for a few of the sarcasms, uttered chiefly by Accursio, which enliven the *Scolastica.* Here are the humanists :

> questi umanisti, che cercano
> Medaglie, e di rovesci si dilettano.

The artistic merit of Ariosto's comedies consists in the perfection of their structure. However involved the intrigues may be, we experience no difficulty in following them; so masterly is their development.[1] It may be objected that he too frequently resorts to the device of anagnorisis, in order to solve a problem which cannot find its issue in the action. This mechanical solution is so obviously employed to make things easy for the author that no interest attaches to the climax of his fables. Yet the characters are drawn with that ripe insight into human nature which distinguished Ariosto. Machiavelli observed that, being a native of Ferrara, cautious in the handling of Tuscan idioms, and unwilling to use the dialect of his own city, Ariosto missed the salt of comedy.[2] There is truth in this criticism. Matched with the best Florentine dialogues, his language wants the raciness of the vernacular. The *sdrucciolo* verse, which he preferred, fatigues the ear and adds to the impression of formality.

Here is Rome :
> Roma, dove intendono
> Che 'l sangue degli Apostoli e de' Martiri
> È molto dolce, e a lor spese è un bel vivere.

Here is Ferrara :
> Ferrara, ove pur vedesi
> Che fino alli barbieri paion nobili.

Here are the Signori of Naples :
> da Napoli.
> Ho ben inteso che ve n' è più copia
> Che a Ferrara di Conti ; e credo ch' abbiano,
> Come questi contado, quei dominio.

[1] Cecchi noticed the lucid order, easy exposition and smooth conduct of Ariosto's plots, ranking him for these qualities above the Latin poets. See the passage from *Le Pellegrine* quoted below.

[2] In an essay on the Italian language, included among Machiavelli's works, but ascribed to him on no very certain ground.

He frequently interrupts the action with tirades, talking, as it were, in his own person to the audience, instead of making his characters speak.[1] Yet foreigners, who study his comedies side by side with Plautus, at almost the same distance of unfamiliarity, will recognise the brilliance of his transcripts from contemporary life. These studies of Italian manners are eminent for good taste, passing at no point into extravagance, and only marred by a certain banality of moral instinct. The *Lena* has the highest value as a picture of Ferrarese society. We have good reason to believe that it was founded on an actual incident. It deserves to rank with Machiavelli's *Mandragola* and Aretino's *Cortigiana* for the light it throws on sixteenth-century customs. And the light is far more natural, less lurid, less partial, than that which either Machiavelli or Aretino shed upon the vices of their century.

Of Machiavelli we have two genuine comedies in prose, the *Mandragola* and the *Clizia*, and two of doubtful authenticity, called respectively *Commedia in Prosa* and *Commedia in Versi*, besides a translation of the *Andria*.[2] Judging by internal evidence alone, a cautious critic would reject the *Commedia in Versi* from the canon of Machiavelli's works ; and if the existence of a copy in his autograph has to be taken as conclusive evidence of its genuineness, we can only accept it as a crude and juvenile production. It is written in

---

[1] Notice the long monologue of the *Cassaria* in which Lucramo describes the fashionable follies of Ferrara. Ariosto gradually outgrew this habit of tirade. The *Scolastica* is freer than any of his pieces from the fault.

[2] *Le Commedie di N. Machiavelli, con prefazione di F. Perfetti*, Firenze, Barbèra, 1863.

various measures, a graceless octave stanza rhyming only in the last couplet being used instead of blank verse, while many of the monologues are lyrical. The language is crabbed, uncertain, archaistic—in no point displaying the incisive brevity of Machiavelli's style. The scene is laid in ancient Rome, and the intrigue turns upon a confusion between two names, Catillo and Cammillo. The conventional parasite of antiquity and the inevitable slaves play prominent parts ; while the plot is solved by a preposterous exchange of wives between the two chief characters. Thus the fabric of the comedy throughout is unnatural and false to the conditions of real life. Were it not for some piquant studies of Italian manners, scattered here and there in the descriptive passages, this *Commedia in Versi* would scarcely deserve passing notice.[1]

The *Commedia in Prosa*, for which we might find a title in the name of the chief personage, Fra Alberigo, displays the spirit and the style of the *Mandragola*. Critics who do not accept it for Machiavelli's own, must assume it to have been the work of a clever and obsequious imitator. It is a short piece in three acts written to expose the corruption of a Florentine house-

---

[1] Take this picture of Virginia (act i. sc. 2) :

Ap. Dilettasi ella dar prova a filare,
    O tessere, o cucire, com' è usanza?
Mis. No, chè far lassa tal cosa a sua madre.
Ap. Di che piglia piacer ?
Mis.   Delle finestre,
    Dove la sta dal mattino alla sera,
    E vaga è di novelle, suoni e canti,
    E studia in lisci, e dorme, e cuce in guanti.

Or the picture of the lovers in church described by the servant, Doria (act iii. sc. 2), or Virginia's portrait of her jealous husband (act iii. sc. 5).

hold. Caterina, the heroine, is a young wife married to an old husband, Amerigo. Their maid-servant, Margherita, holds the threads of the intrigue in her hands. She has been solicited on the one side by Amerigo to help him in his amours with a neighbour's wife, and on the other by the friar, Alberigo, to win Caterina to his suit. The devices whereby Margherita brings her mistress and the monk together, cheats Amerigo of his expected enjoyment, and so contrives that the despicable but injured husband should establish Fra Alberigo in the position of a favoured house-friend, constitute the argument. Short as the play is, it combines the chief points of the *Clizia* and the *Mandragola* in a single action, and may be regarded as the first sketch of two situations afterwards developed with more fulness by the author.[1] The language is coarse, and the picture of manners, executed with remorseless realism, would be revolting but for its strong workmanship.[2] The playwright expended his force on the servant-maid and the friar, those two instruments of domestic immorality. Fra

[1] The scene between Caterina and Amerigo, when the latter is caught in flagrant adultery (act iii. 5), anticipates the catastrophe of the *Clizia*. The final scene between Caterina, Amerigo, and Fra Alberigo bears a close resemblance to the climax of the *Mandragola*. On the hypothesis that this comedy is not Machiavelli's but an imitator's, the playwright must have had both the *Clizia* and the *Mandragola* in his mind, and have designed a pithy combination of their most striking elements.

[2] See especially the scenes between Caterina and Margherita (act i. 3 ; act ii. 1) where the advantages of taking a lover and of choosing a friar for this purpose are discussed. They abound in *gros mots*, as thus :

Cat. Odi, in quanto a cotesta parte tu di' la verità ; ma quello odore, ch' egli hanno poi di salvaggiume, non ch' altro mi stomaca a pensarlo.

Marg. Eh ! eh ! poveretta voi ! i frati, eh ? Non si trova generazione più abile ai servigi delle donne. Voi dovete forse avere a pigliarvi piacere col naso ? etc.

Alberigo is a vulgar libertine, provided with pious phrases to cloak his vicious purpose, but casting off the mask when he has gained his object, well knowing from past experience that the appetites of the woman he seduces will secure his footing in her husband's home.[1] Margherita revels in the corruption she has aided. She delights in sin for its own sake, extracts handfuls of coppers from the friar, and counts on profiting by the secret of her mistress. Her speech and action display the animal appetites and gross phraseology of the proletariate, degraded by city vices and hardened to the spectacle of clerical hypocrisy.[2] One of her exclamations : ' I frati, ah ! son più viziati che 'l fistolo !' taken in conjunction with her argument to Caterina : ' I frati, eh ? Non si trova generazione più abile ai servigi delle donne !' points the satire intended by the playwright. Yet neither Caterina nor Amerigo yield a point of baseness to these servile agents. Plebeian coarseness is stamped alike upon their language and their desires. They have no delicacy of feeling, no redeeming passion, no self-respect. They speak of things unmentionable with a crudity that makes one shudder, and abuse each other in sarcasms borrowed from the rhetoric of the streets.[3] To a refined taste the calculations of Caterina are no

---

[1] Compare his speech to Caterina (act ii. 5) with his dialogue with Margherita (act iii. 4) and his final discourse on charity and repentance (act iii. 6). The irony of these words, ' Certamente, Amerigo, che voi potete vantarvi d' aver la più saggia e casta giovane, non vo' dir di Fiorenza ma di tutto 'l mondo,' pronounced before Caterina a couple of hours after her seduction, fixes the measure of Machiavelli's cynicism.

[2] The quite unquotable but characteristic monologue which opens the third act is an epitome of Margherita's character.

[3] Act iii. 5.

less obnoxious and are far less funny than the rogueries of the friar.

This comedy of Fra Alberigo is a literal transcript from a cynical *Novella*, dramatised and put upon the stage to amuse an audience familiar with such arguments by their perusal of Sacchetti and Boccaccio. Its freedom from Latinising conventionality renders it a striking example of the influence exercised by the *Novellieri* over the theatre. The same may be said about both the *Clizia* and the *Mandragola*, though the former owes a portion of its structure to the *Casina* of Plautus.[1] The *Clizia* is a finished picture of Florentine home-life. Nicomaco and Sofronia are an elderly couple, who have educated a beautiful girl, Clizia, from childhood in their house. At the moment when the play opens, both Nicomaco and his son, Cleandro, are in love with Clizia. Nicomaco has determined to marry her to one of his servants, Pirro, having previously ascertained that the dissolute groom will not object to sharing his wife with his master. Sofronia's family pride opposes the marriage of her son and heir with Clizia ; but she is aware of her husband's schemes, and seeks to frustrate them by giving the girl to an honest bailiff, Eustachio. In the contest that ensues, Nicomaco gains the victory. It is settled that Clizia is to be wedded to Pirro, and on the night of the marriage Nicomaco makes his way into the bridal

---

[1] From an allusion in act ii. sc. 3, it is clear that the *Clizia* was composed after the *Mandragola*. If we assign the latter comedy to a date later than 1512, the year of Machiavelli's disgrace, which seems implied in its prologue, the *Clizia* must be reckoned among the ripest products of his leisure. The author hints that both of these comedies were suggested to him by facts that had come under his notice in Florentine society.

chamber. But here Sofronia proves more than a match for her lord and master. Helped by Cleandro, she substitutes for Clizia a young man-servant disguised as a woman, who gives Nicomaco a warm reception, beats him within an inch of his life, and exposes him to the ridicule of the household.' Sofronia triumphs over her ashamed and miserable husband, who now consents to Clizia's marriage with Eustachio. But at this juncture the long-lost father of the heroine appears like a *deus ex machina.* He turns out to be a rich Neapolitan gentleman. There remains no obstacle to Cleandro's happiness, and the curtain falls upon a marriage in prospect between the hero and the heroine. The weakness of the play, considered as a work of art, is the mechanical solution of the plot. Its strength and beauty are the masterly delineation of a family interior. The *dramatis personæ* are vigorously sketched and act throughout consistently. Nothing can be finer than the portrait of a sober Florentine merchant, regular in his pursuits, punctual in the performance of his duties, exact in household discipline and watchful over his son's education, whose dignified severity of conduct has yielded to the lunacies of an immoderate passion.[2] For the time being Nicomaco forgets his old associates, abandons his business, and consorts

---

[1] The *Clizia* furnished Dolce with the motive of his *Ragazzo* ('Il Ragazzo, comedia di M. Lodovico Dolce. Per Curtio de Navò e fratelli al Leone, MDXLI.'). An old man and his son love the same girl. A parasite promises to get the girl for the old man, but substitutes a page dressed up like a woman, while the son sleeps with the real girl. Readers of Ben Jonson will be reminded of *Epicœne.* But in Dolce's *Ragazzo* the situation is made to suggest impurity and lacks rare Ben's gigantic humour.

[2] See Sofronia's soliloquy, act ii. sc. 4.

with youthful libertines in taverns. His appetite so blinds him that he devises the odious scheme I have described, in order to gratify a senile whim.[1] The lifelong fabric of honesty and honour breaks down in him ; and it is only when lessoned by the punishment inflicted on him by his wife and son, that he returns to his old self and sees the vileness of the situation his folly has created. Sofronia is a notable housewife, rude but respectable. The good understanding between her and her handsome son, Cleandro, whom she loves affectionately, but whom she will not indulge in his caprice for Clizia, is one of the best traits furnished by Italian comedy. Cleandro himself has less than usual of the selfishness and sensuality which degrade the Florentine *primo amoroso.* There is even something of enthusiasm in his passion for Clizia—a germ of sentiment which would have blossomed into romance under the more genial treatment of our drama.[2] Morally speaking, what is odious in this comedy is the willingness of everyone to sacrifice Clizia. Even Cleandro says of her : ' Io per me la torrei per moglie, per amica, e in tutti quei modi, che io la potessi avere.' Nicomaco, when he has failed in

---

[1] Cleandro understands the faint shadow of scruple that suggested this scheme : ' perchè tentare d' averla prima che maritata, gli debbe parere cosa impia e brutta' (act i. sc. 1). This sentence is extremely characteristic of Italian feeling.

[2] His observations on his father are, however, marked by more than ordinary coarseness. ' Come non ti vergogni tu ad avere ordinato, che si delicato viso sia da sì fetida bocca scombavato, sì delicate carni da sì tremanti mani, da sì grinze e puzzolenti membra tocche?' Then he mingles fears about Nicomaco's property with a lover's lamentations. ' Tu non mi potevi far la maggiore ingiuria, avendomi con questo colpo tolto ad un tratto e l' amata e la roba ; perchè Nicomaco, se questo amor dura, è per lasciare delle sue sustanze più a Pirro che a me ' (act iv. sc. 1).

his plot to secure the girl, thinks only of his own shame, and takes no account of the risk to which he has exposed her. Sofronia is merely anxious to get her decently established beyond her husband's reach.

Only long extracts could do justice to the sarcasm and irony with which the dialogue is seasoned. Still a few points may be selected.[1] Sofronia is rating Nicomaco for his unseasonable dissipation. He answers : ' Ah, moglie mia, non mi dire tanti mali a un tratto ! Serba qualche cosa a domane.' Eustachio, in view of taking Clizia for his wife, reflects : ' In questa terra chi ha bella moglie non può essere povero, e del fuoco e della moglie si può essere liberale con ognuno, perchè quanto più ne dai, più te ne rimane.' When Pirro demurs to Nicomaco's proposals, on the score that he will make enemies of Sofronia and Cleandro, his master answers : ' Che importa a te ? Sta' ben con Cristo e fàtti beffe de' santi.' A little lower down Nicomaco trusts the decision of Clizia's husband to lot :

Pirro. Se la sorte me venisse contro ?
Nicom. Io ho speranza in Dio, che la non verrà.
Pirro. O vecchio impazzato ! Vuole che Dio tenga le mani a queste sue disonestà.

Nor can criticism express the comic humour of the scenes, especially of those in which Nicomaco describes the hours of agony he spent in Siro's bed, and afterwards capitulates at discretion to Sofronia.[2] In spite of what is disagreeable in the argument and obscene in the catastrophe, the *Clizia* leaves a wholesomer impression on the mind than is common with Florentine

---

[1] Act iii. scs. 4, 5, 6.   [2] Act v. scs. 2 and 3.

comedies. It has something of Ariosto's *bonhomie*, elsewhere unknown in Machiavelli. Meanwhile the *Mandragola* is claiming our attention. In that comedy, Machiavelli put forth all his strength. Sinister and repulsive as it may be to modern tastes, its power is indubitable. More than any plays of which mention has hitherto been made, more even than Ariosto's *Lena* and *Negromante*, it detaches itself from Latin precedents and offers an unsophisticated view of Florentine life from its author's terrible point of contemplation.

In order to appreciate the *Mandragola*, it is necessary to know the plot. After spending his early manhood in Paris, Callimaco returns to Florence, bent on making the beautiful Lucrezia his mistress. He has only heard of her divine charms; but the bare report inflames his imagination, disturbs his sleep, and so distracts him that he feels forced 'to attempt some bold stroke, be it grave, dangerous, ruinous, dishonourable ; death itself would be better than the life I lead.' Lucrezia is the faithful and obedient wife of Nicia, a doctor of laws, whose one wish in life is to get a son. The extreme gullibility of Nicia and his desire for an heir are the motives upon which Callimaco relies to work his schemes. He finds a parasite, Ligurio, ready to assist him. Ligurio is a friend of Nicia's family, well acquainted with the persons, and so utterly depraved that he would sell his soul for a good dinner. He advises Callimaco to play the part of a physician who has studied the last secrets of his art in Paris, introduces him in this capacity to Nicia, and suggests that by his help the desired result may be obtained

without the disagreeable necessity of leaving Florence
for the baths of San Filippo. In their first interview
Callimaco explains that a potion of mandragora
administered to Lucrezia will remove her sterility, but
that it has fatal consequences to the husband. He
must perish unless he first substitutes another man,
whose death will extinguish the poison and leave
Lucrezia free to be the mother of a future family.
Nicia revolts against this odious project, which makes
him the destroyer of his own honour and a murderer.
But Callimaco assures him that royal persons and
great nobles of France have adopted this method with
success. The argument has its due weight : 'I am
satisfied,' says Nicia, 'since you tell me that a king
and princes have done the like.' But the difficulty
remains of persuading Lucrezia. Ligurio answers :
that is simple enough ; let us work upon her through
her confessor and her mother. 'You, I, our money,
our badness, and the badness of those priests will settle
the confessor ; and I know that, when the matter is
explained, we shall have her mother on our side.'
Thus we are introduced to Fra Timoteo, the chief
agent of corruption. The monk, in a first interview,
does not conceal his readiness to procure abortion and
cover infanticide. For a consideration, he agrees to
convince Lucrezia that the plot is for her good. He
first demonstrates the utility of Callimaco's method to
the mother Sostrata, and then by her help persuades
Lucrezia that adultery and murder are not only venial,
but commendable with so fair an end in view. His
sophistries anticipate the darkest casuistry of Escobar.
Lucrezia, with a woman's good sense, fastens on the

brutal and unnatural loathsomeness of the proposed plan : ' Ma di tutte le cose che si sono tentate, questa mi pare la più strana ; avere a sottomettere il corpo mio a questo vituperio, et essere cagione che un uomo muoia per vituperarmi : chè io non crederei, se io fussi sola rimasa nel mondo, e da me avesse a risurgere l' umana natura, che mi fusse simile partito concesso.' Timoteo replies : ' Qui è un bene certo, che voi ingraviderete, acquisterete un' anima a messer Domenedio. Il male incerto è, che colui che giacerà dopo la pozione con voi, si muoia ; ma e' si truova anche di quelli che non muoiono. Ma perchè la cosa è dubbia, però è bene che messer Nicia non incorra in quel pericolo. Quanto all' atto che sia peccato, questo è una favola : perchè la volontà è quella che pecca, non il corpo ; e la cagione del peccato è dispiacere al marito : e voi gli compiacete ; pigliarne piacere : e voi ne avete dispiacere,' etc. Sostrata, accustomed to follow her confessor's orders, and not burdened with a conscience, clinches this reasoning : ' Di che hai tu paura, moccicona ? E c' è cinquanta dame in questa terra che ne alzarebbero le mani al cielo.' Lucrezia gives way unwillingly : ' Io son contenta ; ma non credo mai esser viva domattina.' Timoteo comforts her with a final touch of monkish irony : ' Non dubitare, figliuola mia, io pregherò Dio per te ; io dirò l'orazione dell' Angiolo Raffaello che t' accompagni. Andate in buon' ora, e preparatevi a questo misterio, che si fa sera.' What follows is the mere working of the plot, whereby Ligurio and Timoteo contrive to introduce Callimaco as the necessary victim into Lucrezia's bed-chamber. The silly Nicia plays the part of pander to his own

shame ; and when Lucrezia discovers the scheme by
which her lover has attained his ends, she exclaims :
' Poi chè l' astuzia tua e la sciochezza del mio marito, la
semplicità di mia madre e la tristizia del mio confessore,
m' hanno condotta a far quello che mai per me
medesima avrei fatto, io voglio giudicare che e'
venga da una celeste disposizione, che abbia voluto
così.   Però io ti prendo per signore, padrone e guida.'
It must be remarked that Lucrezia omits from her
reckoning the weakness which led her to consent.

My excuse for analysing a comedy so indecent as
the *Mandragola*, is the importance it has, not only as
a product of Machiavelli's genius, but also as an illustration of contemporary modes of thought and feeling.
In all points this play is worthy of the author of the
Principe.   The *Mandragola* is a microcosm of society
as Machiavelli conceived it, and as it needs must be to
justify his own philosophy.   It is a study of stupidity
and baseness acted on by roguery.   Credulity and
appetite supply the fulcrum needed by unscrupulous
intelligence.   The lover, aided by the husband's folly,
the parasite's profligacy, the mother's familiarity with
sin, the confessor's avarice, the wife's want of self-
respect, achieves the triumph of making Nicia lead
him naked to Lucrezia's chamber.   Moving in the
region of his fancy, the poet adds *Quod erat demon-
strandum* to his theorem of vileness and gross folly
used for selfish ends by craft.   But we who read it,
rise from the perusal with the certainty that it was
only the corruption of the age which rendered such a
libel upon human nature plausible—only the author's
perverse and shallow view of life which sustained him

in this reading of a problem he had failed to understand. Viewed as a critique upon life, the *Mandragola* is feeble, because the premisses are false ; and
these same false premisses regarding the main forces
of society, render the logic of the *Principe* inconse-
quent. Men are not such fools as Nicia or such
catspaws as Ligurio and Timoteo. Women are not
such compliant instruments as Sostrata and Lucrezia.
Human nature is not that tissue of disgusting mean-
nesses and vices, by which Callimaco succeeds. Here
lay Machiavelli's fallacy. He dreamed of action as
the triumph of astuteness over folly. Virtue with him
meant the management of immorality by bold intelligence. But while, on the one hand, he exaggerated
the stupidity of dupes, on the other he underestimated
the resistance which strongly-rooted moral instincts
offer to audacious villany. He left goodness out of
his account. Therefore, though his reasoning, whether
we examine the *Mandragola* or the *Principe*, seems
irrefragable on the premisses from which he starts, it is
an unconvincing chain of sophisms. The world is not
wholly bad ; but in order to justify Machiavelli's conclusions, we have to assume that its essential forces
are corrupt.

If we turn from the *Mandragola* to the society of
which it is a study, and which complacently accepted
it as an agreeable work of art, we are filled with a
sense of surprise bordering on horror. What must
the people among whom Machiavelli lived, have been,
to justify his delineation of a ruffian so vicious as
Ligurio, a confessor so lost to sense of duty as
Timoteo, a mother who scruples not to prostitute her

daughter to the first comer, a lover so depraved as Callimaco, a wife so devoid of womanly feeling as Lucrezia ?　On first reflection, we are inclined to believe that the poet in this comedy was venting Swiftian indignation on the human nature which he misconceived and loathed.　The very name Lucrezia seems chosen in irony—as though to hint that Rome's first martyr would have failed, if Tarquin had but used her mother and her priest to tame her.　Yet, on a second reading, the *Mandragola* reveals no scorn or anger. It is a piece of scientific anatomy, a demonstration of disease, executed without subjective feeling.　The argument is so powerfully developed, with such simplicity of language, such consistency of character, such cold analysis of motives, that we cannot doubt the verisimilitude of the picture.　No one, at the date of its appearance, resented it.　Florentine audiences delighted in its comic flavour.　Leo X. witnessed it with approval.　His hatred of the monks found satisfaction in Timoteo.　Society, far from rising in revolt against the poet who exposed its infamy with a pen of poisoned steel, thanked the man of genius for rendering vice amusing.　Of satire or of moral purpose there is none in the *Mandragola*.　Machiavelli depicted human nature just as he had learned to know it.　The sinister fruits of his studies made contemporaries laugh.

　　The *Mandragola* was the work of an unhappy man.　The prologue offers a curious mixture of haughtiness and fawning, only comparable to the dedication of the *Principe* and the letter to Vettori.[1]

---

[1] See *Age of the Despots*, pp. 288-292.　Of the two strains of character so ill-blent in Machiavelli, the *Mandragola* represents the vulgar,

A sense of his own intellectual greatness is combined with an uneasy feeling of failure :

> Non è componitor di molta fama.

As an apology for his application to trivialities, he pleads wretchedness and *ennui* :

> E se questa materia non è degna,
> Per esser più leggieri
> D' un uom che voglia parer saggio e grave,
> Scusatelo con questo, che s' ingegna
> Con questi vani pensieri
> Fare el suo tristo tempo più soave;
> Perchè altrove non ave
> Dove voltare el viso;
> Che gli è stato interciso
> Mostrar con altre imprese altra virtue,
> Non sendo premio alle fatiche sue.

These verses, indifferent as poetry, are poignant for their revelation of a disappointed life. Left without occupation, unable to display his powers upon a worthy platform, he casts the pearls of his philosophy before the pleasure-seeking swine. The sense of this degradation stings him and he turns upon society with threats. Let them not attempt to browbeat or intimidate him :

> Che sa dir male anch' egli,
> E come questa fu la sua prim' arte :
> E come in ogni parte
> Del mondo, ove il si suona,
> Non istima persona,
> Ancor che faccia el sergiere a colui
> Che può portar miglior mantel di lui.

Throughout this prologue we hear the growl of a wounded lion, helpless in his lair, yet conscious that

---

and the *Principe* the noble. The one corresponds to his days at Casciano, the other to his studious evenings.

he still has strength to rend the fools and knaves around him.

Aretino completed the disengagement of Italian from Latin comedy. Ignoring the principles established by the Plautine mannerists, he liberated the elements of satire and of realism held in bondage by their rules. His reasoning was unanswerable. Why should he attend to the unities, or be careful to send the same person no more than five times on the stage in one piece? His people shall come and go as they think fit, or as the argument requires.[1] Why should he make Romans ape the style of Athens? His Romans shall be painted from life; his servants shall talk and act like Italian varlets, not mimicking the ways of Geta or Davus.[2] Why should he shackle his style with precedents from Petrarch and Boccaccio? He will seek the fittest words, the aptest phrases, the most biting repartees from ordinary language.[3] Why condescend to imitation, when his mother wit supplies him with material, and the world of men lies open like a book before his eyes[4]? Why follow in the footsteps of the pedants, who mistake their knowledge of grammar for

---

[1] 'Se voi vedessi uscire i personaggi più di cinque volte in scena, non ve ne ridete, perchè le catene che tengono i molini sul fiume, non terrebbeno i pazzi d' oggidì' (Prologue to the *Cortigiana*).

[2] 'Non vi maravigliate se lo stil comico non s' osserva con l' ordine che si richiede, perchè si vive d' un' altra maniera a Roma che non si vivea in Atene' (*Ibid.*).

[3] 'Io non mi son tolto dagli andari del Petrarca e del Boccaccio per ignoranza, chè pur so ciò che essi sono; ma per non perdere il tempo, la pazienza e il nome nella pazzia di volermi trasformare in loro' (Prologue to the *Orazia*).

[4] 'Più pro fa il pane asciutto in casa propria che l' accompagnato con molte vivande su altrui tavola. Imita qua, imita là; tutto è fava, si può dire alle composizioni dei più . . . di chi imita, mi faccio beffe . . . posso giurare d' esser sempre me stesso, ed altri non mai' (*Ibid.*).

genius, and whose commentaries are an insult to the poets they pretend to illustrate ? [1]

Conscious of his own defective education, and judging the puristic niceties of the age at their true value, Aretino thus flung the glove of defiance in the face of a learned public. It was a bold step ; but the adventurer knew what he was doing. The originality of his *Ars Poetica* took the world by surprise. His Italian audience delighted in the sparkle of a style that gave point to their common speech. Had Aretino been a writer of genius, Italy might now have owed to his audacity and self-reliance the starting-point of national dramatic art.[2] He was on the right path, but he lacked the skill to tread it. His comedies, loosely put together, with no constructive vigour in their plots and no grasp of psychology in their characters, are a series of powerfully-written scenes, piquant dialogues, effective situations, rather than comedies in the higher sense of the word. We must not look for Ariosto's lucid order, for Machiavelli's disposition of parts, in these vagaries of a brilliant talent aiming at immediate success. We must be grateful for the filibustering bravado which made him dare to sketch contemporary manners from the life. The merit of these comedies is naturalness. Such affectation of antithesis or

---

[1] 'Io mi rido dei pedanti, i quali si credono che la dottrina consiste nella lingua greca, dando tutta la riputatione allo in *bus* in *bas* della grammatica' (Prologue to *Orazia*). 'I crocifissori del Petrarca, i quali gli fanno dir cose con i loro comenti, che non gliene fariano confessare diece tratti di corda. E bon per Dante che con le sue diavolerie fa star le bestie in dietro, che a questa ora saria in croce anch' egli' (Prologue to *Cortigiana*).

[2] His tragedy *Orazia* has just the same merits of boldness and dramatic movement in parts, the same defects of incoherence. It detaches itself favourably from the tragedies of the pedants.

laboured epigram as mars their style, was part of
Aretino's self. It reveals the man, and is not wearisome like the conceits of the pedantic school. What
he had learned, seen or heard in his experience of the
world—and Aretino saw, heard and learned the worst
of the society in which he lived—is presented with
vigour. The power to express is never shackled by
a back-thought of reserve or delicacy. Each character
stands outlined with a vividness none the less convincing because the study lacks depth. What Aretino
cannot supply, is the nexus between these striking
passages, the linking of these lively portraits into a
coherent whole. Machiavelli's logic, perverse as it
may be, produces by its stringent application a more
impressive æsthetical effect. The doctrine of style for
style's sake, derided by Aretino, satisfies at least our
sense of harmony. In the insolence of freedom he
spoils the form of his plays by discussions, sometimes
dull, sometimes disgusting, in which he vents his spite
or airs his sycophancy without regard for the exigencies
of his subject. Still, in spite of these defects, Aretino's
plays are a precious mine of information for one who
desires to enter into direct communication with the
men of the Renaissance.

Aretino's point of view is that of the successful
adventurer. Unlike Machiavelli, he has no sourness
and reveals no disappointment. He has never fallen
from the high estate of an impersonal ambition. His
report of human depravity is neither scientific nor
indignant. He appreciates the vices of the world, by
comprehending which, as means to ends, he has
achieved celebrity. They are the instruments of his

advance in life, the sources of his wealth, the wisdom he professes. Therefore, while he satirises, he treats them with complacence. Evil is good for its own sake also in his eyes. Having tasted all its fruits, he revels in recalling his sensations, just as Casanova took pleasure in recording his debaucheries. His knowledge of society is that of an upstart, who has risen from the lowest ranks by the arts of the bully, flatterer and pander. We never forget that he began life as a lacquey, and the most valuable quality of his comedies is that they depict the great world from the standpoint of the servants' hall. Aretino is too powerful and fashionable to be aware of this. He poses as the sage and satirist. But the revelation is none the less pungent because it is made unconsciously. The Court, idealised by Castiglione, censured by Guarini, inveighed against by La Casa, here shows its inner rottenness for our inspection, at the pleasure of a charlatan who thrives on this pollution. We hear how the valets of debauched prelates, the parasites of petty nobles, the pimps who battened on the vices of the rich, the flatterer who earned his bread by calumny and lies, viewed this world of fashion, how they discussed it among themselves, how they utilised its corruption. We shake hands with ruffians and cut-throats, enter the Roman brothels by their back-door, sit down in their kitchens, and become acquainted with the secrets of their trade. It may be suggested that the knowledge supplied by Aretino, if it concerns such details, is neither profitable nor valuable. No one, indeed, who is not specially curious to realise the manners of Renaissance Italy, should occupy his leisure with these comedies.

The *Cortigiana* is a parody of Castiglione's *Corte-giano.* A Sienese gentleman, simple and provincial, the lineal descendant of Pulci's Messer Goro, arrives in Rome to make his fortune.[1] He is bent on assuming the fine airs of the Court, and hopes to become at least a Cardinal before he returns home. On his first arrival Messer Maco falls into the clutches of a sharper, who introduces him to disreputable society, under colour of teaching him the art of courtiership. The satire of the piece consists in showing Rome to be the school of profligacy rather than of gentle customs.[2] Before he has spent more than a few days in the Eternal City, the country squire learns the slang of the *demi-monde* and swaggers among courtesans and rufflers. Maestro Andrea, who has undertaken his education, lectures him upon the virtues of the courtier in a scene of cynical irony[3] : 'La principal cosa, il cortigiano vuol sapere bestemmiare, vuole essere giuocatore, invidioso, puttaniere, eretico, adulatore, maldicente, sconoscente, ignorante, asino, vuol sapere frappare, far la ninfa, et essere agente e paziente.' Some of these qualities are understood at once by Messer Maco. Concerning others he asks for further information : 'Come si diventa eretico? questo è 'l caso.—Notate.—Io nuoto benissimo.—Quando alcuno vi dice che in Corte sia bontà, discrezione, amore, o conoscenza, dite no 'l credo . . . . in somma a chi vi dice bene de la Corte, dite: tu sei un bugiardo.' Again, Messer

---

[1] ' Egli è uno di quegli animali di tanti colori che il vostro avolo comperò in cambio d' un papagallo ' (act i. sc. 1).

[2] Its most tedious episode is a panegyric of Venice at the expense of Rome (act iii. sc. 7).

[3] Act i. sc. 22.

Marco asks : 'Come si dice male?' The answer is prompt and characteristic of Aretino [1] : 'Dicendo il vero, dicendo il vero.' What Maestro Andrea teaches theoretically, is expounded as a fact of bitter experience by Valerio and Flamminio, the gentlemen in waiting on a fool of fortune named Parabolano.[2] These men, admitted to the secrets of a noble household, know its inner sordidness, and reckon on the vanity and passions of their patron. A still lower stage in the scale of debasement is revealed by the conversations of the lacqueys, Rosso and Cappa, who discuss the foibles o their master with the coarseness of the stables.[3] In so far as the *Cortigiana* teaches any lesson, it is contained in the humiliation of Parabolano. His vices have made him the slave and creature of foul-minded serving-men, who laugh together over the disgusting details of his privacy, while they flatter him to his face in order to profit by his frivolities.[4] Aretino's own experience of life in Rome enabled him to make these pictures of the servants' hall and antechamber pungent.[5] The venom engendered by years of servitude and adulation is vented in his criticism of the Court as censured from a flunkey's point of view. Nor is he less at home in painting the pleasures of the class whom he has chosen for his critics of polite society. Cappa's soliloquy upon the paradise of the tavern, and Rosso's pranks, when he plays the gentleman in his master's

---

[1] He makes the same point in the prologue to *La Talenta*: 'Chi brama d' acquistarsi il nome del più scellerato uomo che viva, dica il vero.'
[2] Act i. sc. 9; act ii. sc. 6; act ii. sc. 10; act iii. sc. 7.
[3] See especially act i. sc. 7.   [4] Act iv. sc. 6.
[5] Notice the extraordinary virulence of his invective against the *tinello* or common room of servants in a noble household (act v. sc. 15)

fine clothes, owe the effect of humour to their realistic verve.[1] We feel them to be reminiscences of fact. These scenes constitute the salt of the comedy, supported by vivid sketches of town characters—the newsboy, the fisherman of the Tiber, and the superannuated prostitute.[2]

In the *Cortigiana* it was Aretino's object to destroy illusions about Court-life by describing it in all the vileness of reality.[3] The *Marescalco* is a study of the same conditions of society, with less malignity and far more geniality of humour.[4] A rich fool has been recommended by his lord and master, the Duke of Mantua, to take a wife. He loathes matrimony, and shrinks from spending several thousand ducats on the dower. But the parasites, buffoons and henchmen of the prince persuade and bully him into compliance. He is finally married to a page dressed as a woman, and his relief at discovering the sex of his supposed wife forms the climax of the plot. This play is conducted with so much spirit that we may not be wrong in supposing Shakspere in *Twelfth Night* and Ben Jonson in *Epicœne* to have owed something to its humour. We look, however, in vain for such fine creatures of the fancy as Sir Toby Belch, or for a catastrophe so overwhelming as the *crescendo* of noise and bustle which subdue the obstinacy of Morose. On the other hand, the two companion scenes in which Marescalco's nurse enlarges on the luxuries of married life, while Ambrogio

---

[1] Act ii. sc. 1 ; act i. scs. 11–18.
[2] Act i. sc. 4 ; act i. sc. 11 ; act ii. sc. 7.
[3] Act ii. sc. 6.
[4] Of all Aretino's plays the *Marescalco* is the simplest and the most artistically managed.

describes its miseries, are executed with fine sense of comic contrast.[1]

In the *Talanta* we return to Roman society. This comedy is a study of courtesan life, analysed with thorough knowledge of its details. The character of Talanta, who plays her four lovers one against the other, extracting presents by various devices from each of them, displays the author's intimate acquaintance with his subject.[2] Talanta on the stage is a worthy pendant to Nanna in the *Ragionamenti*. But . the intrigue is confused, tedious and improbable; and after reading the first act, we have already seen the best of Aretino's invention. The same may be said about the *Ipocrita* and the *Filosofo*, two comedies in which Aretino attempted to portray a charlatan of Tartufe's type and a student helpless in his wife's hands. These characters are not ill conceived, but they are too superficially executed to bear the weight of the plot laid upon them. In like manner the pedant in the *Marescalco* and the swashbuckler in the *Talanta* are rather silhouettes than finished portraits. Though well sketched, they lack substance. They have neither the lifelike movement of Shakspere's minor persons, nor the impressive mechanism of Jonson's humours. Bobadil and Master Holofernes, though caricatures, move in a higher region of

---

[1] Act i. sc. 6; act ii. sc. 5.

[2] Talanta's apology for her rapacity and want of heart (act i. sc. 1); the description of her by her lover Orfinio, who sees through her but cannot escape her fascination (act i. sc. 7); the critique of her by a sensible man (act i. sc. 12); her arts to bring her lover back to his allegiance and wheedle the most odious concessions (act i. sc. 13); her undisguised marauding (act i. sc. 14); these moments in the evolution of her character are set forth with the decision of a master's style.

the comic art. The characters Aretino could imitate supremely well, were a page like Giannico in the *Marescalco*, a footman like Rosso in the *Cortigiana*, or a woman of the town like Talanta. His comedies are never wanting in bustle and variety of business; while the sarcasm of the author, flying at the best-established reputations, sneering at the most fashionable prejudices of society, renders them effective even now, when all the jealousies he flouted have long been buried in oblivion.[1]

Bibbiena's *Calandra* is a farce, obscene but not malignant. Ariosto's comedies are studies of society from the standpoint of the middle class. If he is too indulgent to human frailty, too tolerant of vice, we never miss in him the wisdom of a genial observer. Machiavelli's *Mandragola* casts the dry light of the intellect on an abyss of evil. Nothing but the brilliance of the poet's wit reconciles us to his revelation of perversity. Aretino, by the animation of his sketches, by his prurient delight in what is vile, makes us comprehend that even the *Mandragola* was possible. Machiavelli stands outside his subject, like Lucifer, fallen but disdainful. Aretino is the Belial who acknowledges corruption for his own domain. Ariosto and Machiavelli are artists each in his kind perfect. Aretino is an *improvvisatore*, clever with the pen he uses like a burin.

It would be difficult to render an account of the

---

[1] The Prologue to the *Cortigiana* passes all the literary celebrities of Italy in review with a ferocity of sarcasm veiled in irony that must have been extremely piquant. And take this equivocal compliment to Molza from the *Marescalco* (act v. sc. 3), ' il Molza Mutinense, che arresta con la sua fistola i torrenti.'

comedies produced by the Italians in the sixteenth century, or to catalogue their authors. A computation has been made which reckons the plays known to students at several thousands. In spite of this extraordinary richness in comic literature, Italy cannot boast of a great Comedy. No poet arose to carry the art onward from the point already reached when Aretino left the stage. The neglect that fell on those innumerable comedies, was not wholly undeserved. It is true that their scenes suggested brilliant episodes to French and English playwrights of celebrity. It is true that the historian of manners finds in them an almost inexhaustible store of matter. Still they are literary lucubrations rather than the spontaneous expression of a vivid nationality. Nor have they the subordinate merit of dealing in a scientific spirit with the cardinal vices and follies of society. We miss the original plots, the powerful modelling of character, the philosophical insight which would have reconciled us to a *Commedia erudita*.

When we examine the plays of Firenzuola, Cecchi, Ambra, Gelli, Il Lasca, Doni, Dolce, we find that a hybrid form of art had been established by the practice of the earlier playwrights. This hybrid implied Plautus and Terence as a necessary basis. It adopted the fusion of Latin arguments with Italian manners which was so ably realised by Ariosto and Machiavelli. It allowed something for the farce traditions which the Rozzi made fashionable at Rome. It assumed ingredients from the *Burle* and *Novelle* of the market-place, reproduced the language of the people, and made use of current scandals to give piquancy to its conventional plots. But notwithstanding the admixture of so many modern elements, the stereotyped Latinism of its form rendered this comedy unnatural. Ingenious *contaminatio*, to use a phrase in vogue among Roman critics, was always more apparent than creative instinct.

The *Commedia erudita* presented a framework ready-made to the playwright, and easily accepted on the strength of usage by the audience he sought to entertain. At the same time it left him free, within prescribed limits, to represent the manners of contemporary life. The main object of a great drama, 'to show the very age and body of the time his form and pressure,' is thrust into the second rank ; and the most valuable portions of these clever works of skill are their episodes—such scenes, for example, as those which in the *Aridosio* of Lorenzino de' Medici reveal the dissoluteness of conventual customs in a scholastic *rifacimento* of the *Adelphi* and the *Mostellaria*.[1] Had the fusion of classical and modern elements been complete as in the *Epicœne* of Jonson, or had the character-drawing been masterly as in Molière's *Avare*, we should have no cause for complaint. But these are just the qualities of success missed by the Italian playwrights. Their studies from nature are comparatively slight. Having exhibited them in the presentation of the subject or introduced them here and there by way of interludes, they work the play to its conclusion on the lines of Latinistic convention.[2]

---

[1] *Lorenzino de' Medici*, Daelli, Milano, 1862.

[2] The pseudo-classical hybrid I have attempted to describe is analogous in its fixity of outline to the conventional framework of the *Sacre Rappresentazioni*, which allowed a playwright the same subordinate liberty of action and saved him the trouble of invention to a like extent.

Such being the form of *cinque cento* comedy, it follows that its details are monotonous. The characters are invariably drawn from the ranks of the rich burgher classes; and if we may trust the evidence furnished by the playwrights, the morality of these classes must have been of an almost inconceivable baseness. We survey a society separated from the larger interests that elevate humanity, without public ambition or the sense of national greatness, excluded from the career of arms, dead to honour, bent upon sensual enjoyment and petty intrigues. The motive which sustains the plot, is illicit love; but in its presentation there is no romance, nothing to cloak the animalism of an unchecked instinct. The young men who play the part of *primi amorosi*, are in debt or without money. It is their object to repair their fortunes by a rich marriage, to secure a maintenance from a neighbour's wife they have seduced, to satisfy the avarice of a greedy courtesan, or to conceal the results of an intrigue which has brought their mistress into difficulties. From the innumerable scenes devoted to these elegant and witty scapegraces, it would be difficult to glean a single sentence expressive of conscience, remorse, sense of loyalty or generous feeling. They submit to the most odious bargains and disreputable subterfuges, sacrificing the honour of their

It may here be noticed that the Italians in general adopted stereotyped forms for dramatic representation. Harlequin, Columbine, and Pantaloon, the Bolognese doctor, the Stenterello of Florence, the Meneghino of Milan, and many other dramatic types, recognised as stationary, yet admitting of infinite variety in treatment by author or actor, are notable examples. In estimating the dramatic genius of Italy this tendency to move within defined and conventional limits of art, whether popular or literary, must never be forgotten.

families or the good fame of the women who depend
upon them, to the attainment of some momentary
self-indulgence.[1]   Without respect for age, they ex-
pend their ingenuity in robbing their parents and
exposing their fathers to ridicule.[2]   Nor is it possible
to feel much sympathy for the elders, who are so
brutally used.   The old man of these comedies is
either a superannuated libertine, who makes himself
ridiculous by his intrigues with a neighbour's wife,
or a parsimonious tyrant, or else an indulgent rake,
who acts the pander for his good-for-nothing rascal of
a son.[3]   Mere simpletons like Machiavelli's Nicia, or
Aretino's Messer Maco, furnish another type of irre-
verent age, unredeemed by the comic humour of Fal-
staff or the gigantic lusts of Sir Epicure Mammon.
Between son and father the inevitable servant plays
the part of clever rogue.   It is he who weaves the
meshes of the intrigue that shall cut the purse-strings
of the stingy parent, blind the eyes of the husband to
his wife's adultery, or cheat the creditor of his dues.
Our sympathy is always enlisted on the side of the
schemers; and however base their tricks may be, we
are invited to applaud the success which crowns them.

[1] Cinthio's conduct towards Emilia in the *Negromante* is a good
instance.

[2] See above, p. 163, note, for Cleandro in the *Mandragola*; and compare Alamanno's conversation with his uncle Lapo, his robbery of his
mother's money-box, and his reflections on the loss he should sustain by
her re-marriage, in Gelli's *La Sporta* (act iii. 5; ii. 2). Camillo's allusions to his father's folly in Gelli's *Errore* (act iv. 2) are no less selfish
and heartless. Alamanno's plot to raise a dower by fraud (*La Sporta*, iv.
1) may be compared with Fabio's trick upon his stepmother in Cecchi's
Martello. In the latter his father takes a hand.

[3] Ghirigoro in Gelli's *Sporta*, Gherardo in Gelli's *Errore*, Girolamo
in Cecchi's *Martello*. It is needless to multiply examples. The analyses
of Machiavelli's comedies will suffice.

The girls are worthy of their lovers. Corrupted by nurses; exposed to the contaminating influences of the convent; courted by grooms and servants in their father's household; tampered with by infamous duennas; betrayed by their own mothers or entrusted by their fathers to notorious prostitutes; they accept the first husband proposed to them by their parents, confident in the hope of continuing clandestine intrigues with the neighbour's son who has seduced them.[1] The wives are such as the *Novelle* paint them, yielding to the barest impulses of wantonness, and covering their debauchery with craft that raises a laugh against the husbands they have cozened. Such are the main actors, the conventional personages, of this domestic comedy. The subordinate characters consist of parasites and flatterers; ignorant pedants and swaggering *bravi*; priests who ply the trade of pimps; astrologers who thrive upon the folly of their clients; doctors who conceal births; prostitutes and their attendant bullies; compliant go-betweens and rapacious bawds; pages, street urchins, and officers of justice. The adulterous intrigue required such minor persons as instruments; and it often happens that scenes of vivid comic humour, dialogues of the most brilliant Tuscan idiom, are suggested by the interaction of these puppets, whose wires the clever valet and the *primo amoroso* pull.

The point of interest for contemporary audiences was the *burla*—the joke played off by a wife upon her

---

[1] It would be easy to illustrate each of these points from the comedies of Ariosto, Cecchi, Machiavelli, Lorenzino de' Medici; to which the reader may be referred *passim* for proof.

husband, by rogues upon a simpleton, by a son upon
his father, by a servant on his master's creditors, by a
pupil on his pedantic tutor. Accepting the conditions
of a comedy so constructed, and eliminating ethical
considerations, we readily admit that these jokes are
infinitely amusing. The scene in Gelli's *Sporta* where
Ghirigoro de' Macci receives the confidences of the
youth who has seduced his daughter, under the impression that he is talking about his money-box, is not
unworthy of Molière's *Avare*. Two scenes in Gelli's
Errore, where Gherardo Amieri, disguised as an old
woman, is tormented by a street urchin whom his son
has sent to teaze him, and afterwards confronted by
his angry wife, might have adorned the *Merry Wives
of Windsor*.[1] Cecchi's comedies in like manner abound
in comical absurdities, involving exquisitely realistic
pictures of Florentine manners.[2] For the student of
language, no less than for the student of Renaissance
life, they are invaluable. But the similarity of form
which marks the comedies of the *cinque cento*, renders
it impossible to do justice to their details in the present
work. I must content myself with the foregoing
sketch of their structure derived from the perusal of
such plays as were accessible in print, and with the
further observation that each eminent dramatist developed some side of the common heritage transmitted
by their common predecessors. Thus Firenzuola continued the Latin tradition with singular tenacity, adapting classical arguments in his *Lucidi* and *Trinuzia* to
modern themes with the same inimitable transparency

---

[1] *Opere di Gio. Battista Gelli* (Milano, 1807), vol. iii.
[2] *Commedie di Giovan Maria Cecchi*, 2 vols, Lemonnier.

of style he had displayed in his *rifacimento* of the *Golden Ass*.[1] Gelli adapted the *Aulularia* in his *Sporta*, and closely followed the *Clizia* in his *Errore*. The devotion professed for Machiavelli by this playwright, was yielded by Cecchi to Ariosto ; and thus we notice two divergent strains of tradition within the circle of Florentine art.[2] Cecchi was a voluminous dramatic writer. Besides his comedies in *sdrucciolo* and *piano* verse, he composed *Sacre Rappresentazioni* and plays of a mixed kind derived from a free handling of that elder form.[3] While Gelli and Cecchi severally followed the example of Machiavelli and Ariosto, Il Lasca attempted to free the Italian drama from the fetters of erudite convention.[4] His comedies are exceedingly witty versions of *Novelle*, forming dramatic pendents to his narratives in that style. Yet though he strove to make the stage a mirror of contemporary

[1] *Opere di Messer Agnolo Firenzuola* (Milano, 1802), vol. v.

[2] E 'l divino Ariosto anco, a chi cedono
  Greci, Latini e Toscan, tutti i comici.
                    Prologue to *I Rivali*.

  Ma che dirò di te, spirito illustre,
  Ariosto gentil, qual lode fia
  Uguale al tuo gran merto, al tuo valore?
  Cede a te nella comica palestra
  Ogni Greco e Latin, perchè tu solo
  Hai veramente dimostrato come
  Esser deve il principio, il mezzo e 'l fine
  Delle comedie, etc.

Le Pellegrine, Intermedio Sesto, published by Barbèra, 1855.

[3] See the 'Esaltazione della Croce,' *Sacre Rappresentazioni*, Lemonnier, vol. iii. Compare those curious hybrid plays, *Il Figliuolo Prodigo*, *La Morte del Re Acab*, *La Conversione della Scozia*, in his collected plays (Lemonnier, 1856). *Lo Sviato* may be mentioned as another of his comedies derived from the *Sacre Rappr.* with a distinctly didactic and moral purpose.

[4] See Prologue to *La Strega*, and above, p. 124.

customs, he could not wholly escape from the mannerism into which the dramatic art had fallen. Nor was
it possible, now that the last gleam of liberty had expired in Italy, when even Florence accepted her fate,
and the Inquisition was jealously watching every new
birth of the press, to create what the earlier freedom
of the Renaissance had missed. The drama was condemned to trivialities which only too faithfully reflected
the political stagnation, and the literary trifling of a
decadent civilisation.[1]

It is worthy of notice, as a final remark upon the
history of the comic stage, that at this very moment of
its ultimate frustration there existed the germ of a
drama analogous to that of England, only waiting to
be developed by some master spirit. That was the
Farsa, which Cecchi, the most prolific, original and
popular of Florentine playwrights, deigned to culti-
vate.[2] He describes it thus : ' The *Farsa* is a new
third species between tragedy and comedy. It enjoys
the liberties of both, and shuns their limitations ; for it
receives into its ample boundaries great lords and
princes, which comedy does not, and, like a hospital or
inn, welcomes the vilest and most plebeian of the
people, to whom Dame Tragedy has never stooped. It
is not restricted to certain motives ; for it accepts all
subjects—grave and gay, profane and sacred, urbane
and rude, sad and pleasant. It does not care for time
or place. The scene may be laid in a church, or a

---

[1] I reserve for another chapter the treatment of the Pastoral, which
eventually proved the most original and perfect product of the Italian
stage.

[2] The titles of his *Farse* given by D' Ancona are *1 Malandrini, Pit-
tura, Andazzo, Sciotta, Romanesca*.

public square, or where you will ; and if one day is not long enough, two or three may be employed. What, indeed, does it matter to the *Farsa* ? In a word, this modern mistress of the stage is the most amusing, the most convenient, the sweetest, prettiest country-lass that can be found upon our earth.'[1] He then goes on to describe the liberty of language allowed in the *Farsa*, rounding off a picture which exactly applies to our Elizabethan drama. The *Farsa*, in the form it had assumed when Cecchi used it, was, in fact, the survival of an ancient, obscure species of dramatic art, which had descended from the period of classical antiquity, and which recently had blent with the traditions of the *Sacre Rappresentazioni*. Had circumstances been favourable to the development of a national drama in Italy, the popular elements of the Pagan farce and the medieval Mystery would have naturally issued through the *Farsa* in a modern form of art analogous to that produced in England. But the Italians had, as we have seen, no public to demand the rehabilitation of the *Farsa* ; nor was Cecchi a Shakspere, or even a Marlowe, to prove, in the face of Latinising playwrights, that the national stage lay in its cradle here. It remained for the poets of a far-off island, who disdained Italian *jigs* and owed nothing to the *Farse* of either Florentine or Neapolitan contemporaries, acting by instinct and in concert with the sympathies of a great nation, to take this ' sweetest, prettiest countrylass ' by the hand and place her side by side with Attic Tragedy and Comedy upon the supreme throne of art.

---

[1] Prologue to the *Romanesca*, Firenze, Cenniniana, 1874.

The Italian comedies offer an even more startling picture of social vice than the *Novelle*.[1] To estimate how far they represent a general truth, is difficult; especially when we remember that they were written in a conventional style, to amuse princes, academicians, and prelates.[2] Comparing their testimony with that of private letters and biographical literature (the correspondence, for example, of Alessandra degli Strozzi, Alberti's treatise on the Family, and statements gleaned from memoirs and *Ricordi*), we are justified in believing that a considerable difference existed at the commencement of this epoch between public and domestic manners in Italy; between the Court and the home, the piazza and the fireside, the diversions of fashionable coteries and the conversation of friends and kinsmen. The family still retained some of its antique simplicity. And it was not as yet vitiated by the institution of Cicisbeism. But the great world was incredibly corrupt. Each Court formed a nucleus of dissolute living. Rome, stigmatised successively by men so different as Lorenzo de' Medici, Pietro Aretino, Gian-Giorgio Trissino, and Messer Guidiccioni, poisoned the whole Italian

---

[1] Dolce in the Prologue to his *Ragazzo* says that, immodest as a comedy may be, it would be impossible for any play to reproduce the actual depravity of manners.

[2] What I have already observed with regard to the *Novelle*—namely, that Italy lacked the purifying and ennobling influences of a real public, embracing all classes, and stimulating the production of a largely designed, broadly executed literature of human nature—is emphatically true also of her stage. The people demand greatness from their authors—simplicity, truth, nobleness. They do not shrink from grossness; they tolerate what is coarse. But these elements must be kept in proper subordination. Princes, petty coteries, academies, drawing-room patrons, the audience of the antechamber and the boudoir, delight in subtleties, *doubles entendre*, scandalous tales, Divorce Court arguments. The people evokes Shakspere; the provincial Court breeds Bibbiena.

nation. Venice entertained a multitude of prostitutes, and called them *benemeritæ* in public acts. Since, therefore, these centres of aristocratic and literary life drew recruits from the burgher and rural classes, the strongholds of patriarchal purity were continually being sapped by contact with fashionable uncleanliness. And thus in the sixteenth century a common standard of immorality had been substituted for earlier severity of manners. The convulsions of that disastrous epoch, following upon a period of tranquillity, during which the people had become accustomed to luxury, submerged whole families in vice. ' Wars, famines, and the badness of the times,' wrote Aretino, 'inclining men to give themselves amusement, have so debauched all Italy (*imputtanita tutta Italia*), that cousins and kinsfolk of both sexes, brothers and sisters, mingle together without shame, without a shadow of conscience.'[1] Though it is preposterous to see Aretino posing as a censor of morals, his acuteness was indubitable; nor need we suppose that his acquaintance with the disease rendered him less sagacious in detecting its causes. What Corio tells us about Lodovico Sforza's capital, what we read about the excess of luxury into which the nobles of Vicenza and Milan plunged, amid the horrors of the French and Spanish occupation, confirms his testimony.[2] After the Black Death, described by Matteo Villani, the Florentines consoled themselves for previous sufferings by an outburst of profligate and reckless living. So now they sought distraction in un-

---

[1] *Cortigiana*, act ii. sc. 10.
[2] See Corio, quoted in *Age of the Despots*, p. 500, note 1. For Milanese luxury, Bandello, vol. i. pp. 219 *et seq.* ; vol. iv. p. 115 (Milan edition, 1814). For Vicenza, Morsolin's *Trissino*, p. 291.

bridled sensuality. Society was in dissolution, and
men lived for the moment, careless of consequences.
The immorality of the theatre was at once a sign and
a source of this corruption. ' O times! O manners!'
exclaims Lilius Giraldus [1] : 'the obscenities of the
stage return in all their foulness. Plays are acted in
every city, which the common consent of Christendom
had banned because of their depravity. Now the very
prelates of the faith, our nobles, our princes, bring them
back again among us, and cause them to be pub-
licly presented. Nay, priests themselves are eagerly
ambitious of the infamous title of actors, in order to
bring themselves into notoriety, and to enrich themselves with benefices.'

It must not be supposed that the immorality of the
comic stage consists in the licence of language, incident
or plot. Had this been all, we should hardly be justified in drawing a distinction between the Italians of the
Renaissance and our own Elizabethan playwrights. It
lies far deeper, in the vicious philosophy of life paraded
by the authors, in the absence of any didactic or satirical aim. Molière, while exposing evil, teaches by
example. A canon of goodness is implied, from which
the deformities of sin and folly are deflections. But
Machiavelli and Aretino paint humanity as simply bad.
The palm of success is awarded to unscrupulous
villany. An incapacity for understanding the immut-
able power of moral beauty was the main disease of
Italy. If we seek the cause of this internal cancer, we
must trace the history of Italian thought and feeling

---

[1] *De Poet. Hist.* Dial. 8.   Giraldi may have had men like Inghirami,
surnamed ' Phædra,' and Cardinal Bibbiena in view.

back to the age of Boccaccio ; and we shall probably form an opinion that misdirected humanism, blending with the impieties of a secularised Papacy, the self-indulgence of the despots, and the coarse tastes of the *bourgeoisie*, had sapped the conscience of society.

CHAPTER XII.

PASTORAL AND DIDACTIC POETRY.

The Idyllic Ideal—Golden Age—Arcadia—Sannazzaro—His Life—The
Art of the *Arcadia*—Picture-painting—Pontano's Poetry—The Nea-
politan Genius—Baiæ and Eridanus—Eclogues—The Play of *Cefalo*
—Castiglione's *Tirsi*—Rustic Romances—Molza's Biography—The
Ninfa Tiberina—Progress of Didactic Poetry—Rucellai's *Api*—Ala-
manni's *Coltivazione*—His Life—His Satires—Pastoral Dramatic
Poetry—The *Aminta*—The *Pastor Fido*—Climax of Renaissance
Art.

THE transition from the middle ages to the Renaissance was marked by the formation of a new ideal,
which in no slight measure determined the type of
Italian literature. The faiths and aspirations of
Catholicism, whereof the *Divine Comedy* remains the
monument in art, began to lose their hold on the imagination. The world beyond the grave grew dim to
mental vision, in proportion as this world, through
humanism rediscovered, claimed daily more attention.
Poliziano's contemporaries were as far removed from
Dante's apprehension of a future life as modern Evan-
gelicals from Bunyan's vivid sense of sin and salvation.
This parallel, though it may seem strained, is close
enough to be serviceable. As the need of conversion
is taken for granted among Protestants, so the other
world was then assumed to be real. Yet neither the
expectation of heavenly bliss nor the fear of purga-
torial pain was felt with that intense sincerity which

inspired Dante's cantos and Orcagna's frescoes. On both emotions the new culture, appearing at one moment as a solvent through philosophical speculation, at another as a corrosive in the sceptical and critical activity it stimulated, was acting with destructive energy. The present offered a distracting tumult of antagonistic passions, harmonised by no great hope. The future, to those inexperienced pioneers of modern thought, was dim, although the haze, through which the vision came to them, seemed golden. Thus it happened that the sensibilities of men athirst for some consoling fancy, took refuge in the dream of a past happy age. Virgil's description of Saturn's reign :

> Au reus hanc vitam in terris Saturnus agebat,
> Necdum etiam audierant inflari classica, necdum
> Impositos duris crepitare incudibus enses :

fascinated their imagination, and they amused themselves with the fiction of a primal state of innocence. Hesiod and the Metamorphoses of Ovid, the Idylls of Theocritus and Virgil's Eclogues, legends of early Greek civility, and romances of late Greek literature, contributed their several elements to this conception of a pastoral ideal. It blent with Biblical reminiscences of Eden, with mediæval stories of the Earthly Paradise. It helped that transfusion of Christian fancy into classic shape, for which the age was always striving.[1] On one side the ideal was purely literary, reflecting the artistic instincts of a people enthusiastic for form, and affording scope for their imitative activity. But on the other side it corresponded to a deep and genuine Italian feeling. That sympathy with rustic

---

[1] See above, Part i. p. 170, for the Golden Age in the *Quadriregio.*

life, that love of nature humanised by industry, that
delight in the villa, the garden, the vineyard, and the
grove, which modern Italians inherited from their
Roman ancestors, gave reality to what might otherwise have been but artificial. Vespasiano's anecdote
of Cosimo de' Medici pruning his own fruit-trees;
Ficino's description of the village feasts at Monte-
vecchio; Flamminio's picture of his Latin farm;
Alberti's tenderness in gazing at the autumn fields—all
these have the ring of genuine emotion. For men who
felt thus, the Age of Gold was no mere fiction, and
Arcady a land of possibilities.

What has been well called *la voluttà idillica*—the
sensuous sensibility to beauty, finding fit expression in
the Idyll—formed a marked characteristic of Renaissance art and literature. Boccaccio developed this
idyllic motive in all his works which dealt with the
origins of society. Poliziano and Lorenzo devoted
their best poetry to the praise of rural bliss, the happiness of shepherd folk anterior to life in cities. The
same theme recurs in the Latin poems of the humanists,
from the sonorous hexameters of the *Rusticus* down
to the delicate hendecasyllables of the later Lombard
school. It pervades the elegy, the ode, the sonnet, and
takes to itself the chiefest honours of the drama. The
vision of a Golden Age idealised man's actual enjoyment of the country, and hallowed, as with inexplicable
pathos, the details of ordinary rustic life. Weary with
Courts and worldly pleasures, in moments of revolt
against the passions and ambitions that wasted their
best energies, the poets of that century, who were nearly
always also men of state and public office, sighed for

the good old times, when honour was an unknown name, and truth was spoken, and love sincere, and steel lay hidden in the earth, and ships sailed not the sea, and old age led the way to death unterrified by coming doom. As time advanced, their ideal took form and substance. There rose into existence, for the rhymesters to wander in, and for the readers of romance to dream about, a region called Arcadia, where all that was imagined of the Golden Age was found in combination with refined society and manners proper to the civil state. A literary Eldorado had been discovered, which was destined to attract explorers through the next three centuries. Arcadia became the wonder-world of noble youths and maidens, at Madrid no less than at Ferrara, in Elizabeth's London and in Marie Antoinette's Versailles. After engaging the genius of Tasso and Guarini, Spenser and Sidney, it degenerated into quaint conventionality. Companions of Turenne and Marlborough told tales of pastoral love to maids of honour near the throne. Frederick's and Maria Theresa's courtiers simpered and sighed like Dresden-china swains and shepherdesses. Crooked sticks with ribbons at the top were a fashionable appendage to red-heeled shoes and powdered perukes. Few phenomena in history are more curious than the prolonged prosperity and widespread fascination of this Arcadian romance.

To Sannazzaro belongs the glory of having first explored Arcadia, mapped out its borders, and called it after his own name. He is the Columbus of this visionary hemisphere. Jacopo Sannazzaro has more than once above been mentioned in the chapters devoted to Latin poetry. But the events of his life have not yet been touched upon.[1] His ancestors claimed to have been originally Spaniards, settled in a village of Pavia called S. Nazzaro, whence they took their name. The poet's immediate forefather was said to have followed Charles of Durazzo in 1380 to the south of Italy, where he received fiefs and lands in the Basilicata. Jacopo was born at Naples in 1458, and was brought up in his boyhood by his mother at S. Cipriano.[2] He studied at Naples under the grammarian Junianus Maius,[3] and made such rapid progress in both Greek and Latin scholarship as soon to be found worthy of a place in Pontano's Academy. In that society he assumed the pseudonym of Actius Sincerus. The friendship between Pontano and Sannazzaro lasted without interruption till the former's death in 1503. Their Latin poems abound in passages which testify to a strong mutual regard, and the life-size effigies of both may still be seen together in the church of Monte Oliveto at Naples.[4] Distinction in scholarship was, after the days of Alfonso the Magnanimous, a sure title to consideration at the Neapolitan Court. Sannazzaro attached himself to the person of Frederick, the second son of Ferdinand I.; and when this prince succeeded to the throne, he conferred upon the poet a

---

[1] The chief sources of Sannazzaro's biography are a section of his *Arcadia* (*Prosa*, vii.), and his Latin poems. The Sannazzari of Pavia had the honour of mention in Dante's *Convito*. Among the poet's Latin odes are several addressed to the patron saint of his race. See *Sannazarii op. omn. Lat. scripta* (Aldus, 1535), pp. 16, 53, 56, 59.

[2] Elegy, ' Quod pueritiam egerit in Picentinis,' *op. cit.* p. 27.

[3] Elegy, ' Ad Junianum Maium Præceptorem,' *op. cit.* p. 20.

[4] I may refer in particular to Sannazzaro's beautiful elegy ' De Studiis suis et Libris Joviani Pontani ' among his Latin poems, *op. cit.* p. 10. For their terra-cotta portraits, see above, *Revival of Learning*, p. 365.

pension of 600 ducats and the pleasant villa of Mer-
goglino between the city and Posilippo.[1] This recom-
pence for past service was considerably below the
poet's expectations and deserts ; nor did he receive any
post of state importance. Yet Sannazzaro remained
faithful through his lifetime to the Aragonese dynasty.
He attended the princes on their campaigns ; espoused
their quarrels in his fierce and potent series of epigrams against the Rovere and Borgia Pontiffs; and
when Frederick retired to France in 1501, he jour-
neyed into exile with his royal master, only returning
to Naples after the ex-king's death. There Sannazzaro
continued to reside until his own death in 1530. His
later years were embittered by the destruction of his
Villa Mergellina during the occupation of Naples by
the imperial troops under the Prince of Orange. But
with the exception of this misfortune, he appears to
have passed a quiet and honourable old age, devoting
himself to piety, contributing to charitable works and
church-building, and employing his leisure in study and
the society of a beloved lady, Cassandra Marchesa.

In his early youth Sannazzaro formed a romantic
attachment for a girl of noble birth, called Carmosina
Bonifacia. This love made him first a poet; and the
majority of his Italian verses may be referred to its
influence. They consist of sonnets and *canzoni*,
modelled upon Petrarch, but marked by independence
of treatment, and spontaneity of feeling. The puristic
revival had not yet set in, and Sannazzaro's style

[1] Sannazzaro's two odes on 'Villa Mergellina' and 'Fons Mergellines'
(*op. cit.* pp. 31, 53), are among his purest and most charming Latin compositions.

shows no servile imitation of his model. It may not
be out of place to give a specimen in translation of
these early *Rime*. I have chosen a sonnet upon
jealousy, which La Casa afterwards found worthy of
rehandling :

> Horrible curb of lovers, Jealousy,
>> That with one force doth check and sway my will ;
>> Sister of loathed and impious Death, that still
>> With thy grim face troublest the tranquil sky ;
> Thou snake concealed in laughing flowers which lie
>> Rocked on earth's lap ; thou that my hope dost kill ;
>> Amid fair fortunes thou malignant ill ;
>> Venom mid viands which men taste and die !
> From what infernal valley didst thou soar,
>> O ruthless monster, plague of mortals, thou
>> That darkenest all my days with misery o'er ?
> Hence, double not these griefs that cloud my brow !
>> Accursèd fear, why camest thou ? Was more
>> Needed than Love's keen shafts to make me bow ?

About the reality of Sannazzaro's passion for Carmosina there can be no doubt. The most directly powerful passages in the *Arcadia* are those in which he
refers to it.[1] His Southern temperament exposed him
to the fiercest pangs of jealousy; and when he found
that love disturbed his rest and preyed upon his health
he resolved to seek relief in travel. For this purpose
he went to France ; but he could not long endure the
exile from his native country, and on his return he
found his Carmosina dead. The elegies in which he
recorded his grief, are not the least poetical of his
compositions both in Latin and Italian.[2] After estab-

---

[1] She is described in *Prosa* iv., and frequently mentioned under the
name of *Arancio* or *Amaranta*.

[2] See the Epitaph ' Hic Amarantha jacet,' the last Eclogue of *Arcadia*,
and the Latin eclogue ' Mirabar vicina Mycon,' in which Carmosina is
celebrated under the name of Phyllis. I may here call attention to Pon-

lishing himself once more at Naples, Sannazzaro began the composition of the *Eclogæ Piscatoriæ*, in which he has been said to have brought the pastoral Muses down to the sea shore. The novelty of these poems secured for them no slight celebrity. Nor are they without real artistic merit. The charm of the sea is nowhere felt more vividly than on the bay of Naples, and nowhere else are the habits of a fishing population more picturesque. Nereids and Sirens, Proteus and Nisa, Cymothoe and Triton, are not out of place in modern verses, which can commemorate Naples, Ischia and Procida, under the titles of Parthenope, Inarime and Prochyte. Happy indeed is the poet, if he must needs write Latin elegies, whose home suggests such harmonies and cadences, for whom Baiæ and Cumæ and the Lucrine Lake, Puteoli and Capreæ and Stabiæ, are household words, and who looks from his study windows daily on scenes which realise the mythology still lingering in names and memories around them by beauty ever-present, inexpressible.

The second mistress of Sannazzaro's heart was a noble lady, Cassandra Marchesa. He paid his addresses to her *more Platonico*, and chose her for the object of refined compliments in classical and modern verse. The Latin elegies and epigrams are full of her praises ; and one of the Eclogues, *Pharmaceutria*, is inscribed with her name. It would scarcely have been necessary to mention this courtly attachment, but for the pleasant light it casts upon Sannazzaro's character. The lady whom he had celebrated and de-

tano's elegy beginning 'Harmosyne jacet hic' in the *Tumuli*, lib. ii. (*Joannis Joviani Pontani Amorum Libri, etc*, Aldus, 1518, p. 87).

fended in his manhood, was the friend of his old age. He is said to have died in her house.

The *Arcadia* was begun at Nocera in Sannazzaro's youth, continued during his first residence in France, and finished on his return to Naples. So much can be gathered from its personal references. The book blends autobiography and fable in a narrative of very languid interest. The poet's circumstances and emotions in exile are described at one moment in plain language, at another are presented with the indirectness of an allegory. Arcadia in some passages stands for a semi-savage country-district in France; in others it is the dream-world of poetry and pastoral simplicity. But in either case its scenery is drawn from Sannazzaro's own Italian home. The inhabitants are shepherds such as Virgil fancied, with even more of personal refinement. Through their lips the poet tells the tale of his own love, and paints his Neapolitan mistress among the nymphs of Mount Parthenion. Throughout, we note an awkward interminglement of subjective and objective points of view. Realism merges into fancy. Experience of life assumes the garb of myth or legend. Neither as an autobiographical romance nor again as a work of pure invention has the *Arcadia* surpassing merit. Loose in construction and uncertain in aim, it lacks the clearness and consistency of perfect art. And yet it is a masterpiece; because its author, led by prescient instinct, contrived to make it reflect one of the deepest and most permanent emotions of his time. The whole pastoral ideal—the yearning after a golden age, the beauty and pathos of the country, the felicity of simple folk, the details of

rustic life, the charm of woods and gardens, the mythology of Pan and Satyrs, Nymphs and Fauns—all
this is expressed in a series of pictures, idyllically graceful, artistically felt. It is not for its story that we read
Arcadia, but for the Feast of Pales, the games at Mas-
silia's shrine, the Sacrifice to Pan, Androgéo's tomb,
the group of girls a-maying, the carved work of the
beechen cup, the passion of Carino, the gardens with
their flowers, and the bands of youths and maidens
meeting under shadowy trees to dance and play. Pictures like these are presented with a scrupulous and
loving sincerity, an anxious accuracy of studied style,
which proves how serious was the author. His heart,
as an artist, is in the realisation of his dream-world;
and his touch is firm and dry and delicate as Mantegna's.
Indeed, we are constantly reminded of the Mante-
gnesque manner, and one reference justifies the belief
that Sannazzaro strove to reproduce its effect.[1] The
sensuousness of the Italian feeling for mere beauty is
tempered with reticence and something of the coldness
of Greek marbles. In point of diction, Boccaccio has
been obviously imitated. But Boccaccio's style is not
revived, as Masuccio strove to revive it, with the fire
and energy of Southern passion substituted for its
Tuscan irony and delicacy. On the contrary, the
periods are still more artificial, the turns of phrase
more tortured. Sannazzaro writes with difficulty in a
somewhat unfamiliar language, rendered all the more
stubborn by his endeavours to add classical refinements. Boccaccio's humour is gone; his sensuality is

---

[1] In *Prosa* xi. he mentions a vase painted by the 'Padoano Mantegna, artefice sovra tutti gli altri accorto ed ingegnosissimo.'

purged by contact with antique examples ; the waving groves of the *Filocopo* are clipped and tutored like box-hedges in an academic garden. If there is less of natural raciness than came unsummoned to Boccaccio's aid, there is more of Virgil and Theocritus than he chose to appropriate. The slow deliberate expansion of each picture, stroke by stroke and touch by touch, reminds us of the *quattrocento* painters ; while the *précieuseté* of the phrasing has affinity to the manner of a late Greek stylist, especially perhaps, though almost certainly unconsciously, to that of Philostratus. This close correspondence of the *Arcadia* to the main artistic sympathies of the Renaissance, rendered it indescribably popular in its own age, and causes it still to rank as one of the representative masterpieces of the epoch. Through its peculiar blending of classical and modern strains—the feasts of Pales and of Pan taking colour from Capo di Monte superstitions ; the nymphs of wood and river modelled after girls from Massa and Sorrento ; the yellow-haired shepherds of Mount Mænalus singing love-laments for Neapolitan Carmosina—we are enabled more nearly than in almost any other literary essay to appreciate the spirit of the classical revival as it touched Italian art. A little earlier, there was more of spontaneity and *naïveté.* A little later, there was more of conscious erudition and consummate skill. The *Arcadia* comes midway between the *Filocopo* and the *Pastor Fido.*

It is time to turn from dissertation, and to detach, almost at haphazard, some of those descriptions which render the *Arcadia* a storehouse of illustrations to the

pictures of the fifteenth century. I will first select the
frescoes on the front of Pales' chapel, endeavouring so
far as possible to reproduce the intricacies and quaint
affectations of the style.[1] The constant abuse of
epithets, and the structure of the period by means
of relatives, pegging its clauses down and keeping
them in their places, will be noticed as part of the
Boccaccesque tradition. 'Intending now to ratify with
souls devout the vows which had been made in former
times of need, upon the smoking altars, all together in
company we went unto the sacred temple, along whose
frontal, raised upon a few ascending steps, we found
above the doorway painted certain woods and hills of
most delightful beauty, full of leafy trees and of a
thousand sorts of flowers, among the which were seen
many herds that went a-pasture, wending at pleasure
through green fields, with peradventure ten dogs to
guard them, the footsteps of the which upon the dust
were traced most natural to the view. Of the shepherds,
some were milking, some shearing wool, others playing
on pipes, and there were there a few, who, as it
seemed, were singing and endeavouring to keep in
tune with these. But that which pleased me to regard
with most attention were certain naked Nymphs,
the which behind a chestnut bole stayed, as it were,
half-hidden, laughing at a ram, who, in his eagerness
to gnaw a wreath of oak that hung before his eyes,
forgot to feed upon the grass around him. In that
while came four Satyrs, with horns upon their heads
and goat's feet, stealing through a shrubbery of lentisks,
softly, softly, to take the maidens from behind. Whereof

[1] *Prosa* iii.

when they were ware, they took to flight through the
dense grove, shunning nor thorns nor aught else that
might annoy them ; and of these one, nimbler than the
rest, was clinging to a hornbeam's branches, and
thence, with a long bough in her hands, defending
herself. The others had cast themselves through
fright into a river, wherethrough they fled a-swimming ;
and the clear water hid little or but nothing of their
snow-white flesh. But whenas they saw themselves
escaped, they sat them down upon the further bank,
fordone with toil and panting, drying their soaked hair,
and thence with word and gesture seemed to mock at
those who had not shown the power to capture
them. And in one of the sides there was Apollo, with
the yellowest hair, leaning upon a wand of wild olive,
and watching Admetus' herds beside a river-bed ; and
thus, intently gazing on two sinewy bulls which jousted
with their horns, he was not ware of wily Mercury,
who in a shepherd's habit, with a kid-skin girded under
his left shoulder, stole the cows away from him. And
in that same space stood Battus, the bewrayer of the
theft, transformed into a stone, stretching his finger
forth in act of one who pointed. A little lower,
Mercury was seen again, seated upon a large stone,
and playing with swollen cheeks upon a rustic pipe,
while his eyes were turned to mark a white calf close
beside him, and with most cunning arts he strove to
cozen Argus of the many eyes. On the other side, at
the foot of an exceeding high oak-tree, was stretched a
shepherd asleep among his goats ; and a dog stayed
near him, smelling at his pouch, which lay beneath his
head ; and he, forasmuch as the moon gazed at him

with glad eyes, methought must be Endymion. Next to him was Paris, who with his sickle had begun to carve *Œnone* on an elm-tree's bark, and being called to judge between the naked goddesses that stood before him, had not yet been able to complete his work. But what was not less subtle in the thought than pleasant in the seeing was the shrewdness of the wary painter, who, having made Juno and Minerva of such extreme beauty that to surpass them was impossible, and doubting of his power to make Venus so lovely as the tale demanded, had painted her with back turned, covering the defect of art by ingenuity of invention. And many other things right charming and most beautiful to look upon, of the which I now have but a faulty memory, I saw there painted upon divers places.' It is clear that Sannazzaro had not read Lessing's *Laocoon* or noted the distinctions between poetry and painting. Yet in this he was true to the spirit of his age ; for actions no less continuous than some of those described by him, may be found represented in the frescoes of Gozzoli or Lippo Lippi.

The finished portrait of Sannazzaro's mistress Carmosina shall supply my next quotation.[1] The exile is listening to shepherds singing, and one of them has mentioned Amaranta. He knows that she is present, and resolves to choose her by her gestures from the rest. 'With wary glance, watching now one and now another, I saw among the maidens one who seemed to me the loveliest. Her hair was covered with a very thin veil, beneath which two eyes, lovely and most brilliant, sparkled not otherwise than the

[1] *Prosa* iv.

clear stars are wont to shine in a serene and limpid
sky ; and her face, inclining somewhat to the oval more
than the round, of fair shape, with a pallor that was not
unpleasing, but tempered, as it were toward dark complexion turning, and relieved therewith by vermeil and
gracious hues, filled with joy of love the eyes that
gazed on her.   Her lips were of the sort that surpass
the morning roses ; between the which, each time she
spoke or smiled, she showed some portion of her teeth,
of such rare and marvellous grace that I could not have
compared them to aught else but orient pearls.   Thence
passing down to her marble and delicate throat, I saw
upon that tender bosom the slight and youthful breasts,
which, like two rounded apples, thrust her robe of
finest texture somewhat forward ; and in the midst of
them I could discern the fairest little way, exceeding
pleasant to the sight, the which, because it ended and
escaped the view, was reason why I dwelt thereon
with greater force of thought.   And she, with most
delicate gait and a gentle and aspiring stature, went
through the fair fields, with her white hand plucking
tender flowers.   With the which when she had filled
her lap, no sooner had the singing youth within her
hearing mentioned Amaranta, than, dropping her
hands and gathered robe, and as it were lost to her
own recollection, without her knowing what befell, they
all slid from her grasp, sowing the earth with peradventure twenty sorts of colours.   Which, as though
suddenly brought to herself, when she perceived, she
blushed not otherwise than sometimes reddens the
enchanted moon with rosy aspect, or as, upon the
issuing of the sun, the red Aurora shows herself to

mortal gaze. Whereupon she, not for any need methinks compelling her thereto, but haply hoping better thus to hide the blushes that came over her, begotten by a woman's modesty, bent toward earth again to pick them up, as though she cared for only that, choosing the white flowers from the crimson and the dark blue from the violet blossoms.' Amaranta makes a pretty picture, but one which is too elaborate in detail. Her sisterhood is described with touches more negligent, and therefore the more artful.[1] 'Some wore garlands of privet with yellow buds and certain crimson intermingled ; others had white lilies and purple mixed with a few most verdant orange leaves between ; one went starred with roses, and yon other whitened with jasmines. So that each by herself and all together were more like to divine spirits than to human creatures. Whereupon many men there present cried with wonder : O blessed the possessor of such beauties !' The young swains are hardly less attractive than their nymphs.[2] 'Logisto and Elpino, shepherds, comely of person and in years within the bounds of earliest youth : Elpino guardian of goats, Logisto of the woolly sheep : both with hair yellower than ripe ears of corn ; both of Arcadia ; both fit alike to sing and to make answer.'

Sannazzaro's touch upon inanimate nature is equally precise. Here is a description of the evening sky.[3] ' It was the hour when sunset embroidered all the west with a thousand varieties of clouds ; some violet, some darkly blue, and certain crimson ; others between yellow and black, and a few so burning with the fire of backward-beaten rays that they seemed as though of

---

[1] *Prosa* iv.　　　[2] *Ibid.*　　　[3] *Prosa* v.

polished and finest gold.'   Here is a garden[1] : 'Moved
by sympathy for Ergasto, many shepherds had moreover wrought the place about with high hedges, not of
thorns or briars, but of junipers, roses and jasmines,
and had delved therein with their mattocks a pastoral
seat, and at even spaces certain towers of rosemary
and myrtles interwoven with the most incomparable
art.'   Here are flowers[2] : 'There were lilies, there
privets, there violets toned to amorous pallor, and in large
abundance the slumberous poppies with their leaning
heads, and the ruddy spikes of the immortal amaranth,
most comely of coronals mid winter's rudeness.'

The same research of phrase marks the exhibition
of emotion.   Carino, the shepherd, tells how, overwhelmed with grief, he lay upon the ground and seemed
lost to life[3] : 'Came the oxherds, came the herdsmen
of the sheep and goats, together with the peasants of
the neighbouring farms, deeming me distraught, as of a
truth indeed I was ; and all with deepest pity asked the
reason of my woe.   Unto whom I made no answer, but,
minding my own weeping, thus with lamentable voice
exclaimed : You of Arcady shall sing among your
mountains of my death ! You of Arcady, who only
have the art of song, you of my death shall sing amid
your mountains !'   His complaint extends to a length
which defies quotation.   But here is an extract from
it[4] : 'O gods of heaven and earth, and whosoe'er ye
are who have regard for wretched lovers, lend, I pray,
your ears of pity to my lamentation, and listen to the
dolent cries my tortured spirit sendeth forth ! O Nai-
ads, dwellers in the running water brooks ! O Napean

nymphs, most gracious haunters of far places and of liquid founts, lift up your yellow tresses but a little from the crystal waves, and receive these my last cries before I perish! O you, O fairest Oreads, who naked on the hanging cliffs are wont to go achase, leave now your lofty mountain realm, and in my misery visit me, for I am sure to win your sorrow by what brings my cruel maid delight! Come forth from your trees, O pitying Hamadryads, ye anxious guardians over them, and turn your thoughts a little toward the martyrdom these hands of mine prepare for me! And you, O Dryads, most beauteous damsels of the woods profound, ye who not once but many and many a time have watched our shepherds at the fall of eve in circle dancing neath the shadow of cool walnut trees, with yellowest curls a-ripple down their snow-white necks, cause now I pray, if you are not with my too changeful fortune changed, that mid these shades my death may not be mute, but ever grow from day to day through centuries to come, so that the tale of years life lacks, may go to lengthen out my fame!'

For English students the *Arcadia* has a special interest, since it begot the longer and more ambitious work of Sir Philip Sidney. Hitherto I have spoken only of its prose ; but the book blends prose and verse in alternating sections. The verse consists of mingled *terza rima, canzoni* and sestines. Not less artificial and decidedly less original than the prose, Sannazzaro's lyrics and eclogues do not demand particular attention. He put needless restraint upon himself by affecting the awkwardness of *sdrucciolo* rhymes [1] ;

---

[1] Even in this Sidney tried to follow him, with an effect the clumsiness

and he lacked the roseate fluency, the winning ease, the unaffected graces of Poliziano. One sestine, sung by himself among the shepherds of Arcady, I have translated, because it paints the actual conditions of life which drove Sannazzaro into his first exile.[1] But the singularly charmless form adopted, which even Petrarch hardly rendered tolerable, seems to check the poet's spontaneity of feeling.

Even as a bird of night that loathes the sun,
I wander, woe is me, through places dark,
The while refulgent day doth shine on earth ;
Then when upon the world descendeth eve,
I cannot, like all creatures, sink in sleep,
But wake to roam and weep among the fields.

If peradventure amid woods and fields,
Where shines not with his radiance the sun,
Mine eyes, o'er-tired with weeping, close in sleep,
Harsh dreams and wandering visions, vain and dark,
Affright me so that still I shrink at eve,
For fear of sleep, from resting on the earth.

O universal mother, kindly earth,
Shall 't ever be that, stretched on verdant fields,
In slumber deep, upon that latest eve,
I ne'er shall wake again, until the sun
Rise to reveal his light to eyelids dark,
And stir my soul again from that long sleep ?

From that first moment when I banished sleep,
And left my bed to lay myself on earth,
The cloudless days for me were drear and dark,
And turned to stubbly straw the flowery fields ;
So that when morn to men brings back the sun,
It darkens round mine eyes in shadowy eve.

My lady, of her kindness, came one eve,
Joyous and very fair, to me in sleep,
And gladdened all my heart, even as the sun,

of which can only be conceived by those who have read his triple-rhyming English *terza rima*.
[1] *Egloga* vii.

When rains are past, is wont to clear the earth ;
And said to me : Come, gather from my fields
Some flow'ret ; cease to haunt those caverns dark.

Fly hence, fly hence, ye tedious thoughts and dark,
That have obscured me in so long an eve !
For I'll go seek the sunny smiling fields,
Taking upon their herbage honeyed sleep :
Full well I know that ne'er man made of earth
More blest than now I am beheld the sun !

Song, in mid eve thou'lt see the orient sun,
And me neath earth among those regions dark,
Or e'er on yonder fields I take my sleep.

Whether the distinctively Neapolitan note can be
discerned in Sannazzaro, seems more than doubtful. As
in his Sapphic Odes and Piscatory Eclogues, so also
in his *Arcadia* we detect the working of a talent self-
restrained within the limits of finely-tempered taste.
The case is very different with Pontano's Latin elegies
and lyrics.[1] They breathe the sensuality and self-
abandonment to impulse of a Southern temperament.
They reflect the profuseness of nature in a region
where men scarcely know what winter means, her
somewhat too nakedly voluptuous beauties, her vol-
canic energies and interminglement of living fire with
barren scoriæ. For this reason, and because there is
some danger of neglecting the special part played by
the Southern Province in Italian literary history, I am

---

[1] From my chapter on Latin poetry in the *Revival of Learning* I purposely omitted more than a general notice of Pontano's erotic verses,
intending to treat of them thereafter, when it should be necessary to
discuss the Neapolitan contribution to Italian literature. The lyrics and
elegies I shall now refer to, are found in two volumes of *Pontani Opera*,
published by Aldus, 1513 and 1518. These volumes I shall quote
together, using the minor titles of *Amorum*, *Hendecasyllabi*, and so forth,
and mentioning the page. I am sorry that I have not a uniform edition
of his Latin poetry (if that, indeed, exists, of which I doubt) before me.

induced to digress from the main topic of this chapter in the direction of Pontano's poetry.

Though a native of Cerreto in Umbria, Pontano passed his life at Naples, and became, if we may trust the evidence of his lyrics, more Neapolitan than the Neapolitans. In him the southern peoples found a voice, which, though it uttered a dead language, expressed their sentiments. It is unlucky that Pontano, who deserves to be reckoned as the greatest poet of Naples, should have made this important contribution to Italian literature in Latin. Whether at that moment he could have spoken so freely in the vulgar tongue is more than doubtful. But be that as it may, we must have recourse to his Latin poems, in order to supply a needed link in the chain of Italian melody. Carducci acutely remarked that, more than any other poems of the century, they embody ' the æsthetic and learned reaction against the mystical idealism of Christianity in a preceding age.' They do so better than Beccadelli's, because, where the *Hermaphroditus* is obscene, the *Eridanus, Baiæ, Amor Conjugalis, Pompæ, Næniæ* of Pontano are only sensual. The cardinal point in Pontano is the breadth of his feeling. He touches the whole scale of natural emotions with equal passion and sincerity. The love of the young man for his sweetheart, the love of the husband for his bride, the love of a father for his offspring, the love of a nurse for her infant charge, find in his verse the same full sensuous expression. In Pontano there is no more of Teutonic *Schwärmerei* than of Dantesque transcendentalism. He does not make us marvel how the young man, who has embroidered odes upon the theme of *Alma Pellegrina,* or who has woven violet and moonshine into some *Du bist wie eine Blume,* can submit to light the hymeneal torch and face the prose of matrimony. Within the limits of unsophisticated instinct he is perfectly complete and rounded to a flawless whole. He does not say one thing and leave another to be understood—a contradiction that imports some radical unreality into the Platonic or sentimental modes of sexual expression. He expects woman to weigh but little less than man in scales of natural appetite. And yet his Muse is no mere vagrant Venus. She is a respectable if not, according to our present views, an altogether decent Juno. The final truth about her is that she revealed to her uniquely gifted bard, on earth and in the shrine of home, that poetry of love which Milton afterwards mythologised in Eden. The note of unadulterated humanity sounds with a clearness that demands commemoration in this poetry of passion. It is, if not the highest, yet the frankest and most decided utterance of mutual, legitimate desire. As such, it occupies an enviable place in the history of Italian love— equally apart from *trecento* sickliness and *cinque cento* corruption; unrefined perchance, but healthy; doing justice to the proletariate of Naples whence it sprung.

Pontano paints all primitive affections in a way to justify his want of reticence. His Fannia, Focilla, Stella, Ariadne, Cinnama—mistress or wife, we need not stop to question—are the very opposite of Dante's or of Petrarch's loves.[1] Liberal of their charms, re-

---

[1] Fannia is the most attractive of these women. See *Amorum,* lib. i. pp. 4, 5, 13. Stella, the heroine of the *Eridani,* is touched with greater

joicing like the waves of the Chiaja in the laughter of
the open day, they think it no shame to unbare their
beauties to their lover's eyes, or to respond with ardour to his caresses. Christian modesty, medieval
asceticism, the strife between the spirit and the flesh,
the aspiration after mystic modes of feeling, have been
as much forgotten in their portraits, as though the
world had never undergone reaction against paganism.
And yet they differ from the women of the Roman
elegiac poets. They are less artificial than Corinna.
Though 'the sweet witty soul of Ovid' passed over
these honeyed elegies, the Neapolitan poet remains a
bourgeois of the fifteenth century. His passion is un-
reservedly sensual and at the same time tenderly affectionate. Its motive force is sexual desire; its depth
and strength are in the love a husband and a father
feels. Given the verses upon Fannia alone, we
should be justified in calling Pontano a lascivious poet.
The three books *De Amore Conjugali* show him in a
different light. He there expounds the duties and
relations of the family with the same robust and unaffected force of feeling he had shown in the description of a wanton. After painting his Stella with the
gusto of an Italian Rubens, he can turn to shed tears
almost sublime in their pathos over the tomb of Lucia
his daughter, or to write a cradle-song for his son
Luciolus.[1] The carnal appetites which are legitimated

delicacy. Cinnama seems to have been a girl of the people. Pontano
borrows for her the language of popular poetry (*Amorum*, i. 19).

> Ipsa tibi dicat, mea lux, mea vita, meus flos,
>> Liliolumque meum, basiolumque meum.
> Carior et gemmis, et caro carior auro,
>> Tu rosa, tu violæ, tu mihi lævis onyx.

[1] Among the most touching of his elegiac verses is the lament

by matrimony and hallowed in domestic relations, but which it is the custom of civilised humanity to veil, assume a tone of almost Bacchic rapture in this fluent Latin verse. This constitutes Pontano's originality. Such a combination has never been presented to the world before or since. The genial bed, from which he draws his inspiration, found few poets to appreciate it in ancient days, and fewer who have dared to celebrate it so unblushingly among the moderns.[1]

The same series of .Pontano's poems may be read with no less profit for their pictures of Neapolitan life.[2] He brings the baths of Baiæ, unspoiled as yet by the eruption from Monte Nuovo, vividly before us; the myrtle-groves and gardens by the bay; the sailors stretched along the shore; the youths and maidens flirting as they bathe or drink the waters, their evening walks, their little dinners, their assignations; all the round of pleasure in a place and climate made for

addressed to his dead wife upon the death of their son Lucius, *Eridanorum*, lib. ii. p. 134. The collection of epitaphs called *Tumuli* bears witness to the depth and sincerity of his sorrow for the dead, to the all-embracing sympathy he felt for human grief. The very original series of lullabies, entitled *Nænia*, illustrate the warmth of his paternal feeling. The nursery has never before or since been celebrated with such exuberance of fancy—and in the purest Ovidian elegiacs ! It may, however, be objected that there is too much about wet-nurses in these songs.

[1] Pontano revels in Epithalamials and pictures of the joys of wedlock. See the series of elegies on Stella, *Eridanorum*, lib. i. pp. 108, 111, 113, 115 ; the congratulation addressed to Alfonso, Duke of Calabria, *Hendecasyllaborum*, lib. i. p. 194 ; and two among the many Epithalamial hymns, *Hendec.* lib. i. p. 195 ; *Lepidina*, Pompa 7, p. 172, with its reiterated ' Dicimus o hymenæe Io hymen hymenææ.' The sensuality of these compositions will be too frank and fulsome for a chastened taste ; but there is nothing in them extra or infra-human.

[2] *Hendecasyllaborum*, lib. i. and ii. pp. 186–218. If one of these lyrics should be chosen from the rest, I should point to ' Invitantur pueri et puellæ ad audiendum Charitas,' p. 209. It begins ' Ad myrtum juvenes venite, myrti.'

love. Or we watch the people at their games, crowded
together on those high-built carts, rattling the tambourine and dancing the tarantella—as near to fauns
and nymphs in shape as humanity well may be.[1]
Each mountain and each stream is personified; the
genii of the villages, the Oreads of the copses, the
Tritons of the waves, come forth to play with men[2]:

> Claudicat hinc heros Capimontius, et de summo
> Colle ruunt misti juvenes mistæque puellæ ;
> Omnis amat chorus, et juncti glomerantur amantes.
> Is lento incedit passu, baculoque tuetur
> Infirmum femur, et choreis dat signa movendis,
> Assuetus choreæ ludisque assuetus amantum.

Nor are these personifications merely frigid fictions.
The landscape of Naples lends itself to mythology, not
only because it is so beautiful, but because human life
and nature interpenetrate, as nowhere else in Europe,
on that bay.   Pontano has a tale to tell of every river
and every grove—how Adonis lives again in the orange
trees of Sorrento, how the Sebeto was a boy beloved
by one of Nereus' daughters and slain by him in anger.[3]
His tendency to personification was irresistible.   Not
content, like Sannazzaro, with singing the praises of his
villa, he feigns a Nympha Antiniana, whom he invokes
as the Muse of neo-Latin lyric rapture.[4]   In the
melodious series of love-poems entitled *Eridanus*, he
exercises the same imaginative faculty on Lombard
scenery.   After closing this little book, we seem to be

---

[1] For such glimpses into actual life, see *Lepidina*, pp. 160–174, in which
a man and woman of Naples discourse of their first loves and wedlock.
The Eclogues abound in similar material.

[2] *Lepidina*, p. 168.   Capimontius is easily recognised as Capo di
Monte.

[3] See *De Hortis Hesperidum*, p. 139, and *Amorum*, lib. ii. p. 33.

[4] *Versus Lyrici*, pp. 91-94.

no less familiar with the 'king of rivers,' Phaethon, and the Heliades, than with the living Stella, to frame whose beauty in a fitting wreath these fancies have been woven.[1] Even the Elegy, which he used so freely and with so complete a pleasure in its movement, becomes for him a woman, with specific form and habit, and a love-tale taken from some Propertian memory of the poet's Umbrian home. To quote Pontano is neither easy nor desirable. Yet I cannot resist the inclination to present Dame Elegia in her Ionian garb in part at least before a modern audience.[2]

> Huc ades, et nitidum myrto compesce capillum,
> Huc ades ornatis o Elegia comis.
> Inque novam venias cultu prædivite formam,
> Laxa fluat niveos vestis adusque pedes.

[1] See, for example, the elegy 'De Venere lavante se in Eridano et quiescente,' *Erid.* lib. i. p. 118.

[2] *De Amore Conjugali*, lib. i. p. 35. 'Hither, and bind with myrtle thy shining hair! O hither, Elegia, with the woven tresses! Take a new form of sumptuous grace, and let thy loose robe flutter to thy snow-white feet. And where thou movest, breathe Arabian nard, and blandest perfume of Assyrian unguents. Let the girl Graces come, thy charge, with thee, and take their joy in dances woven with unwonted arts. Thou in his earliest years dost teach the boy of Venus, and instruct him in thy lore. Wherefore Cytherea gives thee perpetual youth, that never may thy beauty suffer decrease. Come hither, then, and take, O goddess, thy lyre, but with a gentle quill, and move the soft strings to a dulcet sound. Nay, thou thyself hast tried new pleasures, and knowest the sweet thefts of lovers laid on meadow grass. For they say that, wandering once in Umbria, my home, thou didst lie down beside Clitumnus' liquid pools; and there didst see a youth, and dote upon him while he swam, and long to hold him in thine arms. What dost thou, beauteous boy, beneath the wanton waves? These fields are better suited to thy joys! Here canst thou weave a violet wreath, and bind thy yellow hair with flowers of many a hue! Here canst thou sleep beneath cool shade, and rest thy body on the verdant ground! Here join the dances of the Dryads, and leap along the sward, and move thy supple limbs to tender music! The youth inflamed with this, and eager for the beauty and the facile song, wherewith thou captivatest gods, with thee among the willows, under a vine-mantled elm, joined his white limbs upon a grassy bed, and both enjoyed the bliss of love.'

Quaque moves, Arabum spires mollissima nardum,
   Lenis et Assyrio sudet odore liquor.
Tecum etiam Charites veniant, tua cura, puellæ,
   Et juvet insolita ducere ab arte choros.
Tu puerum Veneris primis lasciva sub annis
   Instruis, et studio perficis usque tuo.
Hinc tibi perpetuæ tribuit Cytherea juventæ
   Tempora, neu formæ sint mala damna tuæ ;
Ergo ades, et cape, diva, lyram, sed pectine molli,
   Sed moveas dulci lenia fila sono.
Quinetiam tu experta novos, ni fallor, amores,
   Dulcia supposito gramine furta probas.
Namque ferunt, patrios vectam quandoque per Umbros,
   Clitumni liquidis accubuisse vadis :
Hic juvenem vidisse, atque incaluisse natantem,
   Et cupisse ulnas inter habere tuas.
Quid tibi lascivis, puer o formose, sub undis?
   Deliciis mage sunt commoda prata tuis.
Hic potes e molli viola junxisse coronam,
   Et flavam vario flore ligare comam ;
Hic potes et gelida somnum quæsisse sub umbra,
   Et lassum viridi ponere corpus humo ;
Hic et adesse choris Dryadum, et saluisse per herbas,
   Molliaque ad teneros membra movere modos.
Hic juvenis succensus amor, formamque secutus
   Et facilem cantum, quo capis ipsa deos,
Tecum inter salices, sub amicta vitibus ulmo,
   In molli junxit candida membra toro ;
Inter et amplexus lassi jacuistis uterque,
   Et repetita venus dulce peregit opus.

That this poet was no servile imitator of Tibullus or Ovid is clear. That he had not risen to their height of diction is also manifest. But in Pontano, as in Poliziano, Latin verse lived again with new and genuine vitality.

If it were needful to seek a formal return from this digression to the subject of my chapter, there would be no lack of opportunity. Pontano's Eclogues, the description of his gardens, his vision of the golden age and his long discourse on the cultivation of orange trees, justify our placing him among the strictly pastoral poets.[1] In treating of the country he displays his usual warmth and sensuous realism. He mythologises ; but his myths are the substantial forms of genuine emotion and experience. The Fauns he talks of, are such lads as even now may be seen upon the Ischian slopes of Monte Epomeo, with startled eyes, brown skin, and tangled tresses tossed adown their sinewy shoulders. The Bacchus of his vintage has walked, red from the wine-press, crowned with real ivy and vine, and sat down at the poet's elbow, to pledge him in a cup of foaming must.

While Sannazzaro was exploring Arcadia at Naples, Poliziano had already transferred pastoral poetry to the theatre at Mantua. Of the *Orfeo* and its place in Italian literature, I have spoken sufficiently elsewhere. It is enough to remember, in the present connection, that, while Arcady became the local dreamland of the new ideal, Orpheus took the place of its hero. As the institutor of civil society in the midst of a rude population, he personified for our Italian poets the spirit of their own renascent culture. Arcadia represented the realm of art and song, unstirred by warfare or unworthy passions. Orpheus attuned the simple souls who dwelt in it, to music with his ravishing lyre.

Pastoral representations soon became fashionable. Niccolò da Correggio put the tale of Cephalus and Procrsi on the stage at Ferrara, with choruses of nymphs,

---

[1] I will only refer in detail to the elegy entitled ' Lætatur in villa et hortis suis constitutis' (*De Amore Conjugali*, lib. ii. p. 52). The two books *De Hortis Hesperidum* (Aldus, 1513, pp. 138–159), compose a typical didactic poem.

vows to Diana, eclogues between Corydon and Thyrsis, a malignant Faun, and a *dea ex machinâ* to close
the scene.[1] At Urbino in the carnival of 1506 Baldassare Castiglione and his friend Cesare Gonzaga
recited amœbean stanzas, attired in pastoral dress, before the Court. This eclogue, entitled *Tirsi*, deserves
notice, less perhaps for its intrinsic merits, though
these, judged by the standard of bucolic poetry, are not
slight, than because it illustrates the worst vices of the
rustic style in its adaptation to fashionable usage.[2]
The dialogue opens with the customary lament of one
love-lorn shepherd to another, and turns upon time-
honoured bucolic themes, until the mention of Metau-
rus reminds us that we are not really in Arcadia but
at Urbino. The goddess who strays among her
nymphs along its bank, is no other than the Duchess,
attended by Emilia Pia and the other ladies of her
Court. 'The good shepherd, who rules these happy
fields and holy lands,' is Duke Guidubaldo. Then follow
compliments to all the interlocutors of the *Cortegiano*.
Bembo is the shepherd, 'who hither came from the
bosom of Hadria.' The 'ancient shepherd, honoured
by all, who wears a wreath of sacred laurel,' is Morello
da Ortona. The Tuscan shepherd, 'wise and learned
in all arts,' must either be Bernardo Accolti or else
Giuliano de' Medici. And yonder shepherd from the
Mincio is Lodovico da Canossa. A chorus of shepherds and a morris-dance relieved the recitation, which
was also enlivened by the introduction of one solo,

---

[1] It was printed in 1486.
[2] See the *Poesie Volgari e Latine del Conte B. Castiglione* (Roma,
1760), pp. 7–26.

sung by Iola.   Thus in this early specimen of the
pastoral masque we observe that confusion of things
real and things ideal, of past and present, of imaginary
rustics and living courtiers, which was destined to
prove the bane of the species and to render it a literary
plague in every European capital.   The radical fault
existed in Virgil's treatment of the Syracusan idyll.
But each remove from its source rendered the falsehood more obnoxious.   In Spenser's Eclogues the
awkwardness is greater than in Castiglione's.   Before
Teresa Maria the absurdity was more apparent than
before Elizabeth.   At last the common sense of the
public could no longer tolerate the sham, and Arcadia,
with its make-believe and flattery and allegory,
became synonymous with affectation.

It is no part of my programme to follow the development of the pastoral drama through all its stages
in Italy.[1]   For the end of this chapter I reserve certain
necessary remarks upon its masterpieces, the *Aminta*
and the *Pastor Fido*.   At present it will suffice to indicate the fact that, on the stage, as in the eclogue,
bucolic poetry followed two distinct directions—the
one Arcadian and artificial, the other national and
closely modelled on popular forms.   The *Nencia da*

---

[1] To do so would be almost impossible within lesser limits than those
of a bulky volume.   Anyone who wishes to form a conception of the
multitudes of pastoral plays written and printed in Italy, may consult the
catalogues.   I have before me one list, which I do not believe to be complete, in the *Teatro Italiano*, vol. x.   It occupies twenty-seven closely-
printed pages, and is devoted solely to rural scenes of actual life.   The
Arcadian masques and plays are omitted.   Mutinelli, in the *Annali
Urbani di Venezia*, p. 541, gives a list of the shows performed at Doges'
banquets between 1574 and 1605.   The large majority are pastoral ; and
it is noticeable that, as years go on, the pastorals drive all other forms of
drama out of the field.

Barberino and *Beca da Dicomano* of Lorenzo de' Medici and Luca Pulci belong to the latter class of eclogues.[1] Their corresponding forms in dramatic verse are Berni's *Catrina* and *Mogliazzo*, together with the *Tancia* and *Fiera* of Michelangelo Buonarroti the younger.[2] If it is impossible to render any adequate account of pastoral drama, to do this for bucolic idylls would be no less difficult. Their name in Latin and Italian is legion. Poets so different in all things else as were Girolamo Benivieni, Antonio Tebaldeo, Sperone Speroni, Bernardino Baldi, Benedetto Varchi, and Luigi Tansillo—to mention only men of some distinction—brought Mopsus and Tityrus, Menalcas and Melibæus, Amaryllis and Cydippe, from Virgil's Arcadia, and made them talk interminably of their loves and sheep in delicate Italian.[3] Folengo's sharp satiric wit, as we shall remark in another chapter, finally pursued them with the shafts of ridicule in *Baldus* and *Zanitonella*. Thus pastoral poetry completed the whole cycle of Italian literature—expressed itself through dialogue in the drama, adhered to Virgilian precedent in the Latinists and their Italian followers, adopted the forms of popular poetry, and finally submitted to the degradation of Maccaronic burlesque.

We can well afford to turn in silence from the common crowd of eclogue-writers. Yet one poet emerges from the rank and file, and deserves particular attention. Francesco Maria Molza stood foremost in

---

[1] See above, Part i., pp. 381, 382.

[2] For Berni, see Barbèra's small edition, Florence, 1863. For Buonarroti, Lemonnier's edition in two volumes, 1860.

[3] See *Poesie Pastorali e Rusticali* (Milano, *Classici Italiani*, 1808), for a fairly representative collection of these authors.

his own day among scholars of ripe erudition and literary artists of accomplished skill. His high birth, his genial conversation, his loves and his misfortunes rendered him alike illustrious ; and his *Ninfa Tiberina* is still the sweetest pastoral of the golden age. Molza was born in 1489 at Modena. Since his parents were among the richest and noblest people of that city, it is probable that he acquired the Greek and Latin scholarship, for which he was in after-life distinguished, under tutors at home. At the age of sixteen he went to Rome in order to learn Hebrew, and was at once recognised as a youth of more than ordinary promise by men like Marcantonio Flamminio and Lilio Giraldi. In 1512 he returned to Modena, where he married according to his rank. His wife brought him four children, and he passed a few years at this period with his family. But Molza soon wearied of domestic and provincial retirement. In 1516 he left home again and plunged into the dissipations of Roman life. From this date forward till his death in 1544 he must be reckoned among those Italians for whom Rome was dearer than their native cities. The brilliance of his literary fame and the affection felt for him by men of note in every part of Italy will not distract attention from the ignobility of his career. Faithless to his wife, neglectful of his children, continually begging money from his father, he passed his manhood in a series of amours. Some of these were respectable, but most of them disreputable. A certain Furnia, a low-born Beatrice Paregia, and the notorious Faustina Mancina are to be mentioned among the women who from time to time enslaved him. In the course

of his intrigue with Beatrice he received a stab in the
back from some obscure rival, which put him in peril
of his life.   For Faustina he composed the *Ninfa
Tiberina*.   She was a Roman courtesan, so famous for
her beauty and fine breeding as to attract the sympathy
of even severe natures.   When she died, the town
went into mourning, and the streets echoed with elegiac lamentations.   It is curious that among Michelangelo's sonnets should be found one—not, however, of
the best—written upon this occasion.   While seeking
amusement with the Imperias, who took Aspasia's
place in Papal Rome, Molza formed a temporary
attachment for a more illustrious lady—the beautiful
and witty Camilla Gonzaga.   He passed two years,
between 1523 and 1525, in her society at Bologna.
After his return to Rome, Molza witnessed the miseries
of the sack, which made so doleful an impression on
his mind that, saddened for a moment, he retired like
the prodigal to Modena.   Rome, however, although
not destined to regain the splendour she had lost,
shook off the dust and blood of 1527 ; and there were
competent observers who, like Aretino, thought her
still more reckless in vice than she had been before.
Molza could not long resist the attractions of the Papal
city.   In 1529 we find him once more in Rome,
attached to the person of Ippolito de' Medici, and
delighting the Academies with his wit.   Two years
afterwards, his father and mother died on successive
days of August.   Molza celebrated their death in one
of the most lovely of his many sonnets.   But his ill
life and obstinate refusal to settle at Modena had disinherited him; and henceforth he lived upon his son

Camillo's bounty. To follow his literary biography at this period would be tantamount to writing the history of the two famous Academies *delle Virtù* and *de' Vignaiuoli*. Of both he was a most distinguished member. He amused them with his conversation, recited before them his *Capitoli*, and charmed them with the softness and the sweetness of his manners. Numbers of his sonnets commemorate the friendships he made in those urbane circles.

From the interchange, indeed, of occasional poems between such men as Molza, Soranzo, Gandolfo, Caro, Varchi, Guidiccioni, and La Casa, the materials for forming a just conception of the inner life of men of letters at that epoch must be drawn. They breathe a spirit of gentle urbanity, enlivened by jests, and saddened by a sense, rather uneasy than oppressive, of Italian disaster. The moral tone is pensive and relaxed ; and in spite of frequent references to a corrupt Church and a lost nation, scarcely one spark of rage or passion flashes from the dreamy eyes that gaze at us. Leave us alone, they seem to say; it is true that Florence has been enslaved, and the shadow of disgrace rests upon our Rome ; but what have we to do with it ? And then they turn to indite sonnets on Faustina's hair or elegies upon her modesty[1] ; and when they are tired with these recreations, meet together to invent ingenious obscenities.[2] It was in the midst of such trifling that the great misfortune of Molza's life befell him. The disease of the Renaissance,

---

[1] Of Molza's many sonnets upon this woman and her death, see especially Nos. cxi. cxii.

[2] In the chapter on Burlesque Poetry I shall have to justify this remark.

not the least of Italy's scourges in those latter days of heedlessness and dissolute living, overtook him in some haunt of pleasure. After 1539 he languished miserably under the infliction, and died of it, having first suffered a kind of slow paralysis, in February 1544. During the last months of his illness his thoughts turned to the home and children he had deserted. The exquisitely beautiful Latin elegy, in which he recorded the misery of slow decay, speaks touchingly, if such a late and valueless repentance can be touching, of his yearning for them.[1] In the autumn of 1543, accordingly, he managed to crawl back to Modena; and it was there he breathed his last, offering to the world, as his biographer is careful to assure us, a rare example of Christian resignation and devotion.[2] All the men of the Renaissance died in the odour of piety ; and Molza, as many of his sonnets prove, had true religious feeling. He was not a bad man, though a weak one. In the flaccidity of his moral fibre, his intellectual and æsthetical serenity, his confused and yet contented conscience, he fairly represents his age.

It would be difficult to choose between Molza's Latin and Italian poems, were it necessary to award the palm of elegance to either. Both are marked by the same *morbidezza*, the same pliancy, as of acanthus leaves that feather round the marble of some Roman ruin. Both are languid alike and somewhat tiresome, in spite of a peculiar fragrance. I have sought through upwards of 350 sonnets contained in two collections of

---

[1] See *Revival of Learning*, p. 488.

[2] The best Life of Molza is that written by Pierantonio Serassi, Bergamo, 1747. It is republished, with Molza's Italian poems, in the series of *Classici Italiani*, Milano, 1808.

his Italian works, for one with the ring of true virility,
or for one sufficiently perfect in form to bear trans-
plantation. It is not difficult to understand their
popularity during the poet's lifetime. None are deficient in touches of delicate beauty, spontaneous images,
and sentiments expressed with much lucidity. And their
rhythms are invariably melodious. Reading them, we
might seem to be hearing flutes a short way from us
played beside a rippling stream. And yet—or rather,
perhaps, for this very reason—our attention is not
rivetted. The most distinctly interesting note in them
is sounded when the poet speaks of Rome. He felt
the charm of the seven hills, and his melancholy was
at home among their ruins. Yet even upon this congenial topic it would be difficult to select a single poem
of commanding power.

The *Ninfa Tiberina* is a monody of eighty-one
octave stanzas, addressed by the poet, feigning himself
a shepherd, to Faustina, whom he feigns a nymph. It
has nothing real but the sense of beauty that inspired
it, the beauty, exquisite but soulless, that informs its
faultless pictures and mellifluous rhythms. We are in
a dreamworld of fictitious feelings and conventional
images, where only art remains sincere and unaffected.
The proper point of view from which to judge these
stanzas, is the simply æsthetic. He who would submit
to their influence and comprehend the poet's aim, must
come to the reading of them attuned by contemplation
of contemporary art. The arabesques of the Loggie,
the metal-work of Cellini, the stucchi of the Palazzo del
Te, Sansovino's bas-reliefs of fruits and garlands,
Albano's cupids, supply the necessary analogues.

Poliziano's *Giostra* demanded a similar initiation. But between the *Giostra* and the *Ninfa Tiberina* Italian art had completed her cycle from early Florence to late Rome, from Botticelli and Donatello to Giulio Romano and Cellini. The freshness of the dawn has been lost in fervour of noonday. Faustina succeeds to the fair Simonetta. Molza cannot 'recapture the first fine careless rapture' of Poliziano's morning song—so exuberant and yet so delicate, so full of movement, so tender in its sentiment of art. The *voluttà idillica*, which opened like a rosebud in the *Giostra*, expands full petals in the *Ninfa Tiberina* ; we dare not shake them, lest they fall. And these changes are indicated even by the verse. It was the glory of Poliziano to have discovered the various harmonies, of which the octave, artistically treated, is capable, and to have made each stanza a miniature masterpiece. Under Molza's treatment the verse is heavier and languid, not by reason of relapse into the negligence of Boccaccio, but because he aims at full development of its resources. He weaves intricate periods, and sustains a single sentence, with parentheses and involutions, from the opening of the stanza to its close. Given these conditions, the *Ninfa Tiberina* is all nectar and all gold.

After an exordium, which introduces

> La bella Ninfa mia, che al Tebro infiora
> Col piè le sponde,

Molza calls upon the shepherds to transfer their vows to her from Pales. She shall be made the goddess of the spring, and claim an altar by Pomona's. Here let

the rustic folk play, dance, and strive in song. Hither
let them bring their gifts.[1]

> Io dieci pomi di fin oro eletto,
> Ch' a te pendevan con soave odore,
> Simil a quel, che dal·tuo vago petto
> Spira sovente, onde si nutre amore,
> Ti sacro umil ; e se n' avrai diletto,
> Doman col novo giorno uscendo fuore,
> Per soddisfar in parte al gran disio,
> Altrettanti cogliendo a te gl' invio.

> E d' ulivo una tazza, ch' ancor serba
> Quel puro odor, che già le diede il torno,
> Nel mezzo a cui si vede in vista acerba
> Portar smarrito un giovinetto il giorno,
> E sì 'l carro guidar che accende l' erba,
> E sin al fondo i fiumi arde d' intorno,
> Stolto che mal tener seppe il viaggio,
> E il consiglio seguir fedele e saggio !

The description of the olive cup is carried over the
next five stanzas, when the poet turns to complain that
Faustina does not care for his piping. And yet Pan
joined the rustic reeds ; and Amphion breathed through
them such melody as held the hills attentive ; and
Silenus taught how earth was made, and how the

---

[1] Ten apples of fine gold, elect and rare,
　Which hung for thee, and softest perfume shed,
　Like unto that which from thy bosom fair
　Doth often breathe, whence Love is nourishéd,
　Humbly I offer; and if thou shalt care,
　To-morrow with the dawn yon fields I'll tread,
　My great desire some little to requite,
　Plucking another ten for thy delight.

　Also an olive cup, where still doth cling
　That pure perfume it borrowed from the lathe,
　Where in the midst a fair youth ruining
　Conducts the day, and with such woeful scathe
　Doth guide his car, that to their deepest spring
　The rivers burn, and burn the grasses rathe ;
　Ah fool, who knew not how to hold his way,
　Nor by that counsel leal and wise to stay !

seasons come and go, with his sweet pipings. Even
yet, perchance, she will incline and listen, if only he
can find for her some powerful charm. Come forth, he
cries, repeating the address to Galatea, leave Tiber to
chafe within his banks and hurry toward the sea. Come
to my fields and caves[1]:

> A te di bei corimbi un antro ingombra,
> E folto indora d' elicrisi nembo
> L' edera bianca, e sparge sì dolce ombra,
> Che tosto tolta a le verd' erbe in grembo
> D' ogni grave pensier te n' andrai sgombra ;
> E sparso in terra il bel ceruleo lembo,
> Potrai con l' aura, ch' ivi alberga il colle,
> Seguir securo sonno dolce e molle.

It is perilous for thee to roam the shores where Mars
met Ilia. O Father Tiber, deal gently with so fair a
maiden. It was thou who erewhile saved the infant
hope of Rome, whom the she-wolf suckled near thine
overflow ! But such themes soar too high for shepherd's
pipings. I turn to Caro and to Varchi. Both are
shepherds, who know how to stir the streams of
Mincius and Arethuse. Even the gods have lived
in forest wild, among the woods, and there Anchises
by the side of Venus pressed the flowers. What gifts
shall I find for my Faustina ? Daphnis and Mœris
are richer far than I. How can I contend with them
in presents to the fair ? And yet she heeds them
not :

[1] White ivy with pale corymbs loads for thee
That cave, and with thick folds of helichryse
Gildeth the arch it shades so lovingly ;
Here lapped in the green grass which round it lies,
Thou shalt dismiss grave thoughts, and fancy-free
Spread wide thy skirt of fair cerulean dyes,
And with the wholesome airs that haunt the hill,
Welcome sweet soothing sleep, secure from ill.

Tanto d' ogni altrui dono poco si cura
Questa vaga angioletta umile e pura.

My passion weighs upon me as love weighed on Aristæus. He forgot his flocks, his herds, his gardens, even his beehives for Eurydice. His heartache made him mad, and he pursued her over field and forest. She fled before him, but he followed [1] :

La sottil gonna in preda a i venti resta,
E col crine ondeggiando addietro torna :
Ella più ch' aura, o più che strale, presta
Per l' odorata selva non soggiorna ;
Tanto che il lito prende snella e mesta,
Fatta per paura assai più adorna :
Fende Aristeo la vagha selva anch' egli,
E la man parle aver entro i capegli.

Tre volte innanzi la man destra spinse
Per pigliar de le chiome il largo invito ;
Tre volte il vento solamente strinse,
E restò lasso senza fin schernito :
Nè stanchezza però tardollo o vinse,
Perchè tornasse il pensier suo fallito ;
Anzi quanto mendico più si sente,
Tanto s' affretta, non che il corso allente.

[1] Her rippling raiment, to the winds a prey,
Waves backward with her wavering tresses light ;
Faster than air or arrow, without stay
She through the perfumed wood pursues her flight ;
Then takes the river-bed, nor heeds delay,
Made even yet more beautiful by fright ;
Threads Aristæus, too, the forest fair,
And seems to have his hands within her hair.

Three times he thrust his right hand forth to clasp
The abundance of her curls that lured him on ;
Three times the wind alone deceived his grasp,
Leaving him scorned, with all his hopes undone ;
Yet not the toil that made him faint and gasp,
Could turn him from his purpose still unwon ;
Nay, all the while, the more his strength is spent,
The more he hurries on the course intent.

The story of Eurydice occupies twenty-nine stanzas, and with it the poem ends abruptly. It is full of carefully-wrought pictures, excessively smooth and sugared, recalling the superficial manner of the later Roman painters. Even in the passage that describes Eurydice's agony, just quoted, the forest is *odorata* or *vagha*. Fear and flight make the maiden more *adorna*. The ruffian Aristæus gets tired in the chase. He, too, must be presented in a form of elegance. Not the action, but how the action might be made a groundwork for embroidery of beauty, is the poet's care. We quit the *Ninfa Tiberina* with senses swooning under superfluity of sweetness—as though we had inhaled the breath of hyacinths in a heated chamber.

Closely allied to bucolic stands didactic poetry. The *Works and Days* of Hesiod and the *Georgics* of Virgil—the latter far more effectually, however, than the former—determined this style for the Italians. We have already seen to what extent the neo-Latin poets cultivated a form of verse that, more than any other, requires the skill of a great artist and the inspiration of true poetry, if it is to shun intolerable tedium.[1] The best didactic poems written in Latin by an Italian are undoubtedly Poliziano's *Sylvæ*, and of these the most refined is the *Rusticus*.[2] But Poliziano, in composing them, struck out a new line. He did not follow his Virgilian models closely. He chose the form of declamation to an audience, in preference to the time-honoured usage of apostrophising a patron. This

---

[1] *Revival of Learning*, chap. viii.
[2] *Ibid.* pp. 453–463.

relieves the *Sylvæ* from the absurdity of the poet's feigning to instruct a Memmius or Augustus, a Francis I. or Charles V., in matters about which those warriors and rulers can have felt but a frigid interest. Pontano's *Urania* and *De Hortis Hesperidum* are almost free from the same blemish. The former is addressed to his son Lucius, but in words so brief and simple that we recognise the propriety of a father giving this instruction to his child.[1] The latter is dedicated to Francesco Gonzaga, Marquis of Mantua, who receives complimentary panegyrics in the exordium and peroration, but does not interfere with the structure of the poem. Its chief honours are reserved, as is right and due, for Virgil [2] :—

> Dryades dum munera vati
> Annua, dum magno texunt nova serta Maroni,
> E molli violâ et ferrugineis hyacinthis,
> Quasque fovent teneras Sebethi flumina myrtos.

Pontano's greatness, here as elsewhere, is shown in his mytho-poetic faculty. The lengthy dissertation on the heavens and the lighter discourse on orange-cultivation are adorned and enlivened with innumerable legends suggested to his fertile fancy by the beauty of Neapolitan scenery. When we reach the age of Vida and Fracastoro, we find ourselves in the full tide of Virgilian imitation [3]; and it is just at this point in our

---

[1] Tu vero nate ingentes accingere ad orsus
Et mecum illustres cœli spatiare per oras,
Namque aderit tibi Mercurius, cui cœlifer Atlas
Est avus, et notas puerum puer instruet artes.
> Ed. Aldus (1513), p. 2.

[2] *Ibid.* p. 138.

[3] See *Revival of Learning*, pp. 471–481, for notices of the *Poetica, Bombyces, Scacchia* and *Syphilis*.

enquiry that the transition from Latin to Italian didactic poetry should be effected.

Giovanni Rucellai, the son of that Bernardo, who opened his famous Florentine gardens to the Platonic Academy, was born in 1475. As the author of *Rosmunda*, he has already appeared in this book. When he died, in 1526, he bequeathed a little poem on Bees to his brother Palla and his friend Gian Giorgio Trissino. Trissino and Rucellai had been intimate at Florence and in Rome. They wrote the *Sofonisba* and *Rosmunda* in generous rivalry, meeting from time to time to compare notes of progress and to recite their verses. An eye-witness related to Scipione Ammirato how ' these two dearest friends, when they were together in a room, would jump upon a bench and declaim pieces of their tragedies, calling upon the audience to decide between them on the merits of the plays.' [1] Trissino received the MS. of his friend's posthumous poem at Padua, and undertook to see it through the press. The *Api* was published at Venice in 1539.[2] What remained to be said or sung about bees after the Fourth Georgic ? Very little indeed, it must be granted. Yet the *Api* is no mere translation from Virgil ; and though the higher qualities of variety, invention and imagination were denied to Rucellai, though he can show no passages of pathos to compete with the *Corycius senex*, of humour to approach the battle of the hives, no episode, it need be hardly said, to match with *Pastor Aristæus*, still his modest poem is a monument of pure taste and classical correctness.

[1] See Morsolin's *Giangiorgio Trissino* (Vicenza, 1878), p. 92.
[2] *Ibid.* p. 245.

It is the work of a ripe scholar and melodious versifier, if not of a great singer ; and its diction belongs to the best period of polite Italian.

The same moderate praise might be awarded to the more ambitious poem of Luigi Alamanni, entitled *Coltivazione,* but for its immoderate prolixity.[1] Alamanni resolved to combine the precepts of Hesiod, Virgil and Varro, together with the pastoral passages of Lucretius, in one work, adapting them to modern usage, and producing a comprehensive treatise upon farming. With this object he divided his poem into six books, the first four devoted to the labours of the several seasons, the fifth to gardens, and the sixth to lucky and unlucky days. On a rough computation, the whole six contain some 5,500 lines. *La Coltivazione* is dedicated to Francis I., and is marred by inordinate flatteries of the French people and their king. Students who have the heart to peruse its always chaste and limpidly flowing blank verse, will be rewarded from time to time with passages like the following, in which the sad circumstances of the poet and the pathos of his regrets for Italy raise the style to more than usual energy and dignity[2] :

> Ma qual paese è quello ove oggi possa,
> Glorioso Francesco, in questa guisa
> Il rustico cultor goderse in pace
> L' alte fatiche sue sicuro e lieto ?
> Non già il bel nido ond' io mi sto lontano,
> Non già l' Italia mia ; che poichè lunge
> Ebbe, altissimo Re, le vostre insegne,
> Altro non ebbe mai che pianto e guerra.

---

[1] See *Versi e Prose di Luigi Alamanni,* 2 vols., Lemonnier, Firenze, 1859. This edition is prefaced by a Life written by Pietro Raffaelli.

[2] *Op. cit.* vol. ii. p. 210. It is the opening of the peroration to Book i.

I colti campi suoi son fatti boschi,
Son fatti albergo di selvagge fere,
Lasciati in abbandono a gente iniqua.
Il bifolco e 'l pastor non puote appena
In mezzo alle città viver sicuro
Nel grembo al suo signor ; chè di lui stesso
Che 'l devria vendicar, divien rapina . . .
Fuggasi lunge omai dal seggio antico
L' italico villan ; trapassi l' alpi ;
Truove il gallico sen ; sicuro posi
Sotto l' ali, Signor, del vostro impero.
E se quì non avrà, come ebbe altrove
Così tepido il sol, sì chiaro il cielo,
Se non vedrà quei verdi colli toschi,
Ove ha il nido più bello Palla e Pomona ;
Se non vedrà quei cetri, lauri e mirti,
Che del Partenopeo veston le piagge ;
Se del Benaco e di mill' altri insieme
Non saprà quì trovar le rive e l' onde ;
Se non l' ombra, gli odor, gli scogli ameni
Che 'l bel liguro mar circonda e bagna ;
Se non l' ampie pianure e i verdi prati
Che 'l Po, l' Adda e 'l Tesin rigando infiora,
Quì vedrà le campagne aperte e liete,
Che senza fine aver vincon lo sguardo, &c.[1]

---

[1] ' But what land is that where now, O glorious Francis, the husbandman may thus enjoy his labours with gladness and tranquillity in peace ?
Not the fair nest, from which I dwell so far away ; nay, not my Italy !
She since your ensigns, mighty king, withdrew from her, hath had nought
else but tears and war.   Her tilled fields have become wild woods, the
haunts of beasts, abandoned to lawless men.   Herdsman or shepherd can
scarce dwell secure within the city beneath their master's mantle ; for
those who should defend them, make the country folk their prey. . . .
Let Italy's husbandman fly far from his own home, pass the Alpine
barrier, seek out the breast of Gaul, repose, great lord, beneath thy
empire's pinions !   And though he shall not have the sun so warm, the
skies so clear, as he was wont to have ; though he shall not gaze upon
those green Tuscan hills, where Pallas and Pomona make their fairest
dwelling ; though he shall not see those groves of orange, laurel, myrtle,
which clothe the slopes of Parthenope ; though he shall seek in vain the
banks and waves of Garda and a hundred other lakes ; the shade, the
perfume, and the pleasant crags, which Liguria's laughing sea surrounds
and bathes ; the ample plains and verdant meadows which flower beneath
the waters of Po, Adda, and Ticino ; yet shall he behold glad fields and
open, spreading too far for eyes to follow ! '

Luigi Alamanni was the member of a noble Florentine family, who for several generations had been devoted
to the Medicean cause. He was born in 1495, and
early joined the band of patriots and scholars who
assembled in the Rucellai gardens to hear Machiavelli read his notes on Livy. After the discovery of
the conspiracy against Cardinal Giulio de' Medici, in
which Machiavelli was implicated, and which cost his
cousin Luigi di Tommaso Alamanni and his friend
Jacopo del Diacceto their lives, Luigi escaped across
the mountains by Borgo San Sepolcro to Urbino.
Finally, after running many risks, and being imprisoned
for a while at Brescia by Giulio's emissaries, he made
good his flight to France. His wife and three children
had been left at Florence. He was poor and miserable,
suffering as only exiles suffer when their home is such
a paradise as Italy. In 1527, after the expulsion of
the Medici, Luigi returned to Florence, and took an
active part in the preparations for the siege as well as
in the diplomatic negotiations which followed the fall
of the city. Alessandro de' Medici declared him a
rebel; and he was forced to avail himself again of
French protection. With the exception of a few years
passed in Italy between 1537 and 1540, the rest of his
life was spent as a French courtier. Both Francis I.
and Henri II. treated him with distinction and bounty.
Catherine de Medicis made him her master of the
household; and his son received the bishopric of
Macon. In 1556 he died at Amboise following the
Court.

Luigi Alamanni was the greatest Italian poet of
whose services Francis I. could boast, as Cellini was

the greatest Italian artist. His works are numerous, and all are marked by the same qualities of limpid facility, tending to prolixity and feebleness. Sonnets and *canzoni*, satires, romantic epics, eclogues, translations, comedies, he tried them all. His translation of the *Antigone* deserves commendation for its style. His *Flora* is curious for its attempt to reproduce the comic iambic of the Latin poets. If his satires dealt less in generalities, they might aspire to comparison with Ariosto's. As it is, the poet's bile vents itself in abstract invectives, of which the following verses upon Rome may stand for a fair specimen [1] :

> Or chi vedesse il ver, vedrebbe come
>   Più disnor tu, che 'l tuo Luter Martino,
>   Porti a te stessa, e più gravose some.
> Non la Germania, no, ma l' ozio e 'l vino,
>   Avarizia, ambizion, lussuria, e gola
>   Ti mena al fin, che già veggiam vicino.
> Non pur questo dico io, non Francia sola,
>   Non pur la Spagna, tutta Italia ancora
>   Che ti tien d' eresia, di vizi scola.
> E chi nol crede, ne dimandi ognora
>   Urbin, Ferrara, l' Orso, e la Colonna,
>   La Marca, il Romagnuol, ma più chi plora
> Per te servendo, che fu d' altri donna.

Alamanni is said to have been an admirable improvisatore ; and this we can readily believe, for his verses,

[1] Vol. i. p. 251. It is the end of the third satire. 'He who saw truly, would perceive that thyself brings on thee more dishonour than thy Martin Luther, and heavier burdens too. Not Germany, no, but sloth and wine, avarice, ambition, sensuality, and gluttony, are bringing thee to thy now near approaching end. It is not I who say this, not France alone, nor yet Spain, but all Italy, which holds thee for the school of heresy and vice. He who believes it not, let him enquire of Urbino, Ferrara, the Bear and the Column, the Marches and Romagna, yet more of her who weeps because you make her serve, who was once mistress over nations.'

even when they are most polished, flow with a placidity of movement that betrays excessive ease.

We have traced the pastoral ideal from its commencement in Boccaccio, through the *Arcadia* of Sannazzaro, Poliziano's *Orfeo*, and the didactic poets, up to the point when it was destined soon to find its perfect form in the *Aminta* and the *Pastor Fido*. Both Tasso and Guarini lived beyond the chronological limits assigned to this work. The Renaissance was finished ; and Italy had passed into a new phase of existence, under the ecclesiastical reaction which is called the Counter-Reformation. It is no part of my programme to enter with particularity into the history of the second half of the sixteenth century. And yet the subject of this and the preceding chapter would be incomplete were I not to notice the two poems which combined the drama and the pastoral in a work of art no less characteristic of the people and the age than fruitful of results for European literature. Great tragedy and great comedy were denied to the Italians. But they produced a novel species in the pastoral drama, which testified to their artistic originality, and led by natural transitions to the opera. Poetry was on the point of expiring ; but music was rising to take her place. And the imaginative medium prepared by the lyrical scenes of the Arcadian play, afforded just that generality and aloofness from actual conditions of life, which were needed by the new art in its first dramatic essays.

It would be a mistake to suppose that because the form of the Arcadian romance was artificial, it could not lend itself to the presentation of real passion when

adapted to the theatre. The study of the *Aminta*
and the *Pastor Fido* is sufficient to remove this misconception. Though the latter is the more carefully
constructed of the two, the plot in either case presents
a series of emotional situations, developed with refined art and expressed with lyrical abundance. The
rustic fable is but a veil, through which the everlasting lineaments of love are shown. Arcadia,
stripped of pedantry and affectation, has become the
ideal world of sentiment. Like amber, it encloses in
its glittering transparency the hopes and fears, the
pains and joys, which flit from heart to heart of men
and women when they love. The very conventionality
of the pastoral style assists the lyrical utterance of real
feeling. For it must be borne in mind that both
Aminta and the *Pastor Fido* are essentially lyrical.
The salt and savour of each play are in their choruses
and monologues. The dialogue, the fable and the
characters serve to supply the poet with motives for
emotion that finds vent in song. This being conceded,
it will be understood how from their scenes a whole
world of melodrama issued. Whatever may have
been the subject of an opera before the days of Gluck,
it drew its life-blood from these pastorals.

The central motive of *Aminta* and the *Pastor
Fido* is the contrast between the actual world of ambition, treachery and sordid strife, and the ideal world of
pleasure, loyalty and tranquil ease. Nature is placed
in opposition to civil society, the laws of honour to the
laws of love, the manners of Arcadia to the manners
of Italy. This cardinal motive finds its highest
utterance in Tasso's chorus on the Age of Gold :

O bella età dell' oro,
Non già perchè di latte
Sen corse il fiume, e stillò mele il bosco ;
Non perchè i frutti loro
Dier dall' aratro intatte
Le terre, e gli angui erràr senz' ira o tosco ;
Non perchè nuvol fosco
Non spiegò allor suo velo,
Ma in primavera eterna,
Ch' ora s' accende, e verna,
Rise di luce e di sereno il cielo ;
Nè portò peregrino
O guerra, o merce agli altrui lidi il pino :
Ma sol perchè quel vano
Nome senza oggetto,
Quell' idolo d' errori, idol d' inganno,
Quel che dal volgo insano
Onor poscia fu detto,
Che di nostra natura 'l feo tiranno,
Non mischiava il suo affanno
Fra le liete dolcezze
Dell' amoroso gregge ;
Nè fu sua dura legge
Nota a quell' alme in libertate avvezze :
Ma legge aurea e felice,
Che Natura scolpì, ' S' ei piace, ei lice.'

The last phrase, *S'ei piace, ei lice*, might be written on the frontispiece of both dramas, together with Dafne's sigh : *Il mondo invecchia, E invecchiando intristisce.* Of what use is life unless we love ?

Amiam, che 'l sol si muore, e poi rinasce ;
A noi sua breve luce
S' asconde, e 'l sonno eterna notte adduce.

The girl who wastes her youth in proud virginity, prepares a sad old age of vain regret :

Cangia, cangia consiglio,
Pazzarella che sei ;
Che 'l pentirsi da sezzo nulla giova.

It is the old cry of the Florentine *Canti* and *Ballate*,

'Gather ye rose-buds while ye may!' *Di doman non c' è certezza.* And the stories of *Aminta* and *Pastor Fido* teach the same lesson, that nature's laws cannot be violated, that even fate and the most stubborn bosoms bow to love.

Of the music and beauty of these two dramas, I find it difficult to speak. Before some masterpieces criticism bends in silence. We cannot describe what must be felt. All the melodies that had been growing through two centuries in Italy, are concentrated in their songs. The idyllic voluptuousness, which permeated literature and art, steeps their pictures in a golden glow. It is easy enough to object that their apparent simplicity conceals seduction, that their sentimentalism is unmanly, and their suggestions of physical beauty effeminating :—

> Ma come Silvia il riconobbe, e vide
> Le belle guance tenere d' Aminta
> Iscolorite in sì leggiadri modi,
> Che viola non è che impallidisca
> Sì dolcemente, e lui languir sì fatto,
> Che parea già negli ultimi sospiri
> Esalar l' alma ; in guisa di Baccante,
> Gridando e percotendosi il bel petto,
> Lasciò cadersi in sul giacente corpo ;
> E giunse viso a viso, e bocca a bocca.

This passage warns us that an age of *cicisbei* and *castrati* has begun, and that the Italian sensuousness has reached its final dissolution. Silvia's kisses in *Aminta*, Mirtillo's kisses in *Pastor Fido*, introduce a new refinement of enervation. Marino with his *Adone* is not distant. But, while we recognise in both these poems— the one perfumed and delicate like flowers of spring, the other sculptured in pure forms of classic grace—evident signs of a civilisation sinking to decay; though we almost loathe the beauty which relaxes every chord of manhood in the soul that feels it; we are bound to confess that to this goal the Italian genius had been steadily advancing since the publication of the *Filocopo*. The negation of chivalry, mysticism, asceticism, is accomplished. After traversing the cycle of comedy, romance, satire, burlesque poetry, the plastic arts, and invading every province of human thought, the Italian reaction against the middle ages assumes a final shape of hitherto unapprehended loveliness in the *Aminta* and the *Pastor Fido*. They complete and close the Renaissance, bequeathing in a new species of art its form and pressure to succeeding generations.

CHAPTER XIII.

THE PURISTS.

The Italians lose their Language—Prejudice against the Mother Tongue —Problem of the Dialects—Want of a Metropolis—The Tuscan Classics—Petrarch and Boccaccio—Dante Rejected—False Attitude of the Petrarchisti—Renaissance Sense of Beauty unexpressed in Lyric—False Attitude of Boccaccio's Followers—Ornamental Prose— Speron Sperone—The Dictator Bembo—His Conception of the Problem—The *Asolani*—Grammatical Essay—Treatise on the Language —Poems—Letters—Bembo's Place in the *Cortegiano*—Castiglione on Italian Style—His Good Sense—Controversies on the Language— Academical Spirit—Innumerable Poetasters—La Casa—His Life—*Il Forno*—Peculiar Melancholy—His Sonnets—Guidiccioni's Poems on Italy—Court Life—Caro and Castelvetro—Their Controversies—Castelvetro accused of Heresy—Literary Ladies—Veronica Gambara— Vittoria Colonna—Her Life—Her Friendship for Michelangelo—Life of Bernardo Tasso—His *Amadigi* and other Works—Life of Giangiorgio Trissino—His Quarrel with his Son Giulio—His Critical Works—The *Italia Liberata.*

IT was the misfortune of the Italians that, when culture had become national and the revival of the vulgar literature had been effected, they found themselves in nearly the same relation to their own language as to Latin. After more than a hundred years absorbed in humanistic studies, the authors of the fourteenth century were hardly less remote than the Augustan classics; and to all but Tuscans their diction was almost foreign. At the beginning of the *cinque cento*, the living mother-tongue of Italy which Dante sought—the *Vulgare, quod superius venabamur, quod in qualibet redolet civitate, nec cubat in ulla*—was still to seek.   Since the composition of Dante's essay *De Vulgari Eloquio*, the literary activity of the nation had, indeed, created a desire for some fixed standard of style in modern speech.   But the experiments of the *quattro cento* had not far advanced the matter.   They only proved that Tuscan was the dialect to imitate, and that success in the future must depend on adherence to the Tuscan authors.   Hence it happened that Petrarch and Boccaccio came to be studied with the same diligence, the same obsequious reverence, as Cicero and Virgil.   Italian was written with no less effort after formal purity, no less minute observance of rules, than if it had been a dead language.   At the same time, as a consequence of this system, the vices of the humanistic style—its tendency to servile imitation, emptiness, rhetorical verbosity, and preference of form to matter—were imported into the vernacular literature.

While noting these drawbacks, which attended the resurgence of Italian at an epoch when the whole nation began to demand a common language, we must give due credit to the sagacity displayed by scholars at that epoch in grappling with the problem before them.   The main points at issue were, *firstly* to overcome the prejudice against the mother tongue, which still lingered among educated people ; *secondly*, to adjust Italian to the standards of taste established by the humanistic movement ; and, *thirdly*, to decide whether Tuscan should reign supreme, or be merged in a speech more representative of the Italians as a nation.   Early in the century, the battle of Italian against Latin was practically won.   There remained no obstinate antagonism to a purely national and modern literature. Still the type to which this literature should conform, the laws by which it should be regulated, were as yet unsettled. These questions had to be decided by intelligence rather than by instinct; for the Italians possessed no common medium of conversation, no common opportunities of forensic or parliamentary debate. That insensible process whereby French style has been modelled on the usages of conversation, and English style has been adapted to the tone of oratory, had to be performed, so far as this was possible, by conscious analysis. The Italians were aware that they lacked a language, and they set themselves deliberately to remedy this defect. These peculiar circumstances gave a pedantic tone to the discussion of the problem. Yet the problem itself was neither puerile nor pedantic. It concerned nothing less than the formation of an instrument of self-expression for a people, who had reached the highest grade of artistic skill in the exercise of the dead languages, and who, though intellectually raised to an equality of culture, were divided by tenacious local differences.

That Petrarch and Boccaccio should have been chosen as models of classical Italian style, was not only natural but inevitable. Writers, trained in the method of the humanists, required the guidance of authoritative masters. Just as they used Cicero and Virgil for the correction of medieval Latin, so Petrarch and Boccaccio were needed for the castigation of homespun dialects. Dante, had he been comprehended by such men, would not have satisfied ears educated in the niceties of Latin versification; nor could the builders of Ciceronian perorations have revived the simple prose of the Villani. Petrarch contented their sense of polish; Boccaccio supplied them with intricate periods and cadences of numerous prose. Yet the choice was in either case unfortunate, though for somewhat different reasons.

It was impossible for poets of the sixteenth century to follow Petrarch to the very letter of his diction, without borrowing his tone. Consequently these versifiers affected to languish and adore, wove conceits and complained of cruelty, in the fashion of Vaucluse. Their facile mistresses became Lauras; or else they draped a lay-figure, and wrote sonnets to its painted eyebrows. The confusion between literary ceremony and practical experience of passion wrought an ineradicable discord. Authors of indecent burlesques penned Platonic odes. Bembo, who was answerable for the *Menta* in its Latin form, praised his mistress Morosina in polished sonnets and elegiac threnodies. Firenzuola published the poems to Selvaggia and the *Capitolo* in praise of a specific against infamous diseases. La Casa gratified the same Academies with his panegyric of the Oven and his scholastic exercises in a metaphysical emotion. Reading these diverse compositions side by side, we wake to the ·conviction that the Petrarchistic counterfeits, however excellent in form, have precisely the same mediocrity as Sannazzaro's epic, while the Bernesque effusions express the crudest temper of the men who wrote them. The one class of poems is redolent of affectation, the other of coarse realism. The middle term between these opposites is wanting. Nor could it well be otherwise. The conditions of society in the sixteenth century rendered Petrarch's sentiment impossible. His melancholy, engendered by the contest between passion and religious duty, had become a thing of the far past. The licence of the times rendered this halting between two impulses ridiculous, when no man was found to question the divine right of natural appetite. Even the reverential attitude assumed by Petrarch as a lover, was out of date ; and when his imitators aped it, their insincerity was patent. The highest enthusiasm of the Renaissance revealed itself through the plastic arts in admiration for corporeal beauty. This feeling, while it easily degenerated into sensuality, had no point of contact with Petrarch's medieval Platonism. Therefore the tone of the Petrarchisti was hypocritical, and the love they professed, a sham.

We have a further reason for resenting this devotion to a poet with whose habitual mood the men of that age could not sympathise. We know that they had much to say which remained buried beneath their fourteenth-century disguises. The sincerity of feeling, the fervid passion of poets like Bembo, Molza, or La Casa, cannot be denied. But their emotion found no natural channel of expression. It is not without irritation that we deplore the intellectual conditions of an age, which forced these artists to give forth what they felt in one of two equally artificial forms. Between transcription from the Latin elegists and reproduction of Petrarch there lay for them no choice. Consequently, the Renaissance lacked its full development upon the side of lyric poetry. The secret of the times remained unspoken—a something analogous to Venetian painting, a something indicated in Firenzuola's and Luigini's dialogues on female beauty, a something indirectly presented in Ariosto's episodes, which ought to have been uttered from the heart in song by men who felt the loveliness of plastic form. Instead of this lyrical expression of a ruling passion, we have to content ourselves with pseudo-platonic rhymes and with the fervid sensualities of Pontano's elegiacs. The sensibility to corporeal beauty, which was abundantly represented by Titian, Lionardo, Raphael, Correggio, Michelangelo in art, in literature was either shorn of its essential freedom by the limitations of conventional Platonism, or exaggerated on the side of animalism by imitation of erotic Latin poets. Furthermore, we have some right to regard the burlesque obscenity of academical literature as a partial reaction against the hypocritical refinements of the Petrarchistic mannerism. Thus the deepest instinct of the epoch, that which gave its splendour to the painting of the golden age, found no spontaneous utterance in lyric verse.

The academical study of Boccaccio proved disastrous for a different reason. In this case there was no division between the master and his pupils ; for we have seen already that the author of the Decameron anticipated the Renaissance in the scope and tenor of his work. But he supplied students with a false standard. His Latinising periods, his involved construction of sentences and oratorical amplification of motives encouraged the worst qualities of humanistic style. Boccaccio prevented the Italians from forming a masculine prose manner. Each writer, whatever

might be the subject of his work, aimed at ornate
diction.   Cumbrous and circuitous phrases were
admired for their own sake. The simplicity of the
Chronicles was abandoned for ponderous verbosity, and
Machiavelli's virile force found no successors in the
crowd of academicians who dissected the Decameron
for flowers of rhetoric.

Thus the efforts of the purists took a false direction
from the outset both in prose and verse. The literature which aimed at being national, began with
archaistic exercises; and Italy, at the moment of
attaining self-consciousness, found herself, without a
living language, forced to follow in the steps of
antiquated authors. The industry and earnestness of
the disciples made their failure the more notable; for
while they pursued a track that could not lead to aught
but mannerism, they plumed themselves upon the
soundness of their method. In order to illustrate the
spirit of this movement, I will select a passage from
the works of Speron Sperone, who was by no means
the least successful stylist of the period. He is describing his earlier essays in the art of writing and the
steps by which he arrived at what he clearly thought
to be perfection [1]:

'Being in all truth desirous beyond measure from
my earliest years to speak and to write my thoughts in
our mother tongue, and that not so much with a view
to being understood, which lies within the scope of
every unlettered person, as with the object of placing

[1] I Dialoghi di Messer Speron Sperone (Aldus, Venice, 1542), p. 146.
The passage is taken from a Dialogue on Rhetoric. I have tried to
preserve the clauses of the original periods.

my name upon the roll of famous men, I neglected
every other interest, and gave my whole attention to
the reading of Petrarch and the hundred Novels ; in
which studies having exercised myself for many months
with little profit and without a guide, under the inspiration of God I finally betook me to our revered
Master Trifone Gabrielli [1] ; by whose kindly assist-
ance I arrived at perfect comprehension of those
authors, whom, through ignorance of what I ought to
notice, I had frequently before misunderstood. This
excellent man and true father of ours first bade me
observe the vocables, then gave me rules for knowing
the declension and conjugation of nouns and verbs in
Tuscan, and lastly explained to me articles, pronouns,
participles, adverbs, and other parts of speech ; so
that, collecting all that I had learned, I composed a
grammar for myself, by following the which while
writing I so controlled my style that in a short space of
time the world held me for a man of erudition, and
still considers me as such. When it seemed to me
that I had taken rank as a grammarian, I set myself,
with the utmost expectation of everyone who knew
me, to the making of verses; and then, my head full
of rhythms, sentences and words from Petrarch and
Boccaccio, for a few years, I produced things that
appeared wonderful to my judgment ; but afterwards,
thinking that my vein was beginning to dry up (inas-

---

[1] Trifone Gabrielli was a Venetian, celebrated for his excellent morals
no less than for his learning. He gained the epithet of the Socrates of
his age, and died in 1549. His personal influence seems to have been
very great. Bembo makes frequent and respectful references to him in
his letters, and Giasone de Nores wrote a magnificent panegyric of him
in the preface to his commentary on Horace's *Ars Poetica*, which he professed to have derived orally from Trifone.

into particulars. He carries it through the several topics of tautology, periphrasis, antithesis, and proportion of syllables in words of different length; after which the subject of prosody proper is discussed. Having finished with Petrarch, he then proceeds to render the same account of his studies in Boccaccio, observing the variety and choice of his phrases, but calling special attention to the numbers of his periods, and winding up with this sonorous sentence on prose architecture. 'But you must know that as the composition of prose is a marshalling of the sounds of words in proper order, so its numbers are certain orders in their syllables; pleasing the ear wherewith, the art of oratory opens, continues and finishes a period : forasmuch as every clause has not only a beginning but also a middle and an end; at the beginning it puts itself in motion and ascends ; in the middle, as though weary with exertion, it rests upon its feet awhile ; then it descends, and flies to the conclusion for repose.'[1]

What is admirable, in spite of pedantry and servility, in this lengthy diatribe is the sense of art as art, the devotion to form for its own sake, the effort to grapple with the problems of style, the writer's single-hearted seeking after perfection. Nothing but a highly-developed artistic instinct in the nation could have produced students of this type. At the same time we feel an absence of spontaneity,

---

[1] It should be mentioned that the passage I have paraphrased is put into the lips of Antonio Broccardo, a Venetian poet, whose *Rime* were published in 1538. He attacked Bembo's works, and brought down upon himself such a storm of fury from the pedants of Padua and Venice that he took to his bed and died of grief.

and the tendency to aim at decorative writing is apparent. When the glow of discovery, which impelled Sperone and his fellow-pioneers to open a way across the continent of literature, had failed; when the practice of their school had passed into precepts, and their inventions had been formulated as canons of style; nothing remained for travellers upon this path but frigid repetition, precise observance of conventional limitations, and exercises in sonorous oratory. The rhetoric of the seventeenth century was a necessary outgrowth of pedantic purism. The conceits of Marini and his imitators followed inevitably from a rigorous application of rules that denied to poetry the right of natural expression. It may be urged that for a nation so highly sensitive to form as the Italians, without a metropolis to mould the language in the process of development, and without a spoken dialect of good society, there existed no common school of style but the recognised classics of Tuscany.[1] When each district habitually used a different speech for private and public utterance, men could not write as they talked, and they were therefore forced to write by rule. There is force in these arguments. Yet the

---

[1] The difficulty is well put by one of the interlocutors in Castiglione's dialogue upon the courtier (ed. Lemonnier, p. 41): 'Oltre a questo, le consuetudini sono molto varie, nè è città nobile in Italia che non abbia diversa maniera di parlar da tutte l' altre. Però non vi ristringendo voi a dichiarar qual sia la migliore, potrebbe l'uomo attaccarsi alla bergamasca così come alla fiorentina.' Messer Federigo Fregoso of Genoa is speaking, and he draws the conclusion which practically triumphed in Italy : 'Parmi adunque, che a chi vuol fuggir ogni dubio ed esser ben sicuro, sia necessario proporsi ad imitar uno, il quale di consentimento di tutti sia estimato buono . . . e questo (nel volgar dico), non penso che abbia da esser altro che il Petrarca e 'l Boccaccio ; e chi da questi dui si discosta, va tentoni, come chi cammina per le tenebre e spesso erra la strada.'

consequences of a too minute and fastidious study of the Tuscan authors proved none the less fatal to the freedom of Italian literature ; and, what is more, sagacious critics foresaw the danger, though they were unable to avert it.

The leader in this movement, acknowledged throughout Italy for more than half a century as dictator in the republic of letters, 'foster-father of the language' (*balio della lingua*), 'guide and master of our tongue' (*guida e maestro di questa lingua*), was Pietro Bembo.[1] Though only sixteen years junior to Angelo Poliziano, whom he had himself saluted as 'ruler of the Ausonian lyre,' Bembo outlived his master for the space of fifty-one years, and swayed the literary world at a period when Italian succeeded to the honours of Latin scholarship.[2] He was a Venetian. This fact is not insignificant, since it clearly marks the change that had come over the nation, when the sceptre of learning was transferred to the northern provinces, and the exclusive privilege of correct Italian composition was shared with Tuscans by men of other dialects.[3] In his early youth Bembo had the good sense to perceive that the mother tongue was no less worthy of cultivation than Greek and Latin. The arguments

---

[1] In the famous passage of the *Furioso* where Ariosto pronounces the eulogy of the poets of his day, he mentions Bembo thus (*Orl. Fur.* xlvi. 15).

Pietro

Bembo, che 'l puro e dolce idioma nostro,
Levato fuor del volgar uso tetro,
Quale esser dee, ci ha co 'l suo esempio mostro.

[2] See Bembo's elegy on Poliziano quoted by me in the *Revival of Learning*, p. 484.

[3] See *Revival of Learning*, p. 506, for the transference of scholarship to Lombardy.

advanced by Dante, by Alberti, by Lorenzo de' Medici, recurred with fresh force to his mind. He therefore made himself the champion of Italian against those exclusive students who, like Ercole Strozzi, still contended that the dead languages were alone worthy of attention.[1] He also saw that it was necessary to create a standard of correct style for writers who were not fortunate enough to have been born within the bounds of Tuscany. Accordingly, he devoted himself to the precise and formal study of fourteenth-century literature, polishing his own Italian compositions with a diligence that, while it secured transparent purity of diction, deprived them of originality and impulse. It is said that he passed each of his works through forty successive revisions, keeping as many portfolios to represent the stages at which they had arrived.

Having already sketched the life of Bembo, I shall here restrict myself to remarks upon those of his works which were influential in reviving the practice of Italian composition.[2] Among these the first place must be awarded to *Gli Asolani*, a dialogue on Love, written in his early manhood and dedicated to Lucrezia Borgia. The beauty of its language and the interest of the theme discussed rendered this treatise widely fashionable. Yet it is not possible to study it with pleasure now. Those Platonic conversations, in which the refined society of the Italian Courts delighted, have

---

[1] See the Latin hendecasyllables quoted by me in the *Revival of Learning*, p. 415, and the Defence of Italian in the treatise 'Della volgare Lingua' (Bembo, *Opere*, Milan, *Class. It.* x. 28). Carducci in his essay *Delle Poesie Latine di Ludovico Ariosto*, pp. 179–181, gives some interesting notices of Ercole Strozzi's conversion to the vulgar tongue.

[2] See *Revival of Learning*, pp. 410–415, 481–485.

lost their attraction for us. Nothing but the charming description of Asolo, where the Queen of Cyprus had her garden, surrounded by trimmed laurels and divided crosswise with a leafy *pergola* of vines, retains its freshness. That picture, animated by the figures of the six novitiates of Love, now sauntering through shade and sunlight under the vine-branches, now seated on the grass to hear a lute or viol deftly touched, is in the best idyllic style of the Venetian masters. At the Court of Urbino, where Bembo was residing when his book appeared, it was received with acclamation, as a triumph of divine genius. The illustrious circle celebrated by Castiglione in his *Cortegiano* perused it with avidity, and there is no doubt that the publication gave a powerful impulse to Italian studies. These were still further fostered by Bembo's Defence of the Vulgar Tongue.[1] He had secured the hearing of the world by his *Asolani*. Women and the leaders of fashionable society were with him ; and he pushed his arguments home against the Latinising humanists. ' To abandon our own language for another,' he reminded them, ' is the same as withdrawing supplies from our mother to support a strange woman.' This phrase is almost identical with what Dante had written on the same topic two centuries earlier. But Bembo's standing-ground was different from Dante's. The poet of the fourteenth century felt called to create a language for his nation. The student of the sixteenth, imbued with the assimilative principles of scholarship, too fastidious to risk a rough note in his style, too feeble to attempt a new act of creation, was content to

---

[1] *Opere del Cardinale Bembo (Class. It.* Milano, 1808, vol. x.).

'affect the fame of an imitator.'[1] His piety toward
the mother-tongue was generous; his method of rehabilitation was almost servile.

With the view of illustrating his practice by precepts, Bembo published a short Italian grammar, or
compendium of *Regole Grammaticali.* It went through
fourteen editions, and formed the text-book for future
discussions of linguistic problems. Though welcomed
with enthusiasm, this first attempt to reduce Italian to
system was severely criticised, especially by Sannazzaro,
Caro, Castelvetro and the Florentine Academy.

I have already had occasion to observe that, as a
Latin poet, Bembo succeeded best with memorial
verses. The same may be said about his Italian
poems. The *Canzoni* on the death of his brother, and
that on the death of his mistress Morosina, are justly
celebrated for their perfection of form ; nor are they
so wanting in spontaneous emotion as many of his
Petrarchistic exercises. Bembo was tenderly attached
to this Morosina, whom he first met at Rome, and with
whom he lived till her death at Padua in 1525. She
was the mother of his three children, Lucilio, Torquato
and Elena. The *Canzone* in question, beginning :

> Donna, de' cui begli occhi alto diletto :

was written so late as 1539, three months after Bembo
had been raised to the dignity of Cardinal.[2] As a
specimen of the conceits which he tolerated in poetry,
I have thought it worth while to present the following
translation of a sonnet [3] :

---

[1] See his Latin treatise *De Imitatione.* It is in the form of an epistle.
[2] See Panizzi, *Boiardo ed Ariosto,* vi. lxxxi.
[3] Sonnet xxxvi. of his collected poems.

Ah me, at one same moment forced to cry
  And hush, to hope and fear, rejoice and grieve,
  The service of one master seek and leave,
  Over my loss laugh equally and sigh !
My guide I govern ; without wings I fly ;
  With favouring winds, to rocks and sandbanks cleave ;
  Hate haughtiness, yet meekness misbelieve ;
  Mistrust all men, nor on myself rely.
I strive to stay the sun, set snows on fire ;
  Yearn after freedom, run to take the yoke ;
  Defend myself without, but bleed within ;
Fall, when there's none to lift me from the mire ;
  Complain, when plaints are vain, of fortune's stroke ;
  And power, being powerless, from impuissance win.

In the sixteenth century verses of this stamp passed for masterpieces of incomparable elegance. The same high value was set on Bembo's familiar letters. He wrote them with a view to publication, and they were frequently reprinted during the course of the next fifty years.[1] These may still be read with profit by students for the light they cast upon Italian society during the first half of the *cinque cento*, and with pleasure by all who can appreciate the courtesies of refined breeding expressed in language of fastidious delicacy. The chief men of the day, whether Popes, princes, Cardinals or poets, and all the illustrious ladies, including Lucrezia Borgia, Veronica Gambara, and Vittoria Colonna, are addressed with a mingled freedom and ceremony, nicely graduated according to their rank or degree of intimacy, which proves the exquisite tact developed by the intercourse of Courts in men like Bembo.

Since the composition and publication of such letters

---

[1] My edition is in four volumes, Gualtero Scotto, Vinegia, MDLII. They are collected with copious additions in the *Classici Italiani*.

formed a main branch of literary industry in the period we have reached,[1] it will be well to offer some examples of Bembo's epistolary style ; and for this purpose, the correspondence with Lucrezia Borgia may be chosen, not only because of the interest attaching to her friendship with the author, but also because the topics treated display the refinement of his nature in a very agreeable light.[2] In one of these, written upon the occasion of her father's death, he calls Alexander VI. *quel vostro così gran padre.* In a second, touched with the deepest personal feeling, he announces the death of his own brother Carlo, *mio solo e caro fratello, unico sostegno e sollazzo della vita mia.*[3] In a third he thanks her for her letters of condolence : *Le lagrime alle quali mi scrivete essere stata constretta leggendo nelle mie lettere la morte del mio caro e amato fratello M. Carlo, sono dolcissimo refrigerio stato al mio dolore, se cosa dolce alcuna m' è potuta venire a questo tempo.* In a fourth he turns this graceful compliment : *Pregherei eziandio il cielo, che ogni giorno v' accrescerebbe la bellezza ; ma considero che non vi se ne può aggiungere.* In a fifth he congratulates Lucrezia upon the birth of a son and heir, and in a sixth condoles with her upon his early death. Then another boy is born, just when the Duke of Urbino dies ; and Bembo mingles courtly tears with

---

[1] It will be impossible to do more than make general reference to the vast masses of Italian letters printed in the sixteenth century. I must, therefore, content myself here with mentioning the collections of La Casa, Caro, Bernardo, and Torquato Tasso, Aretino, Guidiccioni, together with the miscellanies published under the titles of *Lettere Scritte al Signor Pietro Aretino*, the *Lettere Diverse* in three books (Aldus, 1567), and the *Lettere di Tredici Uomini Illustri* (Venetia, 1554).

[2] *Lettere*, ed. cit. vol. iv. pp. 1–31.

[3] Another letter, dated Venice, August 1, 1504, is fuller in particulars about this dearly-loved brother.

ceremonious protestations of his joy. It would be impossible to pen more scholarly exercises upon similar occasions; and through the style of the professed epistolographer we seem to feel that Bembo had real interest in the events he illustrates so elegantly. The fatal defect of his letters is, that he is always thinking more of his manner than of his matter. Like the humanists from whom he drew his mental lineage, he laboured for posterity without reckoning on the actual demands posterity would make. Success crowned his efforts in the pleasure he afforded to the public of his day; but this was a success comparable with that of Bernardo Accolti or Tibaldeo of Ferrara, whom he scorned. He little thought that future students would rate an annalist of Corio's stamp, for the sake of his material, at a higher value than the polished author of the *Lettere*. Yet such is the irony of fame that we could willingly exchange Bembo's nicely-turned phrases for a few solid facts, a few spontaneous effusions.

Bembo was a power in literature, the exact force of which it is difficult to estimate without taking his personal influence into consideration. Distinguished by great physical beauty, gifted with a noble presence, cultivated in the commerce of the best society, he added to his insight and his mental energy all the charm that belongs to a man of fashion and persuasive eloquence in conversation. He was untiring in his literary industry, unfailing in his courtesy to scholars, punctual in correspondence, and generous in the use he made of his considerable wealth. At Urbino, at Venice, at Rome, and at Padua, his study was the meeting-place of learned men, who found the graces of the highest aristocracy combined in him with genial enthusiasm for the common interests of letters. Thus the man did even more than the author to promote the revolution he had at heart. This is brought home to us with force when we consider the place assigned to him in Castiglione's *Cortegiano*—a masterpiece of composition transcending, in my opinion, all the efforts made by Bembo to conquer the difficulties of style. Castiglione is no less correct than the dictator strove to be; but at the same time he is far more natural. He treats the same topics with greater ease, and with a warmth of feeling and conviction which endears him to the heart of those who read his golden periods. Yet Castiglione gives the honours of his dialogue to the author of the *Asolani*, when he puts into the mouth of Bembo that glowing panegyric of Platonic love, which forms the close and climax of his dialogue upon the qualities of a true gentleman.[1]

The crowning merit of the *Cortegiano* is an air of good breeding and disengagement from pedantic prejudices. This urbanity renders it a book to read with profit and instruction through all time. Castiglione's culture was the result of a large experience of men and books, ripened by intercourse with good society in all its forms. His sense and breadth of view are peculiarly valuable when he discusses a subject like that which forms the topic of the present chapter. There is one passage in his book, relating to the pro-

---

[1] *Il Cortegiano* (ed. Lemonnier, Firenze, 1854), pp. 296–303. I have already spoken at some length about this essay in the *Age of the Despots*, pp. 116–127, and have narrated the principal events of Castiglione's life in the *Revival of Learning*, pp. 418–422. For his Latin poems see *ib.* pp. 490–497.

blem of Italian style, which, had it been treated with
the attention it deserved, might have saved his fellow-
countrymen from the rigours of pedagogical despotism.[1]

Starting from his cardinal axiom that good manners
demand freedom from all affectation, he deprecates the
use in speech or writing of those antiquated Tuscan
words the purists loved. As usual, he hits the very
centre of the subject in his comments on this theme.
' It seems to me, therefore, exceedingly strange to
employ words in writing which we avoid in all the
common usages of conversation. Writing is nothing
but a form of speaking, which continues to exist after
a man has spoken, and is, as it were, an image or
rather the life of the words .he utters. Therefore in
speech, which, as soon as the voice has issued from
the mouth, is lost, some things may be tolerated that
are not admissible in composition, because writing pre-
serves the words, subjects them to the criticism of the
reader, and allows time for their mature consideration.
It is consequently reasonable to use greater diligence
with a view to making what we write more polished
and correct, yet not to do this so that the written
words shall differ from the spoken, but only so that the
best in spoken use shall be selected for our composition.'
After touching on the need of lucidity, he proceeds :
' I therefore should approve of a man's not only avoiding antiquated Tuscan phrases, but also being careful
to employ such as are in present use in Tuscany and
other parts of Italy, provided they have a certain
grace and harmony.'[2] At this point another inter-

---

[1] Ed. cit. pp. 39–53.
[2] Ariosto's style was formed on precisely these principles.

locutor in the dialogue observes that Italy possesses
no common language. In the difficulty of knowing
whether to follow the custom of Florence or of Bergamo, it is desirable to recognise a classical standard of
style. Petrarch and Boccaccio should be selected as
models. To refuse to imitate them is mere presump-
tion. Here Castiglione states the position of the school
he combats. In his answer to their argument he
makes Giuliano de' Medici, one of the company, declare
that he, a Tuscan of the Tuscans as he is, should never
think of employing any words of Petrarch or Boccaccio which were obsolete in good society. Then the
thread of exposition is resumed. The Italian language,
in spite of its long past, may still be called young and
unformed. When the Roman Empire decayed, spoken
Latin suffered from the corruptions introduced by bar-
barian invaders. It retained greater purity in Tuscany
than elsewhere. Yet other districts of Italy preserved
certain elements of the ancient language that have a
right to be incorporated with the living tongue ; nor
is it reasonable to suppose that a modern dialect
should at a certain moment have reached perfection
any more than Latin did. The true rule to follow is
to see that a man has something good to say. ' Making
a division between thoughts and words is much the
same as separating soul and body. In order, therefore,
to speak or write well, our courtier must have knowledge ; for he who has none, and whose mind is void
of matter worthy to be apprehended, has nought to
say or write.' He must be careful to clothe his
thoughts in select and fitting words, but above all
things to use such 'as are still upon the lips of the

people.' He need not shun foreign phrases, if there
be a special force in them above their synonyms in his
own language. Nor is there cause to fear lest the
vulgar tongue should prove deficient in resources when
examined by grammarians and stylists. ' Even though
it be not ancient Tuscan of the purest water, it will be
Italian, common to the nation, copious and varied,
like a delicious garden full of divers fruits and flowers.'
Here Castiglione quotes the precedent of Greek, showing that each of its dialects contributed something to
the common stock, though Attic was recognised as
sovereign for its polish. Among the Romans likewise,
Livy was not tabooed because of his patavinity, nor
Virgil because the Romans recognised a something in
him of rusticity. ' We, meanwhile, far more severe
than the ancients, impose upon ourselves certain new-
fangled laws that have no true relation to the object.
With a beaten track before our eyes, we try to walk
in bypaths. We take a wilful pleasure in obscurity,
though our language, like all others, is only meant to
express our thoughts with force and clearness. While
we call it the popular speech, we plume ourselves on
using phrases that are not only unknown to the people,
but unintelligible to men of birth and learning, and
which have fallen out of conversation in every district
of the land.' If Petrarch and Boccaccio were living at
our epoch, they would certainly omit words that have
fallen out of fashion since their days ; and it is mere
impertinence for a purist to tell me that I ought to say
Campidoglio instead of *Capitolio* and so forth, because
some elder Tuscan author wrote it, or the peasants of
the Tuscan district speak it so. You argue that only

pride prevents our imitating Petrarch and Boccaccio. But pray inform me whom they imitated? To model Latin poems upon Virgil or Catullus is necessary, because Latin is a dead language. But since Italian is alive and spoken, let us write it as we use it, with due attention to artistic elegance. ' The final master of style is genius, and the ultimate guide is a sound natural judgment.' Do we require all our painters to follow one precedent? Lionardo, Mantegna, Raphael, Michelangelo, Giorgione have struck out different paths of excellence in art. Writers should claim the same liberty of choice, the same spontaneity of inspiration. ' I cannot comprehend how it should be right, instead of enriching Italian and giving it spirit, dignity and lustre, to make it poor, attenuated, humble and obscure, and so to pen it up within fixed limits as that everyone should have to copy Petrarch and Boccaccio. Why should we, for example, not put equal faith in Poliziano, Lorenzo de' Medici, Francesco Diaceto, and others who are Tuscan too, and possibly of no less learning and discretion than were Petrarch and Boccaccio? However, there are certain scrupulous persons abroad nowadays, who make a religion and ineffable mystery of their Tuscan tongue, frightening those who listen to them, to the length of preventing many noble and lettered men from opening their lips, and forcing them to admit they do not know how to talk the language they learned from their nurses in the cradle.' [1]

[1] The preface to the *Cortegiano* may be compared with this passage. When it appeared, the critics complained that Castiglione had not imitated Boccaccio. His answer is marked by good sense and manly logic :

If the Italians could have accepted Castiglione's principles, and approached the problem of their language in his liberal spirit, the nation would have been spared its wearisome, perpetually recurrent quarrel about words. But the matter had already got into the hands of theorists ; and local jealousies were inflamed. The municipal wars of the middle ages were resuscitated on the ground of rhetoric and grammar. Unluckily, the quarrel is not over ; *adhuc sub judice lis est*, and there is no judge to decide it. But in the nineteenth century it no longer rages with the violence that made it a matter of duels, assassinations and lifelong hatreds in the sixteenth. The Italians have recently secured for the first time in their history the external conditions which are necessary to a natural settlement of the dispute by the formation of a common speech through common usage. The parliament, the army, the newspapers of United Italy are rapidly creating a language adequate to all the needs of modern life ; and though purists may still be found, who maintain that Passavanti's *Specchio* is a model of style for leading articles in *Fanfulla*, yet the nation, having passed into a new phase of existence, must be congratulated on having exchanged the 'golden simplicity of the *trecento*' for a powerful and variously-coloured instrument of self-expression.

To stir the dust of those obsolete controversies on the language of Italy—to make extracts from Varchi's, Sperone's or Bembo's treatises upon the Tongues—to

---

see pp. 3, 4. With Castiglione, Aretino joined hands, the ruffian with the gentleman, in this matter of revolt against the purists. See the chapter in this volume upon Aretino.

set Tolommei's claims for Tuscan priority in the balance against Muzio's more modest pleas in favour of Italian [1]—to describe how one set of scholars argued that the vernacular ought to be called Tuscan, how another dubbed it Florentine or Sienese, and how a third, more sensible, voted for Italian [2]—to enumerate the blasts and counterblasts of criticism blown about each sentence in Boccaccio and Petrarch [3]—to resuscitate the orthographical encounters between Trissino and Firenzuola on the matter of the letter K—is no part of my present purpose. It must suffice to have noted that these problems occupied the serious attention of the literary world, and to have indicated by extracts from Sperone and Castiglione the extreme limits of pedantry and sound sense between which the opinion of the learned vibrated. The details of the quarrel may be left to the obscurity of treatises, long since doomed to 'dust and an endless darkness.'

Much unprofitable expenditure of time and thought upon verbal questions of no vital interest was encouraged by the Academies, which now began to sprout like mushrooms in all towns of Italy.[4] The old

---

[1] Varchi's *Ercolano* or *Dialogo delle Lingue*; Sperone's dialogue *Delle Lingue*; Claudio Tolommei's *Cesano*; Girolamo Muzio's *Battaglie*.

[2] Varchi called it *Fiorentina*, Tolommei and Salviati *Toscana*, Bargagli *Senese*, Trissino and Muzio *Italiana*. Castiglione and Bembo agreed in aiming at Italian rather than pure Tuscan, but differed in their proposed method of cultivating style. Bembo preferred to call the language *Volgare*, as it was the common property of the *Volgo*. Castiglione suggested the title *Cortigiana*, as it was refined and settled by the usage of Courts. Yet Castiglione was more liberal than Bembo in acknowledging the claims of local dialects.

[3] For a list of commentators upon Petrarch at this period, see Tiraboschi, lib. iii. cap. iii., section 1. Common sense found at last sarcastic utterance in Tassoni.

[4] See *Revival of Learning*, pp. 365–368.

humanistic societies, founded by Cosimo de' Medici, Pomponius Lætus, Pontano, and Aldo for the promotion of classical studies, had done their work and died away. Their successors, the Umidi of Florence, the Pellegrini of Venice, the Eterei of Padua, the Vignaiuoli of Rome, professed to follow the same objects, with special attention to the reformation of Italian literature. Yet their very titles indicate a certain triviality and want of manly purpose. They were clubs combining conviviality with the pursuit of study; and it too frequently happened that the spirit of their jovial meetings extended itself to the *dicerie, cicalate* and *capitoli* recited by their members, when the cloth was drawn and the society sat down to intellectual banquets. At the same time the Academies were so fashionable and so universal that they gave the tone to literature. It was the ambition of all rising students to be numbered with the more illustrious bodies; and when a writer of promise joined one of these, he naturally felt the influence of his companions. Member vied with member in producing sonnets and rhetorical effusions on the slenderest themes; for it was less an object to probe weighty matters or to discover truth, than to make a display of ingenuity by clothing trifles in sonorous language. Surrounded by a crowd of empty-pated but censorious critics, exercised in the minutiæ of style and armed with precedents from Petrarch, the poet read his verses to the company. They were approved or rejected according as they satisfied the sense of correctness, or fell below the conventional standard of imitative diction. To think profoundly, to feel intensely, to imagine boldly, to invent novelties, to be original in any line, was perilous. The wealth of the Academies, the interest of the public in purely literary questions, and the activity of the press encouraged the publication and circulation of these pedantic exercises. Time would fail to tell of all the poems and orations poured forth at the expense of these societies and greedily devoured by friends prepared to eulogise, or rival bodies eager to dissect and criticise. Students who are desirous of forming some conception of the multitudes of poets at this period, must be referred to the pages of Quadrio with a warning that Tiraboschi is inclined to think that even Quadrio's lists are incomplete. All ranks and conditions both of men and women joined in the pursuit. Princes and plebeians, scholars and worldlings, noble ladies and leaders of the *demi-monde*, high-placed ecclesiastics and penniless Bohemians aspired to the same honours; and the one idol of the motley crowd was Petrarch. There is no doubt that the final result of their labours was the attainment of a certain grace and the diffusion of literary elegance. Yet these gains carried with them a false feeling about poetry in general, a wrong conception of its purpose and its scope. The Italian purists could scarcely have comprehended the drift of Milton's excursion, in his 'Reason of Church Government urged against Prelaty,' upon the high vocation of the prophet-bard. They would have been no less puzzled by Sidney's definition of poetry, and have felt Shelley's last word upon the poetic office, ' Poets are the unacknowledged legislators of the world,' to be no better than a piece of pardonable lunacy.

In this thick-spreading undergrowth of verse,

where, as Tiraboschi aptly remarks, 'beneath the green and ample foliage we seek in vain for fruit,' it is difficult to see the wood by reason of the trees. Poet so closely resembles poet in the mediocrity of similar attainment, that we are forced to sigh for the energy of Michelangelo's unfinished sonnets, or the crudities of Campanella's muse. Yet it is possible to make a representative selection of writers, who, while they belonged to the school of the purists and were associated with the chief Academies of the day, distinguished themselves by some originality of style or by enduring qualities of literary excellence. Foremost among these may be placed Monsignore Giovanni della Casa. He was born in 1503 of noble Florentine parents, his mother being a member of the Tornabuoni family. Educated at Bologna, he entered the service of the Church, and already in 1538 had reached the dignity of Apostolic Clerk. Rome was still what Lorenzo de' Medici had called it, 'a sink of all the vices,' and very few ecclesiastics escaped its immoralities. La Casa formed some permanent connection, the fruit of which was his acknowledged son Quirino.[1] In 1540 he was sent on a special mission to Florence with the title of Apostolic Commissary; and in 1544 he was raised to the Archbishopric of Benevento, and soon afterwards appointed Nuncio at Venice. During the pontificate of Julius III., finding himself out of favour with the

---

[1] Quirino is mentioned as 'legitimatum, seu forsitan legitimandum,' in La Casa's will (*Opp.* Venezia, Pasinelli, 1752, vol. i. p. lxxvii.). From his name and his age at La Casa's death we ought perhaps to refer this fruit of his amours to the Venetian period of his life and his intimacy with the Quirino family. His biographer, Casotti, says that he discovered nothing about the mother's name (*loc. cit.* p. lxxiii.).

Vatican, he continued to reside at Venice, employing his leisure in literary occupations. Paul IV. recalled him to Rome, and made him Secretary of State. But though he seemed upon the point of touching the highest ecclesiastical dignity, La Casa was never promoted to the Cardinalate. It is difficult to find a reason for this omission, unless we accept the traditional belief that the scandal of his *Capitolo del Forno* barred La Casa's entrance to the Sacred College.[1] This burlesque poem, at any rate, supplied the Protestants with a weapon which they used against the Church. The legend based upon its audacious obscenities was credited by Bayle, and in part refuted by the *Antibaillet* of Ménage. Though by no means more offensive to good taste than scores of similar compositions, the high rank of its author and the offices of trust he had discharged for the Papal Curia, emphasised its infamy, and caused La Casa to be chosen as the scapegoat for his comrades. He died in 1556.

La Casa's name is best known in modern literature by his treatise on the manners of the finished gentleman. In this short essay, entitled *Galateo*, he discusses the particulars of social conduct, descending to rules about the proper use of the drinking-glass at table, the employment of the napkin, the dressing of the hair,

[1] La Casa received a special commission at Venice in 1546, to prosecute Pier Paolo Vergerio for heresy. When Vergerio went into exile, he did his best to blacken La Casa's character, and used his writings to point the picture he drew in Protestant circles of ecclesiastical profligacy. The whole subject of La Casa's exclusion from the College is treated by his editor, Casotti (*Opp.* vol. i. pp. xlv.–xlviii.). That the Bishop of Benevento was stung to the quick by Vergerio's invectives may be seen in his savage answer 'Adversus Paulum Vergerium' (*Opp.* iii. 103), and in the hendecasyllables 'Ad Germanos' (*Opp.* i. 295), both of which discuss the *Forno* and attempt to apologise for it.

and the treatment of immodest topics by polite peri-phrases.[1] Galateo is recommended not to breathe hard in the face of the persons he is speaking to, not to swear at his servants in company, not to trim his nails in public, not to tell indecent anecdotes to girls, and so forth. He is shown how to dress with proper pomp, what ceremonies to observe, and which to omit as ser-vile or superfluous, how to choose his words, and how to behave at dinner. The book is an elaborate dis-course on etiquette; and while it never goes far below the surface, it is full of useful precepts based upon the principles of mutual respect and tolerance which govern good society. We might accept it as a sequel to the *Courtier*; for while Castiglione drew the portrait of a gentleman, La Casa explained how this gentleman should conduct himself among his equals. The chief curiosity about the book is, that a man of its author's distinction should have thought it worthy of his pains to formulate so many rules of simple decency. From the introduction it is clear that La Casa meant the *Galateo* to be a handbook for young men entering upon the world. That it fulfilled this purpose, seems proved by the fact that its title passed into a proverb. 'To teach the Galateo' is synonymous in Italian with to teach good manners.

One whole volume of La Casa's collected works is devoted to his official and familiar correspondence, composed in choice but colourless Italian.[2] Another contains his Italian and Latin poems. No poet of the century expressed his inner self more plainly than La

---

[1] *Opp.* vol. i. pp. 237–306. Galateo is said to have been a certain Galeazzo Florimonte of Sessa.

[2] Vol. ii. of the Venetian edition, 1752.

Casa in his verse. The spectacle is stern and grave. From the vocabulary of the Tuscan classics he seems to have chosen the gloomiest phrases, to adumbrate some unknown terror of the soul.[1] Sometimes his sonnets, in their vivid but polished grandeur, rise even to sublimity, as when he compares himself to a leafless wood in winter, beaten by fiercer storms, with days more cold and short in front, and with a longer night to follow.[2] It is a cheerless prospect of old age and death, uncomforted by hope, unvisited by human love. The same shadow, intensified by even a deeper horror of some coming doom, rests upon another sonnet in which he deplores his wasted life.[3] It drapes, as with a funeral pall, the long majestic ode describing his early errors and the vanity of worldly pomp.[4] It adds despair to his lines on jealousy, intensity to his satire on Court-life, and incommunicable sadness to the poems of his love.[5] Very judicious were the Italian critics

[1] Take for instance this outburst from a complimentary sonnet (No. 40, vol. i. p. 70) :

> O tempestosa, o torbida procella,
> Che 'n mar sì crudo la mia vita giri !
> Donna amar, ch' Amor odia e i suoi desiri,
> Che sdegno e feritate onor appella.

Or this opening of the sonnet on Court-honours (No. 26) :

> Mentre fra valli paludose ed ime
> Ritengon me larve turbate, e mostri,
> Che tra le gemme, lasso, e l' auro, e gli ostri
> Copron venen, che 'l cor mi roda e lima.

Or this from a *Canzone* on his love (No. 2) :

> Qual chiuso albergo in solitario bosco
> Pien di sospetto suol pregar talora
> Corrier di notte traviato e lasso ;
> Tal io per entro il tuo dubbioso, e fosco,
> E duro calle, Amor, corro e trapasso.

[2] Sonnet 58, vol. i. 154.
[3] No. 52, *ib.* p. 136.   [4] *Canzone* 4, *ib.* p. 102.
[5] Sonnets 8, 26, 40, *ib.* pp. 12, 39, 70 ; *Canzone* 2, *ib.* p. 79.

who pronounced his style too stern for the erotic muse. We find something at once sinister and solemn in his mood. The darkness that envelops him, issues from the depth of his own heart. The world around is bright with beautiful women and goodly men; but he is alone, shut up with fear and self-reproach. Such a voice befits the age, as we learn to know it in our books of history, far better than the light effusions of contemporary rhymesters. It suits the black-robed personages painted by Moroni, whose calm pale eyes seem gazing on a world made desolate, they know not why. Its accents are all the more melancholy because La Casa yielded to no impulses of rage. He remained sober, cold, sedate; but by some fatal instinct shunned the light and sought the shade. The gloom that envelops him is only broken by the baleful fires of his *Capitoli*. That those burlesque verses, of which I shall speak in another place, were written in his early manhood, and that the *Rime* were perhaps the composition of his age, need not prevent us from connecting them together. The dreariness of La Casa's later years may well have been engendered by the follies of his youth. It is the despondency of exhaustion following on ill-expended energy, the *tædium vitæ* which fell on Italy when she awoke from laughter.

In illustration of the foregoing remarks I have translated six of La Casa's sonnets, which I shall here insert without further comment.[1] In point of form, Italian literature can show few masterpieces superior to the first and second.

---

[1] They are Nos. 58, 50, 25, 26, 8. The sixth, on Jealousy, may be compared with Sannazzaro's, above, p. 200.

Sweet woodland solitude, that art so dear
 To my dark soul lost in doubt's dreadful maze,
 Now that the North-wind, these short sullen days,
 Wraps earth and air in winter's mantle drear,
And thy green ancient shadowy locks are sere,
 White as my own, above the frosty ways,
 Where summer flowers once basked beneath heaven's rays,
 But rigid ice now reigns and snows austere;
Pondering upon that brief and cloudy light
 That's left for me, I walk, and feel my mind
 And members, like thy branches, frozen too;
Yet me, within, without, worse frost doth bind,
 My winter brings a fiercer East-wind's blight,
 A longer darkness, days more cold, more few.

O Sleep, O tranquil son of noiseless Night,
 Of humid, shadowy Night; O dear repose
 For wearied men, forgetfulness of woes
 Grievous enough the bloom of life to blight!
Succour this heart that hath outworn delight,
 And knows no rest; these tired limbs compose;
 Fly to me, Sleep; thy dusky vans disclose
 Over my languid eyes, then cease thy flight.
Where, where is Silence, that avoids the day?
 Where the light dreams, that with a wavering tread
 And unsubstantial footing follow thee?
Alas! in vain I call thee; and these grey,
 These frigid shades flatter in vain. O bed,
 How rough with thorns! O nights, how harsh to me!

It was my wont by day to seek the grove
 Or grot or fount, soothing my soul with song,
 Weaving sweet woes in rhyme, and all night long
 To watch the stars with Phœbus and with Love;
Nor, Bernard, did I fear with thee to rove
 That sacred mount where now few poets throng:
 Till like sea-billows, uncontrollably strong,
 Me too the vulgar usage earthward drove;
And bound me down to tears and bitter life,
 Where founts are not, nor laurel boughs, nor shade,
 But false and empty honour stirs vain strife.
Now, not unmixed with envious regret,
 I watch thee scale yon far-off heights, where yet
 No footstep on the sward was ever laid.

While mid low-lying dells and swampy vales
   Those troubled ghosts and dreams my feet delay,
   Which hide neath gems and gold and proud array
   The barb of poison that my heart impales ;
Thou on the heights that virtue rarely scales,
   By paths untrodden and a trackless way,
   Wrestling for fame with thine own soul, dost stray,
   Free o'er yon hills no earth-born cloud assails.
Whence I take shame and sorrow, when I think
   How with the crowd in this low net accursed
   I fell, and how 'tis doomed that I shall die.
O happy thou ! Thou hast assuaged thy thirst !
   Not Phœbus but grief dwells with me, and I
   Must wait to purge my woes on Lethe's brink.

Now pomps and purple, now clear stream or field
   Seeking, I've brought my day to evensong,
   Profitless, like dry fern or tares, the throng
   Of luckless herbs that no fair fruitage yield.
Wherefore my heart, false guide on this vain quest,
   More than a smitten flint strikes spark and flame ;
   So dulled a spirit must she bring with shame
   To Him who placed it bright within my breast.
Poor heart ! She well deserves to chafe and burn
   Since her so precious and so noble freight,
   Ill-governed, she to loss and woe doth turn !
Nor neath the North-wind do the branches quake
   On yonder bristling oak-trees, as I shake
   Fearing that even repentance comes too late.

Heart-ache, that drawest nutriment from fear,
   And still through growing fear dost gather power ;
   That mingling ice with flame, confusion drear
   And fell disaster on love's realm dost shower !
Forth from my breast, since all thy bitter cheer
   With my life's sweet thou'st blent in one brief hour !
   Hence to Cocytus ! Where hell drinks each tear
   Of tortured souls, self-plagued, self-loathing. cower !
There without rest thy dolorous days drag out,
   Thy dark nights without slumber ! Smart thy worst
   No less with felt pangs than fictitious doubt !
Avaunt ! Why fiercer now than at the first,
   Now when thy venom runs my veins throughout,
   Bring'st thou on those black wings new dreams accurst ?

The vicissitudes of Italy during the first half of the sixteenth century were so tragic, and her ruin was so near at hand, that we naturally seek some echo of this anguish in the verses of her poets. Nothing, however, is rarer than to find direct allusion to the troubles of the times, or apprehension of impending danger expressed in sonnet or *canzone.* While following Petrarch to the letter, the purists neglected his odes to Rienzi and the Princes of Italy. His passionate outcry, *Italia mia,* found no response in their rhetoric. Those sublime outpourings of eloquence, palpitating with alternate hopes and fears, might have taught the poets how to write at least the threnody of Rome or Florence. Had they studied this side of their master's style, the gravity of the matter supplied them by the miseries of their country, might have immortalised their purity of style. As it was, they preferred the *Rime in Vita e Morte di Madonna Laura,* and sang of sentiments they had not felt, while Italy was dying. Only here and there, as in the sombre rhymes of La Casa, the spirit of the age found utterance unconsciously. But for the mass of versifiers it was enough to escape from the real agonies of the moment into academical Arcadia, to forget the Spaniard and the Frenchman in Philiroe's lap with Ariosto, or to sigh for a past age of gold[1] :

> O rivi, o fonti, o fiumi, o faggi, o querce,
> Onde il mondo novello ebbe suo cibo
> In quei tranquilli secoli dell' oro :
> Deh come ha il folle poi cangiando l' esca,
> Cangiato il gusto ! e come son questi anni
> Da quei diversi in povertate e 'n guerra !

[1] La Casa, *Canzone* 4 (*Opp.* i. 151).

This makes the occasional treatment of polîtital subjects the more valuable ; and we hail the patriotic
poems of Giovanni Guidiccioni as a relief from the
limpid nonsense of the amourists.   Born at Lucca in
1500, he was made Bishop of Fossombrone by Paul
III., and died in 1541.   Contemporaries praised him
for the grandeur of his conceptions and the severity of
his diction, while they censured the obscurity that
veiled his unfamiliar thoughts.   'In those songs,'
writes Lilius Giraldus, 'which he composed upon the
woes and miseries of Italy, he set before his readers
ample proofs of his illustrious style.'[1]   One sonnet
might be chosen from these rhymes, reproving the
Italians for their slavery and shame, and pointing to
the cause, now irremediable, of their downfall[2] :

> From deep and slothful slumber, where till now
>   Entombed thou liest, waken, breathe, arise !
>   Look on those wounds with anger in thine eyes,
> Italia, self-enslaved in folly's slough !
> The diadem of freedom from thy brow
>   Torn through thine own misdoing, seek with sighs ;
>   Turn to the path, that straight before thee lies,
> From yonder crooked furrow thou dost plough.
> Think on thine ancient memories !   Thou shalt see
>   That those who once thy triumphs did adorn,
>   Have chained thee to their yoke with fetters bound.
> Foe to thyself, thine own iniquity,
>   With fame for them, for thee fierce grief and scorn,
>   To this vile end hath forced thee, Queen discrowned !

Such appeals were impotent.   Yet they proved a consciousness of the situation, an unextinguished sense of
duty, in the man who penned them.[3]

---

[1] *De Poetis*, Dial. ii.
[2] *Opere di Messer G. Guidiccioni* (Firenze, Barbèra, 1867), vol. i.
p. 12.
[3] We might parallel Guidiccioni's lamentations with several passages

The Court-life followed by professional men of letters made it difficult for them to utter their real feelings in an age of bitter political jealousies. They either held their tongues, or kept within the safer regions of compliment and fancy. The biographies of Annibale Caro and Lodovico Castelvetro illustrate the ordinary conditions as well as the exceptional vicissitudes of the literary career at this epoch. Annibale Caro was born in 1507 at Civitanuova in the March of Ancona. Being poor and of humble origin, he entered the family of Luigi Gaddi at Florence, in the quality of tutor to his children. This patron died in 1541, and Caro then took service under Pier Luigi Farnese, one of the worst princelings of the period. When the Duke was murdered in 1547, he transferred himself to Parma, still following the fortunes of the Farnesi. Employed as secretary by the Cardinal Ranuccio and afterwards by the Cardinal Alessandro of that house, he lived at ease until his death in 1566. Caro's letters, written for his patrons, and his correspondence with the famous scholars of the day, pass for models of Italian epistolography. Less rigid than La Casa's, less manneristic than Bembo's, his style is distinguished by a natural grace and elegance of diction. He formed his manner by translation from the Greek, especially by a version of *Daphnis and Chloe*, which may be compared with Firenzuola's

fro m the Latin elegies of the period, and with some of the obscurer compositions of Italian poetasters. See, for example, the extracts from Cariteo of Naples, Tibaldeo of Ferrara, and Cammelli of Pistoja on the passage of Charles VIII. quoted by Carducci, *Delle Poesie Latine di Ludovico Ariosto*, pp. 83–86. But the most touching expression of sympathy with Italy's disaster is the sudden silence of Boiardo in the middle of a canto of *Orlando*. See above, part i. p. 463.

Asino d' Oro for classic beauty and facility of phrase. But the great achievement of his life was a transcription of the *Æneid* into blank verse. Though Caro's poem exceeds the original by about 5,500 lines, and therefore cannot pass for an exact copy of Virgil's form, Italians still reckon it the standard translation of their national epic. The charm of Caro's prose was communicated to his *versi sciolti*, always easy, always flowing, with varied cadence and sustained melody of rhythm. A *Diceria de' Nasi*, or discourse on noses, and a dissertation called *Ficheide*, commenting on Molza's *Fichi*, prove that Caro lent himself with pleasure to the academical follies of his contemporaries. It seems incredible that a learned man, who had spent the best years of his maturity in diplomatic missions to the Courts of princes, should have employed the leisure of his age in polishing these trifles. Yet such was the temper of the times that this frivolity passed for a commendable exercise of ingenuity.

Caro's original poems have not much to recommend them beyond limpidity of language. The sonnets to an imaginary mistress repeat conventional antitheses and complimentary *concetti*.[1] The adulatory odes are stiff and laboured, as, indeed, they might be, when we consider that they were made to order upon Charles V., the Casa Farnese, and the lilies of France, by a plebeian scholar from Ancona.[2] The last-named of these flatteries, ' Venite all' ombra de' gran gigli d' oro,' is a

---

[1] See, for example, ' Donna, qual mi foss' io,' and ' In voi mi trasformai,' or ' Eran l' aer tranquillo e l' onde chiare.'

[2] See ' Carlo il Quinto fu questi '; ' Nell' apparir del giorno ' ; and ' Venite all' ombra de' gran gigli d' oro.'

masterpiece of prize poetry, produced with labour, filed to superficial smoothness, and overloaded with conceits. On its appearance it was hailed with acclamation as the final triumph of Italian writing. The Farnesi, who had recently placed themselves under the protection of France, and who bore her lilies on their scutcheon, used all their influence to get their servant's work applauded. The Academies were delighted with a display of consummate artifice and mechanical ability. One only voice was raised in criticism. Aurelio Bellincini, a gentleman of Modena, had sent a copy of the ode to Lodovico Castelvetro, with a request that he should pronounce upon its merits. Castelvetro, who was wayward and independent beyond the usual prudence of his class, replied with a free censure of the 'plebeian diction, empty phrases, strange digressions, purple patches, poverty of argument, and absence of sentiment or inspiration,' he detected in its stanzas. At the same time he begged his friend to keep this criticism to himself. Bellincini was indiscreet, and the letter found its way to Caro. Then arose a literary quarrel, which held all Italy suspense, and equalled in ferocity the combats of the humanists.

Lodovico Castelvetro was born in 1505 at Modena. He studied successively at Bologna, Ferrara, Padua, and Siena. Thence he passed to Rome, where strong pressure was put upon him to enter orders. His uncle, Giovanni Maria della Porta, promised, if he did so, to procure for him the bishopric of Gubbio. But Castelvetro had no mind to become a priest. He escaped clandestinely from Rome, and, after a brief sojourn at Siena, returned to Modena. Here in 1542

he subscribed the Formulary of Faith dictated by
Cardinal Contarini, and thereby fell under suspicion of
heresy. Though he escaped inquisitorial censure at
the moment, the charges of Lutheranism were revived
in 1554, when Caro declared open war against him.
Invectives, apologies, censures, and replies were briskly
interchanged between the principals, while half the
scholars of Italy allowed themselves to be drawn into the
fray—Varchi and Molza siding with Caro, Gian Maria
Barbieri and other friends of Castelvetro taking up the
cudgels for the opposite champion.[1] The bitterness of
the contending parties may be gathered from the fact
that Castelvetro was accused of having murdered a
friend of Caro's, and Caro of having hired assassins to
take Castelvetro's life.[2] It seems tolerably certain that
either Caro or one of his supporters denounced their
enemy to the Inquisition. He was summoned to
Rome, and in 1560 was confined in the convent of S.
Maria in Via to await his trial. After undergoing some
preliminary examinations, Castelvetro became persuaded
that his life was in peril. He contrived to escape by
night from Rome, and, after a journey of much anxiety
and danger, took refuge in Chiavenna, at that time a
city of the Grisons. The Holy Office condemned him
as a contumacious heretic in his absence. Wandering
from Chiavenna to Lyons and Geneva, and back again

---

[1] Among the liveliest missiles used in this squabble are Bronzino's
Saltarelli, recently reprinted by Romagnoli, Bologna, 1863.

[2] Alberigo Longo was in fact murdered in 1555, and a servant of
Castelvetro's was tried for the offence. But he was acquitted. Caro, on
his side, gave occasion to the worst reports by writing in May 1560 to
Varchi : 'E credo che all' ultimo sarò sforzato a finirla, per ogni altra
via, e vengane ciò che vuole.' See Tiraboschi, Part 3, lib. iii. chap. 3,
sec. 13.

to Chiavenna, he spent the rest of his life in exile, and died at the last place in 1571.

Castelvetro's publications do not correspond to his fame; for though he gave signs of an acute wit and a biting pen in his debate with Caro, he left but little highly-finished work to posterity. In addition to critical annotations upon Bembo's prose, published in his lifetime, he wrote a treatise upon Rhetoric, which was printed at Modena in 1653, and sent an Italian version of Aristotle's *Poetics* to the press in 1570. This book was the idol of his later years. It is said that, while residing at Lyons, his house took fire, and Castelvetro, careless of all else, kept crying out ' The *Poetics*, the *Poetics*! Save me my *Poetics*!' He may be fairly reckoned among the men who did solid service in the cause of graver studies. Yet, but for the vicissitudes of his career, he could hardly claim a foremost place in literary history.

The ladies who cultivated poetry and maintained relations with illustrious men of letters at this epoch, were almost as numerous as the songsters of the other sex. Lodovico Domenichi in the year 1559 published the poems of no less than fifty authoresses in his *Rime di alcune nobilissime e virtuosissime Donne.* Subjected to the same intellectual training as men, they felt the same influences, and passed at the same moment from humanism to renascent Italian literature.[1] Many of

---

[1] The identity of male and female education in Italy is an important feature of this epoch. The history of Vittorino da Feltre's school at Mantua given by his biographer, Rosmini, supplies valuable information upon this point. Students may consult Burckhardt, *Cultur der Renaissance*, sec. 5, ed. 2, p. 312 ; Gregorovius, *Lucrezia Borgia*, book i. sec. 4 ; Janitschek, *Gesellschaft der Renaissance*, Lecture 3.

these Viragos,[1] as it was the fashion of the age approvingly and with no touch of sarcasm to call them, were dames of high degree and leaders of society. Some, like *la bella Imperia*, were better known in the resorts of pleasure. All were distinguished by intercourse with artists and writers of eminence. It is impossible to render an account of their literary labours. But the names of a few, interesting alike for their talents and their amours, may here be recorded. Tullia di Aragona, the mistress of Girolamo Muzio, who ruled society in Rome, and lived in infamy at Venice[2]—Vittoria Accoramboni, whose tragedy thrilled Italy, and gave a masterpiece to our Elizabethan stage —Tarquinia Molza, grand-daughter of the poet, and maid of honour at Ferrara in Guarini's brilliant days —Laura Terracina, with whose marriage and murder romance employed itself at the expense of probability —Veronica Franco, who entertained Montaigne in her Venetian home in 1580—Ersilia Cortese, the natural daughter of a humanist and wife of a Pope's nephew —Gaspara Stampa, 'sweet songstress and most excellent musician':—such were the women, to whom Bembo and Aretino addressed letters, and whose drawing-rooms were the resort of Bandello's heroes.

Two poetesses have to be distinguished from the common herd. These are Veronica Gambara and Vittoria Colonna. Veronica was the daughter of Count Gianfrancesco Gambara and his wife Alda Pia of Carpi, whose name recalls the fervid days of

---

[1] See Vulgate, Gen. ii. 23 : ' Hæc vocabitur Virago,' &c.

[2] In a rare tract called *Tariffa delle puttane, etc.*, Tullia d' Aragona is catalogued among the courtesans of Venice. See Passano, *Novellieri in Verso*, p. 118.

humanism at its noon.[1] She was born in 1485, and was therefore contemporary with the restorers of Italian literature. Bembo was the guide of her youth, and Vittoria Colonna the friend of her maturer years. In 1509 she married Giberto, lord of Correggio, by whom she had two sons, Ippolito and Girolamo. Her husband died after nine years of matrimony, and she was left to educate her children for the State and Church. She discharged her duties as a mother with praiseworthy diligence, and died in 1550, respected by all Italy, the type of what a noble woman should be in an age when virtue shone by contrast with especial lustre. Her letters and her poems were collected and published in 1759 at Brescia, the city of her birth. Except for the purity of their sentiments and the sincerity of their expression, her verses do not rise far above mediocrity. Like literary ladies of the French metropolis, she owed her fame to personal rather than to literary excellence. 'The house of Veronica,' writes a biographer of the sixteenth century, 'was an Academy, where every day she gathered round her for discourse on noble questions Bembo and Cappello, Molza and Mauro, and all the famous men of Europe who followed the Italian Courts.'[2]

Fabrizio, the father of Vittoria Colonna, was Grand Constable of Naples. He married Agnesina di Montefeltro, daughter of Duke Federigo of Urbino. Their child Vittoria was born at Marino, a feud of the Colonna family, in the year 1490. At the age of four she was betrothed to Ferrante Francesco D' Avalos, a

[1] See *Revival of Learning*, p. 375.
[2] Rinaldo Corso, quoted by Tiraboschi.

boy of the same age, the only son of the Marchese di Pescara. His father died while he was still a child ; and in their nineteenth year the affianced couple were married at Ischia, the residence of the house of D' Avalos. The splendour of two princely families, alike distinguished in the annals of Spanish and Italian history and illustrious by their military honours, conferred unusual lustre upon this marriage. It was, moreover, on the bride's side at least, a love-match. Vittoria was beautiful and cultivated ; the young Marquis of Pescara chivalrous and brave. She was tenderly attached to him, and he had not as yet revealed the darker side of his mixed character. Yet their happiness proved of very short duration. In 1512 he was wounded and made prisoner at the battle of Ravenna ; and though he returned to his wife for a short interval, his duties again called him to the field of war in Lombardy in 1515. Vittoria never saw him after this date ; and before his death the honour of her hero was tarnished by one of the darkest deeds of treason recorded in Italian history. Acting as general for the Spanish emperor, the Marquis entered Milan immediately after the battle of Pavia in 1525. He there and then began his intrigues with Girolamo Morone, Grand Chancellor of Francesco Sforza's duchy. Morone had formed a plan for reinstating his master in Milan by the help of an Italian coalition. With the view of securing the Marquis of Pescara, by which bold stroke he would have paralysed the Spanish military power, Morone offered the young general the crown of Naples, if he would consent to join the league. D' Avalos turned a not unwilling ear to these proposals; but while the plot was hatching, he saw good reason to doubt of its success, and determined to clear himself with Charles V. by revealing the conspiracy. Accordingly, he made his lieutenant, Antonio de Leyva, assist at a privy conference between Morone and himself. Concealed behind the arras, this Spanish officer heard enough to be able afterwards to deliver direct testimony against the conspirators, while the Marquis averred that he had led them on designedly to this end. It may be difficult to estimate the precise amount of Pescara's guilt. But whether he was deceiving Morone from the first, or whether, as seems more probable, he entered the negotiation resolved to side with Charles or with the League as best might suit his purpose, there can be no doubt that he played an odious part in this transaction. He did not long survive the treason; for his constitution had been ruined by wounds received at Pavia. It was also rumoured that Charles accelerated his death by poison. He died on November 25, 1525, execrated by the Italians, and handed down by their historians to perpetual infamy. Something of national jealousy mingled undoubtedly in their resentment. D'Avalos was a Spaniard, and made no concealment of his contempt for the Italian character. Finally, it must be admitted that if he really was acting throughout in his master's interest, his betrayal of Morone was but a bold stroke of policy which Machiavelli might have approved. The game was a dangerous one; but it was thoroughly consistent with statecraft as then understood.[1]

---

[1] See *Ricordi Inediti di Gerolamo Morone*, pubblicati dal C. Tullio Dandolo, Milano, 1855.

No suspicion of her husband's guilt seems to have crossed Vittoria Colonna's mind. Though left so young a widow, beautiful and illustrious by her high rank and education, she determined to consecrate her whole life to his memory and to religion. She survived him two-and-twenty years, which were spent partly in retirement at Ischia, partly in convents at Orvieto and Viterbo, partly in a semi-monastic seclusion at Rome. While still a girl and during her husband's absence in the field, she had amused her leisure with study. This now became her chief resource in the hours she spared from pious exercises. There was no man of great name in the world of letters who did not set his pride on being thought her friend. The collections of letters and poems belonging to that period abound in allusions to her genius, her holiness, and her great beauty. But her chief associates were the group of earnest thinkers who felt the influences of the Reformation without ceasing to be children of the Church. With Vittoria Colonna's name are inseparably connected those of Gasparo Contarini, Reginald Pole, Giovanni Morone, Jacopo Sadoleto, Marcantonio Flamminio, Pietro Carnesecchi, and Fra Bernardino Ochino. The last of these avowed his Lutheran principles; and Carnesecchi was burned for heresy; but Vittoria never adopted Protestantism in any of its dogmatic aspects. She remained an orthodox Catholic to the last, although it seems tolerably certain that she was by no means ignorant of the new doctrines nor unsympathetic to their spirit.[1] Her attitude was prob-

---

[1] The most recent investigations tend rather to confirm the tradition of Vittoria's Lutheran leanings. See Giuseppe Campori's *Vittoria Colonna*

ably the same as that of many Italians who, before the opening of the Council of Trent, desired a reformation from within the Church. To bring it back to purer morals and an evangelical sincerity of faith, was their aim. Like Savonarola, they shrank from heresy, and failed to comprehend that a radical renovation of religion was inseparable, in the changed conditions of modern thought, from a metamorphosis of dogma and a new freedom accorded to the individual conscience. While the Teutonic world struck boldly for the liberation of the reason, the Italians dreamed of an impossible harmony between Catholicism and philosophy. Their compromises led to ethical hypocrisies and to that dogmatic despotism which was confirmed by the Tridentine Council.

A pleasant glimpse into Vittoria's life at Rome is given by the Portuguese artist, Francesco d' Olanda, who visited her about the year 1548. 'Madonna Vittoria Colonna,' he says, 'Marchioness of Pescara and sister to the Lord Antonio Colonna, is one of the most excellent and famous women of Europe—that is, of the whole civilised world. Not less chaste than beautiful, learned in Latin literature and full of genius, she possesses all the qualities and virtues that are praiseworthy in woman. After the death of her hero husband, she now leads a modest and retired life. Tired with the splendour and grandeur of her former state, she gives her whole affections to Christ and to serious studies. To the poor she is beneficent, and is

(Modena, 1878), and the fine article upon it by Ernesto Masi in the *Rassegna Settimanale,* January 29, 1879. Karl Benrath's *Ueber die Quellen der italienischen Reformationsgeschichte* (Bonn, 1876) is a valuable contribution to the history of Lutheran opinion in the South.

a model of true Catholic devotion.' He then proceeds to describe a conversation held with her, in which Michelangelo Buonarroti took a part.[1]

Vittoria Colonna's *Rime* consist for the most part of sonnets on the death of her husband, and on sacred and moral subjects. Penetrated by genuine feeling and almost wholly free from literary affectation, they have that dignity and sweetness which belongs to the spontaneous utterance of a noble heart. Like the poets of an earlier and simpler age, Vittoria listens to the voice of Love, and when he speaks, records the thoughts dictated by his inspiration.[2] That the object of her life-long regret was unworthy of her, does not offend our sense of fitness.[3] It is manifest that her own feeling for the Marquis of Pescara, *il mio bel sole, mio lume eterno*, as she loves to call him with pathetic iteration of the chosen metaphor, had satisfied her un-suspecting nature.[4] Death consecrates her husband for Vittoria, as death canonised Laura for Petrarch.

---

[1] The whole document may be seen in the *Archivio Storico*, nuov. ser. tom. v. part. 2, p. 139, or in Grimm's Life of Michelangelo.

[2] The first lines of the introductory sonnet are strictly true :

> Scrivo sol per sfogar l' interna doglia,
> Di che si pasce il cor, ch' altro non vole,
> E non per giunger lume al mio bel sole,
> Che lasciò in terra si onorata spoglia.

[3] The last biographer of Vittoria Colonna, G. Campori, has shown that her husband was by no means faithful to his marriage vows.

[4] The close of the twenty-second sonnet is touching by reason of its allusion to the past. Vittoria had no children.

> Sterili i corpi fur, l' alme feconde,
> Chè il suo valor lasciò raggio si chiaro,
> Che sarà lume ancor del nome mio.
> Se d' altre grazie mi fu il ciel avaro,
> E se il mio caro ben morte m' asconde,
> Pur con lui vivo ; ed è quanto disio.

He has become divine, and her sole desire is to rejoin him in a world where parting is impossible.[1] The blending of the hero with the saint, of earthly fame with everlasting glory, in this half Christian half Pagan apotheosis, is characteristic of the Renaissance. Michelangelo strikes the same note in the *Capitolo* upon his father's death: ' Or sei tu del morir morto e fatto divo.' It is said that, in her first grief, Vittoria thought of suicide as the means of escaping from this world. But she triumphed over the temptation, and in Bembo's words proved herself *vincitrice di se stessa*. We seem to trace the anguish of that struggle in a sonnet which may possibly have suggested Bembo's phrase.[2]

The religious sonnets are distinguished in general by the same simplicity and sincerity of style.[3] While Vittoria proves herself a Catholic by her invocation of Madonna and S. Francis,[4] it is to the cross of Christ that she turns with the deepest outgoings of pious feeling.[5] Her cry is for lively faith, for evangelical purity of conviction. There is nothing in these meditations that a Christian of any communion may not read with profit, as the heartfelt utterances of a soul athirst for God and nourished on the study of the Gospel.

[1] See, for instance, *Rime Varie*, Sonetto li. and lxxi. xc.
[2] It is No. 31 of the *Rime Varie* (Florence, Barbèra, 1860).
[3] The introductory Sonnet has, however, these ugly *concetti* :

> I santi chiodi ormai sian le mie penne,
> E puro inchiostro il prezioso sangue ;
> Purgata carta il sacro corpo esangue,
> Sì ch' io scriva nel cor quel ch' ei sostenne.

[4] *Rime Sacre*, 119, 120, 86, 87.
[5] *Ibid.* 75, 80, 81.

The memory of Vittoria Colonna is inseparable from that of Michelangelo Buonarroti, who was her intimate companion during the closing years of her life. Of that famous friendship this is not the place to speak at length. It may be enough to report Condivi's words about Michelangelo's grief when he had lost her. ' I remember having heard him say that nothing caused him so much sorrow as that, when he went to visit her upon her passage from this life, he had not kissed her forehead and face, even as he kissed her hand. Her death left him oftentimes astonied and, as it were, deprived of reason.' Some of Michelangelo's best sonnets were composed for Vittoria Colonna in her lifetime. Others record his sorrow for her loss. Those again which give expression to his religious feelings, are animated by her spirit of genuine piety. It is clear that her influence affected him profoundly.

To include any notice of Michelangelo's poetry in a chapter devoted to the purists, may seem paradoxical.[1] His verses are remarkable for the imperfection of their style, and the rugged elevation of their thoughts. With the school of Bembo he has nothing in common except that Platonism which the versifiers of the time affected as a fashion, but which had a real meaning for his creative genius. In the second half of the sixteenth century Michelangelo's sonnets upon the divine idea, lifting the soul by contemplation to her heavenly home, reach our ears like utterances

---

[1] For a brief account of Michelangelo's *Rime*, see *Fine Arts*, Appendix ii. ; also the introduction to my translation of the sonnets, *The Sonnets of Michael Angelo Buonarroti and Tommaso Campanella*, Smith and Elder, 1878.

from some other and far distant age. Both in form
and in spirit they are alien to the *cinque cento*. Yet
the precisians of the time admired these uncouth
verses for the philosophic depth of thought they found
in them. Benedetto Varchi composed a learned treatise
on the sonnet ' Non ha l'ottimo artista '; and when the
poems were printed, Mario Guidicci delivered two
lectures on them before the Florentine Academy.[1]

There is no sort of impropriety in placing Bernardo
Tasso and Giangiorgio Trissino upon the list of literary
purists. The biographies of these two men, more
interesting for the share they took in public life than
for their poetical achievements, shall close a chapter
which has been, almost of necessity, rambling. Bernardo Tasso was a member of the noble and ancient
Bergamasque family Dei Tassi.[2] He was born at
Venice in 1493. Left an orphan in his early childhood, an uncle on his father's side, the Bishop of
Recanati, took charge of him. But this good man
was murdered in 1520, at the time when Bernardo had
just begun a brilliant career in the University of Padua.
The loss of his father and his uncle threw the young
student on the world, and he was glad to take service
as secretary with the Count Guido Rangone. At this
epoch the Rangoni stood high among the first nobility
of Italy, and Count Guido was Captain-General of the
Church. He employed Bernardo in a mission to Paris
in 1528, on the occasion of Ercole d' Este's marriage
to Renée, daughter of Louis XII. Tasso went to

---

[1] Varchi's and Guidicci's *Lezioni* will be found in Guasti's edition of
the *Rime*.

[2] I use the Life prefixed by G. Campori to his *Lettere Inedite di
Bernardo Tasso* (Bologna, Romagnoli, 1869).

France as servant of the Rangoni. He returned to Italy in the employment of the Estensi. But he did not long remain at the Court of Ferrara. About the year 1532, we find him with Ferrante Sanseverino, Prince of Salerno, whom he accompanied in 1535 on the expedition to Tunis. It cannot have been much later than this date that he married the beautiful Porzia de' Rossi, who was the mother of his illustrious son, Torquato. But though this marriage was in all respects a happy one, in none more fortunate than in the birth of Italy's fourth sovran poet, Bernardo was not destined to lead a life of tranquil domesticity. His master, whom he followed whithersoever military service called him, fell out of favour with the Spanish Court in 1547. Maddened by the injustice of his treatment, the Prince deserted from Charles V. to his rival, Francis, was declared a rebel and deprived of his vast domains. Bernardo resolved to share his fortunes, and in return for this act of loyalty, found himself involved in the ruin of the Sanseverini. Henceforth he lived a wandering life, away from Porzia and his family, and ill-contented with the pittance which his patron could afford. In 1556, at Duke Guidubaldo's invitation, he joined the Court of Urbino; and again in 1563 he entered the service of the Duke of Mantua. He died in 1569 at Ostiglia.

It will be seen from this brief sketch that Bernardo Tasso spent his life in mixed employments, as courtier, diplomatist, and military secretary. His career was analogous to that of many nobly-born Italians, for whom there existed no sphere outside the service of a prince. Yet he found time, amid his journeys, campaigns and miscellaneous Court duties, to practise literature. The seven books of his collected poems— sonnets, odes and epithalamial hymns—placed him among the foremost lyrists of the century; while his letters displayed the merits which were usual in that species of composition. Had this been all, he would have deserved honourable mention by the side of Caro, on a somewhat lower level than Bembo. But he was also ambitious of giving a new kind of epic to Italian literature. With this view, he versified the Spanish romance of Amadis of Gaul in octave stanzas. The *Amadigi* is a chivalrous poem in the style of the *Orlando*, but without the irony of Ariosto.[1] It cannot be reckoned a success; for though written with fertile fancy and a flowing vein, its prolixity is tedious. Tasso lacked the art of sustaining his reader's atten- tion. His attempt to treat the ideal of feudalism seriously, without the faith and freshness of the chival- rous epoch, deprived his work of that peculiar charm which belongs to the Italian romantic epic. While still in MS., he submitted his poem to literary friends, and read it at the Court of Urbino. The acclamation it received from men whose literary principles coincided with his own, raised Tasso's expectations high. He imagined that the world would welcome *Amadigi* as a masterpiece, combining the interest of *Orlando* with the dignity and purity of a classic. When it appeared, however, the public received it coldly, and on this occasion the verdict of the people was indubitably

---

[1] The *Amadigi* was printed by Giolito at Venice in 1560 under the author's own supervision. The book is a splendid specimen of florid typography.

right. Another mortification awaited the author. He had dedicated his epic to Philip II. and filled its cantos with adulation of the Spanish race. But the king took no notice of the gift; and two years after the publication of *Amadigi*, it appeared that Tasso's agents at the Spanish Court had not taken the trouble to present him with a copy.[1]

Bernardo Tasso is the representative of a class which was common in Renaissance Italy, when courtiers and men of affairs devoted their leisure to study and composed poetry upon scholastic principles. His epic failed precisely through the qualities for which he prized it. Less the product of inspiration than pedantic choice, it bore the taint of languor and unpardonable dulness. Giangiorgio Trissino, in the circumstances of his life no less than in the nature of his literary work, bears a striking resemblance to the author of the *Amadigi*. The main difference between the two men is that Trissino adopted by preference the career of diplomacy into which poverty drove Tasso.[2] He was born at Vicenza in 1478 of wealthy and noble ancestors, from whom he inherited vast estates. His mother was Cecilia, of the Bevilacqua family. During his boyhood Trissino enjoyed fewer opportunities of study than usually fell to the lot of young Italian nobles. He spent his time in active exercises; and it was only in 1506 that he began his education in earnest. At this date he had been married

---

[1] Besides the *Amadigi*, Bernardo Tasso composed a second narrative poem, the *Floridante*, which his son, Torquato, retouched and published at Mantua in 1587.

[2] *Giangiorgio Trissino*, by Bernardo Morsolin (Vicenza, 1878), is a copious biography and careful study of this poet's times.

nine years, and had already lost his wife, the mother of two surviving children, Francesco and Giulio.[1]

Trissino's inclination toward literature induced him to settle at Milan, where he became a pupil of the veteran Demetrius Chalcondylas. He cultivated the society of learned men, collected MSS., and devoted himself to the study of Greek philosophy. From the first, he showed the decided partiality for erudition which was destined to rule his future career. But scholars at that epoch, even though they might be men of princely fortune, had little chance of uninterrupted leisure. Trissino's estates gave him for a while as much trouble as poverty had brought on Tasso. Vicenza was allotted to the Empire in 1509; and afterwards, when the city gave itself to the Venetian Republic, Trissino's adherence to Maximilian's party cost him some months of exile in Germany and the temporary confiscation of his property. Between 1510 and 1514, after his return from Germany, but before he made his peace with Venice, Trissino visited Ferrara, Florence and Rome. These years determined his life as a man of letters. The tragedy of *Sofonisba*, which was written before 1515, won for its author a place among the foremost poets of the time.[2] The same period decided his future as a courtier. Leo X. sent him on a mission to Bavaria, and upon his return procured his pardon from the Republic of S. Mark. There is not much to be gained by following the intricate details of Trissino's public career. After Leo's death, he was employed by Clement VII. and Paul III. He assisted at the coronation of Charles V., and on this

---

[1] Francesco died in 1514.   [2] See above, pp. 126–128.

occasion was made Knight and Count. Gradually he assumed the style of a finished courtier; and though he never took pay from his Papal or princely masters, no poet carried the art of adulation further.[1]

This self-subjection to the annoyances and indignities of Court-life is all the more remarkable because Trissino continued to live like a great noble. When he travelled, he was followed by a retinue of servants. A chaplain attended him for the celebration of Mass. His litter was furnished with silver plate, and with all the conveniences of a magnificent household. His own cook went before, with couriers, to prepare his table; and the equipage included a train of sumpter-mules and serving-men in livery.[2] At home, in his palace at Vicenza or among his numerous villas, he showed no less magnificence. Upon the building of one country-house at Cricoli, which he designed himself and surrounded with the loveliest Italian gardens, enormous sums were spent; and when the structure was completed, he opened it to noble friends, who lived with him at large and formed an Academy called after him La Trissiniana.[3] Trissino was, moreover, a diligent student and a lover of solitude. He spent many years of his life upon the island of Murano, in a villa secluded from the world, and open to none but a few guests of similar tastes.[4] Yet in spite of the advantages which fortune gave him, in spite of his studious habits, he could not resist the attraction

---

[1] See Morsolin, *op. cit.*, p. 360, for Trissino's own emphatic statement that his services had been unpaid. *Ibid.* p. 344, for a list of the personages he complimented.

[2] *Ibid.* p. 323.

[3] *Ibid.* pp. 219–235.

[4] *Ibid.* p. 301.

which Courts at that epoch exercised over men of birth and breeding throughout Europe. He was for ever returning to Rome, although he expressed the deepest horror for the corruptions of that sinful city.[1] No sooner had he established himself in quiet among the woods and streams of the Vicentine lowlands or upon the breast of the Venetian lagoons, than the hankering to shine before a Prince came over him, and he resumed his march to Ferrara, or made his bow once more in the Vatican.

The end of Trissino's life was troubled by a quarrel with his son Giulio, in which it is difficult to decide whether the father or the son was more to blame. Some years after the death of his first wife, he married a cousin, Bianca Trissino, by whom he had another son, Ciro. Giulio was sickly, and had taken to the ecclesiastical career. His father's preference for Ciro was decided, and he openly expressed it. That Bianca was not entirely responsible for the ensuing quarrel, is certain from the fact that Trissino separated from this second wife in 1535. But it appears that Giulio opened hostilities by behaving with brutal rudeness to his stepmother. Trissino refused to receive him, and cut off his allowance. Giulio then went to law with his father. A hollow peace was patched up, and, after Bianca's death in 1540, Giulio was appointed steward of the family estates. His management of Trissino's property led to new disputes, and new acts of violence. On one occasion the son broke into his father's palace at Vicenza, and tried to turn him by armed force into the streets upon a bitter night of Christmas. Mean-

[1] *Op. cit.* p. 366.

while fresh lawsuits were on foot, and Giulio's cause triumphed in the courts of Venice, whither the case had been removed on appeal from Vicenza. Infuriated by what he deemed a maladministration of justice, the old poet hurled sonnets and invectives against both cities, execrating their infamy in the strongest verse he ever penned.[1] But he could not gain redress against the son he hated. At the age of seventy-two, in the midst of these private troubles, Trissino undertook his last journey to Rome. There he died in 1550, and was buried near John Lascaris in the church of S. Agata in Suburra.

Whatever may have been the crimes of Giulio against his father, Trissino used a cruel and unpardonable revenge upon his eldest son. Not content with blackening his character under the name of Agrilupo in the *Italia Liberata*,[2] he wrote a codicil to his will, in which he brought against Giulio the most dangerous charge it was then possible to make. He disinherited him with a curse, and accused him of Lutheran heresy.[3] It was clearly the father's intention to hand his son down to an immortality of shame in his great poem, to ruin him in his temporal affairs, and to deprive him of his ecclesiastical privileges. Posterity has defeated his first purpose; for few indeed are the readers of Trissino's *Italia Liberata*. In his second and his third objects, he was completely successful. Giulio was prosecuted for heresy in 1551, cited before the Inquisition of Bologna in 1553, excommunicated by the Roman Holy Office in 1554, condemned as a contumacious heretic in 1556, driven into hiding at Venice,

---

[1] *Op. cit.* p. 385.   [2] *Ibid.* p. 413.   [3] *Ibid.* p. 414.

attacked in bed and half murdered there in 1568, and finally thrown into prison in 1573. He died in prison in 1576, without having shown any signs of repentance, a martyr to his Lutheran opinions.[1] Ciro Trissino, the third actor in this domestic tragedy, had already been strangled in his villa at Cornedo in the year 1574.

Trissino's literary labours bring us back to the specific subject of this chapter. He made it the aim of his life to apply the methods of the ancients to the practice of Italian poetry, and to settle the vexed questions of the language on rational principles. Conscious of the novelty and ambitious nature of his designs, he adopted the Golden Fleece of Jason for an emblem, signifying that his voyages in literature led far beyond the ordinary track, with an inestimable prize in view.[2] Had his genius been equal to his enterprise, he might have effected a decisive revolution. But Trissino was a man of sterling parts and sound judgment rather than a poet; a formulator of rules and precepts rather than a creator. His bent of mind was critical; and in this field he owed his success more to coincidence with prevalent opinion than to originality. Though he fixed the type of Italian tragedy by his *Sofonisba*, and tied comedy down to Latin models by his *Simillimi*, we cannot rate his talents as a playwright very high. The

[1] The whole of this extraordinary sequel to Trissino's biography will be read with interest in the last chapter of Signor Morsolin's monograph. It leaves upon my mind the impression that Giulio, though unpardonably ill-tempered, and possibly as ill-conducted in his private life as his foes asserted, was the victim of an almost diabolical persecution.

[2] See Morsolin, *op. cit.*, p. 197. This device was imprinted as early as 1529, upon the books published for Trissino at Verona by Janicolo of Brescia.

Poetica, in which he reduced Horace and Aristotle to Italian prose, and laid down laws for adapting modern literature to antique system, had a wide and lasting influence.[1] We may trace the canon of dramatic unities, which through Italian determined French practice, up to this source; but had not Trissino's precepts been concordant with the tendencies of his age, it is probable that even this treatise would have carried little weight. When he attempted to reform Italian orthography on similar principles, he met with derision and resistance.[2] The world was bent on aping the classics; it did not care about adopting the Greek Kappa, Zeta, Phi, etc. Trissino intervened with more effect in the dispute on language. He pleaded that the vernacular, being the common property of the whole nation, should be called Italian and cultivated with a wise tolerance of local diction. Having discovered a copy of Dante's *De Eloquio,* he communicated this treatise to the learned world in support of his own views, and had a translation of it printed.[3] This publication embittered the strife which was then raging. Some Florentine scholars, led by Martelli, impugned its genuineness. But the *De Eloquio* survived antagonistic criticism, and opened a new stage in the discussion.

In his attempt to add the heroic species of the epic to Italian literature, Trissino was even less successful than in his dramatic experiments. Disgusted with

---

[1] The *Poetica* was printed in 1529; but it had been composed some years earlier.

[2] His grammatical and orthographical treatises were published under the titles of *Epistola a Clemente VII., Grammatichetta, Dialogo Castellano, Dubbi Grammaticali.* Firenzuola made Trissino's new letters famous and ridiculous by the burlesque sonnets he wrote upon them.

[3] Vicenza, Tolomeo Janicolo, 1529.

Ariosto's success in what he regarded as a barbarous style of art, he set himself to make an epic on the model of Homer, with scrupulous obedience to Aristotle's rules. For his subject he chose an episode from Italian history, and used blank verse instead of the attractive octave stanza. The *Italia Liberata* cost its author twenty years of labour.[1] It was a masterpiece of erudition, displaying profound acquaintance with Roman tactics, and a competent knowledge of Roman topography. But in spite of its characters *plaqués* upon those of the *Iliad*, in spite of its learnedly-constructed episodes, in spite of its fidelity to Aristotle, the *Italia Liberata* was not a poem. The good sense of the nation refused it. Tasso returned to the romantic method and the meretricious charms of the *ottava rima*. Only Gravina among critics spoke a good word for it. The subject lacked real grandeur. Italy delivered from the Goths, was only Italy delivered to the Lombards. The unity of the poem was not the unity of an epic, but of a chapter from a medieval Chronicle. The machinery of angels, travestied with classic titles, was ridiculous. The Norcian Sibyl, introduced in rivalry with Virgil's Sibyl of Avernus, was out of place. And though Trissino expunged what made the old romantic poems charming, he retained their faults. Intricate underplots and flatteries of noble families were consistent with a species which had its origin in feudal minstrelsy. They were wholly out of character with a professed transcription from the Greek.

[1] Nine books were first printed at Rome in 1547 by Valerio and Luigi Dorici. The whole, consisting of twenty-seven books, was published at Venice in 1548 by Tolomeo Janicolo of Brescia. This Janicolo was Trissino's favourite publisher.

Neither style nor metre rose to the heroic level. The
blank verse was pedestrian and prolix. The language
was charged with Lombardisms. Thus the *Italia
Liberata* proved at all points that Trissino could make
rules, but that he could not apply them to any purpose.
It is curious to compare his failure with Milton's
success in a not entirely dissimilar endeavour. The
poet achieves a triumph where the pedant only suffers
a defeat ; and yet the aim of both was almost identical.
So different is genius guided by principles from the
mechanical carpentry of imitative talent.

CHAPTER XIV.

BURLESQUE POETRY AND SATIRE.

Relation of Satiric to Serious Literature—Italy has more Parody and Caricature than Satire or Comedy—Life of Folengo—His *Orlandino*—Critique of Previous Romances—Lutheran Doctrines—Orlando's Boyhood—Griffarosto—Invective against Friars—Maccaronic Poetry—The Travesty of Humanism—Pedantesque Poetry—Glottogrysio Ludimagistro—Tifi Odassi of Padua—The Pedant Vigonça—Evangelista Fossa—Giorgio Alione—Folengo employs the Maccaronic Style for an Epic—His Address to the Muses—His Hero Baldus—Boyhood and Youth—Cingar—The Travels of the Barons—Gulfora—Witchcraft in Italy—Folengo's Conception of Witchcraft—Entrance into Hell—The Zany and the Pumpkin—Nature of Folengo's Satire—His Relation to Rabelais—The *Moscheis*—The *Zanitonella*—Maccaronic Poetry was Lombard—Another and Tuscan Type of Burlesque—*Capitoli*—Their Popular Growth—Berni—His Life—His Mysterious Death—His Character and Style—Three Classes of *Capitoli*—The pure Bernesque Manner—Berni's Imitators—The Indecency of this Burlesque—Such Humour was Indigenous—*Terza Rima*—Berni's Satires on Adrian VI. and Clement VII.—His Caricatures—His Sonnet on Aretino—The *Rifacimento* of Boiardo's *Orlando*—The Mystery of its Publication—Albicante and Aretino—The Publishers Giunta and Calvi—Berni's Protestant Opinions—Eighteen Stanzas of the *Rifacimento* printed by Vergerio—Hypothesis respecting the Mutilation of the *Rifacimento*—Satire in Italy.

In all classical epochs of literature comedy and satire have presented their antithesis to ideal poetry, by setting the actual against the imagined world, or by travestying the forms of serious art. Thus the Titanic farce of Aristophanes was counterposed to Æschylean tragedy; and Molière portrayed men as they are, before an audience which welcomed Racine's pictures of men as the age conceived they ought to be.

It is the mark of really great literature when both thesis and antithesis, the aspiration after the ideal and the critique of actual existence, exhibit an equality of scale. The comic and satiric species of poetry attain to grandeur only by contact with impassioned art of a high quality, or else by contrast with a natural greatness in the nation that produces them. Both masque and anti-masque reveal the mental stature of the people. Both issue from the conscience of society, and bear its impress.

If so much be admitted, we can easily understand why burlesque poetry formed the inevitable pendent to polite literature in Italy. There was no national tragedy ; therefore there could be no great comedy. The best work of the age, typified by Ariosto's epic, was so steeped in irony that it offered no vantage-ground for humorous counterpoise. There was nothing left but to exaggerate its salient qualities, and to caricature its form. Such exaggeration was burlesque ; such caricature was parody. In like manner, satire found no adequate sphere. The nation's life was not on so grand a scale as to evolve the elements of satire from the contrast between faculties and foibles. Nor again could a society, corrupt and satisfied with corruption, anxious to live and let live, apply the lash with earnestness to its own shoulders. *Facit indignatio versus*, was Juvenal's motto ; and indignation tore the heart of Swift. But in Italy there was no indignation. All men were agreed to tolerate, condone, and compromise. When vices come to be laughingly admitted, when discords between practice and profession furnish themes for tales and epigrams, the moral conscience is extinct. But without an appeal to conscience the satirist has no *locus standi*. Therefore, in Italy there was no great satire, as in Italy there was no great comedy.

The burlesque rhymesters portrayed their own and their neighbours' immorality with self-complacent humour, calling upon the public to make merry over the spectacle. This poetry, obscene, equivocal, frivolous, horribly sincere, supplied a natural antithesis to the pseudo-platonic, pedantic, artificial mannerism of the purists. In point of intrinsic value, there is not much to choose between the Petrarchistic and the burlesque styles. Many burlesque poets piqued themselves with justice on their elegance, and clothed gross thoughts in diction of elaborate polish. Meanwhile they laid the affectations, conventions and ideals of the age impartially under contribution. The sonnetteers suggested parodies to Aretino, who celebrated vice and deformity in women with hyperboles adapted from the sentimental school.[1] The age of gold was ridiculed by Romolo Bertini.[2] The idyll found its travesty in Berni's pictures of crude village loves and in Folengo's *Zanitonella*. Chivalry became absurd by the simple process of enforcing the prosaic elements in Ariosto, reducing his heroes to the level of plebeian life, and exaggerating the extravagance of his romance. The ironical smile which played upon his lips, expands into broad grins and horse-laughter. Yet though the burlesque poets turned everything they touched into ridicule, these buffoons were not unfre-

---

[1] See the Madrigals in *Opere Burlesche*, vol. iii. pp. 36-38.
[2] *Ibid.* p. 290.

quently possessed of excellent good sense. Not a few
of them, as we shall see, were among the freest thinkers
of their age. Like Court jesters they dared to utter
truths which would have sent a serious writer to the
stake. Lucidity of intellectual vision was granted at
this time in Italy to none but positive and materialistic
thinkers—to analysts like Machiavelli and Pomponazzi,
critics like Pietro Aretino, poets with feet firmly planted
on the earth like Berni and Folengo. The two last-
named artists in the burlesque style may be selected as
the leaders of two different but cognate schools, the
one flourishing in Lombardy, the other in Florence.

Girolamo Folengo was born in 1491 of noble
parents at Cipada, a village of the Mantuan district.
He made his first studies under his father's roof, and
in due time proceeded to Bologna. Here he attended
the lectures of Pomponazzi, and threw himself with
ardour into the pleasures and perils of the academical
career. Francesco Gonzaga, a fantastical and high-
spirited libertine from Mantua, was the recognised
leader of the students at that moment. Duels, challenges, intrigues and street-quarrels formed the staple
of their life. It was an exciting and romantic round
of gaiety and danger, of which the novelists have left
us many an animated picture. Folengo by his extravagant conduct soon exhausted the easy patience of the
university authorities. He was obliged to quit
Bologna, and his father refused to receive him. In
this emergency he took refuge in a Benedictine convent at Brescia. When he made himself a monk,
Folengo changed his Christian name to Teofilo, by
which he is now best known in literature. But he did

not long endure the confinement of a cloister. After
six years spent among the Benedictines, he threw the
cowl aside, and ran off with a woman, Girolama
Dieda, for whom he had conceived an insane passion.[1]
This was in the year 1515. During the next eleven
years he gave himself to the composition of burlesque
poetry. His *Maccaronea* appeared at Venice in 1519,
and his *Orlandino* in 1526. The former was published under the pseudonym of Merlinus Cocaius,
compounded of a slang word in the Mantuan dialect,
and of the famous wizard's title of romance.[2] The
latter bore the *nom de plume* of *Limerno Pitocco*—an
anagram of Merlino, with the addition of an epithet
pointing to the poet's indigence. These works brought
Folengo fame but little wealth, and he was fain to return at last to his old refuge.[3] Resuming the cowl, he
now retired to a monastery in the kingdom of Naples,
visited Sicily, and died at last near Padua, in the convent of S. Croce di Campese. This was in 1544.
The last years of his life had been devoted to religious
poetry, which is not read with the same curiosity as
his burlesque productions.

[1] In *Mac.* xx. (p. 152 of Mantuan edition, 1771), he darkly alludes to
this episode of his early life, where he makes an exposed witch exclaim :
> Nocentina vocor magicis tam dedita chartis,
> Decepique mea juvenem cum fraude Folengum.

[2] I cannot find sufficient authority for the story of Folengo's having
had a grammar-master named Cocaius, from whom he borrowed part of
his pseudonym. The explanation given by his Mantuan editor, which I
have adopted in the text, seems the more probable. *Cocáj* in Mantuan
dialect means a cork for a bottle ; and the phrase *ch' al fà di cocaj* is used
to indicate some extravagant absurdity or blunder.

[3] There seems good reason, from many passages in his *Maccaronea*, to
believe that his repentance was sincere. I may here take occasion to
remark that, though his poems are gross in the extreme, their moral tone
is not unhealthy. He never makes obscenity or vice attractive.

Teofilo Folengo, or Merlinus Cocaius, or Limerno
Pitocco, was, when he wrote his burlesque poems,
what the French would call a *déclassé*. He had com-
promised his character in early youth and had been
refused the shelter of his father's home. He had taken
monastic vows in a moment of pique, or with the baser
object of getting daily bread in idleness. His elope-
ment from the convent with a paramour had brought
scandal on religion. Each of these steps contributed to place him beyond the pale of respectability.
Driven to bay and forced to earn his living, he now
turned round upon society ; and spoke his mind out
with a freedom born of bile and cynical indifference.
If he had learned nothing else at Bologna, he had im-
bibed the materialistic philosophy of Pomponazzi together with Gonzaga's lessons in libertinage. Brutal-
ised, degraded in his own eyes, rejected by the world
of honest or decorous citizens, but with a keen sense
of the follies, vices and hypocrisies of his age, he
resolved to retaliate by a work of art that should
attract attention and force the public to listen to his
comments on their shame. In his humorous poetry
there is, therefore, a deliberate if not a very dignified
intention. He does not merely laugh, but mixes satire
with ribaldry, and points buffoonery with biting sarcasm. Since the burlesque style had by its nature to
be parasitical and needed an external motive, Folengo
chose for the subject of his parody the romance of
Orlando, which was fashionable to the point of extravagance in Italy after the appearance of the *Furioso*.
But he was not satisfied with turning a tale of Paladins
to ridicule. He used it as the shield behind which he

knew that he might safely shoot his arrows at the clergy and the princes of his native land, attack the fortresses of orthodoxy, and vent his spleen upon society by dragging its depraved ideals in the mire of his own powerful but vulgar scorn.

Folengo has told us that the *Orlandino* was conceived and written before the *Maccaronea*, though it was published some years later. It is probable that the rude form and plebeian language of this burlesque romance found but little favour with a public educated in the niceties of style. They were ready to accept the bastard Latin dialect invented for his second venture, because it offended no puristic sensibilities. But the coarse Italian of the *Orlandino* could not be relished by academicians, who had been pampered with the refinements of Berni's wanton Muse.[1] Only eight cantos appeared; nor is there reason to suppose that any more were written, for it may be assumed that the fragment had fulfilled its author's purpose.[2] That purpose was to satirise the vice, hypocrisy and superstition of the clergy, and more particularly of the begging friars. In form the *Orlandino* pretends to be

---

[1] Part of Folengo's satire is directed against the purists. See Canto i. 7–9. He confesses himself a Lombard, and shrugs his shoulders at their solemn criticisms :

> Non però, se non nacqui Tosco, i' piango ;
> Chè ancora il ciacco gode nel suo fango.

To the reproach of ' turnip-eating Lombard' he retorts, ' Tuscan chatterbox.' Compare vi. 1, 2, on his own style :

> Oscuri sensi ed affettate rime,
> Qual' è chi dica mai compor Limerno ?

[2] The first line of the elegy placed upon the edition of 1526 runs thus :

> Mensibus istud opus tribus *indignatio fecit.*

Folengo claims for himself a satiric purpose. The edition used by me is Molini's, Londra, 1775.

a romance of chivalry, and it bears the same relation to the *Orlando* of Boiardo and Ariosto as the *Secchia Rapita* to the heroic poems of Tasso's school. It begins with a burlesque invocation to Federigo Gonzaga, Marquis of Mantua, in which the poet bluntly describes his poverty and begs for largess. Then Folengo passes to an account of his authorities and to the criticism of his predecessors in romantic poetry. He had recourse, he says, to a witch of Val Camonica, who mounted him upon a ram, and bore him to the country of the Goths. There he found forty decades of Turpin's history among the rubbish of old books stolen from Italy. Of these, three decades had already been discovered and translated by Boiardo; but, after versifying a large portion of the second, the poet left the rest of it to Ariosto. The sixth was stolen from him by Francesco Bello. The last he gave with his own hands to Poliziano, who put it into rhyme and allowed Pulci to have the credit of his labours.[1] Folengo himself took a portion of the first decade, and thus obtained material for treating of the birth and boyhood of Orlando. This exordium is chiefly valuable as a piece of contemporary criticism :

> Queste tre Deche dunque sin quà trovo
> Esser dal fonte di Turpin cavate ;
> Ma *Trebisonda, Ancroia, Spagna,* e *Bovo*
> Coll' altro resto al foco sian donate :
> Apocrife son tutte, e le riprovo
> Come nemiche d' ogni veritate ;
> Boiardo, l' Ariosto, Pulci, e 'l Cieco
> Autenticati sono, ed io con seco.

If we may accept this stanza as expressing the opinion

---

[1] See above Part i. p. 455, for the belief that Poliziano was the real author of the *Morgante Maggiore*.

of Italians in the sixteenth century relative to their romantic poets, we find that it almost exactly agrees with that of posterity. Only the *Mambriano* of Bello has failed to maintain its place beside the *Morgante* and *Orlando*.

Embarking upon the subject of his tale, Folengo describes the Court of Charlemagne, and passes the Paladins in review, intermingling comic touches with exaggerated imitations of the romantic style. The peers of France preserve their well-known features through the distorting medium of caricature; while humorous couplets, detonating here and there like crackers, break the mock-heroical monotony. Gano, for example, is still the arch-traitor of the tribe of Judas :

> Figliuol non d' uomo, nè da Dio creato,
> Ma il gran Diavol ebbelo cacato.

The effect of parody is thus obtained by emphasising the style of elder poets and suddenly breaking off into a different vein. Next comes the description of Berta's passion for Milone, with a singularly coarse and out-spoken invective against love.[1] Meanwhile Charlemagne has proclaimed a tournament. The peers array themselves, and the Court is in a state of feverish expectation. *Parturiunt montes*: instead of mailed warriors careering upon fiery chargers, the knights crawl into the lists on limping mules and lean

---

[1] Canto i. 64, 65 ; ii. 1–4 :

> Ed io dico ch' Amor è un bardassola
> Più che sua madre non fu mai puttana, &c.

Folengo, of course, has a mistress, to whom he turns at the proper moments of his narrative. This *mia diva Caritunga* is a caricature of the fashionable Laura. See v. 1, 2 :

> O donna mia, ch' hai gli occhi, ch' hai l' orecchie,
> Quelli di pipistrel, queste di bracco, &c.

asses, with a ludicrous array of kitchen-gear for armour. The description of this donkey-tournament, is one of Folengo's triumphs.[1] When Milone comes upon the scene and jousts beneath his lady's balcony, the style is heightened to the tone of true romance, and, but for the roughness of the language, we might fancy that a page of the *Orlando* were beneath our eyes. A banquet follows, after which we are regaled with a Court-ball, and then ensues the comic chain of incidents which bring Milone and Berta to the fruition of their love. They elope, take ship, and are separated by a series of mishaps upon the open sea. Berta is cast ashore alone in Italy, and begs her way to Sutri, where she gives birth to Orlando in a shepherd's cabin. During the course of these adventures, Folengo diverts his readers with many brilliant passages and bits of satire, at one time inveighing against the licence of balls, at another describing the mixed company on board a ship of passage ; now breaking off into burlesque pedigrees, and then again putting into Berta's mouth a string of Lutheran opinions. Though the personages are romantic, the incidents are copied with realistic fidelity from actual life. We are moving among Italian *bourgeois* in the masquerade of heroes and princesses.

Berta's prayer, when she found herself alone upon the waters in an open boat, is so characteristic of Folengo's serious intention that it deserves more than a passing comment.[2] She addresses herself to God instead of to any Saints :

[1] Canto ii. 9–42.
[2] Canto vi. 40–46. I have placed a translation of this passage in an Appendix to this chapter.

> A te ricorro, non a Piero, o Andrea,
> Chè l' altrui mezzo non mi fa mestiero :
> Ben tengo a mente che la Cananea
> Non supplicò nè a Giacomo nè a Piero.

It is the hypocrisy of friars, Folengo says, who sacrifice to Moloch, while they use the name of Mary to cloak their crimes— it is this damnable hypocrisy which has blinded simple folk into trusting the invocation of Saints. Avarice is the motive of these false priests ; and lust moves them to preach the duty of confession :

> E qui trovo ben spesso un Confessore
> Essere più ruffiano che Dottore.

Therefore, cries Berta, I make my confession to God alone and from Him seek salvation, and vow that, if I escape the fury of the sea, I will no more lend belief to men who sell indulgences for gold. So far the poet is apparently sincere. In the next stanza he resumes his comic vein :

> Cotal preghiere carche d' eresia
> Berta facea, mercè ch' era Tedesca ;
> Perchè in quel tempo la Teologia
> Era fatta Romana e fiandresca ;
> Ma dubito ch' alfin nella Turchia
> Si troverà vivendo alla Moresca ;
> Perchè di Cristo l' inconsutil vesta
> Squarciata è sì che più non ve ne resta.

The blending of buffoonery and earnestness in Folengo's style might be illustrated by the bizarre myth of the making of peasants, where he introduces Christ and the Apostles [1] :

> *Transibat Jesus* per un gran villaggio
> Con Pietro, Andrea, Giovanni, e con Taddeo ;
> Trovan ch' un asinello in sul rivaggio
> Molte pallotte del suo sterco feo.

---

[1] Canto v. 56-58. The contempt for country folk seems unaffected.

> Disse allor Piero al suo Maestro saggio :
> *En, Domine, fac homines ex eo.*
> *Surge, Villane,* disse Cristo allora ;
> E 'l villan di que' stronzi saltò fora.

His fantastic humour, half-serious, half-flippant, spares nothing sacred or profane. Even the Last Judgment receives an inconceivably droll treatment on the slender occasion of an allusion to the disasters of Milan.[1] Folengo has just been saying that Italy well deserves her title of *barbarorum sepultura*.[2]

> Chè veramente in quell' orribil giorno
> Che in Giosafatto suonerà la tromba,
> Facendosi sentire al mondo intorno,
> E i morti salteran fuor d' ogni tomba,
> Non sarà pozzo, cacatojo, o forno,
> Che mentre il tararan del ciel ribomba,
> Non getti fuora Svizzeri, Francesi,
> Tedeschi, Ispani, e d' altri assai paesi ;

---

[1] Canto vi. 55–57. This passage is a caricature of Pulci's burlesque description of the Last Day. See above Part i. p. 449. Folengo's loathing of the strangers who devoured Italy is clear here, as also in i. 43, ii. 4, 59. But there is no force in his invectives or laments.

> L' Italia non più Italia appello,
> Ma d' ogni strana gente un bel bordello.
>
> .   .   .   .   .   .
>
> Che 'l cancaro mangiasse il Taliano,
> Il quale, o ricco, o povero che sia,
> Desidra in nostre stanze il Tramontano.
>
> .   .   .   .   .   .
>
> Chè se non fosser le gran parti in quella,
> Dominerebbe il mondo Italia bella.

> For verily on that most dreadful day,
>   When in the Valley of Jehosaphat
> The trump shall sound, and thrill this globe of clay,
>   And dead folk shuddering leave their tombs thereat,
> No well, sewer, privy shall be found, I say,
>   Which, while the angels roar their rat-tat-tat,
> Shall not disgorge its Spaniards, Frenchmen, Swiss,
> Germans, and rogues of every race that is.

E vederassi una mirabil guerra,
Fra loro combattendo gli ossi suoi :
Chi un braccio, chi una man, chi un piede afferra;
Ma vien chi dice—questi non son tuoi—
Anzi son miei—non sono ; e sulla terra
Molti di loro avran gambe di buoi,
Teste di muli, e d' asini le schiene,
Siccome all' opre di ciascun conviene.

The birth of Orlando gives occasion for a mock-heroic passage, in which Pulci is parodied to the letter.[1] All the more amusing for the assumption of the pompous style, is the ensuing account of the hero's boyhood among the street-urchins of Sutri. When he is tall enough to bestride a broomstick, Orlandino proves his valour by careering through the town and laughing at the falls he gets. At seven he shows the strength of twelve :

Urta, fracassa, rompe, quassa, e smembra ;
Orsi, leoni, tigri non paventa,
Ma contro loro intrepido s' avventa.

The octave stanzas become a cataract of verbs and nouns to paint his tempestuous childhood. It is a spirited comic picture of the Italian *enfant terrible*, stone-throwing, boxing, scuffling, and swearing like a pickpocket. At the same time the boy grows in cunning, and supports his mother by begging from one and bullying another of the citizens of Sutri :—

Then shall we see a wonderful dispute,
As each with each they wrangle, bone for bone ;
One grasps an arm, one grabs a hand, a foot ;
Comes one who says, ' These are not yours, you loon !'
' They're mine !' ' They're not !' While many a limb of brute
Joined to their human bodies shall be shown,
Mule's heads, bull's legs, cruppers and ears of asses,
As each man's life on earth his spirit classes.

[1] Canto vi. 8-11 :
   Quì nacque Orlando, l' inclito Barone ;
   Quì nacque Orlando, Senator Romano, &c.

Io v' addimando per l' amor di Dio
Un pane solo ed un boccal di vino ;
Officio non fu mai più santo e pio
Che se pascete il pover pellegrino :
Se non men date, vi prometto ch' io,
Quantunque sia di membra si piccino,
Ne prenderò da me senza riguardo ;
Chè salsa non vogl' io di San Bernardo.
  Cancar vi mangi, datemi a mangiare,
Se non, vi butterò le porte giuso ;
Per debolezza sentomi mancare,
E le budella vannomi a riffuso.
Gente devota, e voi persone care
Che vi leccate di buon rosto il muso,
Mandatemi, per Dio, qualche minestra,
O me la trate giù dalla finestra.

In the course of these adventures Orlandino meets Oliver, the son of Rainero, the governor, and breaks his crown in a quarrel. This brings about the catastrophe; for the young hero pours forth such a torrent of voluble slang, mixed with imprecations and menaces, that Rainero is forced to acknowledge the presence of a superior genius.[1] But before the curtain falls upon the discovery of Orlandino's parentage and his reception into the company of peers, Folengo devotes a canto to the episodical history of the Prelate Griffarosto.[2] The name of this Rabelaisian ecclesiastic—Claw-the-roast—sufficiently indicates the line of the poet's satire.

Whatever appeared in the market of Sutri fit for the table, fell into his clutches, or was transferred to

---

[1] Canto vii. 61-65.

[2] He has been identified on sufficiently plausible grounds with Ignazio Squarcialupo, the prior of Folengo's convent In the *Maccaronea* this burlesque personage reappears as the keeper of a tavern in hell, who feeds hungry souls on the most hideous messes of carrion and vermin (Book xxiii. p. 217). There is sufficient rancour in Griffarosto's portrait to justify the belief that Folengo meant in it to gratify a private thirst for vengeance.

the great bag he wore beneath his scapulary. His library consisted of cookery books ; and all the tongues he knew, were tongues of swine and oxen.[1] Orlandino met this Griffarosto fat as a stalled ox, one morning after he had purchased a huge sturgeon :

> La Reverenzìa vostra non si parta ;
> Statemi alquanto, prego, ad ascoltare.
> *Nimis sollicita es, o Marta, Marta,*
> *Circa substantiam Christi devorare.*
> Dammi poltron, quel pesce, ch' io 'l disquarta,
> Per poterlo *in communi* dispensare,
> Nassa d' anguille che tu sei, lurcone ;
> E ciò dicendo dagli col bastone.

The priest was compelled to disgorge his prey, and the fame of the boy's achievement went abroad through Sutri. Rainero thereupon sent for Griffarosto, and treated the Abbot to such a compendious abuse of monks in general as would have delighted a Lutheran.[2] Griffarosto essayed to answer him with a ludicrous jumble of dog Latin ; but the Governor requested him to defer his apology for the morrow. The description of Griffarosto's study in the monastery, where wine and victuals fill the place of books, his oratory consecrated to Bacchus, the conversation with his cook, and the *ruse* by which the cook gets chosen Prior in his master's place, carry on the satire through fifty stanzas of slashing sarcasm. The whole episode is a pendent picture to Pulci's Margutte. Then, by a brusque change from buffoonery to seriousness, Folengo plunges into a confession of faith, attributed to Rainero, but presumably his own.[3] It includes the essential

---

[1] In the play on the word *lingue* there is a side-thrust at the Purists.
[2] Canto viii. 23–32.
[3] Canto viii. 73–84. This passage I have also translated and placed in

points of Catholic orthodoxy, abjuring the impostures of priests and friars, and taking final station on the Lutheran doctrine of salvation by faith and repentance. Idle as a dream, says Folengo, are the endeavours made by friars to force scholastic conclusions on the conscience in support of theses S. Paul would have rejected. What they preach, they do not comprehend. Their ignorance is only equal to their insolent pretension. They are worse than Judas in their treason to Christ, worse than Herod, Anna, Caiaphas, or Pilate. They are only fit to consort with usurers and slaves. They use the names of saints and the altar of the Virgin as the means of glutting their avarice with the gold of superstitious folk. They abuse confession to gratify their lusts. Their priories are dens of dogs, hawks, and reprobate women. They revel in soft beds, drink to intoxication, and stuff themselves with unctuous food. And still the laity entrust their souls to these rogues, and there are found many who defraud their kith and kin in order to enrich a convent![1]

It would not be easy to compose an invective more suited to degrade the objects of a satirist's anger by the copiousness and the tenacity of the dirt flung at them. Yet the *Orlandino* was written by a monk, who, though he had left his convent, was on the point of returning to it; and the poem was openly printed during the pontificate of Clement VII. That Folengo should have escaped inquisitorial censure is

---

an Appendix to this chapter, where the chief Lutheran utterances of the burlesque poets will be found together.

[1] In addition to the eighth Canto, I have drawn on iii. 4, 20 ; iv. 13 ; vi. 44, for this list.

remarkable. That he should have been readmitted to the Benedictine order after this outburst of bile and bold diffusion of heretical opinion, is only explicable by the hatred which subsisted in Italy between the rules of S. Francis and S. Benedict. While attacking the former, he gratified the spite and jealousy of the latter. But the fact is that his auditors, whether lay or clerical, were too accustomed to similar charges and too frankly conscious of their truth, to care about them. Folengo stirred no indignation in the people, who had laughed at ecclesiastical corruption since the golden days of the Decameron. He roused no shame in the clergy, for, till Luther frightened the Church into that pseudo-reformation which Sarpi styled a deformation of manners, the authorities of Rome were nonchalantly careless what was said about them.[1] An atrabilious monk in his garret vented his spleen with more than usual acrimony, and the world applauded. *Ha fatto un bel libro!* That was all. Conversely, it is not strange that the weighty truths about religion uttered by Folengo should have had but little influence. He was a scribbler, famous for scurrility, notoriously profligate in private life. Free thought in Italy found itself too often thus in company with immorality. The names of heretic and Lutheran carried with them at that time a reproach more pungent and more reasonable than is usual with the epithets of theological hatred.[2]

---

[1] Leo X.'s complacent acceptance of the *Mandragola* proves this.

[2] The curious history of Giulio Trissino, told by Bernardo Morsolin in the last chapters of his *Giangiorgio Trissino* (Vicenza, 1878), reveals the manner of men who adopted Lutheranism in Italy in the sixteenth century. See above, p. 304. I shall support the above remarks lower down in this chapter by reference to Berni's Lutheran opinions.

In the *Orlandino*, Ariosto's irony is degraded to buffoonery. The prosaic details he mingled with his poetry are made the material of a new and vulgar comedy of manners. The satire he veiled in allegory or polite discussion, bursts into open virulence. His licentiousness yields to gross obscenity. The chivalrous epic, as employed for purposes of art in Italy, contained within itself the germs of this burlesque. It was only necessary to develop certain motives at the expense of general harmony, to suppress the noble and pathetic elements, and to lower the literary key of utterance, in order to produce a parody. Ariosto had strained the semi-seriousness of romance to the utmost limits of endurance. For his successors nothing was left but imitation, caricature, or divergence upon a different track. Of these alternatives, Folengo and Berni, Aretino and Fortiguerra, chose the second; Tasso took the third, and provided Tassoni with the occasion of a new burlesque.

While the romantic epic lent itself thus easily to parody, another form of humorous poetry took root and flourished on the mass of Latin literature produced by the Revival. Latin never became a wholly dead language in Italy; and at the height of the Renaissance a public had been formed whose appreciation of classic style ensured a welcome for its travesty. To depreciate the humanistic currency by an alloy of plebeian phrases, borrowed from various base dialects; to ape Virgilian mannerism while treating of the lowest themes suggested by boisterous mirth or satiric wit; was the method of the so-called Maccaronic poets. It is matter for debate who first invented this style, and who created the title *Maccaronea.* So far back as the thirteenth century, we notice a blending of Latin with French and German in certain portions of the *Carmina Burana.*[1] But the two elements of language here lie side by side, without interpenetration. This imperfect fusion is not sufficient to constitute the genuine Maccaronic manner. The jargon known as Maccaronic must consist of the vernacular, suited with Latin terminations, and freely mingled with classical Latin words. Nothing should meet the ear or eye, which does not sound or look like Latin; but, upon inspection, it must be discovered that a half or third is simple slang and common speech tricked out with the endings of Latin declensions and conjugations.[2] In Italy, where the modern tongue retained close similarity to Latin, this amalgamation was easy; and we find that in the fifteenth century the hybrid had already assumed finished form. The name by which it was then known, indicates its composition. As maccaroni is dressed with cheese and butter, so the maccaronic poet mixed colloquial expressions of the people with classical Latin, serving up a dish that satisfied the appetite by rarity and richness of concoction. At the

---

[1] The political and ecclesiastical satires known in England as the work of Walter Mapes, abound in pseudo-Maccaronic passages. Compare Du Méril, *Poésies Populaires Latines antérieures au xiime Siècle,* p. 142, &c., for further specimens of undeveloped Maccaronic poetry of the middle ages.

[2] Those who are curious to study this subject further, should consult the two exhaustive works of Octave Delepierre, *Macaronéana* (Paris, 1852), and *Macaronéana Andra* (Londres, Trübner, 1862). These two publications contain a history of Maccaronic verse, with reprints of the scarcer poems in this style. The second gives the best text of Odassi, Fossa, and the *Virgiliana.* The *Maccheronee di Cinque Poeti Italiani* (Milano, Daelli, 1864), is a useful little book, since it reproduces Delepierre's collections in a cheap and convenient form. In the uncertainty which attends the spelling of this word, I have adopted the form *Maccaronic.*

same time, since maccaroni was the special delicacy of
the proletariate, and since a stupid fellow was called a
Maccherone, the ineptitude and the vulgarity of the
species are indicated by its title. Among the Maccaronic poets we invariably find ourselves in low Bohemian company. No Phœbus sends them inspiration ;
nor do they slake their thirst at the Castalian spring.
The muses they invoke are tavern-wenches and scul-
lions, haunting the slums and stews of Lombard cities.[1]
Their mistresses are of the same type as Villon's Mar-
got.   Mountains of cheese, rivers of fat broth, are
their Helicon and Hippocrene. Their pictures of manners demand a coarser brush than Hogarth's to do
them justice.

Before engaging in the criticism of this Maccaronic
literature, it is necessary to interpolate some notice of
a kindred style, called *pedantesco*. This was the exact
converse of the Maccaronic manner.   Instead of adapting Italian to the rules of Latin, the parodist now
treated Latin according to the grammatical usages
and metrical laws of Italian. A good deal of the
Hypnerotomachia Poliphili is written in *lingua pedan-
tesca*. But the recognised masterpiece of the species
is a book called *I Cantici di Fidentio Glottogrysio
Ludimagistro*. The author's real name was Camillo
Scrofa, a humanist and schoolmaster of Vicenza.
Though more than once reprinted, together with simi-

----

[1] Take one example, from the induction to Odassi's poems (*Mac.
Andr.* p. 63) :

O putanarum putanissima, vacca vaccarum,
O potifarum potissima pota potaza . . .
Tu Phrosina mihi foveas, mea sola voluptas ;
Nulla mihi poterit melius succurrere Musa,
Nullus Apollo magis.

lar compositions by equally obscure craftsmen, his verses are exceedingly rare.[1] They owe their neglect partly to the absurdity of their language, partly to the undisguised immorality of their subject-matter. Of the *stilo pedantesco* the following specimen may suffice. It describes a hostelry of boors and peasants [2]:

Pur pedetentim giunsi ad un cubiculo,
Sordido, inelegante, ove molti hospiti
Facean corona a un semimortuo igniculo.
Salvete, dissi, et Giove lieti e sospiti
Vi riconduca a i vostri dolci hospitii !
Ma responso non hebbi ; o rudi, o inhospiti !
Io che tra veri equestri e tra patritii
Soglio seder, mi vedi alhor negligere
Da quegli huomini novi et adventitii.
Non sapea quasi indignabundo eligere
Partito ; pur al fin fu necessario
Tra lor per calefarmi un scanno erigere.
Che colloquio, O Dii boni, empio e nefario
Pervenne a l' aure nostre purgatissime,
Da muover nausea a un lenone a un sicario !

One of the most famous and earliest, if not absolutely the first among the authors of Maccaronic verse, was Tifi Odassi, a Paduan, whose poems were given to the press after his death, in at least two editions earlier than the close of the fifteenth century.[3] He chose a commonplace *Novella* for his theme; but the

---

[1] The book was first printed at Vicenza. The copy I have studied is the Florentine edition of 1574. Scrofa's verses, detached from the collection, may be found in the *Parnaso Italiano*, vol. xxv.

[2] *Op. cit.* p. 23.

[3] Bernardino Scardeone in his work *De antiquitate urbis Patavii*, &c. (Basileæ, 1560), speaks of Odassi as the inventor of Maccaronic poetry : 'adinvenit enim primus ridiculum carminis genus, nunquam prius a quopiam excogitatum, quod Macaronæum nuncupavit, multis farcitum salibus, et satyrica mordacitate respersum.' He adds that Odassi desired on his deathbed that the book should be burned. In spite of this wish, it was frequently reprinted during Scardeone's lifetime.

interest of his tale consists less in its argument than in its vivid descriptions of low town-life. Odassi's portraits of plebeian characters are executed with masterly realism, and the novelty of the vehicle gives them a singularly trenchant force. It is unfortunately impossible to bring either the cook-shop-keeper or his female servant, the mountebank or the glutton, before modern readers. These pictures are too Rabelaisian.[1] I must content myself with a passage taken from the description of a bad painter, which, though it is inferior in comic power, contains nothing unpardonably gross.[2]

> Quodsi forte aliquem voluit depingere gallum,
> Quicunque aspiciat poterit jurare cigognam ;
> Depinxitque semel canes in caza currentes,
> Omnes credebant natantes in æquore luzos ;
> Sive hominem pingit, poteris tu credere lignum
> In quo sartores ponunt sine capite vestes ;
> Seu nudos facit multo sudore putinos,
> Tu caput a culo poteris dignoscere nunquam ;
> Sive facit gremio Christum retinere Mariam,
> Non licet a filio sanctam dignoscere matrem ;
> Pro gardelinis depingit sepe gallinas,
> Et pro gallinis depingit sepe caballos :
> Blasfemat, jurat, culpam dicit esse penelli,
> Quos spazzaturas poteris jurare de bruscho ;
> Tam bene depingit pictorum pessimus iste,
> Nec tamen inferior se cogitat esse Bellino.

It will be seen from this specimen that Italian and Latin are confounded without regard to either prosody or propriety of diction. The style, far from being even pedestrian, is reptile, and the inspiration is worthy

---

[1] It is with great regret that I omit Bertapalia, the charlatan—a portrait executed with inimitable verve. Students of Italian life in its lowest and liveliest details should seek him out. *Mac. Andr.* pp. 68–71.

[2] *Ibid.* p. 71. I have altered spelling and punctuation.

of the source imagined by the poet.[1] As Odassi remarks in his induction :

> Aspices, lector, Prisciani vulnera mille
> Gramaticamque novam, quam nos docuere putane.

The note struck by Odassi was sustained by his immediate imitators. Another Paduan author used this parody of humanistic verse to caricature a humanist, whom
he called Vigonça.[2] Like Odassi, he invoked Venus
Volvivaga ; and like Odassi's, very little of his verse is
quotable. The following extracts may be found acceptable for their humorous account of a Professor's inau-
gural lecture in the university of Padua.[3] Vigonça
announces the opening of his course :

> Ipse ante totis facit asavere piacis,
> Et totis scolis mandat bolletina bidelis,
> Quæ bolletina portabant talia verba :
> ' Comes magnificus cavalerius ille Vigonça,
> Patricius Patavus comesque ab origine longa,
> Vos rogat ad primam veniatis quisque legendam ;
> Qui veniet, magnum fructum portabit a casa.'
> Omnes venturos sese dixere libenter ;
> Promissit comes, capitaneus atque potestas,
> Et paduani vechi juvenesque politi.
> Lux promissa aderat, qua se smatare Vigonça
> Debebat, atque suam cunctis monstrare matieram.
> Ille tamen totam facit conçare la scolam,
> De nigro totam facit conzare cathedram,
> In qua debebat matus sprologare Vigonça ;

> [1] Cognosces in me quantum tua numina possunt,
> Quæque tua veniunt stilantia carmina pota.

[1] This anonymous poet has been variously identified with Odassi and
with Fossa of Cremona. The frequent occurrence of Paduan idioms
seems to point to a Paduan rather than a Cremonese author ; and though
there is no authoritative reason for referring the poem to Odassi, it
resembles his style sufficiently to render the hypothesis of his authorship
very plausible. The name of the hero, Vigonça, is probably the Italian
Bigoncia, which meant in one sense a pulpit or a reading-desk, in its
ordinary sense a tub.

[3] Daelli, *Maccheronee di Cinque Poeti Italiani* (Milano, 1864), p. 50 ;
cp. *Mac. Andr.* p. 19.

Cetera fulgebant banchalis atque thapetis,
Et decem in brochis dicit spendidisse duchatos.

After narrating how the whole town responded to Vigonça's invitation, and how the folk assembled to hear his first address, the poet thus describes the great occasion [1] :

Sed neque bastabat ingens intrantibus ussus ;
Rumpebant cupos parietes atque fenestras,
Inque ipso multos busos fecere parete.
Tunc ibi bidelus cunctos ratione pregavit,
Et sibi cavavit nigrum Vigonça biretum,
Et manicas alzans dedit hic sua verba de mato,
Et començavit sanctam faciendo la crucem.
'Magnifice pretor, pariter generose prefecte,
Tu facunde comes auri portando colanam,
Magnus philosophus, lingua in utraque poeta,
'1 u primicerius, Venete spes alma paludis,
Et vos doctores, celeberrima fama per orbem,
Vos cavalerii multum sperone dorati,
Vosque scolares, cives, charique sodales !
Non ego perdivi tempus futuendo putanas,
Non ego zugando, non per bordella vagando ;
Non ego cum canibus lepores seguendo veloces,
Non cum sparveris, non cum falconibus ipse ;
Non ego cum dadis tabulam lissando per ullam ;
Non ego cum chartis volui dissipare dinaros,
Qualiter in Padue faciunt de nocte scolares.
Quum jocant alii, stabat in casa Vigonça
Et studiabat guardando volumina longa.'

This Paduan caricature may be reckoned among the most valuable documents we possess for the illustration of the professorial system in Italy during the ascendancy of humanism. Some material of the same kind is supplied by the *Virgiliana* of Evangelista Fossa, a Cremonese gentleman, who versified a Venetian *Burla* in mock-heroic Latin. He, too, painted the portrait of a pedant, Priscianus [2] :

---

[1] Daelli, *op. cit.* pp. 52, 54.
[2] *Ibid.* p. 112 ; *Mac. Andra*, p. 32.

> Est mirandus homo ; nam sunt miracula in illo,
> Omnes virtutes habet hic in testa fichatas . . .
> Nam quicquid dicit, semper per littera parlat,
> Atque habet in boccham pulchra hæc proverbia semper. . . .
> Est letrutus nam multum, studiavit in omni
> Arte, fuit Padoe, fuit in la citta de Perosa,
> Bononie multum mansit de senno robando.

But Fossa's *Virgiliana*, while aiming at a more subtle sort of parody than the purely maccaronic poems, misses their peculiar salt, and, except for the Hudibrastic description of the author on horseback,[1] offers nothing of great interest.

Brief notice also may be taken of Giovan Giorgio Alione's satire on the Lombards. Alione was a native of Asti, and seasoned his maccaroni with the base French of his birthplace. For Asti, transferred to the House of Orleans by Gian Galeazzo Visconti, was more than half a French city, and its inhabitants spoke the Gallic dialect common to Piedmont.[2] Alione is proud of this subjection, and twits the Lombards of Milan and Pavia with being unworthy of their ancient origin no less than of their modern masters.[3] Unlike the ordinary run of burlesque poems, his *Macharonea* is virulently satirical. Animated by a real rage against the North Italians, Alione paints them as effeminate cowards, devoid of the sense of honour and debased by the vices of ill-bred *parvenus*. The open-

---

[1] ' De fossa compositore quando venit patavio ' (*Mac. Andra.*, p. 39).

[2] Alione says :

> Cum nos Astenses reputemur undique Galli.

[3] See the passage beginning ' O Longobardi frapatores,' and ending with these lines :

> Tunc baratasti Gallorum nobile nomen
> Cum Longobardo, &c.

Daelli, *op. cit.* p. 94.

ing of a *Novella* he relates, may be cited as a fair
specimen of his style [1] :

> Quidam Franzosus, volens tornare Parisum,
> Certum Milaneysum scontravit extra viglianam
> Sine capello docheti testa bagnatum :
> Et cum ignoraret Gallicus hic unde fuisset
> Dixit vulgariter *estes vous moglie mon amicus?*
> Ille qui intelligit a la rebusa, respondit
> *Sy sy mi che ho mogle Milani et anca fiolos.*
> Gallus tunc cernens Lombardum fore loquela,
> Et recordatus quod tempore guerre Salucis
> Alixandrini fecerant pagare menestram
> Scutumque sibi sgrafignarant de gibesera,
> Sfodravit ensem dicens *o tretre ribalde*
> *Rendez moy sa mon escu,* sy non a la morte spazat.

The end of the story is far too crude to quote, and it
is probable that even the most curious readers will
already have had enough of Alione's peculiar gibberish.

The maccaronic style had reached this point when
Folengo took possession of it, stamped it with his own
genius, and employed it for one of the most important
poems of the century. He is said to have begun a
serious Latin epic in his early manhood, and to have
laid this aside because he foresaw the impossibility of
wresting the laurels from Virgil. This story is
probably a legend ; but it contains at least an element
of truth. Folengo aimed at originality ; he chose to
be the first of burlesque Latin poets rather than to
claim the name and fame of a Virgilian imitator.[2] In

---

[1] Daelli, p. 93.

[2] In the first book of the *Moscheis,* line 7, he says :

> Gens ceratana sinat vecchias cantare batajas,
> Squarzet Virgilios turba pedanta suos.

The end of the *Maccaronea* sets forth the impossibility of modern bards
contending with the great poet of antiquity. Pontanus, Sannazzarius, all
the best Latin writers of the age, pale before Virgil :

the proemium to his *Moscheis* he professes to have found the orthodox Apollo deaf to his prayers :

> Illius heu frustra doctas captare sorores
> Speravi ac multa laude tenere polos.

The reason of the god's anger was that his votary had sullied the clear springs of Hippocrene :

> Nescio quas reperi musas, turpesve sorores,
> Nescio quas turpi carmina voce canunt.
> Limpida Pegasidum vitiavi stagna profanus,
> Totaque sunt limo dedecorata meo.

The exordium to the *Maccaronea* introduces us to these vulgar Muses, *grossæ Camœnæ*, who fill their neophytes with maccaronic inspiration :

> Jam nec Melpomene, Clio, nec magna Thalia,
> Nec Phœbus grattando lyram mihi carmina dictet,
> Qui tantos olim doctos fecere poetas ;
> Verum cara mihi foveat solummodo Berta,
> Gosaque, Togna simul, Mafelina, Pedrala, Comina.
> Veridicæ Musæ sunt hæ, doctæque sorellæ ;
> Quarum non multis habitatio nota poetis.

The holy hill of Folengo's Muses is a mountain of cheese and maccaroni, with lakes of broth and rivers of unctuous sauces :

> Stant ipsæ Musæ super altum montis acumen,
> Formajum gratulis durum retridando foratis.

> Non tamen æquatur vati quem protulit Andes,
> Namque vetusta nocet laus nobis sæpe modernis.

This refrain he repeats for each poet with whimsical reiteration. Folengo's own ambition to take the first place among burlesque writers appears in the final lines of *Mac.* book iii. ;

> Mantua Virgilio gaudet, Verona Catullo,
> Dante suo florens urbs Tusca, Cipada Cocajo :
> Dicor ego superans alios levitate poetas,
> Ut Maro medesimos superans gravitate poetas.

The induction to the *Moscheis* points to a serious heroic poem on Mantua, which he abandoned for want of inspiration. We have in these references enough to account for the myth above mentioned.

Here he seeks them, and here they deign to crown
him poet [1]:

> Ergo macaronicas illic cattavimus artes,
> Et me grossiloquum vatem statuere sorores.

We have seen already that the maccaronic style
involved a free use of plebeian Italian, embedded in
a mixed mass of classical and medieval Latinity.
Folengo refined the usage of his predecessors, by
improving the versification, adopting a more uniformly
heroic tone, and introducing scraps of Mantuan dialect
at unexpected intervals, so that each lapse into Italian
has the force of a surprise—what the Greeks called
παρὰ προσδοκίαν. The comic effect is produced by a
sustained epical inflation, breaking irregularly into the
coarsest and least pardonable freaks of vulgarity. It
is as though the poet were improvising, emulous of
Virgil; but the tide of inspiration fails him, he falls
short of classical phrases to express his thoughts, and
is forced in the hurry of the moment to avail himself
of words and images that lie more close at hand. His
Pegasus is a showy hack, who ambles on the bypaths
of Parnassus, dropping now and then a spavined hock
and stumbling back into his paces with a snort. His
war-trumpet utters a sonorous fanfaronnade; but the
blower loses breath, and breaks his note, or suffers it
to lapse into a lamentable quaver.

Tifi Odassi, who may be regarded as Folengo's
master in this species of verse, confined the Maccaronic

---

[1] Compare *Mac.* vii. p. 195.

> Nil nisi crassiloquas dicor scrivisse camœnas,
> Crassiloquis igitur dicamus magna camœnis.

This *great theme* is nothing less than monasticism in its vilest aspects.

Muse to quaintly-finished sketches in the Dutch style.[1] His pupil raised her to the dignity of Clio and composed an epic in twenty-five books. The length of this poem and the strangeness of the manner render it unpalatable to all but serious students at the present time. Its humour has evaporated, and the form itself strikes us as rococo. We experience some difficulty in sympathising with those readers of the sixteenth century, who, perfectly acquainted with Latin poetry and accustomed to derive intellectual pleasure from its practice, found exquisite amusement in so cleverly constructed a parody. Nor is it possible for Englishmen to appreciate the more delicate irony of the vulgarisms, which Folengo adopted from one of the coarsest Italian dialects, and cemented with subtle skill upon the stately structure of his hexameters. Still we may remember that the *Maccaronea* was read with profit by Rabelais, and that much of Butler's humour betrays a strong affinity to this antiquated burlesque.

In substance the *Maccaronea* begins with a rehandling of the *Orlandino*. Guido, peerless among Paladins, wins the love of his king's daughter, Baldovina of France. They fly together into Italy, and she dies in giving birth to a son at Cipada, near Mantua. Guido disappears, and the boy, Baldus, is brought up by a couple of peasants. He believes himself to be their child, and recognises the rustic boor, Zambellus, for his brother. Still the hero's nature reveals itself in the village urchin; and, like the young Orlando, Baldus performs prodigies of valour in his boyhood:

[1] At the end of the *Maccaronea* I think there may be an allusion to Odassi conveyed in these words, *Tifi Caroloque futuris*.

> Non it post vaccas, at sæpe caminat ad urbem,
> Ac ad Panadæ dispectum praticat illam ;
> In villam semper tornabat vespere facto,
> Portabatque caput fractum gambasque macatas.

When he goes to school, he begins by learning his letters with great readiness. But he soon turns away from grammar to books of chivalry :

> Sed mox Orlandi nasare volumina cœpit ;
> Non vacat ultra deponentia discere verba,
> Non species, numeros, non casus atque figuras,
> Non Doctrinalis versamina tradere menti :
> Fecit de norma scartazzos mille Donati
> Inque Perotinum librum salcicia coxit.
> Orlandi solum, nec non fera bella Rinaldi
> Aggradant; animum faciebat talibus altum :
> Legerat Ancrojam, Tribisondam, gesta Danesi,
> Antonæque Bovum, mox tota Realea Francæ,
> Innamoramentum Carlonis et Asperamontem,
> Spagnam, Altobellum, Morgantis facta gigantis.

And so forth through the whole list of chivalrous romances, down to the *Orlando Furioso* and the *Orlandino.* The boy's heart is set on deeds of daring. He makes himself the captain of a band of rogues who turn the village of Cipada upside down. Three of these deserve especial notice—Fracassus, Cingar, and Falchettus ; since they became the henchmen of our hero in all his subsequent exploits. Fracassus was descended in the direct line from Morgante :

> Primus erat quidam Fracassus prole gigantis,
> Cujus stirps olim Morganto venit ab illo,
> Qui bachiocconem campanæ ferre solebat
> Cum quo mille hominum colpo sfracasset in uno.

Cingar in like manner drew his blood from Pulci's Margutte :

> Alter erat Baldi compagnus, nomine Cingar,
> Accortus, ladro, semper truffare paratus ;

Scarnus enim facie, reliquo sed corpore nervis
Plenus, compressus, picolinus, brunus, et atrox,
Semper habens nudam' testam, rizzutus et asper.
Iste suam traxit Marguti a sanguine razzam,
Qui ad calcagnos sperones ut gallus habebat
Et nimio risu simia cagante morivit.

Falchettus boasted a still stranger origin[1] :

Sed quidnam de 'te, Falchette stupende, canemus ?
Tu quoque pro Baldo bramasti prendere mortem.
Forsitan, o lector, quæ dico, dura videntur,
Namque Pulicano Falchettus venit ab illo
Quem scripsere virum medium, mediumque catellum ;
Quapropter sic sic noster Falchettus habebat
Anteriora viri, sed posteriora canina.

It would be too long to relate how Baldus received knightly education from a nobleman who admired his daring; how, ignorant of his illustrious blood, he married the village beauty Berta ; and how he made himself the petty tyrant of Cipada. The exploits of his youth are a satire on the violence of local magnates, whose manners differed little from those of the peasants they oppressed. In course of time Baldus fell under the displeasure of a despot stronger than himself, and was shut up in prison.[2] In the absence of his hero from the scene, the poet now devotes himself to the exploits of Cingar among the peasants of Cipada. Without lowering his epic tone, Folengo fills five books with whimsical adventures, painting the

[1] I do not recognise Pulicanus, who is said to be the ancestor of Falchettus. Is it a misprint for Fulicanus ? Fulicano is a giant in Bello's *Mambriano*, one of Folengo's favourite poems of romance.

[2] *Mac.* iii. The edition I quote from is that of Mantua (?) under name of Amsterdam, 1769 and 1771, 2 vols. 4to. See vol. i. p. 117, for a satire on the frauds and injustice of a country law-court, followed by a mock heroic panegyric of the Casa Gonzaga. The description of their celebrated stud and breed of horses may be read with interest.

manners of the country in their coarsest colours, and introducing passages of stinging satire on the monks he hated.[1]　Cingar, finding himself on one occasion in a convent, gives vent to a long soliloquy which expresses Folengo's own contempt for the monastic institutions that filled Italy with rogues :

> Quo diavol, ait, tanti venere capuzzi ?
> Nil nisi per mundum video portare capuzzos :
> Quisquam vult fieri Frater, vult quisque capuzzum.
> Postquam giocarunt nummos, tascasque vodarunt,
> Postquam pane caret cophinum, celaria vino,
> In Fratres properant, datur his extemplo capuzzus.
> Undique sunt isti Fratres, istique capuzzi.
> Qui sint nescimus ; discernere nemo valeret
> Tantas vestitum foggias, tantosque colores :
> Sunt pars turchini, pars nigri, parsque morelli,
> Pars albi, russi, pars gialdi, parsque bretini.
> Si per iter vado telluris, cerno capuzzos ;
> Si per iter pelagi, non mancum cerno capuzzos ;
> Quando per armatos eo campos, cerno capuzzos ;
> Sive forum subeo, sive barcam, sive tabernam,
> Protinus ante oculos aliquem mihi cerno capuzzum.

There will soon be no one left to bear arms, till the fields, or ply the common handicrafts.　All the villeins make themselves monks, aspiring to ecclesiastical honours and seeking the grade of superiority denied them by their birth.　It is ambition that fills the convents :

> Illic nobilitas sub rusticitate laborat,
> Ambitio quoniam villanos unica brancat.

[1] The episode of Berta's battle with her sister Laena (*Mac.* iv. p. 144), the apostrophe to old age (*Mac.* v. p. 152), the village ball (*ibid.* p. 163), the tricks played by Cingar on Zambellus (*ibid.* p. 168, and *Mac.* vi.), the description of the convent of Motella (*Mac.* vii. 196), the portrait of the ignorant parish-priest (*Mac.* vii. p. 202), the Carnival Mass (*Mac.* viii. p. 212), followed by a drunken *Ker Mess* (*ibid.* p. 214), are all executed in the broad style of a Dutch painter, and abound in realistic sketches of Lombard country-life.

This tirade is followed by the portrait of Prae Jacopinus, a village parson whose stupidity is only equalled by his vices. Jacopino's education in the alphabet is a masterpiece of Rabelaisian humour, and the following passage on his celebration of the Mass brings all the sordidness of rustic ceremonial before our eyes[1] :

> Præterea Missam foggia dicebat in una,
> Nec crucis in fronte signum formare sciebat.
> Inter Confiteor parvum discrimen et Amen
> Semper erat, jam jam meditans adjungere finem ;
> Incipiebat enim nec adhuc in nomine Patris,
> Quod tribus in saltis veniebat ad Ite misestum.

From generalities Folengo passes to particulars in the following description of a village Mass[2] :

> Inde Jacopinus, chiamatis undique Pretis,
> Cœperat in gorga Missam cantare stupendam ;
> Subsequitant alii, magnisque cridoribus instant.
> Protinus Introitum spazzant talqualiter omnem,
> Ad Chyrios veniunt, quos miro dicere sentis
> Cum contrappunto, veluti si cantor adesset
> Master Adrianus, Constantius atque Jachettus.
> Hic per dolcezzam scorlabant corda vilani
> Quando de quintis terzisque calabat in unam
> Musicus octavam noster Jacopinus et ipsas
> Providus octavas longa cum voce tirabat.
> Gloria in excelsis passat, jam Credo propinquat ;
> Oh si Josquinus Cantorum splendor adesset !

Meanwhile Baldus has been left in prison, and it is time for Cingar to undertake his rescue. He effects this feat, by stripping two Franciscan monks, and dressing himself up in the frock he has just filched

---

[1] *Mac.* vii. p. 204.
[2] *Mac.* vii. p. 212. Folengo seems to have been fond of music. See the whimsical description of four-part singing, *Mac.* xx. p. 139, followed by the panegyric of Music and the malediction of her detractors.

from one of them, while he coaxes the unfortunate
Zambellus to assume the other. Then he persuades
the people of Mantua that he has seen himself assassi-
nated on the high road ; gains access to Baldus in the
dungeon, on the plea of hearing his confession ; and
contrives to leave Zambellus there in the clothes of
Baldus, after disguising his friend in one of the friar's
tunics. The story is too intricate for repetition here.[1]
Suffice it to say that Baldus escapes and meets a knight
errant, Leonardus, at the city gate, who has ridden all
the way from Rome to meet so valorous a Paladin.
They swear eternal friendship. The three henchmen
of the hero muster round the new comrades in arms ;
and the party thus formed set forth upon a series of
adventures in the style of Astolfo's journey to the
moon.

This part of the epic is a close copy of the chivalrous romances in their more fantastic details. The
journey of the Barons, as they are now invariably
styled, is performed in a great ship. They encounter
storms and pirates, land on marvellous islands, enter
fairy palaces, and from time to time recruit their forces
with notable rogues and drunkards whom they find
upon their way. The parody consists in the similarity
of their achievements to those of knight-errantry, while
they are themselves in all points unlike the champions
of chivalry. One of their most cherished companions,
for example, is Boccalus, a Bergamasque buffoon, who

---

[1] This episode of Cingar's triumph over the enemies of Baldus, his
craft, his rhetoric, his ready wit, his infinite powers of persuasion, his
monkey tricks and fox-like cunning, is executed with an energy of humour
and breadth of conception, that places it upon a level with the choicest
passages in Rabelais.

distinguishes himself by presence of mind in a great storm [1] :

> Ille galantus homo, qui nuper in æquora bruttam
> Jecerat uxorem, dicens non esse fagottum
> Fardellumque homini plus laidum, plusque pesentum
> Quam sibi mojeram lateri mirare tacatam
> Quæ sit oca ingenio, quæ vultu spazzacaminus.

The tale of adventures is diversified, after the manner of the romantic poets, by digressions, sometimes pathetic, sometimes dissertational. Among these the most amusing is Cingar's lecture on astronomy, in which the planetary theories of the middle ages are burlesqued with considerable irony.[2] The most affecting is the death of Leonardus, who chooses to be torn in pieces by bears rather than yield his virginity to a vile woman. This episode suggests one of the finest satiric passages in the whole poem. Having exhibited the temptress Muselina, the poet breaks off with this exclamation [3] :

> Heu quantis noster Muselinis orbis abundat !

He then enumerates their arts of seduction, and winds up with a powerful dramatic picture, painted from the life, of a *mezzana* engaged in corrupting a young man's mind during Mass-time :

> Dum Missæ celebrantur, amant cantonibus esse,
> Postque tenebrosos mussant chiachiarantque pilastros ;
> Ah miserelle puer, dicunt, male nate, quod ullam
> Non habes, ut juvenes bisognat habere, morosam ! . . .

---

[1] *Mac.* xii. p. 296.

[2] In the course of this oration Folengo introduces an extraordinarily venomous invective against *contadini*, which may be paralleled with his allegory in the *Orlandino*. It begins (*Mac.* xiii. p. 11) :

> Progenies maledicta quidem villana vocatur,

and extends through forty lines of condensed abuse.

[3] *Mac.* xvi. p. 66.

Numquid vis fieri Frater Monachusve, remotis
Delitiis Veneris, Bacchi, Martisque, Jovisque,
Quos vel simplicitas, vel desperatio traxit? . . .
Nemo super-terram sanctus ; stant æthere sancti :
Nos carnem natura facit, quo carne fruamur.

As the epic approaches its conclusion, Baldus discovers
his true father, Guido, under the form of a holy her-
mit, and learns that it is reserved for him by destiny,
first to extirpate the sect of witches under their queen
Smirna Gulfora, and afterwards to penetrate the realms
of death and hell. The last five books of the *Maccaronea* are devoted to these crowning exploits. Merlin
appears, and undertakes the guidance of the Barons on
their journey to Avernus.[1] But first he requires full
confession of their sins from each ; and this humorous
act of penitence forms one of the absurdest episodes,
as may be easily imagined. in the poem. Absolved
and furnished with heroic armour, the Barons march to
the conquest of Gulfora and the destruction of her
magic palace. Folengo has placed it appropriately on
the road to hell ; for under Gulfora he allegorises
witchcraft. The space allotted to Smirna Gulfora and
the importance attached to her overthrow by Baldus
and his Barons, call attention to the prevalence of magic
in Italy at this epoch.[2] It may not, therefore, be out
of place, before engaging in this portion of the analysis,

---

[1] *Mac.* xx. p. 152. From this point onward the poet and Merlin are
one person :

Nomine Merlinus dicor, de sanguine Mantus,
Est mihi cognomen Cocajus Maccaronensis.

[2] The *Novella* of Luca Philippus, who kept a tavern at the door of
Paradise, and had no custom, since no one came that way so long as
Gulfora ruled on earth, forms a significant preface to her episode. See
Mac. xxi. p. 180. The altercation between this host and Peter at the
rusty gate of heaven is written in the purest Italian style of pious parody.

to give some account of Italian witchcraft drawn from other sources, in order to estimate the truth of the satire upon which Folengo expended his force.

' Beautiful and humane Italy,' as Bandello calls his country in the preface to one of his most horrible *Novelle*, was, in spite of her enlightenment, but little in advance of Europe on the common points of medieval superstition. The teaching of the Church encouraged a belief in demons ; and the common people saw on every chapel wall the fresco of some saint expelling devils from the bodies of possessed persons, or exorcising domestic utensils which had been bewitched.[1] Thus the laity grew up in the confirmed opinion that earth, air, and ocean swarmed with supernatural beings, whom they distinguished as fiends from hell or inferior sprites of the elements, called *spiriti folletti*.[2] While the evil spirits of both degrees were supposed to lie beneath the ban of ecclesiastical malediction, they lent their aid to necromancers, witches and wizards, who, defying the interdictions of the Church, had the audacity to use them as their slaves by the employment of powerful spells and rites of conjuration. There was a way, it was believed, of taming both the demons and the elves, of making them the instruments of human avarice, ambition, jealousy and passion. Since all forms of superstition in Italy lent themselves to utilitarian purposes, the necromancer and the witch, having acquired this power over supernatural agents, became the servants of popular lusts. They sold their authority

---

[1] Aretino's *Cortigiana* contains a very humorous exorcism inflicted by way of a practical joke upon a fisherman.

[2] See above, Part i. p. 453, note 2, for the distinction between the fiends and the sprites drawn by Pulci.

to the highest bidders, undertaking to blast the vines or to poison the flocks of an enemy ; to force young men and maidens to become the victims of inordinate appetites ; to ruin inconvenient husbands by slowly-wasting diseases ; to procure abortion by spells and potions ; to confer wealth and power upon aspirants after luxury; to sow the seeds of discord in families—in a word, to open a free path for the indulgence of the vain desires that plague ill-regulated egotisms. A class of impostors, half dupes of their own pretensions, half rogues relying on the folly of their employers, sprang into existence, who combined the Locusta of ancient Rome with the witch of medieval Germany. Such was the Italian *strega*—a loa hsome creature, who studied the chemistry of poisons, philtres, and abortion-hastening drugs, and while she pretended to work her miracles by the help of devils, played upon the common passions and credulities of human kind.[1] By her side stood her masculine counterpart, the *stregone, negromante* or *alchimista*, who plays so prominent a part in the Italian comedies and novels.

Witchcraft was localised in two chief centres—the mountains of Norcia, and the Lombard valleys of the Alps.[2] In the former we find a remnant of antique superstition. The witches of this district, whether male or female, had something of the classical Sibyl in

[1] See Lasca's *Novella* of *Zoroastro* ; Bandello's novels of witchcraft (Part iii. 29 and 52); Cellini's celebrated conjuration in the Coliseum ; and Ariosto's comedy of the *Negromante*. These sources may be illustrated from the evidence given by Virginia Maria Lezia before her judges, and the trial of witches at Nogaredo, both of which are printed in Dandolo's *Signora di Monza* (Milano, 1855). Compare the curious details about Lombard witchcraft in Cantù's *Diocesi di Como*.

[2] It may be remembered that the necromancer in Cellini sent his book

their composition and played upon the terrors of their clients. Like their Roman predecessors, they plied the trades of poisoner, quack-doctor and bawd. In Lombardy witchcraft assumed a more Teutonic complexion. The witch was less the instrument of fashionable vices, trading in them as a lucrative branch of industry, than the hysterical subject of a spiritual disease. Lust itself inflamed the victims of this superstition, who were burned by hundreds in the towns, and who were supposed to hold their revels in the villages of Val Camonica. Like the hags of northern Europe, these Lombard *streghe* had recourse to the black art in the delirious hope of satisfying their own inordinate ambitions, their own indescribable desires. The disease spread so wildly at the close of the fifteenth century that Innocent VIII., by his Bull of 1484, issued special injunctions to the Dominican monks of Brescia, Bergamo and Cremona, authorising them to stamp it out with fire and torture.[1] The result was a crusade against witchcraft, which seems to have increased the evil by fascinating the imagination of the people. They believed all the more blindly in the supernatural powers to be obtained by magic arts, inasmuch as this

to be enchanted in the Apennines of Norcia. Folengo alludes to this superstition :

Qualiter ad stagnum Nursæ sacrare quadernos.

With regard to Val Camonica, see the actual state of that district as reported by Cantù. Folengo in the *Orlandino* mentions its witches. Bandello (iii. 52) speaks of it thus : 'Val Camonica, ove si dice essere di molte streghe.'

[1] Witchcraft in Italy grew the more formidable the closer it approached the German frontier. It seems to have assumed the features of an epidemic at the close of the fifteenth century. Up to that date little is heard of it, and little heed was paid to it. The exacerbation of the malady portended and accompanied the dissolution of medieval

traffic had become the object of a bloody persecution. When the Church recognised that men and women might command the fiends of hell, it followed as a logical consequence that wretches, maddened by misery and intoxicated with ungovernable lusts, were tempted to tamper with the forbidden thing at the risk of life and honour in this world and with the certainty of damnation in the other. After this fashion the confused conscience of illiterate people bred a formidable extension of this spiritual malady throughout the northern provinces of Italy. Some were led by morbid curiosity ; others by a vain desire to satisfy their appetites, or to escape the consequences of their crimes. A more dangerous class used the superstition to acquire power over their neighbours and to make money out of popular credulity.

Born and bred in Lombardy at the epoch when witchcraft had attained the height of popular insanity, Folengo was keenly alive to the hideousness of a superstition which, rightly or wrongly, he regarded as a widespread plague embracing all classes of society. It may be questioned whether he did not exaggerate its importance. But there is no mistaking the verisimilitude of the picture he drew. All the uncleanliness of a diseased imagination, all the extravagances of wanton desire, all the consequences of domestic unchastity— incest, infanticide, secret assassination, concealment of births—are traced to this one cause and identified by him with witchcraft. The palace of the queen Gulfora is a pandemonium of lawless vice :

beliefs in a population vexed by war, famine and pestilence, and vitiated by ecclesiastical corruption.

> Quales hic reperit strepitus, qualemque tumultum,
> Quales mollities turpes, actusque salaces,
> Utile nil scribi posset, si scribere vellem.

Her courts are crowded with devils who have taken human shape to gratify the lusts of her votaries :

> Leggiadros juvenes, bellos, facieque venustos,
> Stringatos, agiles, quos judicat esse diablos,
> Humanum piliasse caput moresque decentes,
> Conspicit, innumeras circum scherzare puellas,
> Quæ gestant vestes auri brettasque veluti.

The multitude is made up of all nations, sexes, ages, classes :

> Obstupet innumeros illic retrovare striones,
> Innumerasque strias vecchias, modicasque puellas.
> Non ea medesimo generatur schiatta paeso ;
> At sunt Italici, Græci, Gallique, Spagnoles,
> Magnates, poveri, laici, fratresque, pretesque,
> Matronæ, monighæ per forzam claustra colentes.

Some of them are engaged in preparing love-potions and poisonous draughts from the most disgusting and noxious ingredients. Others compound unguents to be used in the metamorphosis of themselves on their nocturnal jaunts. Among these are found poets, orators, physicians, lawyers, governors, for whose sins a handful of poor old women play the part of scape-goats before the public :

> Sed quia respectu legis prævertitur ordo,
> Namque solent grossi pisces mangiare minutos,
> Desventuratæ quædam solummodo vecchiæ
> Sunt quæ supra asinos plebi spectacula fiunt,
> Sunt quæ primatum multorum crimina celant,
> Sunt quæ sparagnant madonnis pluribus ignem.

Some again are discovered compiling books of spells :

> Quomodo adulterium uxoris vir noscere possit,
> Quomodo virgineæ cogantur amare puellæ,
> Quomodo non tumeat mulier cornando maritum,

> Quomodo si tumuit fantinum mingat abortum,
> Quomodo vix natos vitient sua fascina puttos,
> Quomodo desiccent odiati membra mariti.

The elder witches keep a school for the younger, and instruct them in the secrets of their craft. Among these Baldus recognises his own wife, together with the principal ladies of his native land.

It is clear that under the allegory of witchcraft, in which at the same time he seems to have believed firmly, Folengo meant to satirise the secret corruption of society. When Gulfora herself appears, she holds her court like an Italian duchess :

> Longa sequit series hominum muschiata zibettis,
> Qui cortesanos se vantant esse tilatos,
> Quorum si videas mores rationis ochialo,
> Non homines maschios sed dicas esse bagassas.

The terrible friar then breaks into a tirade against the courtiers of his day, comparing them with Arthur's knights :

> Tempore sed nostro, proh dii, sæcloque dadessum,
> Non nisi perfumis variis et odore zibetti,
> Non nisi, seu sazaræ petenentur sive tosentur,
> Brettis velluti, nec non scufiotibus auri,
> Auri cordiculis, impresis, atque medallis,
> Millibus et frappis per calzas perque giupones,
> Cercamus carum merdosi germen amoris.

Baldus exterminates the whole vile multitude, while Fracassus pulls Gulfora's palace about her ears. After this, the Barons pursue their way to Acheron, and call upon Charon to ferry them across. He refuses to take so burdensome a party into his boat; but by the strength of Fracassus and the craft of Cingar they effect a passage. Their entry into hell furnishes Folengo with opportunities for new tirades against the vices of Italy. Tisiphone boasts how Rome, through her machinations, has kept Christendom in discord. Alecto exults in her offspring, the Guelph and Ghibelline factions :

> Unde fides Christi paulatim lapsa ruinet,
> Dum gentes Italæ, bastantes vincere mundum
> Se se in se stessos discordant, seque medesmos
> Vassallos faciunt, servos, vilesque famejos
> His qui vassalli, servi, vilesque fameji
> Tempore passato nobis per forza fuere.

After passing the Furies, and entering the very jaws of Hades, Baldus encounters the phantasies of grammarians and humanists, the idle nonsense of the schoolmen, all the lumber of medieval philosophy mixed with the trifles of the Renaissance.[1] He fights his way through the thick-crowding swarm of follies, and reaches the hell of lovers, where a mountebank starts forward and offers to be his guide. Led by this zany, the hero and his comrades enter an enormous gourd, the bulk of which is compared to the mountains of Val Camonica. Within its spacious caverns dwell the sages of antiquity, with astrologers, physicians, wizards, and false poets. But, having brought his Barons to this place, Merlinus Cocajus can advance no further.

---

[1] Hic sunt Grammaticæ populi, gentesque reductæ,
Huc, illuc, istuc, reliqua seguitante fameja :
Argumenta volant dialectica, mille sophistæ
Adsunt bajanæ, pro, contra, non, ita, lyque :
Adsunt Errores, adsunt mendacia, bollæ,
Atque solecismi, fallacia, fictio vatum . . .
Omnes altandem tanto rumore volutant
Ethicen et Physicen, Animam, centumque novellas,
Ut sibi stornito Baldus stopparet orecchias.
Squarnazzam Scoti Fracassus repperit illic,
Quam vestit, gabbatque Deum, pugnatque Thomistas.
Alberti magni Lironus somnia zaffat.

He is destined to inhabit the great gourd himself.
Beyond it he has no knowledge ; and here, therefore,
he leaves the figments of his fancy without a word of
farewell :

> Nec Merlinus ego, laus, gloria, fama Cipadæ,
> Quamvis fautrices habui Tognamque Gosamque,
> Quamvis implevi totum macaronibus orbem,
> Quamvis promerui Baldi cantare batajas,
> Non tamen hanc zuccam potui schifare decentem,
> In qua me tantos opus est nunc perdere dentes,
> Tot, quot in immenso posui mendacia libro.

With this grotesque invention of the infernal pumpkin,
where lying bards are punished by the extraction of
teeth which never cease to grow again, Folengo
breaks abruptly off. His epic ends with a Rabelaisian peal of laughter, in which we can detect a growl of
discontent and anger.

Laying the book down, we ask ourselves whether
the author had a serious object, or whether he meant
merely to indulge a vein of wayward drollery. The
virulent invectives which abound in the *Maccaronea*,
seem to warrant the former conclusion ; nor might it
be wholly impossible to regard the poem as an allegory,
in which Baldus should play the part of the reason,
unconscious at first of its noble origin, consorting with
the passions and the senses, but finally arriving at the
knowledge of its high destiny and defeating the powers
of evil.[1] Yet when we attempt to press this theory
and to explain the allegory in detail, the thread snaps
in our hands. Like the romances of chivalry which

---

[1] This hypothesis receives support from the passage in which Baldus
compares his new love for Crispis, the paragon of all virtues, with his old
infatuation for Berta, who is the personification of vulgar appetite, unrefined natural instinct. See the end of Book xxiii.

it parodies, the *Maccaronea* is a bizarre mixture of heterogeneous elements, loosely put together to amuse an idle public and excite curiosity. If its author has used it also as the vehicle for satire which embraces all the popular superstitions, vices and hypocrisies of his century; if, as he approaches the conclusion, he assumes a tone of sarcasm more sinister than befits the broad burlesque of the commencement; we must rest contented with the assumption that his choleric humour led him from the path of comedy, while the fury of a soul divided against itself inspired his muses of the cook-shop with loftier strains than they had promised at the outset.[1] Should students in the future devote the same minute attention to Folengo that has been paid to Rabelais, it is not improbable that the question here raised may receive solution. The poet is not unworthy of such pains. Regarded merely as the precursor of Rabelais, Folengo deserves careful perusal. He was the creator of a style, which, when we read his epic, forces us to think of the seventeenth century; so strongly did it influence the form of humorous burlesque in Europe for at least two hundred years. On this account, the historian of modern literature cannot afford to neglect him. For the student of Italian manners in Lombardy during the

---

[1] The rage of a man who knows that he has chosen the lower while he might have trodden the higher paths of life and art, flames out at intervals through this burlesque. Take this example, the last five lines of Book xxiii. :

> Sic ego Macronicum penitus volo linquere carmen
> Cum mihi tempus erit, quod erit, si celsa voluntas
> Flectitur et nostris lachrymis et supplice voto.
> Heu heu ! quod volui misero mihi ? floribus Austrum
> Perditus et liquidis immisi fontibus aprum.

height of the Renaissance, the huge amorphous un-
digested mass of the *Maccaronea* is one of the most
valuable and instructive documents that we possess.
I do not hesitate, from this point of view, to rank it
with the masterpieces of the age, with the *Orlando* of
Ariosto, with Machiavelli's comedies, and with the
novels of Bandello.

Folengo used the maccaronic style in two other
considerable compositions.   The one entitled *Moscheis*
is an elegant parody of the *Batrachomyomachia*, relating the wars of ants and flies in elegiac verse.   The
other, called *Zanitonella*, celebrates the rustic loves of
Zanina and Tonello in a long series of elegies, odes
and eclogues.   This collection furnishes a complete
epitome of parodies modelled on the pastorals in vogue.
The hero appears upon the scene in the following
Sonolegia, under which title we detect a blending of
the Sonnet and the Elegy [1] :

> Solus solettus stabam colegatus in umbra,
>   Pascebamque meas virda per arva capras.
> Nulla travajabant animum pensiria nostrum,
>   Cercabam quoniam tempus habere bonum.
> Quando bolzoniger puer, o mea corda forasti ;
>   Nec dedit in fallum dardus alhora tuus.
> Immo fracassasti rationis vincula, quæ tunc
>   Circa coradam bastio fortis erat.

The lament is spun out to the orthodox length of
fourteen verses, and concludes with a pretty point.
Who the *bolzoniger puer* was, is more openly revealed
in another Sonolegia [2] :

> Nemo super terram mangiat mihi credite panem,
>   Seu contadinus, seu citadinus erit,
> Quem non attrapolet Veneris bastardulus iste,
>   Qui volat instar avis, cæcus, et absque braga.

[1] *Zanitonella*, p. 3.   [2] *Ibid.* p. 2.   Compare Sonolegia xiii. *ib.* p. 40.

To follow the poet through all his burlesques of Petrarchistic and elegiac literature, Italian or Latin, would be superfluous. It is enough to say that he leaves none of their accustomed themes untouched with parody. The masterpiece of his art in this style is the sixth Eclogue, consisting of a dialogue between two drunken bumpkins—*interloquutores Tonellus et Pedralus, qui ambo inebriantur.*[1]

The maccaronic style was a product of North Italy, cultivated by writers of the Lombard towns, who versified comic or satiric subjects in parodies of humanistic poetry. The branch of burlesque literature we have next to examine, belonged to Tuscany, and took its origin from the equivocal carnival and dance songs raised to the dignity of art by Lorenzo de' Medici. Its conventional metre was *terza rima*, handled with exquisite sense of rhythm, but degraded to low comedy by the treatment of trivial or vulgar motives. The author of these *Capitoli*, as they were called, chose some common object—a paint-brush, salad, a sausage, peaches, figs, eels, radishes—to celebrate ; affected to be inspired by the grandeur of his subject ; developed the drollest tropes, metaphors and illustrations ; and almost invariably conveyed an obscene meaning under the form of inuendoes appropriate to his professed theme. Though some exceptions can be pointed out, the *Capitoli* in general may be regarded as a species of Priapic literature, fashioned to suit the taste of Florentines, who had been accustomed for many generations to semi-disguised obscenity in their ver-

---

[1] *Op. cit.* p. 42.

nacular town poetry.[1] Taken from the streets and
squares, adopted by the fashionable rhymesters of
academies and courtly coteries, the rude Fescennine
verse lost none of its licence, while it assumed the
polish of urbane art. Were it not for this antiquity and
popularity of origin, which suggests a plausible excuse
for the learned writers of *Capitoli*, and warns us to
regard their indecency as in some measure conventional, it would be difficult to approach the three
volumes which contain a selection of their poems, without horror.[2] So deep, universal, unblushing is the vice
revealed in them.

To Francesco Berni belongs the merit, such as it
is, of having invented the burlesque *Capitolo*. He
gave his name to it, and the term Bernesque has
passed into the critical phraseology of Europe. The
unique place of this rare poet in the history of Italian
literature, will justify a somewhat lengthy account of
his life and works. Studying him, we study the ecclesiastical and literary society of Rome in the age of
Leo X. and Clement. VII.

Francesco Berni was born at Lamporecchio, in the

---

[1] We may ascend to the very sources of popular Tuscan poetry, and
we shall find this literature of *double entendre* in the *Canzoni* of the
Nicchio and *Ugellino*, noticed above, Part i. p. 38. Besides the *Canti Carnascialeschi* edited by Il Lasca, we have a collection of *Canzoni a Ballo*,
printed at Florence in 1569, which proves that the raw material of the
Capitoli lay ready to the hand of the burlesque poets in plebeian
literature.

[2] My references are made to *Opere Burlesche*, 3 vols, 1723, with the
names of Londra and Firenze. Gregorovius says of them : ' Wenn man
diese " scherzenden " Gedichte liest, muss man entweder über die Nichtig-
keit ihrer Gegenstände staunen, oder vor dem Abgrund der Unsittlich-
keit erschrecken, den sie frech entschleiern.' *Stadt Rom.* vol. viii.
p. 345.

Val di Nievole, about the end of the fifteenth century.[1]
His parents were poor; but they were connected with
the family of the Cardinal Bibbiena, who, after the
boy's education at Florence, took him at the age of
nineteen to Rome. Upon the death of this patron in
1520, Berni remained in the service of Bibbiena's
nephew, Agnolo Dovizio. Receiving no advancement
from these kinsmen, he next transferred himself, in the
quality of secretary, to the household of Giammatteo
Giberti, Bishop of Verona, who was a distinguished
Mecænas of literary men. This change involved his
taking orders. Berni now resided partly at Rome and
partly at Verona, tempering the irksome duties of his
office by the writing of humorous poetry, which he
recited in the then celebrated Academy of the Vignaj-
uoli. This society, which numbered Molza, Mauro,
La Casa, Lelio Capilupi, Firenzuola, and Francesco
Bini among its members, gave the tone to polite literature at the Courts of Leo and Clement.

Berni survived the sack of 1527, which proved so
disastrous to Italian scholars ; but he lost everything
he possessed.[2] Monsignor Giberti employed him on
various missions of minor importance, involving journeys
to Venice, Padua, Nice, Florence, and the Abruzzi.
After sixteen years of Court-life, Berni grew weary of
the petty duties, which must have been peculiarly
odious to a man of his lazy temperament, if it is true,
as he informs us, that the Archbishop kept him dancing

[1] The probable date is 1496.

[2] *Orl. Inn. Rifatto da Fr. Berni*, i. 14, 23–28, makes it clear that
Berni was an eye-witness of the Sack of Rome. Panizzi's reference to
this passage (*Boiardo ed Ariosto*, London, 1830, vol. ii. p. cxi) involves
what seems to me a confusion.

attendance till daylight, while he played primiera with his friends. Accordingly, he retired to Florence, where he held a canonry in the cathedral. There, after a quiet life of literary ease, he died suddenly in 1535. It was rumoured that he had been poisoned; and the most recent investigations into the circumstances of his death tend rather to confirm this report. All that is known, however, for certain, is that he spent the evening of May 25 with his friends the Marchionesse di Massa in the Palazzo Pazzi, and that next morning he breathed his last. His mysterious and unexplained decease was ascribed to one of the two Medicean princes then resident in Florence. A sonnet in Berni's best style, containing a vehement invective against Alessandro de' Medici, is extant. The hatred expressed in this poem may have occasioned the rumour (which certainly acquired a certain degree of currency) that Cardinal Ippolito de' Medici attempted to use the poet for the secret poisoning of his cousin, and on his refusal had him murdered. Other accounts of the supposed assassination ascribe a like intention to the Duke, who is said to have suggested the poisoning of the Cardinal to Berni. Both stories agree in representing his tragic end as the price paid for refusal to play the part of an assassin. The matter remains obscure; but enough suspicion rests upon the manner of his death to render this characteristic double legend plausible; especially when we remember what the customs of Florence with respect to poisoning were, and how the Cardinal de' Medici ended his own life.[1]

---

[1] The matter is fully discussed by Mazzuchelli in his biography of Berni. He, relying on the hypothesis of Berni having lived till 1536, if

Such is the uneventful record of Berni's career. He was distinguished among all the poets of the century for his genial vein of humour and amiable personal qualities. That he was known to be stained with vices which it is not easy to describe, but which he frankly acknowledged in his poetical epistles, did not injure his reputation in that age of mutual indulgence.[1] Willing to live and let live, with a never-failing fund of drollery, and with a sincere dislike for work of any sort, he lounged through existence, an agreeable, genial and witty member of society. If this were all, we should not need to write about him now. But with this easy-going temperament he combined a genius for poetry so peculiar and delicate, that his few works mark an epoch in Italian literature.

The best description of Berni is contained in the burlesque portrait of himself, which forms part of his *Boiardo Innamorato.*[2] This has been so well translated by an English scholar, the late W. S. Rose, that I cannot do better than refer the student to his stanzas. They convey as accurate a notion of the Bernesque manner as can be derived from any version in a foreign

---

not till 1543, points out the impossibility of his having been murdered by the Cardinal, who died himself in July 1535. This difficulty has recently been removed by Signor Antonio Virgili's demonstration of the real date of Berni's death in May 1535. See *Rassegna Settimanale*, February 23, 1879, a paper of great importance for students of Berni's life and works, to which I shall frequently refer.

[1] It is enough to mention the *Capitoli* ' Delle Pesche,' ' A M. Antonio da Bibbiena,' ' Sopra un Garzone,' ' Lamentazion d' Amore.' References are made to the *Rime e Lettere di Fr. Berni*, Firenze, Barbèra, 1865. For the *Rifacimento* of the *Orlando Innamorato* I shall use the Milan reprint in 5 vols, 1806, which also contains the *Rime.*.

[2] Book III. canto vii. (canto 67 of the *Rifacimento*, vol. iv. p. 266).

language.[1]　The character he there has given to himself for laziness is corroborated by his extant epistles
in prose.　Berni represents himself as an incur-
ably bad correspondent, pleased to get letters, but
overcome with mortal terror when he is obliged to
answer them.[2]　He confides to his friend Francesco
Bini that the great affair in life is to be gay and to
write as little as possible[3] : ' A vivere avemo sino
alla morte a dispetto di chi non vuole, e il vantaggio è
vivere allegramente, come conforto a far voi, attendando
a frequentar quelli banchetti che si fanno per Roma, e
scrivendo sopra tutto manco che potete.　*Quia hæc est
victoria, quæ vincit mundum.*'　The curse has been
laid upon him of having to drive his quill without ceasing [4] : ' *O ego lævus,* che scrivo d' ogni tempo, e scrivo
ora che ho una gamba al collo, che ieri tornando dalla
Certosa mi ruppe la mia cavalla, cascandomivi sopra.
Sono pure un gran coglione!'　So his pen runs on.
The man writes just as he spoke, without affectation,
mixing his phrases of Latin with the idiom of common
life.　The whole presents an agreeable contrast to the
stilted style of Bembo, La Casa's studied periods, and
the ambitious epistolary efforts of Aretino.　Sometimes
he breaks into doggrel[5] : ' S'io avessi l' ingenio del
Burchiello, Io vi farei volentier un sonetto, Che non
ebbi giammai tema e subietto, Più dolce, più piacevol,
nè piu bello.'　When his friends insist upon his writing

---

[1] This translation will be found in Panizzi's edition of the *Orlando
Innamorato* (London, Pickering, 1830), vol. ii. p. cxiv.
[2] Letter vi. to Messer Giamb. Montebuona.
[3] Letter xvii.
[4] Letter xxiv.
[5] Letter to Ippolito de' Medici (ed. Milan, vol. v. p. 227).

to them, rhyme comes to his aid, and he affects a comic
fit of rage [1] :

> Perchè m' ammazzi con le tue querele,
> Priuli mio, perchè ti duole a torto,
> Che sai che t' amo più che l' orso il miele, &c.

Importuned to publish the poems he recited with
so much effect in private circles, he at last consents
because he cannot help it [2] : 'Compare, io non ho potuto
tanto schermirmi che pure m' è bisognato dar fuori
questo benedetto Capitolo e Comento della Primiera ;
e siate certo che l' ho fatto, non perchè mi consumassi
d' andare in stampa, nè per immortalarmi come il cavalier Casio, ma per fuggire la fatica mia, e la malevol-
enza di molti che domandandomelo e non lo avendo
mi volevano mal di morte.' Nor were these the ordinary excuses of an author eager to conceal his vanity.
The *Capitolo* upon the game of primiera was the only
poem which appeared with his consent.[3] He intended
his burlesque verses for recitation, and is even said to
have preserved no copies of them, so that many of
his compositions, piratically published in his lifetime,
were with difficulty restored to a right text by Il
Lasca in 1548. This indifference to public fame did
not imply any carelessness of style. Mazzuchelli, who
had seen some of his rough copies, asserts that they
bore signs of the minutest pains bestowed upon them.
The melody of versification, richness of allusion, refinement of phrase, equality and flowing smoothness,

---

[1] Letter ix.

[2] Letter vii. Compare the sonnet 'In nome di M. Prinzivalle da
Pontremoli' (ed. Milan, vol. v. p. 3).

[3] It was published at Rome by Calvo in 1526, with the comment of
M. Pietro Paolo da S. Chirico.

which distinguish Berni's work from that of his imitators, confirm the belief that his *Capitoli* and sonnets, in spite of their apparent ease, were produced with the conscientious industry of a real artist.

Berni's theory of poetry revealed a common-sense and insight which were no less rare than commendable in that age of artificial literature.   He refused to write at command, pleading that spontaneity of inspiration is essential to art, and quoting Vida's dictum :

> Nec jussa canas, nisi forte coactus
> Magnorum imperio regum.

Notwithstanding his avoidance of publication and parcimony of production, Berni won an almost unique reputation during his lifetime, and after his death was worshipped as a saint by the lovers of burlesque.[1]   In one of his drollest sonnets he complains that poets were wont to steal their neighbours' verses, but that he is compelled to take the credit of more than he ever wrote [2] :

[1] Il Lasca prefixed a sonnet to his edition of 1548, in which he speaks of ' Il Berni nostro dabbene e gentile,' calls him ' primo e vero trovatore, Maestro e padre del burlesco stile,' says that it is possible to envy but impossible to imitate him, and compares him thus with Burchiello :

> Non sia chi mi ragioni di Burchiello,
> Che saria proprio come comparare
> Caron Dimonio all' Agnol Gabriello.

In another sonnet he climbs a further height of panegyric :

> Quanti mai fur poeti al mondo e sono,
> Volete in Greco, in Ebreo, o in Latino,
> A petto a lui non vagliono un lupino,
> Tant' è dotto, faceto, bello e buono :

and winds up with the strange assurance that :

> da lui si sente
> Anzi s' impara con gioja infinita
> Come viver si debbe in questa vita.

[2] Sonnet xxvii.

A me quei d' altri son per forza dati,
E dicon tu gli arai, vuoi o non vuoi.

A piece of comic prose or verse cannot appear but that it is at once ascribed to him :

E la gente faceta
Mi vuole pure impiastrar di prose e carmi,
Come s' io fussi di razza di marmi :
Non posso ripararmi ;
Come si vede fuor qualche sonetto,
Il Berni l' ha composto a suo dispetto.
E fanvi su un guazzetto
Di chiose e di sensi, che rinnieghi il cielo,
Se Luter fa più stracci del Vangelo.

One of the glosses referred to in this *coda,* lies before me as I write. It was composed by Gianmaria Cecchi on Berni's sonnet which begins 'Cancheri e beccafichi.' The sonnet is an amusing imprecation upon matrimony, written in one paragraph, and containing the sting of the epigram in its short *coda* of three lines.[1] But it did not need a commentary, and Cecchi's voluminous annotations justify the poet's comic anger.

Berni's *Capitoli* may be broadly divided into three classes. The first includes his poetical epistles, addressed to Fracastoro, Sebastian del Piombo, Ippolito de' Medici, Marco Veneziano, and other friends. Except for the peculiar humour, which elevates the trivial accidents of life to comedy, except for the consummate style, which dignifies the details of familiar correspondence and renders fugitive effusions classical, these letters in verse would scarcely detach themselves from a mass of similar compositions. As it is, Berni's personality renders them worthy companions of Ariosto's

[1] Sonnet ix.

masterpieces in a similar but nicely differentiated branch of literature. It remains for the amateurs of autobiographical poetry to choose between the self-revelation of the philosophising Ferrarese poet and the brilliant trifling of the Florentine. The second class embraces a number of occasional poems—the Complaint against Love, the Deluge in Mugello, the Satire upon Adrian VI., the Lamentation of Nardino—descriptive or sarcastic pieces, where the poet chooses a theme and develops it with rhetorical abundance. The third class may be regarded as the special source and fountain of the Bernesque manner, as afterwards adopted and elaborated by Berni's imitators. Omitting personal or occasional motives, he sings the praises of the Plague, of Primiera, of Aristotle, of Peaches, of Debt, of Eels, of the Urinal, of Thistles, and of other trifling subjects. Here his burlesque genius takes the most fantastic flight, soaring to the ether of absurdity and sinking to the nadir of obscenity, combining heterogeneous elements of fun and farce, yet never transgressing the limits of refined taste. These *Capitoli* revealed a new vehicle of artistic expression to his contemporaries. Penetrated with their author's individuality, they caught the spirit of the age and met its sense of humour. Consequently they became the touchstones of burlesque inspiration, the models which tempted men of feebler force and more uncertain tact to hopeless tasks of emulation. We still possess La Casa's *Capitolo* on the Oven ; Molza's on Salad and the Fig ; Firenzuola's on the Sausage and the Legno Santo ; Bronzino's on the Paint-brush and the Radish ; Aretino's on the Quartan Fever ; Franzesi's on Carrots and Chestnuts; Varchi's on Hard Eggs and Fennel; Mauro's on Beans and Priapus; Dolce's on Spittle and Noses; Bini's on the *Mal Franzese*; Lori's on Apples; Ruscelli's on the Spindle—not to speak of many authors, the obscurity of whose names and the obscenity of the themes they celebrated, condemn them to condign oblivion. Not without reason did Gregorovius stigmatise these poems as a moral syphilis, invading Italian literature and penetrating to the remotest fibres of its organism. After their publication in academical circles and their further diffusion through the press, simple terms which had been used to cloak their improprieties, became the bywords of pornographic pamphleteers and poets. Figs, beans, peaches, apples, chestnuts acquired a new and scandalous significance. Sins secluded from the light of day by a modest instinct of humanity, flaunted their loathsomeness without shame beneath the ensigns of these literary allegories. The corruption of society, hypocritically veiled or cynically half-revealed in coteries, expressed itself too plainly through the phraseology invented by a set of sensual poets. The most distinguished members of society, Cardinals like Bembo, prelates like La Casa, painters like Bronzino, critics like Varchi, scholars like Molza, lent the prestige of their position and their talents to the diffusion of this leprosy, which still remains the final most convincing testimony to the demoralisation of Italy in the Renaissance.[1]

[1] The scholars of the day were not content with writing burlesque *Capitoli.* They must needs annotate them. See Caro's Commentary on the *Ficheide* of Molza (Romagnoli, *Scelta di Curiosità Letterarie*, Dispensa vii. Bologna, 1862) for the most celebrated example. There is not

To what extent, it may be asked, was Berni responsible for these consequences? He brought the indecencies of the piazza, where they were the comparatively innocuous expression of coarse instincts, into the close atmosphere of the study and the academical circle, refined their vulgarisms, and made their viciousness attractive by the charm of his incomparable style. This transition from the *Canto Carnascialesco* to the *Capitolo* may be observed in Berni's *Caccia di Amore*, a very licentious poem dedicated to ' noble and gentle ladies.' It is a Carnival Song or *Canzone a Ballo* rewritten in octave stanzas of roseate fluency and seductive softness. A band of youthful huntsmen pay their court in it to women, and the *double entendre* exactly reproduces the style of inuendo rendered fashionable by Lorenzo de' Medici. Yet, though Berni is unquestionably answerable for the obscene *Capitoli* of the sixteenth century, it must not be forgotten that he only gave form to material already sufficiently appropriated by the literary classes. With him, the grossness which formed the staple of Mauro's, Molza's, Bini's, La Casa's and Bronzino's poems, the depravities of appetite which poisoned the very substance of their compositions, were but accidental. The poet stood above them and in some measure aloof from them, employing these ingredients in the concoction of his burlesque, but never losing the main object of his art in their development. A bizarre literary effect, rather than the indulgence of a sensual imagination, was the aim he

a sentence in this long and witty composition, read before the Accademia delle Virtù, which does not contain a grossly obscene allusion, scarcely a paragraph which does not refer to an unmentionable vice.

had in view. Therefore, while we regret that his example gave occasion to coarser debaucheries of talent, we are bound to acknowledge that the jests to which he condescended, do not represent his most essential self. This, however, is but a feeble apology. That without the excuse of passion, without satirical motive or overmastering personal proclivity, he should have penned the *Capitolo a M. Antonio da Bibbiena*, and have joked about giving and taking his metaphorical peaches, remains an ineradicable blot upon his nature.[1]

The Bernesque *Capitoli* were invariably written in *terza rima*, which at this epoch became the recognised metre of epistolary, satirical, and dissertational poetry throughout Italy.[2] Thus the rhythm of the Divine Comedy received final development by lending itself to the expression of whims, fancies, personal invectives and scurrilities. To quote from Berni's masterpieces in this style would be impossible. Each poem of about one hundred lines is a perfect and connected unity, which admits of no mutilation by the detachment of separate passages. Still readers may be referred to the *Capitolo a Fracastoro* and the two *Capitoli della Peste* as representative of the poet's humour in its purest form, without the moral deformities of the still more celebrated *Pesche* or the uncleanliness of the *Orinale*.

---

[1] The six opening lines of the *Lamentazion d' Amore* prevent our regarding Berni's jests as wholly separate from his experience and practice.

[2] A familiar illustration is Cellini's *Capitolo del Carcere*. Curious examples of these occasional poems, written for the popular taste, are furnished by Mutinelli in his *Annali Urbani di Venezia*. See above, Part i. pp. 172, 519, for the vicissitudes of *terza rima* after the close of the fourteenth century.

At the close of the *Capitolo* written on the occasion of Adrian VI.'s election to the Papacy, Berni declared that it had never been his custom to speak ill of people :

> L' usanza mia non fu mai di dir male ;
> E che sia il ver, leggi le cose mie,
> Leggi l' Anguille, leggi l' Orinale,
> Le Pesche, i Cardi e l' altre fantasie :
> Tutte sono inni, salmi, laudi ed ode.

We have reason to believe this declaration. Genial good humour is a characteristic note of his literary temperament. At the same time he was no mean master of caricature and epigram. The *Capitolo* in question is a sustained tirade against the Fleming, who had come to break the peace of polished Rome—a shriek of angry lamentation over altered times, intolerable insults, odious innovations. The amazement and discomfiture of the poet, contrasted with his burlesque utterance, render this composition comic in a double sense. Its satire cuts both ways, against the author and the object of his rage. Yet when Adrian gave place to Giulio de' Medici, and Berni discovered what kind of man the new Pope was, he vented nobler scorn in verse of far more pungent criticism. His sonnet on Clement is remarkable for exactly expressing the verdict posterity has formed after cool and mature enquiry into this Pope's actions. Clement's weakness and irresolution must end, the poet says, by making even Adrian seem a saint[1] :

> [1] A Papacy composed of compliment,
> Debate, consideration, complaisance,
> Of furthermore, then, but, yes, well, perchance,
> Haply, and such-like terms inconsequent ;

Un Papato composto di rispetti,
  Di considerazioni e di discorsi,
  Di più, di poi, di ma, di sì, di forsi,
  Di pur, di assai parole senza effetti ;
Di pensier, di consigli, di concetti,
  Di congetture magre per apporsi
  D' intrattenerti, purchè non si sborsì,
  Con audienze, risposte, e bei detti :
Di piè di piombo e di neutralità,
  Di pazienza, di dimostrazione,
  Di Fede, di Speranza e Carità,
D' innocenza, di buona intenzione ;
  Ch' è quasi come dir, semplicità,
  Per non le dare altra interpretazione,
      Sia con sopportazione,
Lo dirò pur, vedrete che pian piano
Farà canonizzar Papa Adriano.

The insight into Clement's character displayed in this sonnet, the invective against Adrian, and the acerbity of another sonnet against Alessandro de' Medici :

Empio Signor, che de la roba altrui
  Lieto ti vai godendo, e del sudore :

would gain in cogency, could we attach more value to the manliness of Berni's utterances. But when we know that, while he was showering curses on the Duke of Città di Penna, he frequented the Medicean Court and wrote a humorous *Capitolo* upon Gradasso,

Of thought, conjecture, counsel, argument,
    Starveling surmise to summon countenance,
    Negociations, audiences, romance,
    Fine words and shifts, disbursement to prevent ;
Of feet of lead, of tame neutrality,
    Of patience and parade to outer view,
    Of fawning Faith, of Hope and Charity,
Of Innocence and good intentions too,
    Which it were well to dub simplicity,
    Uglier interpretations to eschew ;
        With your permission, you,
To speak the plain truth out, shall live to see
Pope Adrian sainted through this Papacy.

a dwarf of Cardinal Ippolito, we feel forced to place
these epigrammatic effusions among the ebullitions of
personal rather than political animosity. There was
nothing of the patriot in Berni, not even so much as
in Machiavelli, who himself avowed his readiness to
roll stones for the Signori Medici.

As a satirist, Berni appears to better advantage in
his caricatures of private or domestic personages. The
portrait of his housekeeper, who combined in her
single person all the antiquities of all the viragos of
romance :

> Io ho per cameriera mia l' Ancroja
> Madre di Ferraù, zia di Morgante,
> Arcavola maggior dell' Amostante,
> Balia del Turco e suocera del Boja :

Alcionio upon his mule :

> Quella che per soperchio digiunare
> Tra l' anime celesti benedette
> Come un corpo diafano traspare :

Ser Cecco who could never be severed from the Court,
nor the Court from Ser Cecco :

> Perch' ambedue son la Corte e ser Cecco :

the pompous doctor :

> l' ambasciador del Boja,
> Un medico, maestro Guazzaletto :

Domenico d'Ancona, the memory of whose beard,
shorn by some Vandal of a barber, draws tears from
every sympathetic soul :

> Or hai dato, barbier, l' ultimo crollo
> Ad una barba la più singolare
> Che mai fosse descritta in verso o 'n prosa :

these form a gallery of comic likenesses, drawn from
the life and communicated with the force of reality to

the reader. Each is perfect in style, clearly cut like some antique chalcedony, bringing the object of the poet's mirth before us with the exact measure of ridicule he sought to inflict.[1]

This satiric power culminates in the sonnet on Pietro Aretino.[2] The tartness of Berni's more good-humoured pasquinades is concentrated to vitriol by unadulterated loathing. He flings this biting acid in the face of one whom he has found a scoundrel. The sonnet starts at the white heat of fury :

> Tu ne dirai e farai tante e tante,
> Lingua fracida, marcia, senza sale.

It proceeds with execration ; and when the required fourteen lines have been terminated, it foams over into rage more voluble and still more voluble, unwinding the folds of an interminable *Coda* with ever-increasing *crescendo* of vituperation, as though the passion of the writer could not be appeased. The whole has to be read at one breath. No quotation can render a conception of its rhetorical art. Every word strikes home, because every word contains a truth expressed in language of malignant undiluted heart-felt hate. That most difficult of literary triumphs, to render abuse sublime, to sustain a single note of fierce invective without relaxing or weakening the several grades that lead to the catastrophe, has been accom-

---

[1] Sonnets xi. xvi. xiv. iii. xx. The same vivid picturesqueness is displayed in the desecrated Abbey (Sonnet xvii.), which deserves to be called an etching in words.

[2] Sonnet xix. In the *Capitolo* to Ippolito de' Medici, Berni thus alludes to Aretino :

> Com' ha fatto non so chi mio vicino,
> Che veste d' oro, e più non degna il panno,
> E dassi del messere e del divino.

plished. This achievement is no doubt due in some
measure to the exact correspondence between what
we know of Pietro Aretino and what Berni has written
of him. Yet its blunt fidelity to fact does not detract
from the skill displayed in the handling of those triple
series of rhymes, each one of which descends like a
lash upon the writhing back beneath :

> .Ch' ormai ogni paese
> Hai ammorbato, ogn' uom, ogn' animale,
> Il ciel e Dio e 'l diavol ti vuol male.
>> Quelle veste ducale,
> O ducali accattate e furfantate,
> Che ti piangono addosso sventurate,
>> A suon di bastonate
> Ti saran tratte, prima che tu muoja,
> Dal reverendo padre messer boja,
>> Che l' anima di noja,
> Mediante un capestro, caveratti,
> E per maggior favore squarteratti ;
>> E quei tuoi leccapiatti,
> Bardassonacci, paggi da taverna,
> Ti canteranno il requiem eterna.
>> Or vivi e ti governa,
> Bench' un pugnale, un cesso, overo un nodo
> Ti faranno star cheto in ogni modo.

From this conclusion the rest may be divined. Berni
paid dearly for the satisfaction of thus venting his
spleen. Aretino had found more than his match.
Though himself a master in the art of throwing dirt,
he could not, like Berni, sling his missiles with the
certainty of gaining for himself by the same act an
immortality of glory. This privilege is reserved for
the genius of style, and style alone. Therefore he
had to shrink in silence under Berni's scourge. But
Aretino was not the man to forego revenge if only

an opportunity for inflicting injury upon his antago-
nist, full and effectual, and without peril to himself,
was offered. The occasion came after Berni's death ;
and how he availed himself of it, will appear in the
next paragraphs.

Though the *Capitoli* and sonnets won for their
author the high place he occupies among Italian poets,
Berni is also famous for his *rifacimento* or remodelling
of the *Orlando Innamorato*. He undertook this task
after the publication of the *Furioso* ; and though part
was written at Verona, we know from references to
contemporary events contained in the *rifacimento*, that
Berni was at work upon it in the last years of his life
at Florence. It was not published until some time
after his death. Berni subjected the whole of Boiardo's
poem to minute revision, eliminating obsolete words
and Lombard phrases, polishing the verse, and soften-
ing the roughness of the elder poet's style. He
omitted a few passages, introduced digressions, connected the episodes by links and references, and opened
each canto with a dissertation in the manner of Ariosto.
Opinions may vary as to the value of the changes
wrought by Berni. But there can be no doubt that
his work was executed with artistic accuracy, and that
his purpose was a right one. He aimed at nothing
less than rendering a noble poem adequate to the
measure of literary excellence attained by the Italians
since Boiardo's death. The *Innamorato* was to be
made worthy of the *Furioso*. The nation was to
possess a continuous epic of Orlando, complete in all
its parts and uniformly pure in style. Had Berni
lived to see his own work through the press, it is pro-

bable that this result would have been attained. As it happened, the malignity of fortune or the malice of a concealed enemy defeated his intention. We only possess a deformed version of his *rifacimento*. The history, or rather the tragedy, of its publication involves some complicated questions of conjecture. Yet the side-lights thrown upon the conditions of literature at that time in Italy, as well as on the mystery of Berni's death, are sufficiently interesting to justify the requisite expenditure of space and time.

The *rifacimento* appeared in a mutilated form at Venice in 1541, from the press of the Giunti, and again in 1542 at Milan from that of Francesco Calvo. These two issues are identical, except in the title and tail pages. The same batch of sheets was in fact divided by the two publishers. In 1545 another issue, called *Edizione Seconda*, saw the light at Venice, in which Giunta introduced a very significant note, pointing out that certain stanzas were not the work of ' M. Francesco Berni, but of one who presumptuously willed to do him so great an injury.'[1] This edition, differing in many respects from those of 1541 and 1542, was on the whole an improvement. It would seem that the publishers, in the interval between 1541 and 1545, regretted that Berni's copy had been tampered with, and did their best, in the absence of the original, to restore a correct text. Still, as Giunta acknowledged, the *rifacimento* had been irretrievably damaged by some private foe.[2] The introductory

---

[1] 'Di chi presuntuosamente gli ha voluto fare tanta ingiuria.' This note occurs at Stanza 83 of Canto 1.

[2] In some cases the readings of the second edition are inferior to

dedication to Isabella Gonzaga, where we might have expected an allusion to Boiardo, is certainly not Berni's ; and the two lines,

> Nè ti sdegnar veder quel ch' altri volse
> Forse a te dedicar, ma morte il tolse,

must be understood to refer to Berni's and not to Boiardo's death. Comparison of the two editions makes it, moreover, clear that Berni's MS. had been garbled, and the autograph probably put out of the way before the publication of the poem.

Who is to be held responsible for this fraud ? Who was the presumptuous enemy who did such injury to Berni ? Panizzi, so far back as 1830, pointed out that Giovanni Alberto Albicante took some part in preparing the edition of 1541–2. This man prefixed sonnets written by himself to the *rifacimento* ; 'whence we might conclude that he was the editor.'[1] Signor Virgili, to whose researches attention has already been directed, proved further by references to Pietro Aretino's correspondence that this old enemy of Berni had a hand in the same work. Writing to Francesco Calvo

---

those of the first, while both fall short of Boiardo. Boiardo wrote in his description of Astolfo (Canto i. 60) :

> Quel solea dir ch egli era per sciagura,
> E tornava a cader senza paura.

In the *rifacimento* of 1541 we have :

> E alle volte cadeva per sciagura,
> E si levava poi senza paura.

In that of 1545 :

> Un sol dispetto avea : dice Turpino
> Che nel cader alquanto era latino.

I take these instances from Panizzi.

[1] *Boiardo ed Ariosto*, vol. ii. p. cxxxiv.

from Venice on February 16, 1540, Aretino approaches
the subject of the *rifacimento* in these words [1]: 'Our
friend Albicante informs me, with reference to the
printing of *Orlando* defamed by Berni, that you are
good enough to meet my wishes, for which I thank
you. . . . You will see that, for the sake of your own
modesty, you are bound either not to issue the book
at all, or else to purge it of all evil-speaking.' He
then states that it had been his own intention 'to
emend the Count of Scandiano's *Innamoramento*, a
thing in its kind of heroic beauty, but executed in a
trivial style, and expressed with phrases at once plebeian
and obsolete.' This task he renounced upon reflection
that it would bring him no fame to assume the mask
of a dead man's labours. In another letter to the same
Calvo, dated February 17, 1542, Aretino resumes the
subject. Sbernia (so he chooses to call Berni) has
been 'overwhelmed beneath the ruins he pulled down
upon himself by his undoing of the *Innamoramento*.' [2]
Now, it is certain that the ruin proclaimed by Aretino
did really fall on Berni's labours. In 1545 Lodovico
Domenichi published a second *rifacimento*, far inferior
in style to that of Berni, and executed with the sloven-
liness of a literary hack. But this was several times
reprinted, whereas Berni's remained neglected on the
shelves of the librarians until the year 1725, when it

---

[1] *Lettere*, Book ii. p. 121.

[2] *Ibid.* p. 249. We might quote a parallel passage from the Prologue
to the *Ipocrita*, which Aretino published in 1542, just after accomplishing
his revenge on Berni : 'Io non ho pensato al gastigo che io darei a quegli
che pongono il lor nome nei libri che essi guastano nella foggia che un
non so chi ha guasto il Boiardo, per non mi credere che si trovasse cotanta
temerità nella presunzione del mondo.' The hypocrisy of this is worthy
of the play's title.

was republished and welcomed with a storm of exaggerated enthusiasm.

We have therefore reached this conclusion, that Aretino, aided by Albicante, both of them notable literary brigands, contrived to send a mutilated version of the *rifacimento* to press, with the view of doing irreparable mischief to Berni's reputation.[1] We have also seen that there was something dangerous in Berni's work, described by Aretino as *maldicentia*, which he held as a threat over the Milanese publisher. Lastly, Giunta recognised too late that he had made himself the party to some act of malice by issuing a garbled copy. Aretino had, we know, a private grudge to satisfy. He could not forget the castigation he received at Berni's hands, in the sonnet which has been already described. The hatred subsisting between the two men, had been further exasperated by the different parts they took in a literary duel. Antonio Broccardo, a young Venetian scholar, attacked Pietro Bembo's fame at Padua in 1530, and attempted to raise allies against the great dictator. Aretino took up the cudgels for Bembo, and assailed Broccardo with vehement abuse and calumny. Berni ranged himself upon Broccardo's side. The quarrel ended in Broccardo's death under suspicious circumstances in 1531 at Padua. He was, indeed, said to have been killed by Aretino.[2] Berni died mysteriously at Florence

---

[1] Mazzuchelli (*Scrittori d' Italia* : Albicante, Giov. Alberto) may be consulted about the relations between these two ruffians, who alternately praised and abused each other in print.

[2] See Mazzuchelli, *op. cit.*, under ' Brocardo, Antonio.' The spelling of the name varies. Bembo, six years afterwards, told Varchi that Aretino drove Broccardo for him into an early grave. See *Lettere all' Aretino*, vol. ii. p. 186, ed. Romagnoli. The probability is that Broccardo died of

four years later, and Aretino caused his *rifacimento,* 'purged of evil-speaking,' to be simultaneously published at Venice and Milan.

The question still remains to be asked how Aretino, Berni's avowed enemy, obtained possession of the MS. Berni had many literary friends. Yet none of them came forward to avert the catastrophe. None of them undertook the publication of his remains. His last work was produced, not at Florence, where he lived and died, but at Venice ; and Albicante, Aretino's tool, was editor. In the present state of our knowledge it is impossible to answer this question authoritatively. Considerable light, however, is thrown upon the mystery by a pamphlet published in 1554 by the heretic Vergerio. He states that Berni undertook his *rifacimento* with the view of diffusing Protestant doctrines in a popular and unobtrusive form ; but that the craft of the devil, or in other words the policy of the Church, effected its supression at the very moment when it was finished and all but printed.[1] Here, then, we seem to find some missing links in the dark chain of intrigue. Aretino's phrase *maldicentia* is explained ; his menace

fever aggravated by the annoyance caused him by Aretino's calumnies. There is no valid suspicion of poison.

[1] This curious pamphlet was reprinted from a unique copy by Panizzi, *op. cit.* vol. iii. p. 361. In the introduction, Vergerio gives an interesting account of Berni. He represents him as a man of worldly life, addicted to gross pleasures and indecent literature until within a few years of his death. Having been converted to evangelical faith in Christ, Berni then resolved to use the *Orlando* as a vehicle for Lutheran opinions ; and his *rifacimento* was already almost printed, when the devil found means to suppress it. Vergerio is emphatic in his statement that the poem was finished and nearly printed. If this was indeed the case, we must suppose that Albicante worked upon the sheets, cancelling some and leaving others, and that the book thus treated was afterwards shared by Giunta and Calvo.

to Francesco Calvo becomes intelligible ; the silence of
Berni's friends can be accounted for ; and the agency
by which the MS. was placed in Albicante's hands, can
be at least conjectured. As a specimen of Berni's
Lutheran propaganda, Vergerio subjoins eighteen
stanzas, written in the poet's purest style, which were
addressed to Battista Sanga, and which formed the
induction to the twentieth Canto. This induction, as
it stands in Berni's *Innamorato*, is reduced to seven
stanzas, grossly garbled and deformed in diction. Very
few of the original lines have been retained, and those
substituted are full of vulgarisms.[1]   From a comparison
of the original supplied by Vergerio with the mutilated version, the full measure of the mischief practised
upon Berni's posthumous work can be gauged. Furthermore, it must be noticed that these compromising
eighteen stanzas contained the names of several men
alive in Italy, all of whom were therefore interested in
their suppression, or precluded from exposing the fraud.

The inference I am inclined to draw from Signor
Virgili's researches, combined with Vergerio's pamphlet,
is that the Church interfered to prevent the publication of Berni's heretical additions to Boiardo's poem.
Berni's sudden death, throwing his affairs into confusion at the moment when he was upon the point of
finishing the business, afforded an excellent occasion to
his ecclesiastical and personal opponents, who seem
to have put some pressure on his kinsmen to obtain

---

[1] I shall print a translation of the eighteen stanzas in an Appendix
to this volume.   Lines like the following,

Arrandellarsi come un salsicciuolo,

which are common in the mangled version, would never have passed
Berni's censure.

the MS. or the sheets they meant to mutilate.[1] The obnoxious passages may have been denounced by Aretino ; for we know that he was intimate with Vergerio, and it is more than probable that the verses to Sanga were already in circulation.[2] Aretino, strange to say, was regarded in clerical quarters as a pillar of the Church. He therefore found it in his power to wreak his vengeance on an enemy at the same time that he posed as a defender of the faith. That he was allowed to control the publication, appears from his letters to Calvo ; and he confided the literary part of the business to Albicante. His threats to Calvo have reference to Berni's heresy, and the *maldicentia* may possibly have been the eighteen stanzas addressed to Sanga. The terror of the Inquisition reduced Berni's friends to silence. Aretino, even if he had not denounced Berni to the Church, had now identified himself with the crusade against his poem, and he was capable of ruining opponents in this unequal contest by charges they would have found it impossible to refute. The eighteen stanzas were addressed to a secretary of Clement VII. ; and men of note like Molza, Flamminio, Navagero, Fondulo, Fregoso, were distinctly named in them. If, then, there is any

[1] This appears from a reference in Aretino's second letter to Calvo, where he talks of Berni's 'friends and relatives.' It might be going too far to suggest that Berni was murdered by his ecclesiastical enemies, who feared the scandal which would be caused by the publication of his opinions.

[2] Vergerio may have communicated the eighteen stanzas to Aretino ; or conversely he may have received them from him. I have read through the letters exchanged between him and Aretino—and they are numerous— without, however, finding any passage that throws light on this transaction. Aretino published both series of letters. He had therefore opportunity to suppress inconvenient allusions.

cogency in the conclusions I have drawn from various sources, Berni's poem, and perhaps his life, was sacrificed to theological hatred in combination with Aretino's personal malice. The unaccountable inactivity of his friends is explained by their dread of being entangled in a charge of heresy.[1] Enough has been already said about Berni's imitators in the burlesque style. Of satire in the strict sense of the term, the poets of the sixteenth century produced nothing that is worth consideration. The epistolary form introduced by Ariosto, and the comic caprices rendered fashionable by Berni, determined the compositions of Pietro Aretino, of Ercole Bentivoglio, of Luigi Alamanni, of Antonio Vinciguerra, of Giovanni Andrea dell' Anguillara, of Cesare Caporali, and of the minor versifiers whose occasional poems in *terza rima*, seasoned with more or less satirical intention, are usually reckoned among the satires of the golden age.[2] Personal vituperation poured forth in the heat of literary quarrels, scarcely deserves the name of satire. Else it might be necessary in this place to mention Niccolò Franco's sonnets on Pietro Aretino, or the far more elegant compositions of Annibale Caro directed against his

---

[1] We may note the dates and fates of the chief actors in this tragedy. Broccardo died of grief in 1531. Berni died, under suspicion of poison, in 1535. Cardinal Ippolito de' Medici was poisoned a few months later, in 1535. Alessandro de' Medici was murdered by Lorenzino in 1537. Pietro Paolo Vergerio was deprived of his see and accused of heresy in 1544. Berni's old friend, the author of *Il Forno*, M. La Casa, conducted his trial, as Papal Nuncio at Venice. Aretino, who had assumed the part of inquisitor and mutilator to gratify his private spite, survived triumphant.

[2] See the *Raccolta di Poesie Satiriche*, Milano, 1808.

enemy Castelvetro.[1]   Models for this species of poetical
abuse had been already furnished by the sonnets exchanged between Luigi Pulci and Matteo Franco in a
more masculine age of Italian literature.[2]   It is not,
however, incumbent upon the historian to resuscitate
the memory of those forgotten and now unimportant
duels.   The present allusion to them may suffice to
corroborate the opinion already stated that, while the
Italians of the Renaissance were ingenious in burlesque,
and virulent in personal invective, they lacked the
earnestness of moral conviction, the indignation, and
the philosophic force that generate real satire.

[1] See, for the latter series, *Poesie Satiriche*, pp. 138-156.
[2] See *Sonetti di Matteo Franco e di Luigi Pulci*, 1759.   Cp. above,
Part i. p. 431.

CHAPTER XV.

PIETRO ARETINO.

Aretino's Place in Italian Literature and Society—His Birth and Boy-
hood—Goes to Rome—In the Service of Agostino Chigi—At Mantua
Gradual Emergence into Celebrity—The Incident of Giulio
Romano's Postures—Giovanni delle Bande Nere—Aretino settles at
Venice—The Mystery of his Influence—Discerns the Power of the
Press—Satire on the Courts—Magnificent Life—Aretino's Wealth—
His Tributary Princes—Bullying and Flattery—The Divine Aretino—
His Letter to Vittoria Colonna—To Michelangelo—His Admiration
of Artists—Relations with Men of Letters—Epistle to Bernardo
Tasso—His Lack of Learning—Disengagement from Puristic Preju-
dices—Belief in his own Powers—Rapidity of Composition—His Style
- Originality and Independence—Prologue to *Talanta*—Bohemian
Comrades—Niccolò Franco—Quarrel with Doni—Aretino's Literary
Influence—His Death—The Anomaly of the Renaissance—Estimate
of Aretino's Character.

PIETRO ARETINO, as I have already had occasion to
observe, is a representative name in the history of
Italian literature. It is almost as impossible to slur
him over with a passing notice as it would be to dwell
but casually upon Machiavelli or Ariosto, Cellini or
Poliziano, in reviewing the Renaissance. Base in
character, coarse in mental fibre, unworthy to rank
among real artists, notwithstanding his undoubted
genius, Aretino was the typical ruffian of an age which
brought ruffianism to perfection, welcomed it when
successful, bowed to its insolence, and viewed it with
complacent toleration in the highest places of Church,
State, and letters. He was the *condottiere* of the pen

in a society which truckled to the Borgias. He embodied the infamy and cowardice which lurked beneath the braveries of Italian Court-life—the coarseness of speech which contradicted literary purism—the cynicism and gross strength of appetite for which convention was a flimsy veil.[1] The man himself incarnated the dissolution of Italian culture. His works, for the student of that period, are an anti-masque to the brilliant display of Ariosto's or of Tasso's puppets. It is the condemnation of Italy that we are forced to give this prominence to Aretino. If we place Poliziano or Guicciardini, Bembo or La Casa, Bandello or Firenzuola, Cellini or Berni, Paolo Giovio or Lodovico Dolce—typical men of letters chosen from the poets, journalists, historians, thinkers, artists, novel-writers of the age—under the critical microscope, we find in each and all of them a tincture of Aretino. It is because he emphasises and brings into relief one master element of the Renaissance, that he deserves the rank assigned to him. In Athens Aristophanes is named together with Sophocles, Thucydides and Plato, because, with genius equal to theirs, he represented the comic antithesis to tragedy, philosophy and history. In Italy Aretino is classed with Machiavelli and Ariosto for a different reason. His lower nature expressed, not an antithesis, but a quality, which, in spite of intellectual and moral superiority, they possessed in common

[1] The best source of information regarding Pietro Aretino is his own correspondence published in six volumes (Paris, 1609), and the two volumes of letters written to him by eminent personages, which are indeed a rich mine of details regarding Italian society and manners in the sixteenth century. Mazzuchelli's *Vita di Pietro Aretino* (Padua, 1741) is a conscientious, sober, and laborious piece of work, on which all subsequent notices have been based.

with him, which he exhibited in arrogant abundance, and which cannot be omitted from the survey of his century. The alloy of cynicism in Machiavelli, his sordid private pleasures, his perverse admiration for Cesare Borgia, his failure to recognise the power of goodness in the world, condemn him to the company of this triumvir. The profligacy of genius in Ariosto, his waste of divine gifts upon trifles, his lack of noble sentiment, his easy acquiescence in conditions of society against which he should have uttered powerful protest, consign him, however undeservedly, to the same association.[1]

Pietro was born at Arezzo in 1492. His reputed father was a nobleman of that city, named Luigi Bacci. His mother, Tita, was a woman of the town, whose portrait, painted as the Virgin of the Annunciation, adorned the church-door of S. Pietro. The boy, 'born,' as he afterwards boasted, 'in a hospital with the spirit of a king,' passed his childhood at Arezzo with his mother. He had no education but what he may have picked up among the men who frequented Tita's house, or the artists who employed her as a model. Of Greek and Latin he learned nothing either now or afterwards. Before growing to man's estate, he had to quit his native city—according to one account because he composed and uttered a ribald sonnet on indulgences, according to another because he robbed his mother. He escaped to Perugia, and gained his livelihood by binding books. Here he made

---

[1] It may be mentioned that Ariosto has immortalised this bully in the *Orlando* (xlvi. 14), among the most illustrious men and women of his age :

ecco il flagello
De' principi, il divin Pietro Aretino.

acquaintance with Firenzuola, as appears from a letter of the year 1541, in which he alludes to their youthful pranks together at the University. One of Aretino's exploits at Perugia became famous. ' Having noticed in a place of much resort upon the public square a picture, in which the Magdalen was represented at the feet of Christ, with extended arms and in an attitude of passionate grief, he went privily and painted in a lute between her hands.' From Perugia he trudged on foot to Rome, and entered the service of Agostino Chigi, under whose patronage he made himself useful to the Medici, remaining in the retinue of both Leo X. and Clement VII. between 1517 and 1524. This period of seven years formed the man's character; and it would be interesting to know for certain what his employment was. Judging by the graphic descriptions he has left us of the Roman Court in his comedy of the *Cortigiana* and his dialogue *De le Corti*, and also by his humble condition in Perugia, we have reason to believe that he occupied at first the post of lacquey, rising gradually by flattery and baser arts to the position of a confidential domestic, half favourite, half servant.[1]

[1] Aretino's comedies, letters, and occasional poems are our best sources for acquaintance with the actual conditions of palace-life. The *Dialogo de le Corti* opens with a truly terrible description of the debauchery and degradation to which a youth was exposed on his first entrance into the service of a Roman noble. It may have been drawn from the author's own experience. The nauseous picture of the *tinello*, or upper-servants' hall, which occurs in the comedy *Cortigiana* (act v. sc. 15), proves intimate familiarity with the most revolting details of domestic drudgery. The dirt of these places made an ineffaceable impression on Aretino's memory. In his burlesque *Orlandino*, when he wishes to call up a disgusting image, he writes :

Odorava la sala come odora
   Un gran tinel d' un Monsignor Francese,
   O come quel d' un Cardinal ancora
Quando Febo riscalda un bestial mese.

That he possessed extraordinary social qualities, and knew how to render himself agreeable by witty conversation and boon companionship, is obvious from the whole course of his subsequent history. It is no less certain that he allowed neither honour nor self-respect to interfere with his advancement by means which cannot be described in detail, but which opened the readiest way to favour in that profligate society of Rome. His own enormous appetite for sensual enjoyment, his cynicism, and his familiarity with low life in all its forms, rendered him the congenial associate of a great man's secret pleasures, the convenient link of communication between the palace and the stews.[1]

Yet though Pietro resided at this time principally in Rome, he had by no means a fixed occupation, and his life was interrupted by frequent wanderings. He is said to have left Agostino Chigi's service, because he stole a silver cup. He is also said to have taken the cowl in a Capuchin convent at Ravenna, and to have thrown his frock to the nettles on the occasion of Leo's election to the Papacy. We hear of him parading in the Courts of Lombardy, always on the lookout for patronage, supporting himself by what means

---

[1] Aretino's correspondence and the comedy above mentioned throw sufficient light upon these features of Roman society. It will, for the rest, suffice to quote a passage from Monsignore Guidiccioni's letter to Giambattista Bernardi (*Opere di M. Giov. Guidiccioni*, Barbèra, 1867, vol. i. p. 195) : ' Non solamente *da questi illustri per ricchezze* non si può avere, ma non si puote ancora sperare premio che sia di lunghe fatiche o di rischio di morte, se *l' uomo non si rivolge ad acquistarlo per vie disoneste.* Perciocchè essi non carezzano e non esaltano se non adulatori, e *quelli che sanno per alfabeto le abitazioni, le pratiche e le qualità delle cortigiane.*' The whole letter should be read by those who would understand Roman society of the Renaissance. The italics are mine.

is unapparent, but gradually pushing his way to fame and fashion, loudly asserting his own claims to notice, and boasting of each new favour he received. Here is a characteristic glimpse into his nomadic mode of life [1]: 'I am now in Mantua with the Marquis, and am held by him in so high favour that he leaves off sleeping and eating to converse with me, and says he has no other pleasure in life; and he has written to the Cardinal about me things that will not fail to help me greatly to my credit. I have also received a present of 300 crowns. He has assigned to me the very same apartment which Francesco Maria, Duke of Urbino, occupied when he was in exile; and has appointed a steward to preside over my table, where I always have some noblemen of rank. In a word, more could not be done for the entertainment of the greatest prince. Besides, the whole Court worships me. Happy are they who can boast of having got a verse from me. My lord has had all the poems ever writ by me copied, and I have made some in his praise. So I pass my life here, and every day get some gift, grand things which you shall see at Arezzo. But it was at Bologna they began to make me presents. The Bishop of Pisa had a robe of black satin embroidered with gold cut for me; nothing could be handsomer. So I came like a prince to Mantua. Everybody calls me " Messere " and " Signore." I think this Easter we shall be at Loreto, where the Marquis goes to perform a vow; and on this journey I shall be able to satisfy the Dukes

---

[1] Quoted by Philarète Chasles from Gamurrini, *Ist. Gen. delle famiglie nobili Toscane ed Umbre*, iii. 332. I do not know exactly to what period the letter refers.

of Ferrara and Urbino, both of whom have expressed the desire to make my acquaintance.'

On the election of Clement VII., Pietro returned to Rome with a complimentary sonnet in his pocket for the new Pope. He had now acquired an Italian reputation, and was able to keep the state of an in-dependent gentleman, surrounded by a band of dis-reputable hangers-on, the *bardassonacci, paggi da taverna,* of Berni's satirical sonnet. But a misfor-tune obliged him suddenly to decamp. Giulio Ro-mano had designed a series of obscene figures, which Marcantonio Raimondi engraved, and Aretino illustrated by sixteen sonnets, describing and com-menting upon the lewdness of each picture. Put in circulation, these works of immodest art roused the indignation of the Roman prelates, who, though they complacently listened to Berni's *Pesche* or La Casa's *Forno* behind the closed doors of a literary club, dis-liked the scandal of publicity. Raimondi was im-prisoned; Giulio Romano went in the service of the Marquis of Mantua to build the famous Palazzo del Te ; and Aretino discreetly retired from Rome for a season. Of the three accomplices in this act of high treason against art, Aretino was undoubtedly the guiltiest. Yet he had the impudence to defend his sonnets in 1537, and to address them with a letter of dedication, unmatched for its parade of shamelessness, to Messer Battista Zatti of Brescia.[1] In this epistle he takes credit to himself for having procured the engraver's pardon and liberation from Clement VII. However this may be, he fell in 1524 under the special ban of

---

[1] *Lettere,* vol. i. p. 258.

Monsignor Giberti's displeasure, and had to take re
fuge with Giovanni de' Medici delle Bande Nere.[1]
This famous general was a wild free-liver. He conceived a real affection for Aretino, made him the sharer
in his debaucheries, gave him a place even in his own
bed, and listened with rapture to his indecent impro-
visations. Aretino's fortune was secured. It was discovered that he had the art of pleasing princes. He
knew exactly how to season his servility with freedom,
how to flatter the great man by pandering to his passions and tickling his vanity, while he added the pungent sauce of satire and affected bluntness. *Il gran
Diavolo*, as Giovanni de' Medici was called, introduced Aretino to Francis I., and promised, if fortune
favoured him, to make the adventurer master of his
native town, Arezzo.[2]

Aretino's intercourse with these powerful protec-
tors was broken by a short visit to Rome, where he
seems to have made peace with the prelates. It was
probably inconvenient to protract hostilities against a
man who had gained the friendship of a King of
France and of the greatest Italian *condottiere* of his
age. But fortune had ceased to smile on our hero in

---

[1] It may be remembered that Giberti, Bishop of Verona, was Berni's
patron. This helps to account for the animosity between Berni and
Aretino

[2] *Op. Burl.* ii. p. 11 :

> Sotto Milano dieci volte, non ch' una,
> Mi disse : Pietro, se di questa guerra
> Mi scampa Dio e la buona fortuna,
> Ti voglio impadronir della tua terra

Giovanni de' Medici wrote to him thus : 'Vieni presto . . . Il re a buon
proposito si dolse che non ti aveva menato al solito, onde io diedi la colpa
al piacerti più lo stare in Corte che in Campo . . non so vivere senza
l' Aretino.'—*Lettere scritte all' Aretino*, i. 6.

Rome. It so happened that he wrote a ribald sonnet on a scullion-wench in the service of Monsignor Giberti, to whom a certain Achille della Volta was at the same time paying his addresses. The *bravo* avenged this insult to his mistress by waylaying Aretino in the Trastevere and stabbing him several times in the breast and hands. When Aretino recovered from his wounds, he endeavoured in vain to get justice against Achille. The Pope and his Datary refused to interfere in this ignoble quarrel. Aretino once more retired from Rome, vowing vengeance against Clement, whom he defamed to the best of his ability in scurrilous libels and calumnious conversation.[1]

He now remained with Giovanni de' Medici until that general's death in 1526. The great captain died in Aretino's arms at Mantua from the effect of a wound inflicted by an unknown harquebuss in Frundsperg's army.[2] This accident decided Aretino to place no further reliance on princely patronage. He was thirty-two years of age, and had acquired a singular reputation throughout Italy for social humour, pungent wit and literary ability. Though deficient in personal courage, as the affair of Achille della Volta proved, he contrived to render himself formidable by reckless evil-speaking ; and while he had no learning and no style, he managed to pass for a writer of distinction. How he attained this position in an age of

---

[1] The sonnet by Berni quoted above, p. 371, was written to meet these libels of Aretino. It contains an allusion to Achille della Volta's poignard.

[2] See Aretino's Letters, vol. i. pp. 8, 10, for very interesting details concerning the death of Giovanni de' Medici. He here used the interest of his old master to secure the favour of Duke Cosimo.

purists, remains a puzzle; we possess nothing which
explains the importance attached to his compositions
at this early period.   His sonnets had made what the
French call a success of scandal; and the libertines
who protected him, were less particular about literary
elegance than eager to be amused.   If we enquire
minutely into the circumstances of Aretino's career, we
find that he had worked himself into favour with a set
of princes—the Marquis of Mantua, the Dukes of
Ferrara and Urbino, Giovanni de' Medici, and the
King of France—who were powerful enough to confer
fashion upon an adventurer, and to place him in a
position where it would be perilous to contest his
claims, but who were not eminent for literary taste.
In the Court of the two Medici at Rome, who exacted
more scholarship and refinement than Aretino possessed, he never gained firm footing ; and this was perhaps the chief reason of his animosity against Clement.
He had in fact become the foremost parasite, the wittiest and most brilliant companion of debauch, in the
less cultivated Italian Courts.   This reputation he now
resolved to use for his own profit.   From the moment
when he retired to Venice in 1527, resolved to support
himself by literary work, until his death, in 1557, he
enjoyed a princely income, levying tribute on kings
and nobles, living with prodigal magnificence, corresponding with the most illustrious men of all nations,
and dictating his own terms to the society he alternately flattered and insulted.   The history of these
last thirty years, which may be clearly read in the six
bulky volumes of his published correspondence, and
in the four volumes of letters written to him, is one

of the most extraordinary instances on record of celebrity and power acquired by calculated imposture and
audacious brigandism.[1]

Aretino showed prudence in the choice of Venice
for his fixed abode. In Venice there was greater
liberty both of life and speech than elsewhere at that
time in Italy. So long as a man refrained from politics and offered no cause of suspicion to the State, he
might do and publish pretty much what he chose,
without fear of interference and without any serious
peril from the Inquisition. For a filibuster of Aretino's
type, Venice offered precisely the most advantageous
harbour, whence he could make sallies and predatory
excursions, and whither he might always return to rest
at ease beneath the rampart of a proud political indifference. His greatness consisted in the accurate
measure he had taken of the society upon which he
now intended to live by literary speculation. His
acute common sense enabled him to comprehend the
power of the press, which had not as yet been deliberately used as a weapon of offence and an instrument
of extortion. We have seen in another portion of
this book how important a branch of literature the
invectives of the humanists had been, how widely they
were read, and what an impression they produced
upon society. The diatribes of Poggio and Filelfo
circulated in manuscript; but now the press was in
full working order, and Aretino perceived that he

[1] The edition of Aretino's own letters which I shall use is that of
Paris, 1609, in six books. The edition of the *Lettere scritte all'* *Aretino*
is Romagnoli's reprint, *Scelta di Curiosità*, Bologna, 1873–1876, Dispensa
cxxxii., two books divided into four volumes ; to these, for convenience
sake, I shall refer as 1, 2, 3, 4.

might make a livelihood by printing threats and libels mixed with eulogies and personal panegyrics. The unwieldy three-decker of the invective should be reduced to the manageable form of the epistolary torpedo and gunboat. To propagate calumnies and to render them imperishable by printing was the menace he addressed to society. He calculated wisely on the uneasiness which the occasional appearance of stinging pamphlets, fully charged with personalities, would produce among the Italians, who were nothing if not a nation of readers at this epoch. At the same time he took measures to secure his own safety. Professing himself a good Christian, he liberally seasoned his compositions with sacred names; and, though he had no more real religion than Fra Timoteo in Machiavelli's *Mandragola*, he published pious romances under the titles of *I tre libri della Humanità di Christo, I Sette Salmi de la penitentia di David, Il Genesi di Pietro Aretino, La Vita di Catherina Vergine, La Vita di Maria Vergine, La Vita di S. Tommaso Signor d' Aquino.* These books, proceeding from the same pen as the *Sonetti lussuriosi* and the pornographic *Ragionamenti*, were an insult to piety. Still they served their author for a shield, behind which he shot the arrows of his calumnies, and carried on the more congenial game of making money by pandering to the licentiousness or working on the cowardice of the wealthy.[1]

Aretino, who was able to boast that he had just

---

[1] It is clear from a perusal of the *Lettere all' Aretino* that his reputation depended in a great measure upon these pious romances. The panegyrics heaped on them are too lengthy and too copious to be quoted. They are curiously mixed with no less fervent praises of the *Dialoghi*.

refused a flattering invitation from the Marquis of Montferrat, was received with honour by the State of Venice. Soon after his arrival he wrote thus to the Doge Andrea Gritti[1]: 'I, who, in the liberty of so great and virtuous a commonwealth, have now learned what it is to be free, reject Courts henceforth for ever, and here make my abiding tabernacle for the years that yet remain to me ; for here there is no place for treason, here favour cannot injure right, here the cruelty of prostitutes exerts no sway, here the insolence of the effeminate is powerless to command, here there is no robbing, no violence to the person, no assassination. Wherefore I, who have stricken terror into kings, I, who have restored confidence to virtuous men, give myself to you, fathers of your people, brothers of your servants, sons of truth, friends of virtue, companions of the stranger, pillars of religion, observers of your word, executors of justice, treasuries of charity, and subjects of clemency.' Then follows a long tirade in the same stilted style upon the majesty of Venice. The Doge took Aretino by the hand, reconciled him with Clement and the Bishop of Verona, and assured him of protection, so long as the illustrious author chose to make the city of the lagoons his home. Luigi Gritti, the Doge's son, assigned him a pension ; and though invitations came from foreign Courts, Aretino made his mind up to remain at Venice. He knew that the very singularity of his resolve, in an age when men of letters sought the patronage of princely houses, would enable him to play the game he had in view. Nor could he forget the degradation

[1] *Lettere*, vol. i p. 3.

he had previously undergone in courtly service.
'Only let me draw breath outside that hell! Ah!
your Court! your Court! To my mind a gondolier
here is better off than a chamberlain there. Look
you at yonder poor waiting man, tortured by the cold,
consumed by the heat, standing at his master's
pleasure—where is the fire to warm him? where is the
water to refresh him? When he falls ill, what
chamber, what stable, what hospital will take him in?
Rain, snow, mud! Faugh, it murders a man to ride
in such weather with his patron or upon his errands.
Think how cruel it is to have to show a beard grown
in the service of mere boys, how abject are white
hairs, when youth and manhood have been spent in
idling around tables, antechamber doors, and privies?
Here I sit when I am tired ; when I am hungry, eat;
when I feel the inclination, sleep ; and all the hours
are obedient to my will.' [1]   He revels in the sense of
his own freedom.   ' My sincerity, and my virtue, which
never could stomach the lies that bolster up the Court
of Rome, nor the vices that reign in it, have found
favour in the eyes of all the princes of the world.
Emperors, thank God, are not Popes, nor Kings Cardinals!   Therefore I enjoy their generosity, instead
of courting that hypocrisy of priests, which acts the
bawd and pander to our souls.   Look at Chieti, the
parasite of penitence!   Look at Verona, the buffoon
of piety!   They at least have solved the doubts in
which their ambitious dissimulation held those who
believed that the one would not accept the hat, and the

other was not scheming for it. I meanwhile praise
God for being what I am. The hatred of slaves, the
rancours of ambition no longer hem me round. I rob
no man's time. I take no delight in seeing my neighbours go naked through the world. Nay, I share
with them the very shirts off my back, the crust of
bread upon my plate. My servant-girls are my
daughters, my lacqueys are my brothers. Peace is the
pomp of my chambers, and liberty the majordomo of
my palace. I feast daily off bread and gladness ; and,
wishing not to be of more importance than I am, live
by the sweat of my ink, the lustre of which has never
been extinguished by the blasts of malignity or the
mists of envy.'[1]   At another time he breaks into
jubilant descriptions of his own magnificence and popularity. ' I swear to you by the wings of Pegasus
that, much as may have reached your ears, you have
not heard one half the hymn of my celebrity. Medals
are coined in my honour ; medals of gold, of silver, of
brass, of lead, of stucco. My features are carved
along the fronts of palaces. My portrait is stamped
upon comb-cases, engraved on mirror-handles, painted
on majolica. I am a second Alexander, Cæsar, Scipio.
Nay more : I tell you that some kinds of glasses they
make at Murano, are called Aretines. Aretine is the
name given to a breed of cobs—after one Pope Clement sent me and I gave to Duke Frederick. They
have christened the little canal that runs beside my
house upon the Canalozzo, Rio Aretino. And, to make
the pedants burst with rage, besides talking of the
Aretine style, three wenches of my household, who

' *Lettere*, ii. 58.

have left me and become ladies, will have themselves
known only as the Aretines.'[1]

These self-congratulations were no idle vaunts.
His palace on the Grand Canal was crowded with
male and female servants, thronged with visitors,
crammed with costly works of art and presents received
from every part of Italy and Europe. The choicest
wines and the most exquisite viands—rare birds, delicate fruits, and vegetables out of season—arrived by
special messengers to furnish forth his banquets. Here
he kept open house, enjoying the society of his two
bosom friends, Titian and Sansovino, entertaining the
magnificent Venetian prostitutes, and welcoming the
men of fashion or of learning who made long journeys
to visit him.[2] 'If I only spent in composition one
third of the time I fling away, the printers would do
nothing but attend to the issuing of my works. And
yet I could not write so much if I would ; so enormous
is the multitude which comes incessantly to see me.
I am often forced to fly from my own house, and leave
the concourse to take care of itself.'[3] 'So many lords
and gentlemen are eternally breaking in upon me with
their importunities, that my stairs are worn by their
feet like the Capitol with wheels of triumphal chariots.

---

[1] *Lettere*, iii. 145 ; cp. iii. 89. The whole of the passage translated
above is an abstract of a letter professedly written to Aretino by Doni
(*Lett. all' Ar.* vol. iv. p. 395), which may be read with profit as an instance
of flattery. The occurrence of the same phrases in both series of epistles
raises a doubt whether Aretino did not tamper with the text of the correspondence he published, penning panegyrics of himself and printing them
under fictitious names as advertisements. Doni was a man who might
have lent himself to such imposture on the public.

[2] See *Lettere all. Ar.* vol. iv. p. 352, for a vivid description, written by
Francesco Marcolini, of Aretino's train of living and prodigal hospitality.
It realises the vast banquetting-pictures of Veronese.

[3] *Lettere* iii. 72.

Turks, Jews, Indians, Frenchmen, Germans, Spaniards, flock to see me. You can fancy how many Italians come! I say nothing about the common folk. You could not find me without a flock of friars and priests. I have come to be the Oracle of Truth, the Secretary of the Universe : everybody brings me the tale of his injury by this prince or that prelate.'[1] This sumptuous train of life demanded a long purse, and Aretino had nothing but his brains to live by. Yet, by the sale of his books and the contributions levied on great folk, he accumulated a yearly income sufficient to his needs. 'Thanks to their Majesties of Spain and France, with the addition of a hundred crowns of pension allowed me by the Marquis of Vasto, and the same amount paid by the Prince of Salerno, I have six hundred crowns of fixed income, besides the thousand or thereabouts I make yearly with a quire of paper and a bottle of ink.'[2] In another place he says that in the course of eighteen years 'the alchemy of his pen had drawn over twenty-five thousand crowns from the entrails of various princes.'[3] It was computed that, during his lifetime, he levied blackmail to the extent of about 70,000 crowns, or considerably more than a million of francs, without counting his strictly professional earnings. All this wealth he spent as soon as he laid hands upon it, boasting loudly of his prodigality, as though it were a virtue. He dressed splendidly, and denied himself no sensual indulgence. His house contained a harem

---

[1] *Lettere* i. 206. This passage occurs also in a letter addressed to Aretino by one Alessandro Andrea (*Lett. all' Ar.* vol. iii. p. 178); whence Mazzuchelli argues that Aretino tampered with the letters written to him, and interpolated passages before he sent them to the press. See last page, note 1.

[2] *Lettere*, ii. 213.   [3] *Lettere*, iii. 70.

of women, devoted to his personal pleasures and those, apparently, of his familiar friends. He had many illegitimate daughters, whom he dowered. Moreover, he was liberal to poor people; and while squandering money first upon his vices, he paid due attention to his reputation for generosity.[1] The bastard of Arezzo vaunted he had been born in a hospital with the soul of a king.[2] Yet he understood nothing of real magnanimity; his charity was part of an openhanded recklessness, which made him fling the goods of fortune to the wind as soon as gained—part of the character of *grand seigneur* he aspired to assume.[3]

It would fatigue the patience of the reader to furnish forth a complete list of the presents made to Aretino and acknowledged by him in his correspondence. Chains, jewels, horses, pictures, costly stuffs, cups, mirrors, delicacies of the table, wines—nothing came amiss to him; and the more he received, the more he cried continually give, give, give! There was hardly a reigning prince in Europe, hardly a noble of distinction in Italy, who had not sent some offering to his shrine. The Sultan Soliman, the pirate Barbarossa, the Pope, the Emperor, were among his tributaries.[4] The Empress gave him a golden collar worth three hundred crowns. Philip, Infante of Spain, presented him with another worth four hundred. Francis I. bestowed

---

[1] See *Lettere*, ii. 257; iii. 340; v. 251.

[2] See the *Capitolo al Duca di Fiorenza*.

[3] Marcolini's letter (*Lettere all' Aretino*, vol. iv. p. 352), and some letters from obscure scholars (for example, *ib.* vol. ii, pp. 118-121), seem to prove that he was really openhanded in cases of distress.

[4] There is a letter from Barbarossa to Aretino in the *Lettere all' Ar.* vol. iii. p. 269.

on him a still more costly chain, wrought of pure gold,
from which hung a row of red enamelled tongues,
bearing the inscription *Lingua ejus loquetur mendacium.*
Aretino received these presents from the hands of
ambassadors, and wore them when he sat to Titian or
to Tintoretto for his portrait. Instead of resenting the
equivocal compliment of the French king's motto, he
gloried in it. Lies, no less than flattery, were among
the openly-avowed weapons of his armoury.[1] Upon
the medals struck in his honour he styled himself
Divus P. Aretinus, Flagellum Principum, the Divine
Pietro Aretino, Scourge of Princes. Another inscription ran as follows : *I Principi tributati dai popoli il
Servo loro tributano*—Princes who levy tribute from
their people, bring tribute to their servant. And there
is Aretino seated on a throne, with noble clients laying
golden vases at his feet.[2]

It is incredible that arrogance so palpable should
have been tolerated, inconceivable how such a braggart
exercised this fascination. What had Emperors and
Kings to gain or lose by Aretino's pen ? What was
the secret of his power ? No satisfactory answer has
yet been given to these questions. The enigma does
not, indeed, admit of solution. We have to deal in
Aretino's case with a blind movement among ' the better
vulgar,' expressing itself as fashion ; and nothing is
more difficult to fathom than the fashion of a bygone
age.[3] The prestige which attached itself to people

---

[1] See the frank admissions in *Lettere*, ii. 52 ; iv. 168 ; i. 19, 30, 142.

[2] See the plates prefixed to Mazzuchelli's Life of Aretino. Compare
a passage in his Letters, vi. 115, and the headings of the Letters addressed
to him, *passim*.

[3] After studying the *Lettere scritte all' Aretino*—epistles, it must be

like Cagliostro or S. Germains or Beau Nash is quite incalculable. Yet some account may be rendered of what seems to have been Aretino's method. He assiduously cultivated a reputation for reckless freedom of speech. He loudly trumpeted his intention of speaking evil when and where it pleased him. He proclaimed himself the champion of veracity, asserted that nothing was so damnatory as the truths he had to tell, and announced himself the 'Censor of the world,' the foe of vice, the defender of virtue. Having occupied the ear of society by these preliminary fanfaronnades, he proceeded to satirise the Courts in general, and to vilify the manners of princes, without mentioning any in particular.[1] It thus came to be believed that Aretino was a dangerous person, a writer it would be wiser to have upon one's side, and who, if he were not coaxed into good humour, might say something eminently disagreeable.[2] There was pungency enough

remembered, from foreign kings and princes, from cardinals and bishops, from Italian dukes and noblemen, from illustrious ladies and great artists, and from the most distinguished men of letters of his day—I am quite at a loss to comprehend the *furore* of fashion which accompanied this man through his career. One and all praise him as the most powerful, the most virtuous, the bravest, the wittiest, the wisest, or, to use their favourite phrase, the *divinest* man of his century. Was all this a mere convention? Was it evoked by fear and desire of being flattered in return? Or, after all, had Aretino some now occult splendour, some real, but now unintelligible, utility for his contemporaries?

[1] The Papal Court was attacked by him ; but none other that I can discover. The only Prince who felt the rough side of his tongue was the Farnese :

> Impara tu, Pierluigi ammorbato,
> Impara, Ducarel da sei quattrini,
> Il costume d' un Rè si onorato.

Cardinal Gaddi and the Bishop of Verona were pretty roughly treated. So was Clement VII. But all these personages made their peace with Aretino, and paid him homage.

[2] See the curious epistle written to Messer Pompeo Pace by the Conte

in his epigrams, in the slashing, coarse, incisive brutality of his style, to make his attack formidable. People shrank from it, as they now shrink from articles in certain libellous weekly papers. Aretino was recognised as a Cerberus, to whom sops should be thrown. Accordingly, the custom began of making him presents and conferring on him pensions. Then it was discovered that if he used a pen dipped in vitriol for his enemies, he had in reserve a pen of gold for his patrons, from which the gross mud-honey of flatteries incessantly trickled.[1] To send him a heavy fee was the sure way of receiving an adulatory epistle, in which the Scourge of Princes raised his benefactor of the moment to the skies. In a word, Aretino's art consisted in making each patron believe that the vigilant satirist of other people's vices bestowed just eulogy on him alone, and that his praises were wrung from the mouth of truth by singular and exceptional merit. The fact is that though Aretino corresponded with all the princes of Europe and with at least thirty Cardinals, his letters are nothing but a series of the grossest flatteries. There is a hint here and there that the

di Monte Labbate, and included among the *Lettere all' Aretino*, vol. iv. p. 385. Speaking of Aretino's singular worth and excellent qualities, it discusses the question of the terror he inspired, which the author attributes to a kind of justifiable *chantage*. That Aretino was the inventor of literary *chantage* is certain ; but that it was justifiable, does not appear.

[1] Aretino made no secret of his artificial method of flattery. In a letter to Bembo (*Lettere*, ii. 52), he openly boasts that his literary skill enables him to 'swell the pride of grandees with exorbitant praises, keeping them aloft in the skies upon the wings of hyperboles.' 'It is my business,' he adds, 'to transform digressions, metaphors, and pedagogeries of all sorts into capstans for moving and pincers for opening. I must so work that the voice of my writings shall break the sleep of avarice ; and baptise that conceit or that phrase which shall bring me crowns of gold, not laurels.'

benefactor had better loosen his purse strings, if he wishes the stream of sycophancy to continue When Cerberus has been barking long without a sop, we hear an angry growl, a menace, a curt and vicious snarl for gold.[1] But no sooner has the gift been sent, than the fawning process recommences. In this way, by terrorism and toad-eating, by wheedling and bullying, by impudent demands for money and no less impudent assertions of his power to confer disgrace or fame, the rascal held society at his disposal. He boasted, and not without reason, that from his study in Venice he could move the world by a few lines scribbled on a piece of paper with his pen. What remains inconceivable, is that any value should have been attached to his invectives or his panegyrics—that persons of distinction should have paid him for the latter, and have stooped to deprecate the former. But it had become the fashion to be afraid of Aretino, the fashion to court his goodwill, the fashion to parade his praises. Francis I. and Charles V. led this vogue. The other princes followed suit. Charles wished to knight Aretino ; but the adventurer refused a barren honour. Julius III. made him knight of S. Peter with a small

---

[1] As a sample of his begging style, we may extract the following passage from a letter (1537), referring to the king of France (*Lettere,* i. 111) : ' I was and ever shall be the servant of his Majesty, of whom I preached and published what appears in all my utterances and in all my works. But since it is my wonted habit not to live by dreams, and since certain persons take no care for me, I have with glory to myself made myself esteemed and sought by those who are really liberal. The chain was three years delayed, and four have gone without so much as a courtesy to me from the King's quarter. Therefore I have turned to one who gives without promising—I speak of the Emperor. I adored Francis ; but never to get money from the stirring of his liberality, is enough to cool the furnaces of Murano.'

pension.   Henry VIII. sent him a purse of 300 crowns
for a dedicatory epistle.[1]   It was even talked of ele-
vating him to the rank of Cardinal, and engrossing
his talents for the service of the Church.[2]   Nobody
thought of addressing him without the prefix of *Divino*.[3]   And yet, all this while, it was known to everyone in Italy that Aretino was a pander, a coward, a
liar, a debauchee, who had wallowed in every lust, sold
himself to work all wickedness, and speculated on the
grossest passions, the basest curiosities, the vilest vices
of his age.[4]

[1] See Cromwell's letter, in the *Lettere all' Aretino*, vol. ii. p. 15.

[2] *Lettere all' Aretino,* vol. i. p. 245 ; vol. iv. pp. 281, 289, 300, contain
allusions to this project, which is said to have originated with the Duke
of Parma.   The first citation is a letter of Titian's.

[3] 'Divino,' 'Divinissimo,' 'Precellentissimo,' 'Unichissimo,' 'Onnipo-
tente,' are a few of the epithets culled from the common language of his
flatterers.

[4] I will translate passages from two letters, which, by their very
blasphemies, emphasise this contradiction.   'One might well say that
you, most divine Signor Pietro, are neither Prophet nor Sibyl, but rather
the very Son of God, seeing that God is highest truth in heaven, and you
are truth on earth ; nor is any city but Venice fit to give you harbourage,
who are the jewel of the earth, the treasure of the sea, the pride of heaven ;
and that rare cloth of gold, bedecked with gems, they place upon the
altar of S. Mark's, is nought but you ' (*Lettere scritte a P. Aretino*, vol.
iii. p. 176).   The next is more extraordinary, since it professes to be
written by a monk : 'In this our age you are a column, lantern, torch
and splendour of Holy Church, who, could she speak, would give to you
the revenues of Chieti, Farnese, Santa Fiore, and all those other idlers,
crying out—Let them be awarded to the Lord Pietro, who distinguishes,
exalts and honours me, in whom unite the subtlety of Augustine, the
moral force of Gregory, Jerome's profundity of meaning, the weighty style
of Ambrose.   It is not I but the whole world that says you are another
Paul, who have borne the name of the Son of God into the presence of
kings, potentates, princes of the universe ; another Baptist, who with
boldness, fearing nought, have reproved, chastised, exposed iniquities,
malice, hypocrisy before the whole world ; another John the Evangelist,
for exhorting, entreating, exalting, honouring the good, the righteous, and
the virtuous.   Verily he who first called you Divine, can claim the words
Christ spake to Peter : Beatus es, quia caro et sanguis non revelavit tibi,
sed Pater noster qui in coelis est ' (*Ibid.* p. 142).

Sometimes he met with men stout enough to treat him as he deserved. The English ambassador at Venice cudgelled him within an inch of his life. Pietro Strozzi threatened to assassinate him if he showed his face abroad, and Aretino kept close so long as the *condottiere* remained in Venice. Tintoretto offered to paint his portrait ; and when he had got the fellow inside his studio, grimly took his measure with a cutlass. Aretino never resented these insults. Bully as he was, he bowed to blows, and kissed the hand that dared to strike him. We have already seen how he waited till Berni's death before he took revenge for the famous sonnet. All this makes the general adulation of society for the 'divine Aretino' the more unintelligible. We can only compare the treatment he received with the mingled contempt and flattery, the canings and the invitations, showered at the present time on editors of scandal-mongering journals.

The miracle of Aretino's dictatorship is further enhanced by the fact that he played with cards upon the table. His epistles were continually being printed —in fact, were sent to the press as soon as written. Here all the world could see the workings of his mind, his hypocrisies, his contradictions, the clamorousness of his demands for gold, the grossness and universality of his flatteries, his cynical obscenity, his simulation of a superficial and disgusting piety. Yet the more he published of his correspondence, the louder was the acclamation of society. The charlatan of genius knew his public, and won their favour by effronteries that would have ruined a more cautious impostor. Some of his letters are masterpieces of infernal malice. The Marchioness of Pescara had besought him to change his mode of life, and to dedicate his talents only to religion.[1] *This is how he answers her*[2] *:* 'It gives me pleasure, most modest lady, that the religious pieces I have written do not displease the taste of your good judgment. Your doubt, whether to praise me or to dispraise me for expending my talents on aught else than sacred studies, is prompted by that most excellent spirit which moves you to desire that every thought and every word should turn toward God, forasmuch as He is the giver of virtue and of intellectual power. I confess that I am less useful to the world, and less acceptable to Christ, when I exhaust my studious energies on lying trifles, and not on the eternal verities. But all this evil is caused by the pleasure of others, and by my own necessities ; for if the princes were as truly pious as I am indigent, I would employ my pen on nothing else but Misereres. Excellent my lady, all men are not gifted with the graces of divine inspiration. *They* are ever burning with lustful desires, while *you* are every hour inflamed with angelic fire. For *you* the services of the Church and sermons are what music and comedies are for *them*. *You* would not turn your eyes to look at Hercules upon his pyre, nor yet on Marsyas without his skin : while *they* would hardly keep a S. Lawrence on the gridiron or a flayed Bartholomew in their bedroom. There's my bosom friend Bruciolo ; five years ago he dedicated his Bible to the King, who calls himself Most Christian, and yet

---

[1] Her letter may be read in the *Lettere all' Aretino*, vol. iii. p. 28.
[2] *Lettere*, ii. 9.

he has not had an answer.　Perhaps the book was neither well translated nor well bound.　On this account my *Cortigiana*, which drew from his Majesty the famous chain of gold, abstained from laughing at his *Old Testament*; for this would be indecent.　So you see I ought to be excused if I compose jests for my livelihood and not for evil purpose.　Anyhow, may Jesus inspire you with the thought of paying me through M. Sebastiano of Pesaro—from whom I received your thirty crowns—the rest, which I owe, upon my word and honour.　From Venice.　The 9th of January, 1537.'

This letter, one long tissue of sneers, taunts and hypocritical sarcasms, gives the complete measure of Aretino's arrogance.　Yet the illustrious and pious lady to whom it was addressed, suffered the writer— such was this man's unaccountable prestige—to remain her correspondent.　The collection of his letters contains several addressed to Vittoria Colonna, of which the date is subsequent to 1537.[1]　Not less remarkable were Aretino's dealings with the proud, resentful, solitary Michelangelo.　Professing the highest admiration for Buonarroti's genius, averring that 'the world has many kings but one only Michelangelo,' Aretino wrote demanding drawings from the mighty sculptor, and giving him advice about his pictures in the Sistine.　Instead of treating these impertinent advances with silence or sending a well-merited rebuff, we have a letter from Michelangelo addressed to 'M. Pietro,

---

[1] She wrote to him again in 1539 ; see *Lettere all' Aretino*, vol. iii. p. 30.　The series of letters from the virtuous Veronica Gambara are equally astonishing (*ib.* vol. i. pp. 318-333).

my lord and brother,' requesting the dictator to write something concerning him [1] : 'Not only do I hold this dear, but I implore you to do so, since kings and emperors regard it as the height of favour to be mentioned by your pen.' Was this the depth of humility, or the acme of irony, or was it the acquiescence of a noble nature in a fashion too prevalent to be examined by the light of reason ? Let those decide who have read a portion of Aretino's letters to his "singularly divine Buonaruoto.' For my own part, in spite of their strange but characteristic fusion of bullying and servility, I find in these epistles a trace of Aretino's most respectable quality—his worship of art, and his personal attachment to great artists. It may be said in passing that he never shows so well as in the epistles to Sansovino and Titian, men from whom he could gain but indirectly, and to whom he clung by an instinct of what was truest and sincerest in his nature. It is, therefore, not improbable that Michelangelo gave him credit for sincerity, and, instead of resenting his importunity, was willing to accept his advances in a kindly spirit.[2]

Thus far we have been dealing with Aretino's relation to sovereigns, ladies, and people of importance in the world of art. That he should have imposed upon them is singular. But his position in the republic of letters offers still stranger food for reflection. In an age of literary refinement and classical erudition, this untaught child of the people arrogated to himself the fame of a prominent author, and had his claims

---

[1] *Lettere all' Aretino*, vol. ii. p. 335.

[2] Giorgio Vasari, the common friend of Pietro Aretino and M. A. Buonarroti, had no doubt something to do with the acquiescent courtesy of the latter.

acknowledged by men like Bembo, Varchi, Molza, Sperone.[1] All the Academies in Italy made him their member with extraordinary honours, and he corresponded with every writer of distinction. He treated the scholars of his day as he treated the princes of Italy, abusing them collectively for pedantry, and showering the epithets of *divino, divinissimo,* upon them individually. With his usual sagacity, Aretino saw how to command the public by running counter to the prejudices of his century, and proclaiming his independence of its principles. He resolved to win celebrity by contrast, by piquancy of style, by the assertion of his individual character, by what Machiavelli termed *virtù.* As he had boasted of the baseness of his origin, so now he piqued himself upon his ignorance. He made a parade of knowing neither Latin nor Greek, derided the puristic veneration for Petrarch and Boccaccio then in vogue, and asserted that his mother-wit was the best source of inspiration. This audacity proved

---

[1] The adulation with which all the chief literary men of Italy greeted Aretino, is quite incredible. One must read their letters in the *Lettere all' Aretino* to have any conception of it. See in particular those of Varchi (*ib.* vol. ii. pp. 186-202), of Dolce (vol. ii. pp. 277–295), of Paolo Giovio (vol. iii. pp. 59–64), of Niccolò Martelli (vol. iii. pp. 116–125), of Annibale Caro (*ib.* p. 163), of Sperone (*ib.* pp. 324–330), of Firenzuola (*ib.* p. 345), of Doni (vol. iv. p. 395). Molza, terrified by one of Aretino's threats, cringes before him (vol. i. p. 340). Doni signs himself ' Il Doni dell' Aretino,' and Vergerio, Bishop of Capo d' Istria, ' Il Vescovo dell' Aretino.' Even the excellent Bishop of Fossombrone pays him courtly compliments (vol. ii. pp. 61–67). The pitch attained by these flatteries may be understood from this opening of a letter : ' Bella armonia, e soave concento, dovea essere nel cielo, Signor Pietro divino, e fra le stelle amiche, il dì, che Iddio e la Natura di voi fece altero dono a questa nostra etade,' etc. *ad inf.* (vol. iv. p. 269). Here is another fragment : ' Manifestamente si vede e si conosce che da Iddio per conservazione de la sua gloria e per utilità del mondo v' abbi fra tanti avversari,' etc. (vol iv. p. 398).

successful. While the stylists of the day were polishing their laboured periods to smoothness, he expressed
such thoughts as occurred to him in the words which
came first to hand, seeking only vivacity, relief and
salience. He wrote as he talked; and the result was
that he acquired a well-won reputation for freshness,
wit, originality and vigour. This is how he dictates the
terms of epistolary style to Bernardo Tasso [1] : ' I, who
am more your brother in benevolence than you show
yourself to be my friend in honour, did not believe that
the serenity of my mind would ever again be dimmed
by those clouds, which, after thunders and lightnings,
burst in the bolt that sent Antonio Broccardo beneath
the earth. Pride and vanity, for certain, prompted you
to tell the excellent and illustrious Annibale Caro that
no writer of letters is worthy to be imitated at the
present day, sagaciously hinting at yourself as the right
man to be imitated. Without doubt, your inordinate
self-love, combined with your inattention to the claims
of others, brought your judgment to this pass. I published letters before you, and you borrowed your style,
in so far as it is worth anything, from me. Yet you
cannot produce even a counterfeit of my manner.
My sentences and similes are made to live ; yours issue
stillborn from your mind. It is time that you copy a
few of my familiar phrases, word by word. What
else can you do? Your own taste is rather inclined
to the scent of flowers than the savour of fruits. You
have the graces of a certain celestial style, fit for epithalamial odes and hymns. But all that sweetness is out

---

[1] *Lettere*, v. 184. The above is only a condensed paraphrase of a very
long tirade.

of place in epistles, where we want the salience of invention, not the illuminated arabesques of artifice. I am not going to sing my own praises, nor to tell you that men of merit ought to mark my birthday with white chalk—I, who without scouring the post-roads, without following Courts, without stirring from my study, have made every living duke, prince, sovereign, tributary to my virtue—I, who hold fame at my discretion through the universe—I, whose portrait is revered, whose name is honoured in Persia and the Indies. To end this letter, I salute you with the assurance that nobody, so far as your epistles go, blames you for envy's sake, while many, very many, praise you through compassion for your having written them.' There was no limit to his literary self-confidence.' 'Of the three opinions current respecting the talents which keep my name alive, time has refuted that, which, hearing I had no erudition, judged my compositions to be nonsense, together with that other, which, finding in them some gust of genius, affirmed they were not mine. Whence it follows that only one remains, the opinion, to wit, that I, who never had a tutor, am complete in every branch of knowledge. All this comes from the poverty of art, which ever envies the wealth of nature, from whom I borrow my conceptions. Wherefore, if you are of the number of those who, in order to deprive me of nature's favour, attribute to me the learning that comes from study, you deceive yourself, for I swear by God I hardly understand my mother tongue.' Meanwhile his tirades against the purists are full of excellent good sense. 'O mistaken multitude, I tell you again, and yet

again that poetry is a caprice of nature in her moments
of gladness; it depends on a man's own inspiration,
and if this fails, a poet's singing is but a tambourine
without rattles, a bell-tower without bells.   He who
attempts to write verses without the gift is like the
alchemists, who, for all their industry and eager avarice,
never yet made gold, while nature, without labour,
turns it out in plenty, pure and beautiful.   Take
lessons from that painter, who, when he was asked
whom he imitated, pointed to a crowd of living men,
meaning that he borrowed his examples from life and
reality.   This is what I do, when I write or talk.
Nature herself, of whose simplicity I am the secretary,
dictates that which I set down.' [1]   And again: ' I
laugh at those pedants, who think that learning consists
in Greek and Latin, laying down the law that one who
does not understand these languages, cannot open his
mouth.   It is not because I do not know them, that I
have departed from Petrarch's and Boccaccio's precedents; but because I care not to lose time, patience,
reputation, in the mad attempt to convert myself into
their persons.   The true aim of writing is to condense
into the space of half a page, the length of histories,
the tedium of orations; and this my letters clearly
show that I have done '   ' It is far better to drink out
of one's own wooden cup than another's golden goblet ;
and a man makes a finer show in his own rags than in
stolen velvets.   What have we to do with other people's
property ? ' [2]   'What have we to do with words which,
however once in common use, have now passed out of
fashion ? ' [3]   At times he bursts into a fury of invective

[1] *Lettere*, i. 123.   [2] *Lettere*, ii. 182.   [3] *Lettere*, i. 210.

against erudition : ' Those pedants, the asses of other people's books, who, after massacring the dead, rest not till they have crucified the living! It was pedantry that murdered Duke Alessandro, pedantry that flung the Cardinal of Ravenna into prison, and, what is worse, stirred up heresy against our faith through the mouth of that arch-pedant Luther.'[1] This is admirable. It plunges to the very root of the matter. Sharpened by his hostility to the learning he did not share, and the puerile aspects of which he justly satirised, this acute and clairvoyant critic is enabled to perceive that both Italian tyrannicide and German Reformation had their origin in the humanistic movement of the fifteenth century. He is equally averse to either consequence. Erudition spoils sport, stiffens style, breaks in upon the pastimes of the principalities and papacies, which breed the lusts on which an Aretino lives.

It was Aretino's boast that he composed as fast as the pen would move across the paper, and that his study contained no books of reference—nothing but the quire of paper and the bottle of ink, which were necessary to immortalise the thick-crowding fancies of his brain. His comedy of the *Filosofo* was written in ten mornings ; the *Talanta* and the *Ipocrita* in 'the hours robbed from sleep during perhaps twenty nights.'[2] Referring to his earlier fertility in 1537, he says[3] : ' Old age begins to stupefy my brains, and love, which ought to wake them up, now sends them off to sleep. I used to turn out forty stanzas in a morning ; now I can with difficulty produce one. It took me only seven morn-

---

[1] *Lettere*, i. 143.   [2] *Lettere*, iii. 84.   Letter at the end of the *Talanta*.
[3] *Lettere*, i. 99.

ings to compose the *Psalms*; ten for the *Cortigiana* and the *Marescalco*; forty-eight for the two *Dialogues*; thirty for the *Life of Christ.*' The necessary consequences of this haste are discernible in all his compositions. Aretino left nothing artistically finished, nothing to which it is now possible to point in justification of his extraordinary celebrity. His sonnets are below contempt. Frigid, inharmonious, pompous, strained, affected, they exhibit the worst vices to which this species of poetry is liable. His *Capitoli*, though he compared them to 'colossal statues of gold or silver, where I have carved the forms of Julius, a Pope, Charles, an Emperor, Catherine, a Queen, Francesco Maria, a Duke, with such art that the outlines of their inner nature are brought into relief, the muscles of their will and purpose are shown in play, the profiles of their emotions are thrown into salience'[1]—these *Capitoli* will not bear comparison for one moment with Berni's. They are coarse and strident in style, threadbare in sentiment, commonplace in conception, with only one eminent quality, a certain gross prolific force, a brazen clash and clangour of antithesis, to compensate for their vulgarity. Yet, such as they are, the *Capitoli* must be reckoned the best of his compositions in verse. Of his comedies I have already spoken. These will always be valuable for their lively sketches of contemporary manners, their free satiric vein of humour. The *Dialoghi*, although it is scarcely possible to mention them in a decent book of history, are distinguished by the same qualities of veracity, acumen, prolific vigour, animal spirits, and outspokenness.

· *Lettere*, vi. 4.

Aretino's religious works, it need hardly be said, are worthless or worse. Impudent romances, penned by one of the most unscrupulous of men, frankly acknowledged by their author to be a tissue of 'poetical lies,' we are left to marvel how they could have deceived the judgment and perverted the taste of really elevated natures.[1] That the Marchioness of Pescara should have hailed the coarse fictions of the Life of S. Catherine, which Aretino confessed to have written out of his own head, as a work of efficient piety, remains one of the wonders of that extraordinary age.

What then, it may finally be asked, was Aretino's merit as an author? Why do we allude to him at all in writing the history of sixteenth-century literature? The answer can be given in two words—originality and independence. It was no vain boast of Aretino that he trusted only to nature and mother-wit. His intellectual distinction consisted precisely in this confidence and self-reliance, at a moment when the literary world was given over to pedantic scruples and the formalities of academical prescription. Writing without the fear of pedagogues before his eyes—seeking, as he says, relief, expression, force, and brilliancy of phrase, he produced a manner at once singular and attractive, which turned to ridicule the pretensions of the purists. He had the courage of his personality, and stamped upon his style the very form and pressure of himself. As a writer, he exhibited what Machiavelli demanded from the man of action—*virtù*, or the virility of self-reliance. That was the secret of his success. The

---

[1] See *Lettere*, ii. 168, iii. 169, for his method of composing these books.

same audacity and independence characterise all his utterances of opinion—his criticisms of art and literature—his appreciation of natural beauty. In some of the letters written to painters and sculptors, and in a description of a Venetian sunset already quoted in this book, we trace the dawnings of a true and natural school of criticism, a forecast of the spontaneity of Diderot and Henri Beyle. This naturalness of expression did not save Aretino from glaring bad taste. His letters and his dedicatory introductions abound in confused metaphors, extravagant *concetti*, and artificial ornaments. It seems impossible for him to put pen to paper without inventing monstrous and ridiculous periphrases. Still the literary impropriety, which would have been affectation in anyone else, and which became affectation in his imitators, was true to the man's nature. He could not be true to himself without falseness of utterance, because there was in him an inherent insincerity, and this was veiled by no scholastic accuracy or studied purity of phrase.

Much of the bad taste of the later Renaissance (the tropes of Marini and the absurdities of *seicentismo*) may be ascribed to the fascination exercised by this strange combination of artificiality and naturalness in a style remarkable for vigour. Who, for instance, does not feel that the mannerism of our euphuistic prosaists is shadowed forth in the following passage from the introduction to the *Talanta*?[1] The Prologue, on the drawing of the curtain, takes the

---

[1] I have purposely chosen an extract where the style is keen and mobile. Had I taken examples from the Letters, I could have produced a far closer parallel to Lilly's rhetoric.

audience into his confidence, and tells them that he
long had hesitated which of the Immortal Gods to
personate.   Mars, Jupiter, Phœbus, Venus, Mercury,
and all the Pantheon in succession were rejected,
for different appropriate reasons, till the God of
Love appeared.   'When at last it came to Cupid's
turn, I immediately said Yes! and having so assented,
I felt wings growing at my shoulders, the quiver at my
side, the bow within my hands.   In a moment I became all steel, all fire; and eager to be ware what
things are done in love, I cast a glance upon the crowd
of lovers; whence I soon could see who has the rendez-
vous, who is sent about his business, who prowls around
his mistress' house, who enters by the door, who clam-
bers up the walls, who scales the rope, who jumps
from the window, who hides himself within a tub, who
takes the cudgel, who gets a gelding for his pains, who
is stowed away by the chambermaid, who is kicked
out by the serving-man, who goes mad with anxiety,
who bursts with passion, who wastes away in gazing,
who cuts snooks at hope, who lets himself be hoodwinked, who spends a fortune on his mistress to look
grand, who robs her for a freak, who saps her chastity
with threats, who conjures her with prayers, who
blabs of his success, who hides his luck, who bolsters
up his vaunt with lies, who dissembles the truth, who
extols the flame that burns him, who curses the cause
of his heart's conflagration, who cannot eat for grief,
who cannot sleep for joy, who compiles sonnets, who
scribbles billets-doux, who dabbles in enchantments,
who renews assaults, who takes counsel with bawds,
who ties a favour on his arm, who mumbles at a flower

the wench has touched, who twangles the lute, who hums a glee, who thrusts his rival through the body, who gets killed by his competitors, who eats his heart out for a mylady, who dies of longing for a strumpet. When I understood the things aforesaid, I turned round to these female firebrands, and saw how the devil (to chastise them for the perverse ways they use toward men who serve them, praise them, and adore them) gives them up, easy victims, to a pedant, a plebeian, a simpleton, a loon, a groom, a graceless clown, and to a certain mange that catches them.'

Aretino congregated round him a whole class of literary Bohemians, drawing forth the peccant humours of more than one Italian city, and locating these greedy adventurers in Venice as his satellites. It is enough to mention Niccolò Franco, Giovanni Alberto Albicante, Lorenzo Veniero, Doni, Lodovico Dolce. They were, most of them, hack writers, who gained a scanty livelihood by miscellaneous work for the booksellers and by selling dedications to patrons. More or less successfully, they carried on the trade invented and developed by Aretino; remaining on terms of intimacy with him, at first as friends or secretaries, afterwards as enemies and rivals. We have already seen what use was made of Albicante for the mutilation of Berni's *Innamoramento*. This poetaster was a native of Milan, who published a history of the war in Piedmont, which Aretino chose to ridicule in one of his *Capitoli*.[1] Albicante replied with another poem in *terza rima*, and Aretino seems to have perceived that he had met a

---

[1] See the article on Albicante in Mazzuchelli's *Scrittori Italiani*, vol. i.

worthy adversary. It was Albicante's glory to be called *furibondo* and *bestiale*. He affected an utter indifference to consequences, an absolute recklessness concerning what he did and said. Whether Aretino was really afraid of him, or whether he wished to employ him in the matter of Berni's *Innamoramento*, is not certain. At any rate, he made advances to Albicante in a letter which begins : ' My brother, the rage of poets is but a frenzy of stupidity.' The antagonists were reconciled, and the Academy of the Intronati at Siena thought this event worthy of commemoration in a volume : ' Combattimento poetico del divino Aretino e del bestiale Albicante occorso sopra la Guerra di Piemonte, e la pace loro celebrata nella Accademia de gli Intronati a Siena.'

Niccolò Franco was a native of Benevento, whom Aretino took into his service as a kind of secretary.[1] Being deficient in scholarship, he needed a man capable of supplying him with Greek and Latin quotations, and who could veneer his coarse work with a show of humanistic erudition. Franco undertook the office ; and it is probable that some of Aretino's earlier works of piety and learning—the *Genesis*, for instance—issued from this unequal collaboration. But their good accord did not last long. Franco proved to be a ruffian of even fiercer type than his master. If Aretino kept a literary poignard in the scabbard, ready to strike when his utility demanded, Franco went about the world with unsheathed dagger, stabbing for the pleasure of the sport. ' I would rather lose a dinner,' he writes, ' than omit to fire my pen off when

[1] For what follows see Tiraboschi, tom. vii. part 3, lib. iii.

the fancy takes me.' The two men could not dwell together in union. When Aretino published the first series of his letters, Franco issued a rival volume, in the last epistle of which, addressed to Envy, he made an attack on his patron. Ambrogio degli Eusebi, an *âme damnée* of the Aretine, about whom many scurrilous stories were told, stabbed Franco, while Aretino published invective after invective against him in the form of letters. Franco left Venice, established himself for a while at Casale in the lordship of Montferrat, opened a school at Mantua, and ran a thousand infamous adventures, pouring forth satirical sonnets all the while at Aretino. In the course of his wanderings, he completed a Latin commentary on the *Priapea.* These two works together—the centuries of sonnets against Aretino, and the Priapic lucubrations—obtained a wide celebrity. Speaking of the book, Tiraboschi is compelled to say that 'few works exist which so dishonour human nature. The grossest obscenities, the most licentious evil-speaking, the boldest contempt of princes, Popes, Fathers of the Council, and other weighty personages, are the gems with which he adorned his monument of perverse industry.' Franco proved so obnoxious to polite society that he was, at last taken and summarily hanged in 1569. The curious point about this condemnation of a cur is, that he was in no whit worse than many other scribblers of the day. But he made more noise; he had not the art to rule society like Aretino; he committed the mistake of trusting himself to the perilous climates of Lombardy and Rome. His old master drove him out of Venice, and the unlucky reprobate paid the penalty of his misdeeds by becoming the scapegoat for men whom he detested.

Doni began his Venetian career as a friend of Aretino, whose companion he was in the famous Academy of the Pellegrini. They quarrelled over a present sent to Doni by the Duke of Urbino, and the bizarre Florentine passed over to the ranks of Aretino's bitterest enemies. In 1556 he declared war, with a book entitled ' Terremoto del Doni Fiorentino.' The preface was addressed to ' the infamous and vicious Pietro Aretino, the source and fountain of all evil, the stinking limb of public falsehood, and true Antichrist of our century.' Soon after the appearance of this volume, followed Aretino's death. But Doni pursued his animosity beyond the grave, and was instrumental in causing his rival's writings to be subjected to ecclesiastical interdiction.

We tire of these low literary quarrels. Yet they form an integral part of the history of Italian civilisation ; and the language of invective used in them, originating with Aretino and improved upon by Doni and Franco, became the model of vituperative style in Europe. Doni's ' Earthquake, with the Ruin of a great Bestial Colossus, the Antichrist of our age,' brings to mind a score of pamphlets, published in Europe during the conflict of the Church with Reformation. We find an echo of its strained metaphors in the polemical writings of Bruno and Campanella. The grotesque manner of the seventeenth century begins with Aretino and his satellites, just as its far-fetched conceits may be traced in the clear language of Guarini. Gongora, Marini, Euphues, and the *Précieuses Ridicules* of the

Hôtel Rambouillet are contained, as it were, in germ among this little knot of refugees at Venice, who set their wits against the academical traditions of pure Italian taste.

A characteristic legend is told of Aretino's death. Two of his sisters kept, it is said, a house of ill fame ; and the story runs that he died of immoderate laughter, flinging himself backward in his chair and breaking his neck, on hearing some foul jest reported by them. It is difficult to believe that this tale has any foundation in fact. We must take it as a scurrilous invention, proving the revolution of public opinion, which, since his books had been put upon the Index in 1559, undoubtedly took place. Of like tenor is the epitaph which was never really placed upon his grave [1] :

> Qui giace l' Aretin poeta tosco,
> Che disse mal d' ognun fuorchè di Cristo,
> Scusandosi col dir : non lo conosco.

His features, though formed upon a large and not ignoble type, bore in later life a mixed expression of the wolf and the fox ; nor was it without oblique satire that the engraver of his portrait, Giuseppe Patrini, surrounded the medallion with a wolf's hide, the grinning snarl and slanting eyes of the brute mimicking the man's physiognomy. It was a handsome face, no doubt, in youth, when, richly attired in the satin

---

[1] These lines have been, without authority, ascribed to Giovio ; they may thus be rendered :

> Here lieth Aretine, in prose and poem
> Who spake such ill of all the world but Christ,
> Pleading for this neglect, I do not know him.

Giovio, we may remember, styled Aretino *divino, divinisimo, unichissimo, precellentissimo*, in his letters.

mantle cut for him by a bishop, and mounted on his white charger, he scoured the streets of Reggio at Giovanni de' Medici's side, curling his blue-black beard, and fixing his bold bright eyes upon the venal beauties they courted in company. But the thick lips and open sensual mouth, the distended nostrils, and the wicked puckers of the wrinkles round his eyes and nose, show that the beast of prey and appetite had been encouraged through a life of self-indulgence, until the likeness of humanity yielded to victorious animalism. The same face, at once handsome and bestial, never to be forgotten after a first acquaintance, leans out, in the company of Sansovino and Titian, from the bronze door of the Sacristy in S. Mark's Church.[1] The high relief is full of life and movement, one of Sansovino's masterpieces. And yet it strikes one here with even greater strangeness than the myths of Ganymede and Leda on the portals of S. Peter's at Rome.

Aretino is, in truth, not the least of the anomalies which meet us everywhere in the Italian Renaissance. Was he worse, was he not even in some respects better than his age? How much of the repulsion he inspires can be ascribed to altered taste and feeling? To what extent was the legend of the man, so far as

---

[1] Among the many flatteries addressed to Aretino none is more laughable than a letter (*Lettere all' Aretino*, vol. iii. p. 175) which praises his physical beauty in most extravagant terms : ' Most divine Lord Peter ; if, among the many and so lovely creatures that swinish Nature sends into this worst of worlds, you alone are of such beauty and incomparable grace that you combine all qualities the human frame can boast of : for the which cause there is no need to wonder that Titian, when he seeks to paint a face that has in it true beauty, uses his skilled brush in only drawing you,' &c. &c. The period is too long to finish.

this is separable from the testimony of his writings, made black by posthumous malevolence and envy? These are the questions which rise in our mind when we reflect upon the incidents of his extraordinary career, and calmly estimate his credit with contemporaries. The contradictions of the epoch were concentrated in his character. He was a professed ✓ Christian of the type formed by Rome before the Counter-Reformation. He helped the needy, tended the sick, dowered orphans, and kept open house for beggars. He was the devoted friend of men like Titian, a sincere lover of natural and artistic beauty, an acute and enthusiastic critic. At the same time he did his best to corrupt youth by painting vice in piquant colours. He led a life of open and voluptuous debauchery. He was a liar, a bully, a braggart, venomous in the pursuit of private animosities, and the remorseless foe of weaker men who met with his displeasure. From the conditions of society which produced Cesare and Lucrezia Borgia, Pier Luigi Farnese and Gianpaolo Baglioni, it was no wonder that a writer resolved on turning those conditions to account, should have arisen. The credit of originality, independence, self-reliant character—of what Machiavelli called *virtù*—does certainly belong to him. It is true that he extracted the means of a luxurious existence from patrons upon whom he fawned. Yet he was superior to the common herd of courtiers, in so far as he attached himself to no master, and all his adulation masked a ✓ battery of menaces. The social diseases which emasculated men of weaker fibre, he turned to the account of his rapacious appetites. His force consisted in the clear notion he had formed of his own aim in life, and the sagacity with which he used the most efficient means for attaining it. The future, whether of reputation or of literary fame, had no influence over his imagination. He resolved to enjoy the present, and he succeeded beyond expectation. Corruption is itself a kind of superiority, when it is consummate, cynical, self-conscious. It carries with it its own clairvoyance, its own philosophy of life, its own good sense. More than this, it imposes on opinion and fascinates society. Aretino did not suffer from a divided will. He never halted between two courses, but realised the ideal of the *perfettamente tristo.* He lived up to Guicciardini's conception of the final motive, which may be described as the cult of self. Sneering at all men less complete in purpose than himself, he disengaged his conduct from contemporary rules of fashion ; dictated laws to his betters in birth, position, breeding, learning, morals, taste ; and vindicated his virility by unimpeded indulgence of his personal proclivities. He was the last, the most perfect, if also the most vitiated product of Renaissance manners. In the second half of the sixteenth century, when hypocrisy descended like a cloud upon the ineradicable faults of Italy, there was no longer any possibility for the formation of a hero after Aretino's type.

Thus at the close of any estimate of Aretino, we are forced to do justice to the man's vigour. It is not for nothing that even a debased society bows to a dictatorship so autocratic ; nor can eminence be secured, even among the products of a decadent civilisation, by undiluted defects. Aretino owed his influence to genuine qualities—to the independence which underlay his arrogance, to the acute common sense which almost justified his vanity, to the outspokenness which made him satirise the vices that he shared and illustrated.[1] We have abundant and incontrovertible testimony to the fact that his *Dialoghi*, when they were first published, passed for powerful and drastic antidotes to social poisons[2] ; and it is clear that even his religious works were accepted by the pious world as edifying. The majority of his contemporaries seem to have beheld in him the fearless denouncer of ecclesiastical and civil tyrants, the humble man's friend, and the relentless detective of vice. The indescribable nastiness of the *Dialoghi*, the false feeling of the *Vita di. S. Catherina*, which makes us turn with loathing from their pages, did not offend the taste of his century. While, therefore, he comprehended and expressed his age in its ruffianism and dissoluteness, he stood outside it and above it, dealing haughtily and like a potentate with evils which subdued less hardened spirits, and with

---

[1] I should not be surprised to see an attempt soon made to whitewash Aretino. Balzac, in his *Catherine de Médicis*, has already indicated the line to be followed : ' L'Arétin, l'ami de Titien et le Voltaire de son siècle, a, de nos jours, un renom en complète opposition avec ses œuvres, avec son caractère, et que lui vaut une débauche d'esprit en harmonie avec les écrits de ce siècle, où le drolatique était en honneur, où les reines et les cardinaux écrivaient des contes, dits aujourd'hui licentieux.'

[2] I will only refer to a very curious epistle (*Lettere a P. Aretino*, vol. iii. p. 193), which appears to me genuine, in which Aretino is indicated as the poor man's friend against princely tyrants ; and another from Daniello Barbaro (*ibid.* p. 217), in which the Dialogue on Courts is praised as a handbook for the warning and instruction of would-be courtiers. The Pornographic Dialogues made upon society the same impression as Zola's *Nana* is now making, although it is clear to us that they were written with a licentious, and not an even ostensibly scientific, intention.

personages before whom his equals grovelled. We must not suffer our hatred of his mendacity, uncleanliness, brutality, and arrogance to blind us to the elements of strength and freedom which can be discerned in him.

¹ While these sheets are passing through the press, I see announced a forthcoming work by Antonio Virgili, *Francesco Berni con nuovi documenti.* We may expect from this book more light upon Aretino's relation to the Tuscan poet.

CHAPTER XVI.

HISTORY AND PHILOSOPHY.

Frivolity of Renaissance Literature—The Contrast presented by Machia-
velli—His Sober Style—Positive Spirit—The Connection of his Works
—Two Men in Machiavelli—His Political Philosophy—The *Patria*—
Place of Religion and Ethics in his System—Practical Object of his
Writings — Machiavellism — His Conception of Nationality—His
Relation to the Renaissance — Contrast between Machiavelli and
Guicciardini—Guicciardini's Doctrine of Self-interest—The Code of
Italian Corruption—The Connection between these Historians and
the Philosophers—General Character of Italian Philosophy—The
Middle Ages in Dissolution—Transition to Modern Thought and
Science—Humanism counterposed to Scholasticism—Petrarch—Pico
Dialogues on Ethics—Importance of Greek and Latin Studies—
Classical substituted for Ecclesiastical Authority — Platonism at
Florence—Ficino—Translations—New Interest in the Problem of
Life—Valla's Hedonism—The Dialogue *De Voluptate*—Aristotle at
Padua and Bologna—Arabian and Greek Commentators—Life of
Pietro Pomponazzi—His Book on Immortality—His Controversies—
Pomponazzi's Standpoint—Unlimited Belief in Aristotle—Retrospect
over the Aristotelian Doctrine of God, the World, the Human Soul—
Three Problems in the Aristotelian System—Universals—The First
Period of Scholastic Speculation—Individuality—The Second Period
of Scholasticism—Thomas Aquinas—The Nature of the Soul—New
Impulse given to Speculation by the Renaissance—Averroism— The
Lateran Council—Is the Soul Immortal?—Pomponazzi reconstructs
Aristotle's Doctrine by help of Alexander Aphrodisius—The Soul is
Material and Mortal—Man's Place in Nature—Virtue is the End of
Man—Pomponazzi on Miracles and Spirits—His Distinction between
the Philosopher and the Christian—The Book on Fate—Pomponazzi
the Precursor—Coarse Materialism—The School of Cosenza—Aris-
totle's Authority Rejected — Telesio — Campanella — Bruno — The
Church stifles Philosophy in Italy—Italian Positivism.

THE literature which has occupied us during the last
nine chapters, is a literature of form and entertainment.

Whether treating chivalrous romance, or the Arcadian ideal, or the conditions of contemporary life, these poets, playwrights and novelists had but one serious object—the perfection of their art, the richness and variety of their pictures. In the conscious pursuit of beautiful form, Poliziano and Ariosto, Bembo and Berni, Castiglione and Firenzuola, Il Lasca and Molza, were alike earnest. For the rest, they sought to occupy their own leisure, and to give polite society the pastime of refined amusement. The content of this miscellaneous literature was of far less moment to the authors and their audience than its mode of presentation. Even when they undertook some theme involving the realities of life, they dwelt by preference upon externals. In the *Cortegiano* and *Galateo*, for example, conduct is studied from an æsthetical far more than from a moral point of view. The questions which stirred and divided literary coteries, were questions of scholarship, style, language. Matter is everywhere subordinated to expression ; the writer's interest in actuality is slight ; the power or the inclination to think is inferior to the faculty for harmonious construction. These characteristics of literature in general, render the exceptions noticeable, and force me, at some risk of repetition, to devote a chapter to those men in whom the speculative vigour of the race was concentrated. These were the historians and a small band of metaphysicians, who may be fitly represented by a single philosopher, Pietro Pomponazzi. Of the Florentine historiographers, from Villani to Guicciardini, I have already treated at some length in a previous portion of this work.[1] I

[1] *Age of the Despots*, chaps. v. and vi.

shall therefore confine myself to resuming those points in which Machiavelli and Guicciardini uttered the reflections of their age on statecraft and the laws that govern political life.

When we compare Machiavelli with his contemporaries, we are struck by his want of sympathy with the prevalent artistic enthusiasms. Far from being preoccupied with problems of diction, he wrote with the sole object of making what he had to say plain. The result is that, without thinking about expression, Machiavelli created Italian prose anew, and was the first to form a monumental modern style. Language became, beneath his treatment, a transparent and colourless medium for presenting thoughts to the reader's mind ; and his thoughts were always removed as little as possible from the facts which suggested them. He says himself that he preferred in all cases the essential reality of a fact to its modification by fancy or by theory.[1] His style is, therefore, the reverse of that which the purists cultivated. They uttered generalities in ornamented and sonorous phrases. Machiavelli scorned ornament, and ignored the cadence of the period. His boldest abstractions are presented with the hard outline and relief of concrete things. Each sentence is a crystal, formed of few but precise words by a spontaneous process in his mind. It takes shape from the thought; not from any preconceived type of rhythm, to which the thought must be accommodated. It is perfect or imperfect according as the thinking process has been completely or incompletely

---

[1] ' Mi è parso più conveniente andare dietro alla verità effettuale della cosa che all' immaginazione di essa (*Principe*, cap. xv.).

victorious over the difficulties of language. It is figurative only when the fact to be enforced derives new energy from the imagination. Beauty is never sought, but comes unbidden, as upon the limbs and muscles of an athlete, whose aim has been to gain agility and strength. These qualities render Machiavelli's prose a model worthy of imitation by all who study scientific accuracy.

The style is the man ; and Machiavelli's style was the mirror of his mind and character. While the literary world echoed to the cry of Art for Art, he followed Science for the sake of Science. Occupied with practical problems, smiling at the supra-mundane aspirations of the middle ages, scorning the æsthetical ideals of the Renaissance, he made the political action of man, *l'homme politique*, the object of exclusive study. His resolute elimination of what he considered irrelevant or distracting circumstances from this chosen field of research, justifies our placing him among the founders or precursors of the modern scientific method. We may judge his premisses insufficient, his conclusions false ; but we cannot mistake the positive quality of his mind in the midst of a rhetorical and artistic generation.

There is a strict link of connection between Machiavelli's works. These may be divided into four classes—official, historical, speculative and literary. To the first belongs his correspondence with the Florentine Government ; to the second, his Florentine History and several minor studies, the *Vita di Castruccio,* the *Ritratti,* and the *Metodo tenuto dal Duca Valentino* ; to the third, his *Discorsi, Principe, Arte della Guerra* and *Discorso sopra la Riforma di Fi-*

renze; to the fourth, his comedies, poems, novel of *Belfagor*, and *Descrizione della Peste.* The familiar letters should be used as a key to the more intimate understanding of his character. They illustrate some points in his political philosophy, explain his personal motives, and throw much light upon his purely literary compositions. We learn from them to know him as a friend, the father of a family, the member of a little social circle, and finally as the ever-restless aspirant after public employment. Valuable as these letters are for the student of Machiavelli's writings, his private reputation would have gained by their destruction. They show that the man was inferior to the thinker. In spite of his logical consistency of intellect, we become convinced, while reading them, that there were two persons in Machiavelli. The one was a faithful servant of the State, a student of books and human nature, the inaugurator of political philosophy for modern Europe. The other was a boon companion, stooping to low pleasures, and soiling his correspondence with gossip which breathes the tainted atmosphere of Florentine vice. These letters force us to reject the theory that he wrote his comedies with any profound ethical purpose, or that he personally abhorred the moral corruption of which he pointed out the weakening results for Italy. The famous epistle from San Casciano paints the man in his two aspects—at one moment in a leathern jerkin, playing games of hazard with the butcher, or scouring the streets of Florence with a Giuliano Brancaccio; at another, attired in senatorial robes, conversing with princes, approaching the writers of antiquity on equal terms, and penning works which place him on a level with Ariosto and Galileo. The second of these Machiavellis claims our exclusive attention at the present moment. Yet it is needful to remember that the former existed, and was no less real. Only by keeping this in mind can we avoid the errors of those panegyrists who credit the *Mandragola* with a didactic purpose, and refuse to recognise the moral bluntness betrayed in Machiavelli's theorisation of human conduct. The man who thought and felt in private what his familiar letters disclose, was no right censor of the principles that rule society. We cannot trust his moral tact or taste.

Machiavelli was not a metaphysician. He started with the conception of the State as understood in Italy. His familiarity with the Latin classics, and his acquaintance with the newly-formed monarchies of Europe, caused him, indeed, to modify the current notion. But he did not enquire into the final cause of political communities, or present to his own mind a clear definition of what was meant by the phrase *patria*. We are aware of a certain hesitancy between the ideas of the Commune and the race, the State and the Government, which might have been removed by a more careful preliminary analysis. Between the Roman Republic, on the one hand, and the modern nation, on the other, we always find an Italian city. From this point of view, it is to be regretted that he did not appropriate Plato's *Republic* or Aristotle's *Politics.*[1] He might by such a course of study have

---

[1] The section on the types of commonwealths in the *Discorsi* (cap. ii,) comes straight from Polybius. But I am not aware of any signs in Machiavelli of a direct study of the elder Greek philosophical writings.

avoided the severance of politics from ethics, which renders his philosophy unnatural. We must, however, remember that he did not propose to plan a scientific system. His works have a practical aim in view. They are directed toward the grand end of Italy's restoration from weakness and degeneracy to a place among the powerful peoples of the world. This purpose modifies them in the most minute particulars. It is ever present to Machiavelli's mind. It makes his philosophy assume the form of a critique. It explains the apparent discord between the *Discorsi* and the *Principe*. It enables us to comprehend the nature of a patriotism which subordinates the interests of the individual to the body politic, even though the State were in the hands of an unscrupulous autocrat. The salvation of Italy, rather than any metaphysical principle, is the animating motive of Machiavelli's political writings. Yet we may note that if he had laid a more solid philosophical basis, if he had striven more vigorously to work out his own conception of the *patria*, and to understand the laws of national health, instead of trusting to such occasional remedies as the almost desperate state of Italy afforded, he would have deserved better of his country and more adequately fulfilled his own end.

Though Machiavelli had not worked out the conception of a nation as an organic whole, he was penetrated with the thought, familiar to his age, that all human institutions, like men, have a youth, a manhood, and a period of decline. Looking round him, he perceived that Italy, of all the European nations, had advanced farthest on the path of dissolution. He calls

the Italians the reproach and corruption of the world—
la corruttela, il vituperio del mondo. When he enquires
into the causes of this ruin, he is led to assign (i) the
moral debasement of his country to the Roman Church ;
(ii) her sloth and inefficiency in warfare to the despots
and the mercenaries ; (iii) her inability to cope with
greater nations to the want of one controlling power in
the peninsula. A nation, he argues, cannot be a nation
while divided into independent and antagonistic States.
It needs to be united under a monarch like France,
reduced beneath the sway of a presiding commonwealth like ancient Rome, or connected in a federation
like the Swiss. This doctrine of the nation, or, to use
his own phrase, of the *patria*, as distinguished from
the Commune and the Empire, was highly original in
Italy at the time when Machiavelli gave it utterance.
It contained the first logically reasoned aspiration after
that independence in unity, which the Italians were
destined to realise between the years 1858 and 1871.
He may be said to have formed it by meditating on
the Roman historians, and by comparing Italy with
the nascent modern nations. The notion of ethnology
did not enter into it so much as the notion of political
and social cohesion. Yet nationality was not excluded ;
for he conceived of no power, whether Empire or
Church, above the people who had strength to define
themselves against their neighbours. To secure for
the population of the Italian peninsula that unity which
he rightly considered essential to the *patria*, and the
want of which constituted their main inferiority, was
the object of all his speculations.

The word *patria* sounds the keynote of his political theory, and a patriot is synonymous for him with a completely virtuous man. All energies, public and private, are only valuable in so far as they build up the fabric of the commonwealth. Religion is good because it sustains the moral fibre of the people. It is a powerful instrument in the hands of a wise governor; and the best religion is that which develops hardy and law-loving qualities. He criticises Christianity for exalting contemplative virtues above the energies of practical life, and for encouraging a spirit of humility. He sternly condemns the Church because she has been unfaithful even to the tame ideal of her saints, and has set an example of licentious living. Religion is needed as the basis of morality; and morality itself must be encouraged as the safeguard of that discipline which constitutes a nation's vigour. A moralised race is stronger than a corrupt one, because it has a higher respect for law and social order, because it accepts public burdens more cheerfully, because it is more obedient to military ordinances. Thus both religion and morality are means to the grand end of human existence, which is strenuous life in a united nation. I need hardly point out how this conception runs counter to the transcendentalism of the Middle Ages.

Machiavelli admires the Germans for their discipline and sobriety, which he ascribes to the soundness of their religious instincts. France and Spain, he says, have been contaminated by the same corrupting influence as Italy; but they owe their present superiority to the fact of their monarchical allegiance. This opens a second indictment against the Church. Not only has the Church demoralised the people; but it is chiefly due to the ambition of the Popes that Italy has never passed beyond the stage of conflict and disunion.

An important element in this conception of the *patria* is that it should be militant. Races that have ceased from war, are on the road to ruin ; and only those are powerful which train the native population to arms. The feebleness of Italy can be traced to the mercenary system, introduced by despots, adopted by commercial republics, and favoured by ecclesiastics. If the Italians desire to recover freedom, they must form a national militia ; and this can best be done by adapting the principles of the Roman army to modern requirements. The *Art of War* is a development of this theme. At its close, Machiavelli promises the sceptre of Italy, together with the glory of creating Italian nationality, to any State clear-sighted and self-denying enough to arm its citizens and take the lead in the peninsula. That State, he says, shall play the part of Macedon. Reading the peroration of the *Art of War* by the light of recent history, its paragraphs sound like a prophecy. What Machiavelli there promised, has been achieved, much in the way he indicated, by Piedmont, the Macedon of United Italy.

When Machiavelli discusses the forms of constitutions, he is clearly thinking of cities rather than of nations as we understand them. He has no conception of representative government, but bases all his observations on the principle of burghership. There is no sound intermediate, he says, between a commonwealth and a principality. In the former, the\burghers have equal rights. In the latter there will be a hierarchy of classes. Though his sympathies are with the former (since he holds that the equality of the citizens is the best safeguard for the liberties and law-abiding virtues of the State), he is yet by no means unfavourable to despotism. The decadence of Italy, indeed, had gone so far that her best chance of restoration depended on a prince. Therefore, while he suggests measures for converting despotic States into republics by crushing the aristocracy, and for creating principalities out of free commonwealths by instituting an order of nobles, he regards the latter as the easier task of the two. Upon such topics we must always bear in mind that what he says is partly speculative, and partly meant to meet the actual conditions of Italian politics. The point of view is never simply philosophical nor yet simply practical. So long as the great end could be achieved, and a strong military power could rise in Italy, he is indifferent to the means employed. The peroration of the *Art of War* is an appeal to either prince or republic. The peroration of the *Riforma di Firenze* is an appeal to a patriotic Nomothetes. He there says to Clement : You have one of those singular opportunities offered to you, which confer undying glory on a mortal ; you may make Florence free, and, by wise regulations, render her the bulwark of renascent Italy. The peroration of the *Principe* is an appeal to an ambitious autocrat. Follow the suggestions of ancient and contemporary history, which all point to the formation of a native army. Comprehend the magnitude of the task, and use the right means for executing it ; and you will earn the fame of restoring your country to her place among the nations.

The case of Italy is almost desperate. Yet there is still hope. A prudent lawgiver may infuse life into the decaying commonwealth of Florence. A spirited despot may succeed in bringing the whole peninsnla by force of arms beneath his sway. Machiavelli will not scrutinise the nature of the remedy too closely. He is ready to sacrifice his republican sympathies, and to welcome the saviour who comes even in the guise of Cesare Borgia. When the salvation of the *patria* is at stake, none but precisians can hesitate about the choice of instruments.

This indifference to means, provided the end be secured, is characteristic of the man. Machiavelli's Machiavellism consists in regarding politics as a game of skill, where all ways are justified, and fixity of purpose wins. He does not believe in Fortune, though he admits the favourable circumstances which smoothed the way for men like Cesare. With Juvenal, he says : *Nos te, nos facimus, Fortuna, deam.* Again, he does not believe in Providence. Though a prophet speak with the voice of God, he will not succeed unless, like Moses, he be provided with a sword to ratify his revelation. History is a logical sequence of events, the sole intelligible nexus between its several links being the human will. Virtue is decision of character, accompanied by intellectual sagacity ; it is the strong man's subordination of his passions, prejudices, predilections, energies, to the chosen aim. We all admit that it is better to be good than bad. Yet morality has little to do with political success. What lies in the way of really great achievement, is the mediocrity of human nature. Men will not be completely bad or

perfectly good. They spoil their best endeavours by
vacillation and incompetence to guide their action
with regard to the sole end in view.

Enough has been said in different portions of this
book about the morality of Machiavelli's political
essays. Yet this much may be here repeated. Those
who wish to understand it, must not forget the medieval background of the despots—Ezzelini, Visconti,
Scaligeri, Estensi, Carreresi—which lay behind Machiavelli. The sinfulness, treason, masterful personality,
Thyestean tragedies, enormous vices and intolerable
mischief of the Renaissance—all this was but a pale
reflex of the middle ages. In those earlier tyrants,
the Centaur progenitors of feebler broods, through
generations in which men gradually discriminated the
twy-formed nature of their ancestry, the lust and luxury
of sin had been at their last apogee. *In istis peccandi
voluptas erat summa.* What followed in Machiavelli's
age, was reflection succeeding to action—evil philosophised in place of evil energetic.

Though Machiavelli perceived that the decadence
of Italy was due to bad education, corrupt customs,
and a habit of irreligion, he did not insist on the necessity of reformation. He was satisfied with invoking
a Dictator, and he counselled this Dictator to meet
the badness of his age with fraud and violence. Thus
he based his hope of national regeneration upon those
very vices which he indicated as the cause of national
degeneracy. Whether we ascribe this error to the
spirit of the times in which he lived, or to something
defective in his own character, it is clear he had not
grasped the fundamental principle of righteousness, as

that which can alone be safely trusted by a people or its princes. Perhaps he thought that, for practical purposes, the method of radical reformation was too tardy. Perhaps he despaired of seeing it attempted. Of all Italian institutions, the Church, in his opinion, was the most corrupted. Yet the Church held religious monopoly, and controlled education. And the Church had severed morality from religion, religion from the State; making both the private concern of individuals between their conscience and their God.

Just as Machiavelli proved himself incapable of transcending the corruption of his age, though he denounced it; so, while he grasped the notion of a *patria* superior to the commune, he was not able to disengage his mind from the associations of Italian diplomacy. He perceived that the *débris* of medieval society in Italy—the Papacy, the nobles, the *condottieri*—afforded no foundation for the State he dreamed of building. He relied on the masses of the people as the only sound constituent of his ideal *patria*. He foresaw a united nation, to which the individual should devote himself, and which should absorb the dispersed forces of the race. And yet he had not conceived of the nation as a living whole, obeying its own laws of evolution and expansion. He regarded the State as a mechanical or artificial product, to be moulded by the will of a firm ruler. In his theory there is always a Nomothetes, a Dictator, the *intervenient skill* of a constructor, whom he imagines capable of altering the conditions of political existence by a *coup d'état* or by a readjustment of conflicting rights and interests.

Even while praising the French monarchy for its stability, in words that show a just appreciation of constitutional government, he hypothesises a lawgiver in the past. *Chi ordinò quello stato, volle che quelli rè*— he who organised that State, willed that those kings, etc. The *ordinò* and *volle* are both characteristic of his habitual point of view. Probably this faith in manipulation arose from his lifelong habit of regarding small political communities, where change was easily effected. In his works we do not gain any broad prospect from the vantage-ground of comprehensive principles, but a minutely analytical discussion of statecraft, based in the last resort upon the observation of decadent Italian cities. The question always presents itself : how, given certain circumstances, ought a republic or a prince to use them to the best advantage ? The deeper problem, how a nation stirred by some impulse, which combines all classes in a common heroism or a common animosity, must act, hardly occurs to his mind. England, with forces intellectual, emotional and practical at fullest strain, in combat with the Spanish tyranny, adopting a course of conduct which reveals the nation to itself by the act of its instinctive will—such a phase of the larger, more magnetic life of peoples, which Milton compared to the new youth of the eagle, had not been observed by Machiavelli. The German Reformation, the French Revolution, the American War of Independence, might have taught him to understand that conception of the modern nation which he had divined, but which the conditions of his experience prevented his appropriating. Had he fully grasped it, we can scarcely believe that the

Principe would have been written. The good faith
of that essay depends upon a misconception.

In like manner Machiavelli discerned the weaknesses
of the Renaissance without escaping from its enthusiasms. He despised the æsthetical ideal of his age.
He was willing to sacrifice form, beauty, rhythm, the
arts of culture and learned leisure, to stern matters of
fact and stringent discipline. Yet he believed as firmly
as any humanist, that the regeneration of his country
must proceed from a revival of the past. It is the loss
of antique virtues that has enervated our character, he
cries. It is the neglect of historical lessons that renders
our policy so suicidal. We need to recover the Roman
military system, the Roman craft of conquest, the
Roman pride and poverty, the Roman subordination
of the individual to the State. What we want is a
dictator or a lawgiver after the Roman fashion—a
Romulus, a Numa, a Camillus, a Coriolanus. The
patria, as he imagines it, is less the modern nation
than the Roman Commonwealth before the epoch of
the Empire. This unquestioning belief in the efficacy
of classical revival finds vent, at the close of the *Arte
della Guerra*, in a sentence highly characteristic of the
Renaissance. ' This province, Italy,' he says, ' seems
made to give new birth to things dead, as we have seen
in poetry, in painting, and in sculpture.' Hence, he
argues, it may be her vocation to bring back the
military system and supremacy of ancient Rome.

Thus, to resume what has been said, Machiavelli
ascribed the weakness of the Italians to their loss of
morality ; but he was not logical enough to insist that
their regeneration must begin with a religious revolu-

tion. He foresaw the modern nation; but he attempted to construct it on the outlines of antiquity. Believing that States might be formed or reformed by ingenious manipulation of machinery, he acquired no true notion of constitutional development or national evolution. His neglect to base his speculations on a thorough-going definition of the State and its relation to man as a social being, caused him to assume a severance between ethics and politics, which no sound philosophy of human life will warrant.

On what, then, if these criticisms are just, is founded his claim to rank among the inaugurators of historical and political science? The answer has been already given. It was not so much what he taught, as the spirit in which he approached the problems of his enquiry, which was scientific in the modern sense. Practical, sincere and positive, Machiavelli never raises points deficient in actuality. He does not invite us to sympathise with the emotions of a visionary, or to follow the vagaries of a dreamer. All that he presents, is hard, tangible fact, wrought into precise uncompromising argument, expressed in unmistakeably plain language. Not only do his works cast floods of light upon Italian history; but they suggest questions of vital importance, which can still be discussed upon the ground selected by their author. They are, moreover, so penetrated with the passion of a patriot, however mistaken in his plan of national reconstitution, that our first sense of repulsion yields to a warmer feeling of admiration for the man who, from the depths of despair, could thus hope on against hope for his country.

Studying Guicciardini, we remain within the same

sphere of conceptions, limited by the conditions of Italian politics in the beginning of the sixteenth century. There is no less stringency of minute analysis, an even sharper insight into motives, an equal purity and precision of language.[1] But the moral atmosphere is different. The corruption which Machiavelli perceived and criticised, is now accepted. In the place of desperate remedies suggested by the dread of certain ruin, Guicciardini has nothing to offer but indifference and self-adjustment to the exigencies of the moment. Machiavelli was a visionary and an idealist in spite of his positive bias. Guicciardini is a practical diplomatist, bent on saving his own State and fortune from the wreck which he contemplated. What gives grandeur to Machiavelli's speculation is the conception of the *patria*, superior to the individual, demanding unlimited self-sacrifice, and repaying the devotion of the citizens by strength in union. This idea has disappeared in Guicciardini's writings. In its stead he offers us self-interested egotism. Where Machiavelli wrote *patria*, he substituted *il particolare*. It follows from this cold acquiescence in a base theory of public conduct, adapted to a recognised state of social anarchy, that Guicciardini's philosophy is far more immoral than Machiavelli's. The *Ricordi*, in which, under the form of aphorisms, he condensed the results of his experience and observation, have been well described as the 'code of Italian corruption.' Resistance has to be abandoned. Remedies are hopeless. Let us sit down and calmly criticise the process of decay. A wise man will seek

---

[1] I refer to the *Opere Inedite*. In the *Istoria d' Italia*, Guicciardini's style is inferior to Machiavelli's.

to turn the worst circumstances to his own profit ; and what remains for political sagacity is the accumulation of wealth, honours, offices of power on the ambitious individual.

Machiavelli and Guicciardini had this in common, that their mental attitude was analytical, positive, critically scientific. It negatived the *a priori* idealism of medieval political philosophy, and introduced a just conception of the method of enquiry. This quality connects them on the one hand with the practical politicians of their age, and on the other with its representative thinkers in the field of metaphysics.

It is no part of my plan to attempt a general history of Italian philosophy during the Renaissance period, or even to indicate its leading moments. On the scale of my present work, any such endeavour would of necessity be incomplete ; for the material to be dealt with is obscure, and the threads of thought to be interwoven are scattered, requiring no little patience and no slight expenditure of exposition on the part of one who seeks to place them in their proper relations. Of philosophy, in the strict sense of the term, the Italian Renaissance had not much to offer. We do not revert to that epoch, expecting to meet with systematic theories of the universe, plausible analyses of the laws of thought, or ingenious speculations upon the nature of being. It is well known that the thinkers of the fifteenth and sixteenth centuries can scarcely claim to have done more than lead the revolt of reason against scholastic tyranny and obsolete authorities, appealing with often misdirected enthusiasm to original sources, and suggesting theories and methods which, in the hands

of abler speculators, at a more fortunate epoch, generated the philosophies of modern Europe. Yet even
so the movement of thought in Italy was of no slight
moment, and the work accomplished deserves to be
recorded with more honour than it has hitherto received
from the historians of philosophy.

The Renaissance in general may be called the
Middle Ages in dissolution. That the period was
transitional in its chief aspects, has often already been
insisted on. The massive fabrics of feudalism and the
Church were breaking up. The vast edifice of
scholastic theology was being undermined by men who
had the energy to free themselves from orthodox
tradition, but scarcely force enough or opportunity to
mould the thought of the new age. The Italians who
occupied themselves with philosophical problems, from
Petrarch to Campanella, hold an intermediate place
between the schoolmen and the founders of modern
metaphysics. They accomplish the transition from S.
Thomas and Occam to Bacon, Descartes and Spinoza.
It is possible to mark three phases in this process of
transition, each of which was necessary in the progress
of the mind from theological ontology to science and
free speculation. The thinkers of the first stage began
by questioning the authority of dogma. Those of the
second stage accepted the authority of the ancients.
Those of the third appealed to Nature against ecclesiastical and classical authority alike. Humanism was
thus intermediate between scholasticism and what, for
want of a more definite phrase, may be termed rationalism. Succeeding to the schoolmen, the scholars
cleared the groundwork of philosophy of old encum-

brances, and reappropriated antique systems of thought. After them, the schools of Lower Italy, including Telesio, Campanella and Bruno, prepared the path to be immediately followed ; with what profit is apparent to the dullest intellect. Clearly, and beyond the possibility of question, they propounded the main problems which have agitated all the scientific schools of modern Europe. To them belongs the credit of having first speculated knowledge and reality from no external standpoint, but from the immediate consciousness. The *Interrogatio Naturæ* and the *Cogito, ergo sum,* which became the watchwords of modern empiricism and rationalism, are theirs. But, at the very moment when the Italians of the Revival had performed their pioneering task-work, all vital vigour in the nation was extinguished or suspended by the deadly influences of Spanish domination and Papal terrorism.[1] It was left for other races to enter on the promised land which they had conquered.

Upon its first appearance, it was clear that humanism would run counter to both currents of medieval thought, the orthodox and the heretical, the Thomistic and Averroistic. Dante designed his epic

---

[1] I cannot refrain from translating a paragraph in Spaventa's Essay upon Bruno, which, no less truly than passionately, states the pith of this Italian tragedy. ' The sixteenth century was the epoch, in which the human spirit burst the chains that up to then had bound it, and was free. There is no more glorious age for Italy. The heroes of thought and freedom, who then fought for truth, were almost all her sons. They were persecuted and extinguished with sword and fire. Would that the liberty of thought, the autonomy of the reason, they gave to the other nations of Europe, had borne fruit in Italy ! From that time forward we remained as though cut off from the universal life ; it seemed as if the spirit which inspired the world and pushed it onward, had abandoned us ' (*Saggi di Critica,* Napoli, 1867, p. 140).

in accordance with the fixed outlines of Thomistic
theology. The freethinkers of the Lombard universities expressed a not uncertain adhesion to the materialistic doctrines which passed for Averroism. But
Petrarch, the hero of the coming age, pronounced his
contempt for scholastic quibbles, and at the same time
waged war against the tenets of Averroes. He introduced a new spirit into philosophical discussion, a new
style of treatment, literary rather than scientific, which
tended to substitute humane culture for logical pedantry. The departure from medieval lines of thought,
thus signalised by Petrarch, was followed by the students of the next two centuries. Questions which had
agitated Europe since the days of Roscelin, now
seemed to lose the interest of actuality. The distinctions of Nominalism and Realism retained no
attraction for men who were engaged in discovering
manuscripts, learning to write correct Latin, acquiring
Greek, and striving to penetrate the secret of antiquity.
The very style of the schoolmen became a byword
for ineptitude and barbarism. It required no little
courage and a prestige as brilliant as Pico's to sustain
the cause of Albertus Magnus or Johannes Scotus.[1]
Scholars of the type of Poggio and Filelfo, Beccadelli
and Poliziano, abhorred their ponderous metaphysics,
as though they were grotesque chimeras generated by
the indigestion of half-starved intellectual stomachs.
Orpheus had reappeared. He bade the world thenceforward move to music and melodious rhythms both of
thought and language. The barbarians might harbour

---

[1] *Epistolæ Angeli Poliziani,* lib. ix. p. 269 (ed. Gryphius, 1533).

Mercury within their hearts, to quote Pico's apology; they might display wisdom in unvarnished plainness; but what were these claims worth in an age that required the lips rather than the soul to be eloquent, and when a decorated fiction found more favour than a naked truth? No more decided antithesis than that of scholastic philosophy to the new classical ideal is conceivable.

Thus the first movement of the Revival implied an uncompromising abandonment of medieval thought as worse than worthless. If men educated by the humanistic method were to speculate, they would do so upon lines different from those suggested by the schoolmen. Cicero and Seneca became their models; and the rhetorical treatment of moral topics passed muster with them for philosophy. A garrulous colloquial skimming in fair Latin over the well-trodden ground of ethics supplanted the endeavour to think strictly upon difficult subjects. Much of this literature—the dialogues of Alberti, for example, and Landino's Camaldolese Disputations—can still be read with profit. But regarded from the point of view of systematic thought, it has slight importance. We value it principally for the light it casts upon contemporary manners and modes of opinion.

The study of Greek and Latin texts revealed a world to the Italians far wider than the regions where the medieval mind had moved in narrow limits. The immediate effect of this discovery was not, however, wholly salutary. The ancients began to exercise a kind of despotism; and a new authority, no less stringent than that of dogma, bound the scholars of the Revival beneath the tyranny of classical names. It was impossible for the intellect to free itself from fetters at a single leap. This second servitude seemed destined to be even more pernicious than the first; for as yet there was no criticism, and the superincumbent masses of antique literature, extending from the earliest dawn of Greek history to the latest commentators of Byzantium and Ravenna, underwent but little process of sifting. It was enough for the Italians of that epoch to assimilate. Nothing which bore the stamp of antiquity came amiss to their omnivorous appetite. Compilations from second or third sources were valued as equally precious with original texts. The testimony of hearsay reporters passed for conclusive evidence in matters of history. Masters in philosophy were confounded with expositors, who flourished at the distance of some centuries. Athens and Alexandria, Rome and Constantinople, were indiscriminately regarded as a single Holy Land of wisdom.

While this fermentation of assimilative erudition was still at its height, Gemistos Plethon preached his Neo-platonic mysticism at Florence; and the first attempt at a new philosophy for Western Europe, independent of the schoolmen, uninfluenced by orthodoxy, proceeded from the Medicean academy. The Platonism of Ficino and Pico, we now know, was of a very mixed and ill-determined quality. Uncontrolled by critical insight, and paralysed by the prestige attaching to antiquity, the Florentine school produced little better than an unintelligent eclecticism. Their so-called philosophical writings were commonplace-books of citations, anthologies of ill-digested abstracts, in which Greek and Asiatic and Christian opinions issued in an incoherent theosophy. It must be reckoned a great misfortune for Italian thought that the Platonists were able to approach the masterpieces of their Attic teacher through a medium of Alexandrian and Byzantine enthusiasm. Had they been forced to attack the 'Republic' without the intervention of Plotinus and Gemistos, they might have started on some fruitful line of speculation. They would at least have perceived that Plato's theology formed a background to his psychological, ethical, educational and political theories, instead of fastening upon those visionary systems which his later Greek expositors extracted from the least important portions of his works. At the same time, this Neo-platonic mysticism was only too sympathetic to the feebler pietism of the middle ages for men who had discovered it, to doubt its inspiration.

What was finally accomplished for sound scholarship by Ficino, lay in the direction, not of metaphysics or of history, but of translation. The enduring value of Pico's work is due, not to his Quixotic quest of an accord between Pagan, Hebrew and Christian traditions, but to the noble spirit of confidence and humane sympathy with all great movements of the mind, which penetrates it. If we cannot rate the positive achievements of the Florentines in philosophy at a high value, still the discussion of Platonic and Aristotelian doctrines which their investigations originated, caused the text of the Greek philosophers to be accurately examined for the first time in Western Europe. Their theories, though devoid of originality and clogged at every point with slavish reverence for classical authority, marked a momentous deviation from the traditional methods of medieval speculation.

Thus a vast and tolerably accurate acquaintance with the chief thinkers of antiquity, reinforced by the translation of their principal works, was the main outcome of the Platonic revival at Florence. Uncritically, and with many a blundering divergence into the uncongenial provinces of Oriental thought, the Italian intellect appropriated Greek philosophy. A groundwork was laid down for the discussion of fundamental problems in the forms under which they had presented themselves to the ancient world. But while the Platonists were wrangling with the Aristotelians about the superiority of their respective masters; while the scholars were translating from the original languages; while the mystics were building castles in the air, composed of fragments from Neo-platonic and Neo-pythagorean systems, cementing them with the mortar of Christianity and adding quaint outbuildings of Cabbalistic and astrological delusions; the writers of ethical treatises pursued another line of enquiry, which was no less characteristic of the age and no less fruitful of results. During the middle ages thought of every kind had been concentrated on the world beyond this life. The question of how to live here was answered with reference to eternal interests solely. Human existence had no meaning except as the prelude to heaven or hell. But contact with antiquity introduced a new class of problems. Men began once more to ask themselves how they ought to live in this world, not with the view of avoiding misery and securing happiness in the next, but with the aim of making their terrestrial home most comfortable and their sojourn in it most effective for themselves and their companions. The discussion of the fundamental question how to live to best advantage, without regard for the next world and unbiassed by the belief in a a rigid scheme of salvation, occupies an important place in the philosophical essays of the time. Landino, for example, in his Camaldolese Disputations, raises the question whether the contemplative or the practical life offers superior attractions to a man desirous of perfecting self-culture. Alberti touches the same topic in his minor dialogues, while he subjects the organism of the Family in all its relations to a searching analysis in his most important essay.

Valla, in the famous dialogue *De Voluptate*, attacks the problem of conduct from another point of view.[1] Contrasting the Stoical with the Epicurean ideals, asceticism with hedonism, he asks which of the two fulfils the true end of human life. His treatise on Pleasure is, indeed, a disputation between renascent paganism, naturalism, and humanism on the one side, and the medieval scheme of ethics on the other. Man according to nature contends with man according to grace; the soul, obeying the desires of the flesh, defends her cause against the spirit, whose life is hid with a crucified Christ in God. Thus the two points of view between which the Renaissance wavered, are placed in powerful contrast; and nowhere has their antagonism been more ably stated. For the champion of hedonism Valla appropriately chose the poet Bec-

---

[1] *Laurentius Valla: Opera omnia*, Basileæ, 1465. The 'De Voluptate' begins at p. 896 of this edition.

cadelli, while he committed the defence of asceticism to Niccolò Niccoli. Though at the close of the argument he awarded the palm of victory to the latter,[1] it is clear that his sympathies lay with the former, and all the strength of his reasoning faculty is employed in the statement and support of Beccadelli's thesis. The first and far the longest part of the dialogue, where we detect a true note of sincerity, is a remorseless onslaught upon monasticism under the name of Stoicism, resulting in a no less uncompromising defence of physical appetite. Some of the utterances upon sexual morality are penetrated with the rancour of rebellion.[2] It is the revolt of the will against unnatural restrictions, the reassertion of natural liberty, emboldened by the study of classical literature, embittered by long centuries of ecclesiastical oppression. Underlying the extravagances of an argument which owes its crudity and coarseness to the contradictions of the century, we find one central thought of permanent importance. Nature can do nothing wrong ; and that must be wrong which violates nature.[3] It is man's duty, by interrogation of nature, to discover the laws of his own being and to obey those. In other words, Valla, though in no sense a man of

---

[1] ' Uterque pro se de laudibus Voluptatis suavissime quidem quasi cantare visus est ; sed Antonius hirundini, Nicolaus philomelæ (quam lusciniam nominant) magis comparandus' (*ib.* lib. iii. p. 697).

[2] ' Meâ quidem sententiâ odiosus est si quis in mœchos, si rerum naturam intueri volumus, invehat' (*ib.* lib. i. cap. 38). ' Quisquis virgines sanctimoniales primus invenit, abominandum atque in ultimas terras exterminandum morem in civitatem induxisse. . . . Melius merentur scorta et postribula quam sanctimoniales virgines ac continentes' (*ib.* lib. i. cap. 43).

[3] ' Quod natura finxit atque formavit id nisi sanctum laudabileque esse non posse' (*ib.* lib. i. cap. 9).

science, proclaims the fundamental principle of science, and inaugurates a new criterion of ethics.

Three main points may be discriminated in the intellectual movement briefly surveyed in the preceding paragraphs. The first is an abrupt breach with scholasticism. The whole method of philosophy has been changed, and the canon of authority has altered. The second is the acquisition of classical thought, and the endeavour, especially at Florence, among the Platonists, to appropriate it and adapt it to Christianity. The third is the introduction of a new problem into philosophical discussion. How to make the best of human life, is substituted for the question how to ensure salvation in the world beyond the grave. It will be observed that each of these three points implies departure from the prescribed ground of medieval speculation, which always moved within the limits of theology. Theology, except in the mysticism of the Platonists, except in occasional and perfunctory allusions of the rhetoricians, has no place in this medley of scholarship, citation, superstition, and frank handling of practical ideals.

While the Florentine Platonists were evolving an eclectic mysticism from the materials furnished by their Greek and Oriental studies; while the Ciceronian humanists were discussing the fundamental principles which underlie the various forms of human life; the universities of Lombardy continued their exposition of Aristotle upon the lines laid down by Thomistic and Averroistic schoolmen. Padua and Bologna extended the methods of the middle ages into the Renaissance. Their professors adhered to the formal definitions and distinctions of an earlier epoch, accumulating comment upon comment, and darkening the text of their originals with glosses. Yet the light shed by the Revival penetrated even to the lecture-rooms of men like Achillini. Humanism had established the principle of basing erudition on the study of authentic documents. The text of Aristotle in the Greek or in first-hand translations, had become the common property of theologians and philosophers. It was from these universities that the first dim light of veritable science was to issue. And here the part played by one man in the preparation of a new epoch for modern thought is so important that I may be allowed to introduce him with some prolixity of biographical details.[1]

Pietro Pomponazzi was born of noble lineage at Mantua in 1462. He completed his studies at Padua, where he graduated in 1487 as laureate of medicine. It may be remarked incidentally that teachers of philosophy at this era held the degree of physicians. This point is not unimportant, since it fixes our attention on the fact that philosophy, as distinguished from theology, had not yet won a recognised position. Logic formed a separate part of the educational curriculum. Rhetoric was classed with humanistic literature. Philosophy counted as a branch of Physics. At Florence, in the schools of the Platonists, metaphysical enquiries assumed a certain hue of mysticism. At Padua and Bologna, in the schools of the physicians, they assimi-

---

[1] For the following sketch of Pomponazzi's life, and for help in the study of his philosophy, I am indebted to Francesco Fiorentino's *Pietro Pomponazzi*, Firenze, Lemonnier, 1868, 1 vol. I may here take occasion to mention a work by the same author, *Bernardino Telesio*, *ibid.* 1872, 2 vols. Together, these two books form an important contribution to the history of Italian philosophy.

lated something of materialism. During the middle ages they had always flourished in connection with theology. But that association had been broken ; and as yet a proper place had not been assigned to the science of the human mind. A new department of knowledge was in process of formation, distinct from theology, distinct from physics, distinct from literature. But at the epoch of which we are now treating, it had not been correctly marked off from either of these provinces, and in the schools of Lombardy it was confounded with physical science.

In 1488 Pomponazzi, soon after taking his degree as a physician, was appointed Professor Extraordinary of Philosophy at Padua. He taught in concurrence with the veteran Achillini, who was celebrated for his old-world erudition and his leaning toward the doctrines of Averroes. Pomponazzi signalised his *début* in the professorial career, by adopting a new method of instruction. Less distinguished for learning than acuteness, he confined himself to brilliant elucidations of his author's text. For glosses, citations and hair-splitting distinctions, he substituted lucid and precise analysis. It is probable that he was a poor Greek scholar. Paolo Giovio goes so far, indeed, as to assert that, of the two classical languages, he only knew Latin ; nor is there anything in his own writings to demonstrate that he had studied Greek philosophy in the original. But he proved himself a child of the new era by his style of exposition, no less than by a strict adherence to Alexander of Aphrodisias, the Greek commentator of Aristotle. What that divergence from the system of his rival, Achillini, who still adhered to the commentaries of Averroes, implied, I shall endeavour to make clear in the sequel. For the present, we must follow his career as a professor. Before the year 1495 he had been appointed to the ordinary chair of Natural Philosophy at Padua ; and there he resided until 1509, when the schools of Padua were closed. He spent this period chiefly in lecturing on Aristotle's Physics, for the sake presumably of the medical students who crowded that university. Forced by circumstances to leave Padua, Pomponazzi found a home in Ferrara, where he began to expound Aristotle's treatise *De Animâ.* Unlike Padua, the University of Ferrara had a literary bias ; and we may therefore conclude that Pomponazzi availed himself of this first favourable opportunity to pursue the studies in Aristotelian psychology for which he had a decided personal preference. In 1512 he was invited to Bologna, where he remained until his death, in the capacity of Professor of Natural and Moral Philosophy. His stipend, increased gradually through a series of engagements, varied from a little over 200 to 600 golden ducats. Bologna, like Ferrara, was not distinguished for its school of medicine. Consequently, we find that from the date of his first settlement in that city, Pomponazzi devoted himself to psychological and ethical investigations. All the books on which his fame are founded were written at Bologna. In the autumn of 1516 he published his treatise *De Immortalitate Animæ.* It was dedicated to Marcantonio Flavio Contarini ; and, finding its way to Venice, it was immediately burned in public because of its heretical opinions. A long and fierce controversy followed this first publication. Contarini, Agostino Nifo,

Ambrogio Fiandino, and Bartolommeo di Spina issued treatises, in which they strove to combat the Aristotelian materialism of Pomponazzi with arguments based on Thomistic theology or Averroistic mysticism. He replied with an *Apologia* and a *Defensorium*, avowing his submission to the Church in all matters of faith, but stubbornly upholding a philosophical disagreement with the doctrine of the immortality of the human soul. During this discussion Pomponazzi ran some risk of being held accountable for his opinions. The friars and preachers of all colours were loud in their denunciations ; and it is said that Bembo's intercession with Pope Leo in behalf of his old master was needed to secure Pomponazzi from ecclesiastical procedure. During the last years of his life the professor of Bologna completed two important treatises, *De Incantationibus* and *De Fato*. They were finished in 1520 but not published until after his death, when they appeared in the Basle edition of his collected works. He died in 1525, and was buried at Mantua. Pomponazzi had been thrice married. He left behind him an unsullied reputation for virtuous conduct and sweet temper. He was, physically, a little man, and owed to this circumstance the *sobriquet* of *Peretto*. We gain a glimpse of him in one of Bandello's novels. But, with this exception, the man is undiscernible through the mists of three intervening centuries. With the author the case is different. In his books Pomponazzi presents a powerful and unmistakeable personality. What remains to be said about him and his influence over Italian thought must be derived from an examination of the three treatises already mentioned.

In order to make Pomponazzi's position intelligible,
it will be needful to review the main outlines of Aristotelian thought, as it was transmitted through the
middle ages to the men of the Renaissance. Pomponazzi claimed to be no more than an expositor of
Aristotle's system. If he diverged from the paths of
orthodox philosophy, it was because he recognised a
discrepancy upon vital points between Thomas of
Aquino and the Peripatetic writings. If he rejected
some fashionable theories of the freethinkers who
preceded him, it was because he saw that Averroes
had misinterpreted their common master. He aimed
at stating once again the precise doctrine of the Greek
philosopher. He believed that if he could but grasp
Aristotle's real opinion, he should by that mental act
arrive at truth. The authority of the Stagirite in all
matters of human knowledge lay for him beyond the
possibility of question; or, what amounted to nearly
the same thing, his interest in speculative questions
was confined to making Aristotle's view intelligible.
Thus, under the humble garb of a commentator, one
of the boldest and in some respects the most original
thinkers of his age stepped forth to wage war with
superstition and ecclesiastical despotism. The Church,
since the date of Thomas Aquinas, had so committed
herself to Aristotle that proving a discrepancy between her dogma and the Aristotelian text upon any
vital point, was much the same as attacking the dogma
itself. This must be kept steadily in mind if we
wish to appreciate Pomponazzi.[1] His attitude cannot

---

[1] It will be remembered that in the controversy between Galileo and
the Inquisition, the latter condemned Copernicus on the score that he
contradicted Aristotle and S. Thomas of Aquino.

easily be understood at the present day, when science has discarded authority, and the *ipse dixit* of a dead man carries no weight outside religious or quasi-religious circles. This renders the prefatory remarks I have to make necessary.

In the Platonic system it was impossible to explain the connection between ideas, conceived as sole realities, and phenomena, regarded as distinct from that ideal world to which they owed their qualities of relative substantiality and cognisability. Aristotle attempted to solve Plato's problem by his theory of form and matter, activity and passivity, energy and potentiality, inseparable in the reality of the individual. He represented the intelligible world as a scale of existences, beginning with form and matter coherent in the simplest object, and ending in God. God was the form of forms, the thought of thoughts, independent of matter, immoveable and unchangeable, although the cause of movement and variety. The forms resumed in God, as species are included in the Summum Genus, were disseminated through the universe in a hierarchy of substances, from the most complex immediately below God, to the most simple immediately above the groundwork given by incognisable matter. In this hierarchy matter was conceived as the mere base; necessary, indeed, to every individual but God; an essential element of reality; but beyond the reach of knowledge. The form or universal alone was intelligible. It may already be perceived that in this system, if the individual, composed of form and matter, alone is substantial and concrete, while the universal alone is cognisable, Aristotle admitted a division between reality and truth. The former attribute belongs to the individual, the latter to the universal. The place of God, too, in the system is doubtful. Is He meant to be immanent in the universe, or separated from it? Aristotle uses language which supports each of these views. Again, God is immaterial, universal, the highest form ; and yet at the same time He is an individual substance ; whereas, by the fundamental conception of the whole scheme, the coherence of form and matter in the individual is necessary to reality. It might seem possible to escape from these difficulties by regarding Aristotle's Deity as the Idea of the Universe, and each inferior form in the ascending series of existences as the material of its immediate superior, until the final and inclusive form is reached in God. But what, then, becomes of matter in itself, which, though recognised as unintelligible, is postulated as the necessary base of individual substances ?

In Aristotle's theory of life there is a similar ascending scale. The soul ($\psi v \chi \dot{\eta}$) is defined as the form of the body. Its vegetative, motive, sensitive, appetitive faculties ($\psi v \chi \dot{\eta}$ $\theta \rho \epsilon \pi \tau \iota \kappa \dot{\eta}$, $\kappa \iota \nu \eta \tau \iota \kappa \dot{\eta}$, $a \dot{\iota} \sigma \theta \eta \tau \iota \kappa \dot{\eta}$, $\dot{o} \rho \epsilon \kappa \tau \iota \kappa \dot{\eta}$), are subordinated to the passive intellect ($\nu o \hat{\upsilon} s$ $\pi a \theta \eta \tau \iota \kappa \dot{o} s$), which receives their reports ; and this in its turn is subordinated to the active intellect ($\nu o \hat{\upsilon} s$ $\pi o \iota \eta \tau \iota \kappa \dot{o} s$), which possesses the content of the passive intellect as thought. The intellect ($\nu o \hat{\upsilon} s$) is man's peculiar property : and Aristotle in plain words asserts that it is separate from the soul ($\psi v \chi \dot{\eta}$). But he has not explained whether it is separate as the highest series of an evolution may be called distinct from the lower, or as something alien and communicated from without is separate. The passive intellect, being a receptacle for images and phantasms furnished by the senses, perishes with the soul, which, upon the dissolution of the body, whereof it is the form, ceases to exist. But the active intellect is immortal and eternal, being pure thought, and identifiable in the last resort with God. So much Aristotle seems to have laid down about the immortality of the intellect. It is tempting to infer that he maintained a theory of man's participation in the divine Idea—that is to say, in the complex of the categories which render the universe intelligible and distinguish it as a cosmos. But, just as Aristotle failed to explain the connection of God with the world, so he failed to render his opinion regarding the relation of God to the human intellect, and of the immortal to the perishable part of the soul, manifest. It can, however, be safely asserted that he laid himself open to a denial of the immortality of each individual person. This, at any rate, would follow from the assumption that he believed us to be persons by reason of physical existence, of the soul's faculties, and of that blending of the reason with the orectic soul which we call will. As the universe culminates in God, so man culminates in thought, which is the definition of God ; and this thought is eternal, the same for all and for ever. It does not, however, follow that each man who has shared the divine thought, should survive the dissolution of his body. The person is a complex, and this complex perishes. The active intellect is imperishable, but it is impersonal. In like manner the whole hierarchy of substances between the ground of matter and the form of forms is in perpetual process of combination and dissolution. But the supreme Idea endures, in isolation from that flux and reflux of the individuals it causes. Whether we regard the ontological or the psychological series, only the world of pure thought, the Idea, is indissoluble, subject to no process of becoming, and superior to all change. The supreme place assigned to Thought in either hierarchy is clear enough. But the nexus between (i) God and the Universe (ii) God and the active intellect (iii) the active intellect, or pure thought, and the inferior faculties of the soul, which supply it with material for thought, is unexplained.

Three distinct but interpenetrating problems were presented by the Aristotelian system. One concerns the theory of the Universal. Are universals or particulars prior? Do we collect the former from the latter; or do the latter owe their value as approximate realities to the former? The second concerns the theory of the Individual. Assuming that the Individual is a complex of form and matter, are we to regard the matter or the form as its essential substratum? The third concerns the theory of the human Soul. Is it perishable with the body, or immortal? If it is immortal, does the incorruptible quality perpetuate the person who has lived upon this globe; or is it the common property of all persons, surviving their decease, but not ensuring the prolongation of each several consciousness? The first of these problems formed the battle-field of Nominalists, Realists and Conceptualists in the first period of medieval thought. It was waged upon the data supplied by Porphyry's abstract of the Aristotelian doctrine of the predicaments. The

second problem occupied the encyclopædic thinkers of
the second period, Albertus Magnus, Duns Scotus and
Thomas of Aquino. Their contest was fought out
over the Metaphysics of Aristotle. The third problem
arrested the attention of speculators in the age of the
Renaissance. The text which they disputed was
Aristotle's essay *De Animâ*. This movement of
medieval thought from point to point was not unnatural nor unnecessitated. In the first period Aristotle
was unknown ; but the creeds of Christianity supplied
a very definite body of conceptions to be dealt with.
About the personality of God, the immortality of the
soul, and the concrete reality of the human individual,
there was then no doubt. Theology was paramount ;
and the contention of the schoolmen at this epoch regarded the right interpretation of the Universal. Was
it a simple conception of the mind, or an external and
substantial reality ? Was it a name or an entity ?
The Nominalists, who adopted the former of these two
alternatives, fell necessarily beneath the ban of ecclesiastical censure and suspicion ; not because their
philosophical conclusions were unwarranted, but because these ran counter to the prevailing spirit of the
Christian belief. Their definitions sapped the basis of
that transcendentalism on which the whole fabric of
medieval thought reposed. Nevertheless, at the end
of the battle, the Nominalists virtually gained the day.
Abelard's Conceptualism was an attempt to harmonise
antagonistic points of view by emphasising the abstrac-
tive faculty of the human subject. In the course of
this warfare the problem of the Individual had been
neglected. The reciprocity of form and matter had

not been expressly made a topic of dispute. Meanwhile a flood of new light was being cast upon philosophical questions by the introduction into Europe of Latin texts translated by Jewish scholars from the Arabic versions of Aristotle, as well as by the commentaries of Averroes. This rediscovery of Aristotle forced the schoolmen of the second period to consider the fundamental relation of matter to form. The master had postulated the conjunction of these two constituents in the individual. Thomas of Aquino and Duns Scotus advanced opposing theories to explain the ground and process of individualisation. With regard to the elder problem of the Universal, S. Thomas declared himself for modified Conceptualism. With regard to the second problem, he pronounced matter to be the substratum of individuals—matter stamped as with a seal by the form impressed upon it. Thus he adhered as closely as was possible for a theologian to the Peripatetic doctrines. For a student of philosophy to advance opinions without reckoning with Aristotle was now impossible. The great Dominican Doctor achieved the task of bringing Aristotle into satisfactory accord with Christian dogma. Nor was this so difficult as it appears. Aristotle, as we have seen, did not define his views about the soul and God. Moreover, he had written no treatise on theology proper. Whether he ascribed personality or conscious thought to God was more than doubtful. His God stood at the apex of the world's pyramid, inert, abstract, empty, and devoid of life. Christendom, meanwhile, was provided with a robust set of theological opinions, based on revelation and held as matters of faith. To transfer these to the account of the Aristotelian Deity, to fill out the vacuous and formal outline, and to theosophise the whole system was the work of S. Thomas. To the fixed dogmas of the Latin Church he adjusted the more favourable of Aristotle's various definitions, and interpreted his dubious utterances by the light of ecclesiastical orthodoxy.

Up to this point the doctrine of personal immortality had been accepted by all Christians as requiring no investigation. Human life was only studied in relation to the world beyond the grave, where each man and woman was destined to endure for all eternity. To traverse this fundamental postulate, was to proclaim the grossest heresy ; and though Epicureans, as Dante calls them, of that type were found, they had not formulated their opinions regarding the soul's corruptibility in any scientific theory, nor based them on the authority of Aristotle. S. Thomas viewed the soul as the essential form of the human body; he further affirmed its separate existence in each person, and its separate immortality. The soul, he thought, although defined as the form of a physical body, acquired a habit of existence in the body, which sufficed for its independent and perpetual survival. These determinations were clearly in accordance with the Christian faith. But the time was approaching when the problem of the soul itself should be narrowly considered. Averroes had interpreted Aristotle to mean that the active intellect alone, which he regarded as common to all human beings, was immortal. This was tantamount to denying the immortality of the individual. Men live and die, but the species is eternal. The active intellect arrives continually at human consciousness in persons, who participate in it and perish. Knowledge is indestructible for the race, transitory for each separate soul. At one end of the universal hierarchy is matter; at the other end is God. Between God and man in the descending scale are the intelligences of the several spheres. From the lowest or lunar sphere humanity derives the active intellect. This active intellect is a substantial entity, separate no less from God than from the human soul on which it rains the knowledge of a lifetime. It is not necessary to point out how much of mystical and Oriental material Averroes engrafted on Aristotle's system. His doctrine, though vehemently repudiated by orthodox schoolmen, found wide acceptance; and there were other heretics who asserted the perishable nature of the human soul, without distinction of its faculties. These heterodoxies gained ground so rapidly through the first two centuries of the Italian revival (1300—1500), that in December 1513 it was judged needful to condemn them, and to reassert the Thomistic doctrine by a Council of the Lateran over which Leo X. presided.[1]

If we consider the intellectual conditions of the Renaissance, it becomes clear why the problem of Immortality acquired this importance, and why heretical opinions spread so widely as to necessitate a confirmation of the orthodox dogma. Medieval speculation had

---

[1] 'These are the words : 'Hoc sacro approbante Concilio damnamus et reprobamus omnes asserentes *animam intellectivam mortalem esse*, aut *unicam in cunctis hominibus*, et hæc in dubium vertentes, cum illa non solum vere per se et essentialiter humani corporis forma existat . . . verum et immortalis, et pro corporum quibus infunditur multitudine, singulariter multiplicabilis et multiplicata et multiplicanda sit.'

a perpetual tendency to transcend the sphere of this earth. The other world gave reality and meaning to human life. All eyes were fixed on the Beyond, at first with an immediate expectation of the Judgment, afterwards with a continued looking forward to Paradise or Punishment. This attitude toward eternity was an absorbing preoccupation. But with the dawn of the new age our life on earth acquired a deeper significance; and the question was not unnaturally posed—this soul, whose immortality has been postulated, on whose ultimate destiny so many anticipations of weal and woe have been based, what is it? Are we justified in assuming its existence as an incorruptible and everlasting self? What did Aristotle really think about it? The age inclined with overmastering bias toward a practical materialism. Men were eager to enjoy their lives and to indulge their appetites. They tired of the restrictions imposed upon their nature by the prospect of futurity. They found in their cherished classics, whose authority had triumphed over Church and Council, but vague and visionary hints of immortality. Even in the highest ecclesiastical quarters it was fashionable to speak lightly of the fundamental dogmas of the Christian creed. Leo X., who presided over the Lateran Council of 1513, did not disguise his doubts concerning the very doctrine it had reinforced. The time had come for a reconsideration *ab initio* of a theory which the middle ages had accepted as an axiom. The battle was fought out on the ground of Aristotle's treatise on the soul. Independent research had not yet asserted its claims against authority; and the problem which now presented itself to the professors and students of Italy, was not : Is the soul immortal ? but : Did Aristotle maintain the immortality of the soul ? The philosopher of Stagira, having been treated on his first appearance as a foe of the faith and then accepted as its bulwark, was now to be used as an efficient battering-ram against the castles of orthodox opinion.

There were two ways of regarding Aristotle's doctrine of the active intellect. The one was to view the Nous as a development from the soul, which in its turn should be conceived as a development from the senses. The other was to recognise it as separate from the soul and imported from without. Each claimed substantial support in various dicta of the master. The latter found able exposition at the hands of his Arabic commentator Averroes. The former was maintained by the fullest and latest of the Greek peripatetics, Alexander of Aphrodisias. In the later middle ages free thought, combating the Thomistic system, inclined to Averroism. Pomponazzi, the chief Aristotelian of the Renaissance, declared for Alexander. His great work, *De Immortalitate Animæ*, is little more than an attempt to reconstruct the doctrine of Aristotle by the help of Alexander. Pomponazzi starts by laying down the double nature of the human soul. It is both sensitive and intelligent. On this point philosophers are agreed ; the questions at issue relate to the mode of connection between the two portions, and the prospect of immortality for both or either. He next proceeds to state the opinions of Averroes, the Platonists, and Thomas of Aquino, meeting their several arguments, and showing how and where they diverge from Aristotle, and endeavouring to prove the superiority of his master's doctrine. Pomponazzi agrees with S. Thomas as to the division of the soul and its relation to the body. He differs with him on the point of immortality, declaring with sufficient clearness that no portion of the human soul can be other than perishable. If we admit that the soul in general is the act or form of the body, the intelligent portion of the soul is included in this definition. It cannot dispense with the body, at least as the object of its intelligent activity. But if it be thus intimately bound up with the body, it must suffer corruption with the body ; or even should we suppose it to survive, it will have no images or phantasms furnished by the senses, which are the necessary pabulum of its thinking faculty.[1] The order of nature admits of no interruption. It will not do to say that the soul thinks in one way during life on earth, and in another way after death. This contradicts the first principle of continuity. Man occupies a middle place between imperishable and perishable things.[2] He has a certain odour of immateriality, a mere shadow of intellect, because he stands upon the confine between these

---

[1] Cap. viii. 'Cum et Aristoteles dicat, necesse esse intelligentem phantasma aliquod speculari.' Again, *ibid.* : 'Ergo in omni suo intelligere indiget phantasia, sed si sic est, ipsa est materialis ; ergo anima intellectiva est materialis.' Again, *ibid* : 'Humanus intellectus corpus habet caducum, quare vel corrupto corpore ipse non esset, quod positioni repugnat, vel si esset, sine opere esset, cum sine phantasmate per positionem intelligere non posset et sic otiaretur.'

[2] Cap. ix. 'Et sic medio modo humanus intellectus inter materialia et immaterialia est actus corporis organici.' Again, *ibid.* : 'Ipse igitur intellectus sic medius existens inter materialia et immaterialia.' Again, *ibid.* : 'Homo est medius inter Deos et bestias, quare sicut pallidum comparatum nigro dicitur album, sic homo, comparatus bestiis, dici potest Déus et immortalis, sed non vere et simpliciter.'

regions.[1] But his very conduct shows how vain and unsubstantial is his claim to pure reason. If we see a few men elevate themselves toward God, there are thousands who descend toward the brutes ; and of those who spend their lives in clarifying their intelligence, none can boast of more than an obscure and cloudy vision.[2] In the hierarchy of souls we can broadly distinguish three grades ; the pure intelligences of the astral spheres, who have no need of physical organs ; the souls of brutes, immersed in matter, and no better than a mode of it ; the souls of men, which occupy a middle place, requiring matter as the object of their thought, but rising by speculation above it. Even so within the mind of man we may discern a triple series—the factive, practical, and speculative intellects. The first subserves utility ; man shares it with the brutes. The third enables him to lift himself toward God. The second is essentially human ; he uses it in moral action, and performs his duty by obeying it. Both the sensitive soul and the intellect are material in the full sense of extension.[3] To conceive of them otherwise is contradictory to reason and to Aristotle. It is therefore impossible to hold that either soul or intellect, although the latter has certain affinities to imperishable intelligence, should survive the body. The senses supply the object of thought ;

---

[1] Cap. viii. 'Vixque sit umbra intellectûs.' Again, cap. ix. : 'Cum ipsa sit materialium nobilissima, in confinioque immaterialium, aliquid immaterialitatis odorat, sed non simpliciter.'

[2] See (cap. viii.) the passage which begins ' Secundò quia cum in ista essentia.'

[3] See the passages quoted above ; and compare *De Nutritione,* lib. i. cap. 11, which contains Pomponazzi's most mature opinion on the material extension of the soul, which he calls, *in all its faculties, realiter extensa.*

the phantasms dealt with by the intellect depend upon the physical organs : abstract these, and where is the cogitative faculty ? Having thus attempted to demonstrate the mortality of the human soul, Pomponazzi feels bound to attack the problem of the final end of human beings. Hitherto, throughout the ages of Christianity, men had lived on this world with eternity in view. That was their aim and goal. He has removed this object ; and he anticipates hostile argument by affirming that virtue itself is the proper end of man on earth. The practical intellect is the attribute of humanity as distinguished both from the brutes and from the separate intelligences of the spheres. To act in accordance with the nature of this specific quality— in other words, to follow virtue—is the end of man. Virtue is her own reward, as vice is its own punishment.[1] The question whether the soul be mortal or immortal, whether we have a right to expect future judgment or not, has really nothing to do with the matter.[2] With this ethical conclusion Pomponazzi terminates his argument. He is careful, however, to note that though he disbelieves in the immortality of the soul as a philosopher, he accepts it in the fullest sense as a Christian.[3] It has been suggested that the

---

[1] *De Immortalitate*, cap. xiv. After demonstrating that the *intellectus practicus*, as distinguished from the *speculativus* and the *factivus*, is the special property of man, and that consequently in Ethics we have the true science of humanity, he lays down and tries to demonstrate the two positions that (1) 'præmium essentiale virtutis est ipsamet virtus quæ hominem felicem facit ;' (2) 'pœna vitiosi est ipsum vitium, quo nihil miserius, nihil infelicius esse potest.'

[2] For this argument he refers to Plato in cap. xiv. : 'Sive animus mortalis sit, sive immortalis, nihilominus contemnenda est mors, neque alio pacto declinandum est a virtute quicquid accidat post mortem.'

[3] See especially the exordium to cap. viii.

orthodox doctrine of the resurrection of the body might have supplied Pomponazzi with a link between science and faith.[1] However, he did not avail himself of it; and his philosophy stands in abrupt and open conflict with his creed.

The treatise *De Incantatione* presents the same antithesis between Peripatetic science and Christian faith. Pomponazzi composed it at the instance of a physician, his friend, who begged him to offer an explanation of some apparently supernatural phenomena. It is, in fact, an essay upon demons and miracles. As a philosopher, Pomponazzi stoutly rejects both. The order of nature cannot be interrupted. Angels and devils only exist in the popular imagination. Miracles are but imperfectly comprehended manifestations of natural forces, which the vulgar ascribe to the intervention of God or spirits.[2] Each religion has its own miracles and its own saints, to whom the common folk attribute supernatural power.[3] But Moses, Mahomet and Christ stand upon the same level; the thaumaturgists of every creed are equally unable to alter the universal order.[4] Credulity and ignorance ascribe to all of them faculties they cannot possess. Having, as a philosopher, expressed these revolutionary ideas, as a Christian, he briefly and summarily states his belief in all that he has just denied.[5]

Basing his argument upon the ground of reason, which, for him, was no other than the Aristotelian doctrine of the Cosmos, Pomponazzi recognises no

---

[1] Ritter, *Geschichte der Christlichen Philosophie*, part v. p. 426, quoted by Fiorentino, *op. cit.*

[2] *De Incant.* cap. 3.

[3] *Ibid.* cap. 4.

[4] *Ibid.* cap. 12.

[5] Peroration of *De Incant.*

agency that interrupts the sequence of cause and effect in nature. But the astral intelligences are realities, and their operation has been as clearly ascertained as that of any other natural force. Therefore Pomponazzi refers to the planets many extraordinary exhibitions of apparently abnormal power, conceding upon this point as much as could have been desired by the most superstitious of his contemporaries. Not only are the lives of men subject to planetary influence; but all human institutions rise, flourish and decay in obedience to the same superior laws. Even religions have their day of inevitable decline, and Christianity is no exception to the general rule. At the present moment, says Pomponazzi, we may discern signs of approaching dissolution in the fabric of our creed.[1] He is careful to add, as usual, that he holds this doctrine as a philosopher; but that, as a Christian, he believes in the permanence of revealed religion. Faith and reason could not be brought into more glaring antagonism, nor is it possible to affirm contradictory propositions with less attempt at reconciliation. Pomponazzi seems determined to act out by anticipation Pascal's axiom, *Il faut être Pyrrhonniste accompli et Chrétien soumis.* What the real state of his mind was, and whether the antithesis which seems to us so untenable, did not present itself to him as an anomaly, hardly admits of explanation. A similar unresolved discord may be traced in nearly all the thinkers of this epoch.

It remains to mention one more treatise of Pomponazzi, the Book on Fate. Here he raises the question of human freedom face to face with God and

[1] *De Incant.* cap. 12.

the unbroken order of the Universe. The conclusions at which he arrives are vacillating and unsatisfactory; nor is there much in his method of handling this ancient problem to arrest attention. The essay, however, contains one sentence which deserves to be recorded. 'A very Prometheus,' he says, 'is the philosopher. Seeking to penetrate the secret things of God, he is consumed with ceaseless cares and cogitations ; he forgets to thirst, to hunger, to eat, to sleep, to spit; he is derided of all men, and held for a fool and sacrilegious person ; he is persecuted by inquisitors; he becomes a gazing-stock to the common folk. These, then, are the gains of the philosophers; these are their guerdons.'[1] Not only were these words spoken from the man's own heart, smarting under the attacks to which his treatise on the soul had exposed him ; but they were in a profound sense prophetic. While reading them, we think of Campanella's lifelong imprisonment and sevenfold tortures ; of Bruno's death by fire, and Vanini's tongue torn out before his execution ; of Galileo's recantation and disgrace ; of Carnesecchi, Paleario and Montalcino burned or strangled. A whole procession of Italian martyrs to free thought and bold avowal of opinion passes before our eyes.

Reviewing Pomponazzi's work, we find that, though he occupied for the most part the modest place of a commentator and expositor, he valiantly asserted the rights of reason face to face with ecclesiastical authority. Under the ægis of the formula *salvâ fide*, he attacked the popular belief, disputed the fiats

[1] *De Fato*, lib. iii. cap. 7.

of Church Councils, denied miracles, rejected supernatural causes, and proclaimed that science must be
based upon the axiom of an unalterable permanence
in the order of the universe. The controversy which
his treatise on immortality inflamed in Italy, popular-
ised the two conceptions of God's immanence in nature
and of the evolution of the human soul from corporeal
organs. In other words it struck a powerful blow at
transcendental, extra-mundane speculation, and prepared the way for sounder physical investigations.
The positive spirit appeared in Pomponazzi, never
thenceforward to be set at rest until the cycle of
modern scientific illumination shall be accomplished.

The deep impression produced by this controversy
on the mind of the Italians, may be illustrated by a
little story. Pomponazzi's disciple, Simone Porzio,
when invited to lecture at Pisa, opened Aristotle's
meteorological treatises at the commencement of his
course. The assembly, composed of students and
people of the town, who had assembled, as was then
the custom, to gaze upon the new professor and to
judge his manner,[1] cried in a loud voice : ' *Quid de
animâ?* Speak to us about the soul !' He had to
close his book, and take up the *De Animâ*. This
Porzio frankly professed his belief that the human
soul differed in no essential point from the soul of a
lion or a plant, and that those who thought otherwise,
were prompted by a generous pity for our mean estate.[2]

---

[1] An interesting description of a humanist opening his course at
Padua, and of the excitement in the town about it, is furnished by the
anonymous Maccaronic poet who sang the burlesque praises of *Vigonça*.
See Delepierre, *Macaronéana Andra*, London, 1862. Above, p. 331.

[2] He makes these assertions in a treatise *De Mente Humanâ*.

Materialism of the purest water became fashionable, and expressed itself in pithy sentences, which, though devoid of historical accuracy, sufficiently paint the temper of the folk who gave them currency. Of this type is the apocryphal epitaph of Cesare Cremonini, one of the latest of the Italian peripateticians. He died in 1631, and on his grave was said to have been written at his own request *Hic jacet Cremoninus totus.* To the same Cremonini is ascribed the Jesuitical motto *Foris ut moris, intus ut libet,* which may be regarded as a cynical version of Pomponazzi's oft-repeated protestation of belief in dogmas he had demonstrated contrary to reason.[1] Had it been possible for the Church to continue her tolerance of Leo's age, or had the Counter-Reformation taken a direction less inimical to free enquiry, the studied hypocrisy of this epigram, so painfully characteristic of the age that gave it birth, might have been avoided. The men who uttered it and acted by it, were the same of whom Milton spoke in *Areopagitica* : ' I have sat among their learned men (for that honour I had), and been counted happy to be born in such a place of philosophic freedom as they supposed England was, while themselves did nothing but bemoan the servile condition into which learning amongst them was brought; that this was it which had damped the glory of Italian wits ; that nothing had been written now these many years but flattery and fustian.'

Central and Northern Italy performed the first two

---

[1] In the peroration of his treatise on Incantation, Pomponazzi says : ' Habes itaque, compater charissime, quæ, ut mea fert opinio, Peripatetici ad ea quæ quæsivisti, dicere verisimiliter haberent. Habes et quæ veritati et Christianæ religioni consona sunt.'

stages of Renaissance thought. Florence, true to the destiny which made her artful and form-giving, attempted to restore Platonic philosophy in accordance with the conditions determined by the middle ages. Bologna, gifted with a personality no less substantial, adhered to scholastic traditions, but accommodated their rigid subject-matter to the spirit breathed upon them by more liberal scholarship. It remained for the South of Italy to complete the work, and to supply the fulcrum needed for the first true effort of modern science. Hitherto, whether at Florence or Bologna, philosophy had recognised authority. Discarding the yoke of the Church, both Platonists and Aristotelians recognised masters, whose words they were contented to interpret. Reason dared not declare herself, except beneath the mask of some great teacher—Plato or Plotinus, Aristotle or Alexander or Averroes. The school of Cosenza cut itself adrift from authority, ecclesiastical or classical. This is the import of the first sonnet in Campanella's series, preserved for us by the fortunate mediation of his disciple, the German with the Italianised patronymic, Tobia Adami [1] :

> Born of God's Wisdom and Philosophy,
>> Keen lover of true beauty and true good,
>> I call the vain self-traitorous multitude
>> Back to my mother's milk ; for it is she,
> Faithful to God her spouse, who nourished me,
>> Making me quick and active to intrude
>> Within the inmost veil, where I have viewed
>> And handled all things in eternity.

[1] From my *Sonnets of Michael Angelo and Campanella*, p. 119.

> If the whole world's our home where we may run,
>   Up, friends, forsake those secondary schools
>   Which give grains, units, inches for the whole !
> If facts surpass mere words, melt pride of soul,
>   And pain, and ignorance that hardens fools,
>   Here in the fire I've stolen from the Sun !

Campanella calls the students of truth back to Nature from the 'secondary schools' of the philosophers, Plato, Aristotle, Thomas of Aquino, or Averroes; who imposed upon their reason by the word 'authority.' In his fifth sonnet he enforces the same theme [1] :

> The world's the book where the eternal sense
>   Wrote his own thoughts ; the living temple where,
>   Painting his very self, with figures fair
>   He filled the whole immense circumference.
> Here then should each man read, and gazing find
>   Both how to live and govern, and beware
>   Of godlessness ; and, seeing God all-where,
>   Be bold to grasp the universal mind.
> But we tied down to books and temples dead,
>   Copied with countless errors from the life,—
>   These nobler than that school sublime we call.
> O may our senseless souls at length be led
>   To truth by pain, grief, anguish, trouble, strife !
>   Turn we to read the one original !

Tyrants, hypocrites and sophists—that is to say, the triple band of State and Church oppressors, of interested ecclesiastics, and of subtle logicians—have drawn their threefold veil between the human intelligence and the universe, from which alone, as their proper home and *milieu*, men must derive the knowledge that belongs to them. Campanella, with the sincerity of one to whom the truth is dearer than his own reputation, yields the *spolia opima* of this latest victory over the strongholds of authority to his master—the master

---

[1] *Ibid.* p. 123.

whom he never knew in life, but over whose bier he
wept and prayed in secret, hiding the fire of modern
freedom and modern science beneath the black cowl of a
Dominican friar [1] :

> Telesius, the arrow from thy bow
>   Midmost his band of sophists slays that high
>   Tyrant of souls that think ; he cannot fly :
>   While Truth soars free, loosed by the self-same blow,
> Proud lyres with thine immortal praises glow,
>   Smitten by bards elate with victory :
>   Lo, thine own Cavalcante, stormfully
>   Lightning, still strikes the fortress of the foe !
> Good Gaieta bedecks our saint serene
>   With robes translucent, light-irradiate,
>   Restoring her to all her natural sheen ;
> The while my tocsin at the temple-gate
>   Of the wide universe proclaims her queen,
>   Pythia of first and last ordained by fate.

In these verses, the saint and queen proclaimed by
Campanella is Nature. During the middle ages truth
had seemed to descend as by a sort of inspiration upon
man from an extra-mundane God. During the first
and second periods of the Renaissance the human
intellect repudiated this transcendentalism, but yielded
itself, a willing victim, to the authority of books, Plato
or Aristotle, and their commentators. Now the mind
of man stands face to face with nature, and knows that
there, and there alone, is inspiration. The great
Baconian secret, the Interrogation of Nature, has been
revealed. It is now acknowledged on all sides that
not what Telesio or Campanella, or their famous disciple, Bacon, achieved in actual discovery, was noteworthy. But the spirit communicated from Telesio
and Campanella to Bacon, is the spirit of modern
science. Meanwhile, another native of South Italy,

[1] *Ibid.* p. 174.

Giordano Bruno, proclaimed the immanence of God in the world, the identification of the universe with God in thought, the impossibility of escaping from God in nature, because nature, realising God for the human soul, is divine. The central conception of the third age of Italian thought, underlying the apparently divergent systems of Campanella and Bruno—the conception, namely, of a real and indestructible correlation between the human spirit and the actual universe, and the consequent reliance of the human consciousness upon its own testimony in the search for truth—contained the germ of all that has, in very various regions, been subsequently achieved by French, Dutch, English, and German speculators. Telesio and Campanella, long before Bacon, founded empirical science. Campanella and Bruno, long before Descartes, established the principle of idealistic philosophy in the self-conscious thinking faculty of man. The sensualism of Telesio, the spiritualism of Bruno, and Campanella's dualism, foreshadow all possible sects of empiricists, rationalists and eclectics, which have since divided the field of modern speculation. It is easy enough now to look down either from the height of full-blown transcendental metaphysics or from the more modest eminence of solid physical science upon the intellectual abortions generated by this potent conception in its earliest fusion with medieval theology. Yet it is impossible to neglect the negative importance of the work effected by men who declared their independence of ecclesiastical and classical authority in an age when the Church and antiquity contended for the empire of the human reason. Still less possible is it to deny the place of Galileo,

Descartes, Bacon, Spinoza, among the offspring begotten of the movement which Pomponazzi, Telesio, Campanella and Bruno inaugurated and developed.

Thus, therefore, by the substitution of human for revealed authority ; by the suggestion of new and real topics of enquiry, and finally by the repudiation of all authority except that of nature's ascertained laws ; by the rending of all veils between the human reason and the universe, the Italian philosophers of the Renaissance effected for Europe the transition from the middle ages to the modern era.

What is the link of connection between Machiavelli and Pomponazzi, the two leaders of Italian thought at the height of the Renaissance ? It may be expressed in one formula—a vivid sense of man and the world as they are; or, in other words, positivism. Machiavelli dispenses with Providence, smiles incredulously at Fortune, explains all social and historical problems by reference to the will and thought of men in action. He studies human nature as he finds it, not as it ought to be according to some ideal standard. Pomponazzi shatters transcendentalism at a blow. He proves that there is no convincing argument for immortality. He demonstrates that the end of man is to be found in conduct. He treats religions without exception as transitory institutions, subject to the universal laws of birth and corruption, useful to society in their day of vigour, but destined to succeed each other with the waxing and the waning of the influences that control our globe and all that it contains. On this point Machiavelli and Pomponazzi are in complete accord. Both of them interpret the spirit of their century.

As Machiavellism existed in Italian politics before
Machiavelli theorised it, so materialism leavened society
before Pomponazzi gave it the consistency of demonstration. The middle ages with their political and theological idealism were at an end. Machiavelli and Pomponazzi contemporaneously philosophised the realism
on which science was destined to be founded. They
were the deicides of elder faiths; the hierophants of a new
revelation, as yet but dimly apprehended; the Columbus
and Vespucci of an intellectual hemisphere which it
remained for their posterity to colonise. The conditions of public and private life in the Italian cities—the
decline of religious feeling, the corruption of morality,
the paganising tendencies of humanism, the extinction
of political activity, the decay of freedom, the survival
of the Church and Commune when their work was
ended—rendered any such movement as that of the
German Reformation wholly impossible. The people
lacked the spiritual stuff for it. We have seen that it
was chiefly men like Berni and Folengo who gave
open utterance to Lutheran opinions; and from sources
like those no pure or vivifying waters could be drawn.
Italy's work lay in another direction. Those very conditions which unfitted her for a religious revival, enabled
her to perform her true mission. It was no slight
achievement to have set up the pillars of Hercules for
transcendentalism, and at the same time to have discovered the continent of positive science. For the
fruits and recognition of her labours she has had to
wait   Her history since the date of Machiavelli's
  h has been obscure until the middle of this cen-
  t , and in the race of the nations she has been left

behind.[1] But the perturbation of the intellectual current caused by the Reformation is now nearly over, and the spirit of modern science still finds itself in harmony with that of the Italian thinkers who gave it earliest expression.

[1] It may be worth reminding the reader that Pomponazzi died in 1525, and Machiavelli in 1527—the year of Rome's disaster. Their births also were nearly synchronous. Pomponazzi was born in 1462, Machiavelli in 1469.

CHAPTER XVII.

CONCLUSION.

Retrospect—Meaning of the Renaissance—Modern Science and Demo-cracy—The Preparation of an Intellectual Medium for Europe—The Precocity of Italy—Servitude and Corruption—Antiquity and Art— The Italian Provinces — Florence — Lombardy and Venice — The March of Ancona, Urbino, Umbria—Perugia — Rome—Sicily and Naples—Italian Ethnology—Italian Independence on the Empire and the Church—Persistence of the Old Italic Stocks—The New Nation —Its Relation to the Old—The Revival of Learning was a National Movement—Its Effect on Art—On Literature—Resumption of the Latin Language—Affinities between the Latin and Italian Genius— Renascence of Italian Literature combined with Humanism—Greek Studies comparatively Uninfluential—The Modern Italians inherited Roman Qualities—Roman Defects—Elimination of Roman Satire— Decay of Roman Vigour—Italian Realism—Positivism—Sensuous-ness—Want of Mystery, Suggestion, Romance—The Intellectual Atmosphere—A Literature of Form and Diversion — Absence of Commanding Genius—Lack of Earnestness—Lack of Piety—Mater-ialism and Negation—Idyllic Beauty—The Men of the Golden Age —The Cult of Form—Italy's Gifts to Europe—The Renaissance is not to be Imitated—Its Importance in Human Development—Feudalism, Renaissance, Reformation, Revolution.

AT the end of a long journey it is natural to review the stages of the way that has been traversed. We resume the impressions made upon our mind, and extract that element of generality from recollection, which the rapid succession of scenes, incidents and interests denied to the experience of travel. In like manner, those who have been engaged in some his-torical enquiry, after examining each province of the subject separately, seek a vantage-ground of contemplation, whence the conclusions they have reached can be surveyed in their relation to each other.

What we call, for want of a better name, the Renaissance, was a period of transition from the middle ages to the first phase of modern life. It was a step which had to be made, at unequal distances of time and under varying influences, by all the peoples of the European community. Its accomplishment brought the several members of that community into international relationship, and formed a confederation of reciprocally balanced powers out of the Occidental races who shared the inheritance of imperial Rome. At the commencement of this period, the modern nations acquired consistency and fixity of type. Mutually repelled by the principle of nationality, which made of each a separate organism, obeying its own laws of growth according to peculiarities of climate, blood and social institutions, they were at the same time drawn and knit together by a common bond of intellectual activities and interests. The creation of this international consciousness or spirit, which, after the lapse of four centuries, justifies us in regarding the past history of Europe as the history of a single family, and encourages us to expect from the future a still closer interaction of the Western nations, can be ascribed in a great measure to the Renaissance. One distinctive feature of that epoch was, reaction against the main forces of the middle ages. And since reaction implies a vivid principle of vitality, we find, in the further progress of this movement, the new ideas of democracy and science counterposed to feudalism and the Church. So vast a revolution as the reconstruction of society upon new bases, could not be effected by any simple or continuously progressive process. The nations educated by the Church and disciplined by feudalism, could not pass into a new phase of being without checks, hesitations, retrogressions, hindrances innumerable. Nor was it to be expected that the advance of each member in the European community should proceed upon an exactly similar method, or with equally felicitous results. It was inevitable that both feudalism and the Church should long remain in liquidation, resisting the impact of scepticism inherent in the Reformation; opposing stubborn resistance to republican energy liberated by the Revolution; crystallising the counter-movement of the modern spirit at one point in monarchical absolutism, at another in Protestant establishments; receding from this rebellious province to fortify and garrison that loyal stronghold; tolerating no compromise here, and there achieving a temporary triumph by transaction with the steadily-advancing forces ranged against them. The battle even now is being waged with varying success over the wide field of Europe; and whatever may be our conviction as to the ultimate issue of the struggle, it is impossible to foresee a definite end, or to assign even probable limits to the extent and the duration of the conflict.

Although we may hold the opinion that science and democracy constitute the fundamental points in modern as distinguished from medieval history, it would be paradoxical to assert that they emerged into prominence during the initial stage of the Renaissance. A common intellectual atmosphere had first to be prepared for Europe. The sense of human freedom had to be acquired by studies and discoveries which made man master of himself and of the world around him.   His attention had to be diverted from the life beyond the grave to his life upon this planet.   The culture, which formed the great achievement of the Italian Renaissance and which was diffused through Europe, uniting men of all races and all creeds in speculative and literary activity, evoking sympathies and stimulating antagonisms upon vital questions of universal import, was necessary for the evolution of the modern world as we now know it.   In many senses we have already transcended the original conditions of that culture.   But we owe to it our spiritual solidarity, our feeling of intellectual identity, our habit of pouring convergent contributions from divers quarters into the stock of indestructible experience.

Quickened to livelier consciousness by contact with the masterpieces of antiquity, in the dawn of that new age, the reason rapidly engaged in exploratory expeditions.   Both human nature and the material universe presented themselves with altered aspect to thought and senses, which had lain dormant during centuries of incubation.   At first, like the blind man of the miracle, the awakening intelligence saw confusedly.   It is easy with our clearer vision to despise the hybrid fancies of a time when things old and new were so romantically blent—'the men as trees, walking,' of that inexperienced intuition, the childish science and the scarce-fledged criticism of discoverers, who, while they reached forth to the future, still retained the hold of custom and long reverence on the past.   A note of imperfection, vacillation, tentative endeavour, can be traced in all the productions of the Renaissance—everywhere, in fact, but in the fine arts, where a simpler insight and more unimpeded faculties were exercised at that period than the last three centuries have boasted. In another important department the men of that age proved themselves more than merely precocious and immature. The humanistic system of mental training has survived with little alteration to the present day, and still forms the basis of what is called a liberal education.

This transition from the middle ages to the modern era, which we designate by the metaphor of Renascence or new birth, made itself first powerfully felt in Italy. Of all the European nations, the Italians alone can boast of a great and uninterrupted history, extending over the twenty-five centuries which are known to us by tolerably trustworthy records. They first gave the civilisation of republican and imperial Rome to the Western world. They formed the Latin Church, and extended the organisation of ecclesiastical Rome to European Christendom. This was their double work in what we call the ancient and medieval periods. At the close of the latter, they inaugurated the age of culture, science and associated intellectual endeavour, in which we are now living. In Italy the people preserved unbroken memories of their classical past ; and, as we have seen throughout these volumes, the point of departure for modern reconstruction was a renewed and vital interest in antiquity. Here, too, the characteristic institutions of feudalism had taken but slight hold, while the secularisation of the Papacy had undermined the spiritual prestige of the Church. Thus the forces to be overcome were feebler in Italy than elsewhere, while the current of fresh energy was stronger.

The conditions under which the Italians performed their task in the Renaissance were such as seem at first sight unfavourable to any great achievement. Yet it is probable that, the end in view being the stimulation of mental activity, no better circumstances than they enjoyed could have been provided. Owing to a series of adverse accidents, and owing also to their own instinctive preference for local institutions, they failed to attain the coherence and the centralised organisation which are necessary to a nation as we understand that word. Their dismemberment among rival communities proved a fatal source of political and military weakness, but it developed all their intellectual energies by competition to the utmost.

At the middle of the fifteenth century their communes had lost political liberty, and were ruled by despots. Martial spirit declined. Wars were carried on by mercenaries ; and the people found itself in a state of practical disarmament, when the neighbouring nations quarrelled for the prize of those rich provinces. At the same time society underwent a rapid moral deterioration. When Machiavelli called Italy 'the corruption of the world,' he did not speak rhetorically. An impure and worldly clergy; an irreligious, though superstitious, laity ; a self-indulgent and materialistic middle class; an idle aristocracy, excluded from politics and unused to arms ; a public given up to pleasure and money-getting ; a multitude of scholars, devoted to trifles, and vitiated by studies which clashed with the ideals of Christianity—from such elements in the nation proceeded a widely-spread and ever-increasing degeneracy. Public energy, exhausted by the civil wars and debilitated by the arts of the tyrants, sank deep and deeper into the lassitude of acquiescent lethargy. Religion expired in laughter, irony and licence. Domestic simplicity yielded to vice, whereof the records are precise and unmistakeable. The virile virtues disappeared. What survived of courage assumed the forms of ruffianism, ferocity and treasonable daring. Still, simultaneously with this decline in all the moral qualities which constitute a powerful people, the Italians brought their arts and some departments of their literature to a perfection that can only be paralleled by ancient Greece. The anomaly implied in this statement is striking; but it is revealed to us by evidence too overwhelming to be rejected. We must be careful not to insist on any causal link of connection between the moral and intellectual conditions of Italian society at this epoch. Still we are forced to admit that servitude and corruption are the commanding features of the age in which Italy for the third time in her history won and held the hegemony of the world. In politics, in religion, in ethics, she seemed to have been left devoid of guiding principles ; and tragic interest is added to the climax of her greatness by the long series of disasters, culminating in Spanish enslavement and ecclesiastical tyranny, which proved her interral rottenness and put an end to her unrivalled intellectual triumphs.

It has been my object in this work to review the part played by the Italians at the beginning of modern history, subjecting each department of their activity to

separate examination. In the first of the five volumes
I described the social and political conditions under
which the renascence of the race took place. In the
second I treated of that retrogressive movement toward
antiquity, which constitutes the most important factor
in the problem offered by that age. The third volume
was devoted to the Fine Arts, wherein the main originality of modern Italy emerged. It was through art
that the creative instincts of the people found their
true and adequate channel of expression. Paramount
over all other manifestations of the epoch, fundamental
beneath all, penetrative to the core of all, is the
artistic impulse. The slowly self-consolidating life of
a great kingdom, concentrating all elements of national
existence by the centripetal force of organic unity, was
wanting. Commonwealths and despotisms, representing a more imperfect stage of political growth, achieved
completion and decayed. But art survived this dis-
integration of the medieval fabric; and in art the
Italians found the cohesion denied them as a nation.
While speaking thus of art, it is necessary to give a
wide extension to that word. It must be understood
to include literature. Nor, in the case of Italy, does
this imply an undue strain upon its meaning. The
last two volumes of my work have been devoted to the
stages whereby vernacular literature absorbed into
itself the elements of scholarship, and gave form to
the predominating thoughts and feelings of the people.
This process of form-giving was controlled, more or
less consciously throughout, by the artistic instincts of
which I have been speaking. Thus we are justified in
regarding the literary masterpieces of the sixteenth

century as the fullest and most representative expression of the Italian temperament at the climax of its growth. The literature of the golden age implies humanism, implies painting. It will be seen that the logic of the whole subject necessitated the reservation of this department for final treatment, and justified a more minute investigation than had been accorded to the rest.

It is not only possible but right to speak of Italy collectively when we review her work in the Renaissance. Yet it should not be forgotten that Italy at this time was a federation, presenting upon a miniature scale the same diversities in her component parts as the nations of Europe do now. If for this reason alone, we may profitably survey the different shares claimed by her several communities in the general achievement.

At the beginning of such a review, we cannot fail to be struck with the predominance of Florence. The superiority of the Tuscans was threefold. In the first place, they determined the development of art in all its branches. In the second place, they gave a language to Italy, which, without obliterating the local dialects, superseded them in literature when the right moment for intellectual community arrived. That moment, in the third place, was rendered possible by the humanistic movement, which began at Florence. The humanists prepared the needful literary medium by introducing classical studies into every town of the peninsula. Without this discipline, Tuscan could not so speedily have produced Italian, or have been so readily accepted by North and South. It may, indeed, be affirmed without exaggeration that, prior to the close of the fifteenth century, what we call the Italian genius was, in truth, the genius of Florence.

What the Lombards and Venetians produced in fine art and literature was of a later birth.[1] Yet the novelists of Lombardy, the Latin lyrists of Garda, the school of romantic and dramatic poets at Ferrara, the group of sculptors and painters assembled in Milan by the Sforza dynasty, the maccaronic Muse of Mantua, the unrivalled magnificence of painting at Venice, the transient splendour of the Parmese masters, the wit of Modena, the learning of the princes of Mirandola and Carpi, must be catalogued among the most brilliant and characteristic manifestations of Italian genius. In pure literature Venice contributed but little, though she sent forth a dictator, Pietro Bembo, to rule the republic of letters at the moment when the sceptre was about to pass from Florence. Her place, as the home of Aldo's Greek press, and as the refuge for adventurers like Aretino and Folengo, when the rest of Italy was yielding to reactionary despotism, has to be commemorated. Of the northern universities, Padua preserved the tradition of physical studies, and Bologna that of legal erudition, onward from the middle ages. Both became headquarters of materialistic philosophy in the sixteenth century. The school of Vicenza had flourished in humane letters at the commencement of the epoch. But it declined early ; while that of Ferrara, on the contrary, succeeded to the honours of Florence and Pisa. Genoa was almost

[1] I need hardly guard this paragraph by saying that I speak within the limits of the Renaissance.

excluded from the current of Italian culture. Her
sumptuous palaces and churches, her sensual unsympathetic painting, belong to the last days of Italian
energy. Her few great scholars owed their fame to
correspondence and connection with the students of
more favoured districts.

From Romagna, the Marches of Ancona, and the
Umbrian cities, more captains of adventure than men
of letters or artists swelled the muster-roll of Italian
worthies. We must not, however, forget the unique
place which Urbino, with its refined society, pure
Court, and concourse of accomplished men and women,
occupies in the history of Italian civilisation. The
position of Perugia, again, is not a little singular.
Situated upon the borders of Tuscany and Umbria,
sharing something of the spirit of both districts, over-
shadowed by Papal Rome, yet harbouring such broods
of *bravi* as the Baglioni, conferring a tyranny on
Braccio and the honour of her name on Pietro Van-
nucci, this city offers a succession of picturesque and
perplexing contradictions. Perugia was the centre of
the most religious school of painting which flourished
in the fifteenth century, and also the cradle of the religious drama. For the student of Italian psychology,
very much of serious moment is contained in this
statement.

Rome continued to be rather cosmopolitan than
Italian. The power, wealth, and prestige of the Popes
made their Court a centre ; and men who settled in the
Eternal City, caught something of its greatness. There
is, however, no reason to recapitulate the benefits conferred by ecclesiastical patronage at various times on

fine arts, scholarship, and literature. Rather must it be borne in mind that the Romans who advanced Italian culture, were singularly few. The work of Rome was done almost exclusively by aliens, drawn for the most part from Tuscany and Lombardy.

After Frederick II.'s brilliant reign, the Sicilians shared but little in the intellectual activity of the nation. That this was not due to want of capacity in the people, seems proved by their aptitude for poetry first shown at Frederick's Court, and next by the un-rivalled richness of their dialectical literature, both popular and cultivated. Whether the semi-feudalism which oppressed the Southern provinces, checked the free expansion of mental faculty, admits of question. But it is certainly remarkable that, during the Renaissance, the wide districts of the *Regno* produced so little. Antonio Beccadelli was, indeed, a native of Palermo; but Pontano owned Cerreto for his birthplace. Valla claimed to be a Roman, and Sannazzaro traced his ancestry through Piacenza into Spain. These are the four greatest names of the period when Naples formed a literary centre under the Aragonese dynasty. We have already seen that Naples, though not prolific of native genius, gave specific tone of warmth and liberty to literature. This may be ascribed partly to the free manners, bordering on licence, of the South, and partly to the permanent jealousy subsisting between the Kingdom and the Papacy. The *Novella* produced humorous pictures of society at Florence, facetiæ in Rome, but bitter satires on the clergy at Naples. The scandals of the Church provoked the frigid animosity of Florentines like Machiavelli and

Guicciardini; in Naples they led to Valla's ponderous critique and Sannazzaro's envenomed epigrams. The sensuousness of Poliziano assumed voluptuous fervour in Pontano's lyrics. Lastly, the Platonic mysticism of Florence, and the Peripatetic materialism of Bologna ended in the new philosophy of the Calabrian school. This crowning contribution of the south to Italy, this special glory of the sixteenth century, came less from Naples than from minor cities of Calabria. Telesio of Cosenza, Bruno of Nola, Campanella of Stilo, showed that something of the old Greek speculative genius—the spirit of Parmenides and Pythagoras—still lingered round the shores of Magna Græcia. Just as the Hellenic colonists at Elea and Tarentum anticipated the dawn of Attic philosophy, so did those robust and innovating thinkers shoot the arrows of their speculation forward at the mark of modern science.

It is tempting to pass from this review of the Italian provinces to meditations on a further problem. How far may the qualities of each district have endured from remote antiquity? To what extent may they have determined the specific character of Italian production in the modern age? Did the population of Calabria, we ponder, really inherit philosophical capacity from their Greek ancestors? Dare we connect the Tuscan aptitude for art with that mysterious race who built their cities on Etrurian hill-tops? Can the primitive ethnology of the Ligurian and Iapygian stocks be used to explain the silence of the Genoese Riviera and the Apulian champaign? Is a Teutonic strain discernible in the gross humour of the Mantuan Muse, or in the ballads of Montferrat? It would be easy to multiply these questions. But the whole subject of national development is still too obscure to admit of satisfactory answers.[1] All we can affirm without liability to error, amounts to this ; that Rome never completely fused the divers races of the Italian peninsula, nor obliterated their characteristic differences. After the dissolution of her empire, we find the Italian provinces presenting local types in language, manners, sentiments, and intellectual proclivities. It is not unreasonable, therefore, to conjecture that certain of these differences sprang from the persistence of ethnological qualities, and others from the infusion of fresh blood from without.

The decisive fact of Italian history in all its branches at this epoch is the resurgence of the Latin, or shall we rather say, of the Italic spirit ? The national consciousness survived, though dimly, through the middle ages ; nor had the people suffered shipwreck in the break-up of the Roman power. This was due in no small measure to the fact that the Empire was the creation of this people, and that consequently they were in a sense superior to its fall. Roman civilisation, Roman organisation, Roman institutions, Roman law, were the products of the Italian

[1] Those who are curious in such matters, may be referred to the following works by Giustiniano Nicolucci : *La Stirpe Ligure in Italia,* Napoli, 1864 ; *Sulla Stirpe Iapigica,* Napoli, 1866 ; *Sull' Antropologia della Grecia,* Napoli, 1867 ; *Antropologia dell' Etruria,* Napoli, 1869 ; *Antropologia dell' Lazio,* Napoli, 1873. Also to Luigi Calori's *Del Tipo Brachicefalo negli Italiani odierni,* Bologna, 1868, and a learned article upon this work by J. Barnard Davis in the *Journal of the Anthropological Institute,* Jan. July, 1871. Nicolucci's and Calori's researches lead to opposite results regarding the distribution of brachycephalic skulls in Italy. Nicolucci adopts in its entirety the theory of an Aryan immigration from the North ; Barnard Davis rejects it. It seems to me impossible in our present state of knowledge to draw conclusions from the extremely varied and interesting observations recorded in the treatises cited above.

genius; and when the Roman State declined, the home province suffered a less thorough-going transformation than, to take an instance, either Gaul or Spain. It would be paradoxical to maintain that the imperial despotism exercised a more controlling authority over the outlying provinces than over Italy proper. Yet something of this kind might be advanced, when we reflect upon the self-indulgent majesty of Rome herself; upon the sovereign privileges accorded to the chief Italian cities; upon the prosperity and vastness of Mediolanum, Aquileia and Ravenna. Local ties and local institutions kept a lasting hold upon the ancient no less than the medieval Italian; and long after Rome became the *colluvies omnium gentium* so bitterly described by Juvenal, the country towns, especially in the valley of the Po, retained a vigorous personality. In this respect the relation in which men of state and letters, like the Plinies, stood on one side to the capital and on the other to their birthplace, is both interesting and instructive. The citizens of the provincial *municipia* gloried in the might of Rome. Rome was for them the fulcrum of a lever which set the habitable globe in movement at their touch. Still the Empire existed for the world, while each Italian city claimed the duty and affection of its own inhabitants. When Rome failed, the cosmopolitan authority of the Empire was extended to the Church, or, rather, fell into abeyance between the Church and the resuscitated Empire. Just as the *municipia* flourished beneath the shadow of old Rome, so now the Communes grew beneath the Church and the new Empire. These two creations of the earlier middle ages, though formulated and legalised in Italy, weighed less heavily there than on some other parts of Europe. The Italians resisted imperial authority, and preserved their own local independence. The Northern Emperors were never really strong below the Alps except on sufferance and by the aid of faction. In like manner the Italian burghers tolerated ecclesiastical despotism only in so far as they found it convenient to do so. In spite of Gothic, Lombard, Frankish and German attempts at solidification, the cities succeeded in asserting their autonomy. The Italic stock absorbed the several foreign elements that mingled with it. Vernacular Latin, surviving the decay of literature, repelling the influence of alien dialects, prevailed and was the language of the people.

Notwithstanding this persistence of the antique type, the Italian nation, between the ages of Constantine and Frederick Barbarossa, was intellectually and actually remade. It was not a new nation like the English, French or Germans ; for its life had continued without cessation on the same soil from a period antecedent to the birth of Rome. It had no fund of myth and legend, embodying its memories in popular epical poetry. Instead of Siegfried, Arthur or Roland, it looked back to the Virgilian Aeneas.[1] Still it underwent, together with the rest of Europe, the transformation from Paganism to Christianity. It felt the influences of feudalism, while repelling them with obstinate and finally victorious jealousy. It owed something

---

[1] That the *Æneid* was still the Italian Epos is proved by the many local legends which connected the foundation of cities with the Trojan wars.

to chivalry, though the instincts of the race were rather practical and positive than romantic. It suffered the eclipse of antique culture, and borrowed from its conquerors a tincture of their style in art and literature. When these new Italians found a voice, they spoke in tones which lacked the ring of Roman eloquence. The massy fabric of the Roman syntax was dismembered. And yet their speech had more affinity to Roman style than that of any Northern people. The greatest jurists, ecclesiastics and statesmen of the middle ages, the interpreters of Roman law, the fabricators of solid theological edifices, the founders of the Catholic Church, the champions of the Imperial idea, were Italians, proving by their grasp of practical affairs and by the positive turn they gave to speculative enquiries, a participation in the ancient Latin spirit.[1] Even when it is least classical, the medieval work of the Italian genius betrays this ancestry—in Lombard no less than in Tuscan architecture, in the monumental structure of the Divine Comedy, in the comprehensive digest of the *Summa*, in the rejection of sentimentalism from the tradition of Provençal poetry, in Petrarch's conception of scholarship, in the sensuous realism of Boccaccio.

The Revival of Learning was the acquisition of complete self-consciousness by this new race, which still retained so much of its old temperament. Ill at ease among the customs and ideals of Teutonic tribes; stubbornly refusing to merge their local independence

---

[1] It is enough to mention a few names—Gregory the Great, Lanfranc, S. Anselm, Peter the Lombard, Hildebrand, S. Thomas Aquinas, Accursius, Bartolus—to prove how strong in construction, as opposed to criticism, were the Italian thinkers of the middle ages.

in a kingdom ; struggling against feudalism ; accepting
Chivalry and Gothic architecture as exotics ; without
national legends ; without crusading enthusiasms ; the
Italians were scarcely themselves until they regained
the right use of their energies by contact with the
classics. This makes the Revival of Learning a
national, a patriotic, a dramatic movement. This
gives life and passion to a process which in any other
country, upon any other soil, might have possessed but
little more than antiquarian interest. This, and this
alone, explains the extraordinary fervour with which
the Italians threw themselves into the search, abandoning the new-gained laurels of their modern tongue,
absorbing the intellectual faculties of at least three
generations in the labour of erudition, and emerging
from the libraries of the humanists with a fresh sense
of national unity. At the same moment, and by the
same series of discoveries, they found themselves and
found for Europe the civilisation of the modern world.

It is only by remembering that the Italic races,
clogged by the ruins of the Roman Empire, and
tardily receptive of Teutonic influences, resumed their
natural activity and recognised their vocation in the
Revival of Learning, that we can comprehend the
radical revolution effected in all departments of thought
by this event. In Architecture, the Gothic style,
which had been adopted as it were with repugnance
and imperfectly assimilated, was at once abandoned.
Brunelleschi, Alberti, Bramante, San Gallo, Michelangelo, Palladio, strove, one and all, to effect a right
adjustment of the antique style to modern requirements.
Foreign elsewhere, the so-called Palladian manner is

at home and national in Italy. Sculpture, even earlier
than architecture, took and followed the same hint.
What chiefly distinguishes the work of the Pisan
school from contemporary work of French or German
craftsmen is, that here the manner of Græco-Roman
art has been felt and partly comprehended. Painting,
though more closely connected with Christianity, more
perfectly related to conditions of contemporary life,
owed strength and vigour in great measure to the
same conditions. During the fifteenth century classical
influences continued increasingly to modify the practice
of the strongest masters. In literature, the effect of
the Revival was so decisive as to demand a somewhat
closer investigation.

The awakened consciousness of the Italic people
showed itself first in the creation of a learned literature, imitating as closely as possible in a dead language
the models recovered from ancient Rome. It was not
enough to appropriate the matter of the Latin authors.
Their form had to be assimilated and reproduced.
These pioneers in scholarship believed that the vulgar
tongue, with its divergent dialects, had ever been and
still remained incapable of higher culture. The refined
diction of Cicero and Virgil was for them a separate
and superior speech, consecrated by infallible precedent, and no less serviceable for modern than it formerly had been for antique usage. Recovering the
style of the Augustan age, they thought they should
possess an instrument of utterance adapted to their
present needs, and correlated to the living language of
the people as it had been in the age of Roman greatness. They attacked the easier branches of composi-

tion first. Epistolography and rhetoric assumed the
Roman habit. Then the metres of Horace, Ovid,
and Virgil were analysed and copied. In the inevitable compromise between classical modes of expression and modern necessities of thought, concessions
were always made to the advantage of the former.
The Persons of the Trinity, the saints and martyrs of
the Church, pranked themselves in phrases borrowed
from an obsolete mythology. Christ figured as a hero.
The councils of each petty Commune arrogated the
style of Senate and People. *Condottieri* masqueraded
as Scipio, Hannibal, and Fabius Cunctator. Cecco
and Tonino assumed the graceful garb of Lycidas and
Thyrsis. So fervid was the sense of national resurgence that these literary conventions imposed on men
who ruled the politics of Italy—on statesmen with
subtle insight into practical affairs; on generals with
egotistic schemes to be developed from the play and
counter-play of living interests. When Poliziano ruled
the republic of letters, this acclimatisation of the Latin
classics was complete. Innumerable poems, reproducing the epic, elegiac and lyric measures of the
Romans, poured from the press. Moralists draped
themselves in the Hortensian toga. Orators fulmi-
nated copious floods of Ciceronian rhetoric. Critics
aped Quintilian. Historians stuffed their chapters
with speeches and descriptions modelled upon Livy.
Pastoral and didactic poets made centos from Virgil.
The drama flourished under the auspices of Plautus,
Terence, and Seneca. Preachers were more scrupulous to turn their sentences in florid style than to clinch
a theological argument. Upon the lips of Popes the

God of Sinai or Calvary was Jupiter Optimus Maximus. Even envoys and ambassadors won causes for their States by paragraphs, citations, perorations in the manner of the ancients.

This humanistic ardour at first effected a division between the lettered and unlettered classes. The people clung to their dialects. Educated folk despised all forms of speech but Latin. It seemed as though the national literature might henceforth follow two separate and divergent courses. But with the cessation of the first enthusiasm for antique culture, the claims of vernacular Italian came to be recognised. No other modern nation had produced masterpieces equal to Dante's, Petrarch's, and Boccaccio's. The self-esteem of the Italians could not suffer the exclusion of the Divine Comedy, the *Canzoniere* and the Decameron from the rank of classics. Men of delicate perception, like Alberti and Lorenzo de' Medici, felt that the honours of posterity would fall to the share of those who cultivated and improved their mother tongue. Thus the earlier position of the humanists was recognised as false. Could not their recent acquisitions be carried over to the account and profit of the vernacular? A common Italian language, based upon the Tuscan, but modified for general usage, was now practised in accordance with the rules and objects of the scholars. Upon the briar of the popular literature were grafted the highly-cultivated roses of the classic gardens. It was thus that the masterpieces of *cinque cento* literature came into being —the *Orlando* and the comedies of Ariosto, Machiavelli's histories and Sannazzaro's *Arcadia—*Tasso's

Gerusalemme, and Guarini's *Pastor Fido*, together with
the multitudinous and multifarious work of lesser
craftsmen in prose and verse.

Steeped in classical allusion and reminiscence, the
form of this new literature was modern; but its spirit
was in a true sense Latin. The Italic people had
found their proper mode of self-expression, and proclaimed their hereditary affinities to the makers of
Roman art. In the history of the Italian Renaissance
Greek studies form but an episode. The Platonic
school of Florence, the Venetian labours of Aldus,
exercised a partial and imperfect influence over Italian
culture. They proved more important for Europe at
large than for the peninsula, more valuable in their
remote than their immediate consequences. With the
whole of classic literature to choose from, this instinctive preference of Latin illustrates the point I am engaged in demonstrating—namely, that in Italy the
Revival of Learning was a resurgence of the Italic
genius modified and formed by Roman influence.
True to their ancestry, the Italians assimilated Roman
types, and left the Greek aside.

If we pause to consider the qualities of the Roman
spirit in art and literature, we shall see in how real a
sense the modern people reproduced them and remained
within their limits. Compared with the Hellenic and
Teutonic races, the Romans were not myth-making,
nor in the sincerest sense poetical. In like manner the
Italians are deficient on the side of legend and romance.
This defect has been insisted on in the preceding
volumes, where the practical and positive quality of
Italian poetry, its leaning to realism and abstinence

from visionary flights of the imagination, have more
than once been pointed out. Roman literature was
composite and cultured, rather than simple or spontaneous. The Roman epic was literary; based on
antecedent models, and confined within the sphere of
polished imitation. The Roman Comedy and Tragedy
were copies of the Greek. In these highest departments of art the Roman poets gave new form to
foreign matter, and infused their national spirit into
works that might be almost ranked with free translations. The same is true of their lyrics. Even the
metres in all these species are appropriated. The
Italians in like manner invented but little. They
borrowed from every source—from the Arthurian and
Carolingian romances, from Provençal love-poetry,
and lastly in copious quantities from Roman literature.
But they stamped their own genius on the materials
adopted, retouched the form, and modified the sentiment, converting all they took to their own genuine
uses. In this respect the Italians, though apparently
so uncreative, may be called more original than the
Romans. Their metrical systems, to begin with—the
sonnet, the octave stanza, and *terza rima*—are their own.
Their touch upon Teutonic legend is more characteristic than the Roman touch on Greek mythology.
Dante and Petrarch deal more freely with Provençal
poetry than Horace or Catullus with the lyrics of their
predecessors. In the matter of dramatic composition,
the Italians stand in much the same relation to the
Romans as the Romans to the Greeks; and this may
be repeated with reference to elegiac and pastoral
poetry, and some minor species. The Italic race, in

its later as in its earlier development, seems here, also, satisfied with form-giving and delicacy of execution.

If we turn to the indigenous and characteristic qualities of Roman literary genius, we find these reappearing with the force of spontaneity among the Italians. First of all may be reckoned the strong love of country-life which lends undying freshness to Catullus, Horace, and the poetical episodes of Lucretius. This is a no less marked feature of Italian literature. The very best poetry of the humanists is that which deals with villa-life among the Tuscan hills, beside the bay of Naples, or on the shores of Garda. The purest passages in the *Novelle*, the least intolerable descriptions in the treatises of the essayists, are those which celebrate the joys of field and wood and garden. The most original products of the Italian stage are the *Aminta* and the *Pastor Fido*, penetrated through and through with a real love of the country—not with any feeling for Nature in her sublimer and wilder aspects, but with the old Saturnian pathos and fresh clinging loveliness of nature made the friend of man and humanised by labour. The tears shed by Alberti over the rich fields of autumn, as he gazed upon them from some Tuscan summit, seem to have fallen like a dew of real emotion upon the driest places of a pastoral literature which is too often conventional.

Resuming the main thread of the argument, it may be said that the Italians also shared the Roman partiality for didactic poetry. The Latin poems of Poliziano, Vida, and Fracastoro, together with the Italian work of Alamanni, Rucellai, and other authors,

sufficiently prove this. Nor does it seem to me that
we need suppose these essays in a style of inevitable
weariness to have been merely formal imitations of the
ancients. The delight with which they were first
received and even now sometimes are read in Italy, and
the high reputation they have won for their authors,
show that there is something in the Italian geniussym-
pathetic to their spirit. One department of their Roman
heritage was left uncultivated by the Italians. They
produced no really great satire ; but, on the other
hand, that indigenous satiric humour, inclining to caricature and obscenity, which found vent in the fescennine songs of Roman festivals and triumphs, endured
without material change through all modifications of
the national life. The earliest monuments of the vernacular literature afford instances of its popularity
throughout the middle ages. It gave a special quality
to the Florentine Carnival ; it assumed high literary
form in Lorenzo's *Canti* and Berni's burlesque *Capitoli* ;
it flourished on the quays of Naples, and sheltered at
Rome under the protection of Pasquino.

Leaving pure literature aside, we may trace the
Latin ancestry of the Italians in their strong forensic
bias. Just as the Forum was the centre of Roman, so
was the Piazza the centre of Italian life. The declam-
atory emphasis that spoils much Latin prose and verse
for Northern ears, sounds throughout Italian literature.
Their writers too easily assume a rhetorical tone, and
substitute sonorousness of verbiage for solid matter or
sound feeling. The recitations of the Romans find an
analogue in the Italian Academies. The colloquial
taint of Roman philosophical discussion is repeated in

the moral diatribes of the humanists. But with equal justice we might urge that the practical and legal qualities of the Latin race, and its powerful organising faculty, survived, and found expression in the modern nation. The Italians, as we have already said, were the greatest Churchmen, Statesmen, and Jurists of medieval Europe. They created the Papacy. They formulated the conception of the Empire. They preserved, explained, and taught Roman law. But this element was already worked out and exhausted at the close of the medieval period. We find it in abeyance during the Renaissance. The political vigour, the martial energy, the cohesive force, the indomitable will of the Romans, have clearly deserted their Italian inheritors. There is a massive architecture, as of masonry, in Roman writing, which Italian almost always misses.

If it were permissible to venture here upon a somewhat bold hypothesis, we might ask whether the Italic races now displayed themselves as they might have been without the centralising and controlling genius of Rome ? In the history of the Italian peninsula, can we regard the ascendancy of Rome as a gigantic episode ? Rome bound the various tribes together in a common system, formed one language, and used Italy as the throne of world-wide empire. But Rome's empire passed, and the tribes remained—indelibly stamped, it is true, with her mark, and subsequently modified by a succession of intrusive incidents—yet yielding to the world in a new form a second crop of flowers and fruitage similar to that which they had borne for Rome. It will not do to press these speculations. They suggest themselves when we observe that, what the Italians lacked in the Renaissance was precisely what Rome, or the Latin confederacy, gave to Italy in the ancient days of her supremacy. It is as though the great Saturnian mother, exhausted by the production of Rome and all that Rome implied through Empire and through Papacy for Europe, had little force left but for amenities and subtleties in modern literature. To the masonry of Rome succeeds the filigree work' of the *cinque cento.*

There is no mistaking the positive, materialistic, quality possessed by the Italians in common with their Latin ancestors. This, after all is said, constitutes the true note of their art and literature. Realism, preferring the tangible and concrete to the visionary and abstract, the defined to the indefinite, the sensuous to the ideal, determines the character of their genius in all its manifestations. We find it even in the Divine Comedy. Dante's pictures appeal to our eyes ; his songs of angels and cries of damned souls reach our ears ; he makes us shrink with physical loathing from the abominations of Malebolge, and feel upon our foreheads the cool morning wind of Purgatory. His imaginary world can be mapped out ; his journey through it has been traced and measured, inch by inch, and hour by hour. The same realism determined the speculation of the Italians, deflecting it from metaphysics to problems of practical life. Again it leavened their religion. We find it in S. Catherine's visions, in the stigmata of S. Francis, in the miracle of Bolsena. Under its influence the dogmas of the Church assumed a kind of palpability. It was against Italian sensuousness that the finer spiritual perceptions of the Teutonic races rose in revolt; and the Italians, who had transmitted their own religious forms to Europe, could not understand the point at issue. Feeble or insufficient as we may judge this realism in the regions of pure thought or pious feeling, it was supremely powerful in art. It enabled the Italians so to apprehend the mysteries of the faith, and so to assimilate the classic myths, as to find for both a form of beauty in sculpture and in painting. Had they inclined more to the abstract or to the visionary, Christian art would have remained impossible. Had they been less simply sensuous, they might perhaps have shrunk from pagan legends, or have failed to touch them with the right sincerity. How ill these legends fared at the hands of contemporary Teutonic artists, is notorious. In the realm of literature the same quality gave to Petrarch's treatment of chivalrous love a new substantiality. It animated Boccaccio, and through his influence created a literature of fiction, indescribably rich in objective realism and spontaneous passion. Ariosto owed to it the incomparable brilliance of his pictures. And, since such sensuousness has perforce its evil side, we find it, in the last resort, no longer clothing unsubstantial thoughts with forms of beauty, lending reality to the poet's visions, or humanising the austerities of faith, but frankly and simply subordinating its powers to a debased imagination. The Italian sensuousness too often degenerates into mere sensuality in the period of our enquiry. Nor is this the only defect of the quality. When we complain that the Italians are deficient in the highest tragic imagination, that their feeling for nature lacks romance, or that none but their rarest works of art attain sublimity, we are but insisting on the realistic bias which inclined them to things tangible, palpable, experienced, compassable by the senses. How much of tragedy is due to horror the soul alone can gauge; how much of romance depends upon a sense of mystery and unexplored capacities in natural things ; how much of the sublime consists of incorporeal vagueness, need not here be insisted on. The sensuousness of the Italians, simpler and less finely tempered with spiritual substance than that of the Greeks, while it gave them so much of serene beauty and intelligible form, denied them those high and rare touches which the less evenly balanced genius of the Northern races can command at will. The poverty of imaginative suggestion in their lyrical and dramatic poetry has been already indicated. We feel this even in their music. The most adorable melodies, poured forth like nightingale songs in the great schools of the eighteenth century, owe their perfection to purity of outline ; their magic depends on a direct appeal to sensibility. There is not in them 'more than the ear discovers.' They are not, to quote Sir Thomas Browne again, 'a hieroglyphical and shadowed lesson of the whole world and creatures of God.' Palestrina and Stradella, Pergolese and Salvator Rosa, move in a region less mystical and pregnant with accumulated meaning than that which belongs to Bach and Beethoven.

The intellectual medium formed in Italy upon the dissolution of the middle ages was irreligious and indifferent; highly refined and highly cultivated ; instinctively æsthetic and superbly gifted, but devoid of moral earnestness or patriotic enthusiasm, of spiritual passion or political energy. Society, enslaved, disfranchised, and unwarlike, was composed of peasants and artisans, sleek citizens, effeminated nobles, courtiers and scholars of a hundred types, monks and clergy of manifold variety and almost incalculable multitude, despots more or less successful in their arts of imposition and seduction, and the countless dependents on the wants and whims and vices of this motley population. Among the last may be reckoned artists of all but the first rank, men of letters, parasites and captains of adventure, courtesans and Abbés, pamphleteers and *bravi*, orators and secretaries. Outside the universities, the factories and the market-place, there were few callings that could be reckoned honourable or honest, independent or respectable. Over the rest hung the shadow of servitude and corruption, of ecclesiastical depravity and private debauchery, of political stagnation and haughty patronage. Still the qualities of intellectual sagacity, determined volition, and a certain æsthetical good taste, were all but universal. We find them in such works as Cellini's biography, Lorenzino de' Medici's apology, and the memoirs of his murderer— to mention only documents where the last-named quality might well have been absent. Even the lowest instruments of public or private profligacy maintained an independence face to face with art, and recognised a higher law than their employer's in the duties imposed upon them by the ideal after which they strove as men of letters, painters or the like. We trace this loyal service and artistic freedom even in Pietro Aretino.

A literature, corresponding to this medium, of necessity arose. It was a literature of form and style, of pleasure and diversion, without intensity of passion, earnestness of purpose, or profundity of thought. It could boast no Shakspere, no Pindar, no Dante, no Descartes. The prevailing types which it developed, were idyllic, descriptive, melodramatic, narrative, elegiac, sentimental, burlesque, and licentious. Poliziano, Sannazzaro, Lorenzo de' Medici, Pulci, the writers of sonnets and *Capitoli*, the novelists and the satirists, are each and all of them related by no superficial tie to Boccaccio. He is the morning star of this multifarious and brilliant band of artist-authors, until the moment when Ariosto rises above the horizon, and the *cinque cento* finds adequate expression in the *Orlando Furioso*. In that poem the qualities by which the age is characterised, are concentrated, and the advance in artistic faculty and feeling since the period of the Decameron is manifested. Amid the many writers of the century we seek in vain a true philosopher. We have, instead, to content ourselves with the ethical dissertations of the humanists ; with sketches like the *Cortegiano*, the *Galateo*, the *Governo della Famiglia*; with erudite fancies like the speculations of Ficino, or the scholastic triflings of Pico della Mirandola. Yet out of the very indifferentism of the age philosophy will spring. Pomponazzi formulates the current materialism. It remains for Telesio, Campanella, Bruno, Galileo to found the modern scientific method. Meanwhile, the political agitations of despotisms and republics alike, and the diplomatic relations of so many petty States, have stimulated observation and developed the powers of analysis. Therefore the most vigorous and virile product of this literature is such work as the *Principe* and *Discorsi* of Machiavelli, the *Ricordi* of Guicciardini, together with the histories and reflective treatises on statecraft published by the statists of their school.

The absence of seriousness in the literature of the golden age is striking to a Northern student. It seems to have been produced for and by men who had lost their ethical and political conscience, and had enthroned an æsthetical conscience in its room. Their religious indifference is deadlier than atheism. Their levity is worse than sarcasm. They fulfil the epigram of Tacitus, who wrote: *corrumpere et corrumpi sæculum vocant.* Yet no one has the vigour to be angry. It is difficult to detect the true note of satire in their criticism of society. Ariosto is playful, Aretino scurrilous, Alamanni peevish, Folengo atrabilious. The purely religious compositions of the period lack simplicity and sincerity. The *Sacre Rappresentazioni* are sentimental and romantic. The Christian epics of the Latin poets are indescribably frigid. The *Laudi* are either literary like Lorenzo's, or hysterical like Benivieni's praise of Christian madness. The impertinent biographies of Aretino pass muster for genuinely pious work with Vittoria Colonna. It is only in some heartfelt utterance of the aged Michelangelo, in the holy life of a S. Antonino, or the charity of Luca della Robbia's mission to young Boscoli, or the fervour of Savonarola's sermons, that here and there the chord of real religious feeling vibrates. Philosophy entrenches herself, where she is strongest, in negation—in Valla's negation of any ethical standard

superior to sensuous hedonism, in Pomponazzi's negation of immortality, in Machiavelli's negation of Providence. So complete an antithesis to the medieval
ground of thought was necessary ; and its results for
the future of science are incontestable. But at the
moment it meant a withdrawal from spiritual interests,
an insistance on the material side of human life, which
was correlated to religious indifference and social dissolution.

The drama abounds in comedies and masques, of
wonderful variety and great artistic beauty. But
there is no tragedy worthy of the name. And the
tragic element, as distinguished from romance and
pathos, is conspicuous by its absence in the novels of
the period. Lyrical poets prefer the conscious shams
of Petrarchism to any genuine utterance of emotion.
The gravity of La Casa's sonnets, wrenched from an
uneasy and unwilling conscience, the sublimity of
Michelangelo's Platonic mysticism, the patriotic indignation of Guidiccioni's laments for Italy enslaved
and sunk in sensual sloth, must rank as luminous exceptions. In the romantic epic, chivalry, the ideal of
an earlier age, is turned to gentle ridicule. Honour is
sneered at or misunderstood. The absurd, the marvellous, the licentious are mingled in a form of incomparable artistic suavity. Tasso's graver epic
belongs to another epoch. Trissino's heroic poem is
unreadable. Like the tragedies of the scholars, it
lacks life and stands in no relation to the spirit of the
age.

Over the whole art and literature of the epoch is
shed an agreeable light of quietude and acquiescence,

a glow of contentment and well-being, which contrasts strangely with the tragic circumstances of a nation crumbling into an abyss of ruin. It is not precisely the *bourgeois* felicity of Boccaccio, but a tranquillity that finds choicest expression in the painted idylls of Giorgione and the written idylls of Sannazzaro. Its ultimate ideal is the Golden Age, when no restraints were placed on natural inclination, and no ambition ruffled the spirit rocked in halcyon ease. This prevailing mood of artists and writers was capable of sensuous depth, as in the *Baiæ* of Pontano. It was capable of refined irony, as in the smile of Ariosto. It was capable of broad laughter, as in the farce of Bibbiena. It was capable of tenderness, as in the *Ballate* of Poliziano. It was capable of cynical licentiousness, as in Aretino's *Ragionamenti*, and the Florentine *Capitoli*. But it was incapable of tragic passion, lyrical rapture, intensity, sublimity, heroism. What ears would there have been in Italy for Marston's prologue to *Antonio and Mellida* or for Milton's definition of the poet's calling? The men who made this literature and those with whom they lived, for whom they wrote, were well-bred, satisfied with inactivity, open at all pores to pleasure, delighting in the refinements of tact and taste, but at the same time addicted to gross sensuality of word and deed. The world was over for them. The arenas of energy were closed. About the future life they entertained a suave and genial scepticism, a delicate *peut-être* of blended affirmation and negation, lightly worn, which did not interrupt the observance of ceremonial piety. They loved their villa, like Flamminio, Ficino, Bembo, all the poets of

Benacus. They spent their leisure between a grove
of laurels and a study. They met in courtly circles
for polite discourse and trifling dissertation, with no in-
fluencing passion, no speculative enthusiasm, no insight into mysteries deeper than the subtleties of poetry
and art. Not one of them, amid the crash and conflict
of three nations on their soil, exclaimed in darkness
Imus, imus præcipites! When the woes of Italy
touched them with a shade of melancholy, they sought
relief in pastimes or in study. Cinthio, prefacing his
novels with the horrors of the Sack of Rome, Bargagli
using Siena's agony as introduction to his love-ro-
mances, are parables of what was happening in the
world of fact and feeling. The portrait of Castiglione,
clear-browed, sedate, intelligent, humane, expresses the
best men of the best moment in that age. The *Aminta*
is their dream-world, modelled on reality. Vida's
apostrophe to *pulcherrima Roma* utters their sentiment of nationality.

There is a beautiful side to all this. It is the
idyllic ideal of life, revealed in Titian's picture of the
Three Ages of Man, the ideal which results in golden
and consummate art, tranquillised to euthanasia, purged
of all purpose more earnest than may be found in
melodies played beside a fountain in the fields by
boys to listening girls, on flute or viol. For this
ideal a great future was in store, when the animating motive of idyllic melody expressed itself in the
opera music of the eighteenth century, and Italy gave
the last of her imperishable gifts, a new and perfect
art of song, to Europe. But there is also an ugly
side to all this. The ultimate corruption of the age—

in its absence of energy, its avoidance of serious endeavour, its courtly adulation, its ruffianism, servility,
cynicism and hypocrisy—is incarnated in Aretino.
Here the vices of the Italian Renaissance show their
cloven hoofs. Through the orange and laurel
bowers, flooded with Tintoretto's golden sunlight,
grins a bestial all-devouring satyr, a satyr far less innocent or gentle than Greek poets feigned, with a
wolf's jaws as well as a goat's legs. And in Aretino
is already foreshadowed Baffo, the prurient and porcine
Caliban of verse, more barbarously bestial than Venetian Casanova. Meanwhile amid apparent civility of
manner, the violent crimes of a corrupt and servile
race were frequent. Poisoning and secret assassination, acts of personal vengeance and the employment
of hired cut-throats, rendered life unsafe in that idyllic
Italy.

The historian of this epoch, though he feels its
splendour and would fain bless, finds himself forced to
insist upon the darker details of the subject. The
triumphal pæan of his opening pages ends, too often
for his sympathy, in dissonance and wailing echoes.
Yet it would be unjust and unscientific to close on any
note of lamentation, when the achievements of the
eldest-born of Europe's daughters stand arrayed before
him. It has often been said that the Renaissance
presents an insoluble problem. Twy-natured and indeterminate, the spirit of the age has been likened to
the Sphinx, whose riddle finds no Œdipus. But this
language is at best rhetorical. The anomalies and
contradictions of a period to which we owe so much
of our spiritual and intellectual force, are due to its

transitional character. The middle ages were closed. The modern world was scarcely formed. This interval was chosen for the re-birth of the Italian spirit. On the Italians fell the complicated and perplexing task of modulating from the one phase to the other. And, as I have attempted to explain, the Italians were a peculiar people. They had resisted the Teutonic impact of the medieval past; but they had failed to prepare themselves for the drama of violence and bloodshed which the feudal races played out on the plains of Lombardy. When we say that it was their duty to have formed themselves into a nation like the French, we are criticising their conduct from a modern point of view. Experience proved that their policy of municipal independence was a kind of suicide. But the instincts of clanship, slowly transmuted through feudal institutions into a monarchical system, had from time immemorial been absent in Italy. Rome herself had never gathered the Italian cities into what we call a nation. And when Rome, the world's head, fell, the municipalities of Italy remained, and the Italian people sprang to life again by contact with their irrecoverable past.[1] Then, though the Church swayed Europe from Italian soil, she had nowhere less devoted subjects than in Italy. Proud as the Italians had been of the Empire, proud as they now were of the Church, still neither the Roman Empire nor the Roman Church imposed on the Italian character. Pondering on the unique circumstances of this new nation, unorganised like her sisters, conscious of an immense past and a

---

[1] ' Roma, caput mundi,' is a significant phrase. It marks the defect of Italian nationality as distinguished from cosmopolitan empire.

persistent vitality, shrewdly apathetic to the religious enthusiasms of the younger races, yet obliged to temporise and acquiesce and cloak indifference with hypocrisy, we are brought to feel, though we may not fully explain, the inevitableness of many distracting discords in what was still an incomplete phase of national existence.

As a final consideration, after reviewing the anomalies of Italian society upon the dissolution of the Middle Ages, we are fully justified in maintaining that the race which had produced Machiavelli and Columbus, Campanella and Galileo—that is to say, the firmest pioneers and freest speculators of the dawning modern age—was capable, left but alone, of solving its own moral contradictions by some virile effort. Pioneering energy, speculative boldness, virility of effort (however masked by pedantry and purism, by the urbanities and amenities of polite culture, by the baseness of egotism and the immorality of social decadence), were the deepest notes of the bewildering age which forms our theme. But this freedom from interference, this luck of being left alone, was just what the Italians could never get. The catastrophes of several successive invasions, followed by the petrifying stagnation of political and ecclesiastical tyranny, checked their natural evolution and suspended their intellectual life, before the fruit-time had succeeded to the flower-time of the Renaissance. The magnificent audacity of their impulse fell checked in mid-career. Their achievement might be likened to an arch ascending bravely from two mighty piers, whereon the keystone of completion was not set.

When all her deities were decayed or broken, Italy
still worshipped beauty in fine art and literary form.
When all her energies seemed paralysed, she still pursued her intellectual development with unremitting
ardour. This is the true greatness of those fifty years
of glorious achievement and pitiful humiliation, during
which the Italians, like Archimedes in his Syracusan
watch-tower, turned deaf ears to combatant and con-
queror, intent on problems that involved the future
destinies of man. The light of the classics had fallen
on their pathway at the close of the middle ages. The
leading of that light they still pursued, as though they
had been consecrated to the service of a god before
unknown in modern Europe. Their first and foremost gift to nations who had scourged and slain them,
was a new and radiant conception of humanity. This
conception externalised itself in the creation of a
common mental atmosphere, in the expression of the
modern spirit by fine art and literature, in the diffusion
of all that is contained for us in culture. They
wrought, thought, painted, carved and built with the
antique ideal as a guiding and illuminative principle
in view. This principle enabled them to elevate and
harmonise, to humanise and beautify the coarser elements existing in the world around them. What they
sought and clung to in the heritage of the ancients,
was the divinity of form—the form that gives grace,
loveliness, sublimity to common flesh and blood in
art; style to poetry and prose; urbanity to social
manners; richness and elegance. to reflections upon
history and statecraft and the problems of still infan-
tine science. Lastly, whatsoever is implied in the

double formula of the discovery of man and of the world—the resuscitation of learning by scholars; the positive study of human motives and action by historians; the new philosophy prepared by speculators of the Southern school; the revival of mathematical and astronomical researches after a sound method; the endeavour to base physical science on experiment and observation; the exploration of the western hemisphere by navigators—all this we owe to the Italians of the fifteenth and sixteenth centuries.

We may allow that their execution of a task so arduous and beneficial was accomplished under conditions of social corruption and political apathy, which somewhat dimmed the lustre of their triumph. It may be admitted that they failed, even in their own domains of art and poetry, to realise the highest possible ideals; and we may ascribe this failure partly to their moral feebleness, which contradicts our sense of manhood. Still these are no reasons why we should not pay the homage due to their achievement. The deepest interest in the Italian Renaissance, the warmest recognition of its services to modern Europe, are compatible with a just conviction that the tone of that epoch is not to be imitated. Such imitation would, in point of fact, be not merely anachronistic but impossible. To insist on anything so obvious would be impertinent to common sense, were we not from time to time ad monished from the chair of criticism that a new Gospel, founded on the principles of the Renaissance, has been or is being preached in England. Criticism, however, is fallible; and in this matter its mistake is due to the English incapacity for understanding that scientific curiosity may be engaged, without didactic objects, on moral and historical problems. We cannot extract from the Renaissance a body of ethical teaching, an ideal of conduct, or a discipline of manners, applicable to the altered conditions of the nineteenth century. But we can exercise our ingenuity upon the complex questions which it offers ; we can satisfy the passion of enquiry, which prompts men to examine, analyse, reflect upon, and reappropriate the past. We can attempt to depict the period, as we recover a phase of our own youth by recollection, extenuating nothing, setting nothing down in malice, using the results of our researches for no purposes of propaganda, but aiming, in so far as our capacity sustains us, at the simple truth about it.

For a student animated with this passion of curiosity, the Italian Renaissance, independently of any sympathies he may have formed for the Italian people, or any fascination which an age and race so picturesque may exercise, must be a subject worthy of most patient contemplation. As we grow in knowledge, corroborating and confirming those views about the world and man which originated with the new direction given to enquiry in the fifteenth century, we learn with ever stronger certainty, that as there is no interruption in the order of nature, so the history of civilisation is continuous and undivided. In the sequence of events, in the growth of human character, no arbitrary freaks, no flaws of chance, are recognisable. Age succeeds to age ; nations rise and perish ; new elements are introduced at intervals into the common stock ; the drama is not played out with one set of actors. But, in spite of all change, and though we cannot as yet demonstrate the law of evolution in details, we are reasonably convinced that the development of human energy and intellectual consciousness has been carried on without cessation from the earliest times until the present moment, and is destined to unbroken progress through the centuries before us. History, under the influence of this conception, is rapidly ceasing to be the record of external incidents, of isolated moments, or of brilliant episodes in the epic of humanity. We have learned to look upon it as the biography of man. To trace the continuity of civilisation through the labyrinths of chance and error and suspended energy, apparent to a superficial glance or partial knowledge, but on closer observation and a wider sweep of vision found to disappear, is the highest aim of the historian. The germ of this new notion of man's life upon our planet was contained in the cardinal intuition of the Renaissance, when the ancient and the modern worlds were recognised as one. It assumed the dignity of organised speculation in the German philosophies of history, and in the positive philosophy of Auguste Comte. It has received its most powerful corroboration from recent physical discoveries, and has acquired firmer consistency in the Darwinian speculation. Whether we approach the problem from a theological, a positive, or a purely scientific point of view, the force of the hypothesis remains unaltered. We are obliged to think of civilised humanity as one.

In this unbroken sequence of events, a place of prime importance must be assigned to the Renaissance; and the Italian race at that moment must be regarded, for a short while at least, as the protagonist of the universal drama. The first stage of civilisation is by common consent assigned to the Eastern empires of remote antiquity ; the second to the Hellenic system of civic liberty and intellectual energy; the third to Roman organisation. During the third period a new spiritual force was evolved in Christianity, and new factors were introduced into Europe by the immigration of the Northern races. The fourth historical period is occupied by the Church and feudalism, the first inheriting Roman organisation, the second helping to constitute the immigrant races into new nationalities. The fifth great epoch is the emancipation of modern Europe from medieval influences. We may be said to live in it; for though the work of liberation has in large measure been accomplished, no new social principle or comprehensive system has yet supervened. Three movements in the process can, however, be discerned ; and these are respectively known by the names of Renaissance, Reformation, Revolution. It was in the first of these three stages that Italy determined the course of civilisation. To neglect the work achieved by Italy, before the other nations of Europe had emerged from feudalism, is tantamount to dropping a link indispensable to the strength and cohesion of the whole chain.

Accustomed to regard the Church as a political member of their own confederation, and withdrawn from the feudal system by the action of their communes, the Italians were specially fitted to perform their task. The conditions under which they lived as the inheritors of Rome, obliged them to look backward instead of forward; and from this necessity emerged the Revival of Learning, which not only restored the interrupted consciousness of human unity, but supplied the needful starting-point for a new period of intellectual growth. The connection between the study of classical literature, scientific investigation, and Biblical criticism, has been already insisted on in this work. From the Renaissance sprang the Reformation, veiling the same spirit in another form, before the Church bethought herself of quenching the new light in Italy. Without the sceptical and critical industry of the Italians; without their bold explorations in the fields of philosophy, theology and political science; without their digging round the roots of human knowledge; without their frank disavowal of past medieval transcendentalism; neither the German Reformation nor the advance of speculative thought in France, Holland and England, would have been possible.

To pursue the subject further is not necessary. How the Revolution was linked to the Reformation by the intermediate action of Holland, England and America; and how the European peoples, educated after the type designed by Italian humanists, formed their literatures, built up philosophies, and based positive enquiry on solid foundations, are matters too well known and have too often been already noted to need illustration. It is enough for a student of the Renaissance to have suggested that the peculiar circumstances and sympathies of the Italians, at a certain moment of this modern evolution, forced and enabled them to do what was imperatively demanded for its after progress. That they led the van of liberation; that, like the Jews and Greeks, their predecessors, they sacrificed their independence in the very triumph of achievement ; are claims upon our everlasting gratitude.   This lends the interest of romance or drama to the doleful tale of depredation and enslavement which concludes the history of the Italian Renaissance.

APPENDICES.

APPENDIX I.

(See above, chapter xi.)

Italian Comic Prologues.

THE current of opinion represented by the prologues to Italian comedies deserves some further illustration.

Bibbiena, in the *Calandra*, starts with what is tantamount to an apology for the modern style of his play. 'Voi sarete oggi spettatori d' una nuova commedia intitolata Calandra, in prosa non in versi, moderna non antica, volgare non latina.' He then explains why he has chosen the language of his age and nation, taking great pains to combat learned prejudices in favour of pure Latin. At the close he defends himself from the charge of having robbed from Plautus, confessing at the same time that he has done so, and thus restricting his earlier boast of novelty to the bare point of diction.

In the prose *Cassaria*, which was contemporaneous with the *Calandra*, Ariosto takes the same line:

> Nuova commedia v' appresento, piena
>> Di vari giuochi ; che nè mai latine
>> Nè greche lingue recitarno in scena.
> Parmi vedere che la più parte incline
>> A riprenderla, subito ch' ho detto
>> Nuova, senza ascoltarne mezzo o fine :
> Chè tale impresa non gli par suggetto
>> Delli moderni ingegni, e solo stima
>> Quel, che gli antiqui han detto, esser perfetto.

He then proceeds to defend his own audacity, which really consists in no more than the attempt to remodel a Latin play. In the prologue to the prose *Suppositi* Ariosto follows a different course, apologising for his *contaminatio* of Plautus and Terence by the argument that they borrowed from Menander and Apollodorus.

Machiavelli in the prologue to the *Clizia* says that history repeats itself. What happened at Athens, happened yesterday at Florence. He has, therefore, laid his scene at Florence : 'perchè Atene è rovinata, le vie, le piazze, i luoghi non vi si riconoscono.' He thus justifies the modern *rifacimento* of an ancient comedy conducted upon classical principles.

Gelli in the *Sporta* reproduces Ariosto's defence for the *Suppositi*. If he has borrowed from Plautus and Terence, they borrowed from Menander. Then follows an acute description of comedy as it should be : 'La commedia, per non essere elleno altro ch' uno specchio di costumi della vita privata e civile sotto una imaginazione di verità, non tratto da altro che di cose, che tutto 'l giorno accaggiono al viver nostro, non ci vedrete riconoscimenti di giovani o di fanciulle che oggidì non ne occorre.'

Cecchi in the *Martello* says he has followed the *Asinaria* :

> Rimbustata a suo dosso, e su compostovi
> (Aggiungendo e levando, come meglio
> Gli è parso ; e ciò, non per corregger Plauto,
> Ma per accomodarsi ai tempi e agli uomini
> Che ci sono oggidì) questa sua favola.

In the *Moglie* and the *Dissimili* he makes similar statements, preferring ' la opinione di quelli maestri migliori ' (probably Ariosto and Machiavelli), and also :

> perchè il medesimo
> Ved ' egli che hanno fatto li più nobili
> Comici che vi sieno.

Lorenzino de' Medici in his prologue to the *Aridosio* tells the audience they must not be angry if they see the usual lover, miser, and crafty servant, ' e simil cose delle quali non può uscire chi vuol fare commedie.'

These quotations may suffice. If we analyse them, it is clear that at first the comic playwrights felt bound to apologise for writing in Italian ; next, that they had to defend themselves against the charge of plagiarism ; and in the third place that, when the public became accustomed to Latinising comedies in the vulgar tongue, they undertook the more difficult task of justifying the usage which introduced so many obsolete, monotonous, and anachronistic elements into dramatic literature. At first they were afraid to innovate even to the slight extent of adaptation. At last they were driven to vindicate their artificial forms of art on the score of prescribed usage. But when Cecchi and Lorenzino de' Medici advanced these pleas, which seem to indicate a desire on the part of their public for a more original and modern comedy, the form was too fixed to be altered. Aretino, boldly breaking with tradition, had effected nothing. Il Lasca, laughing at the learned unrealities of his contemporaries, was not strong enough to burst their fetters. Nothing was left for the playwrights but to go on cutting down the old clothes of Plautus and Terence to fit their own backs—as Cecchi puts it.

APPENDIX II.

(See above, chapter xiv.)

*Passages translated from Folengo and Berni, which illustrate
the Lutheran opinions of the Burlesque Poets.*

ORLANDINO VI. 41.

' To Thee, and not to any Saint I go ;
How should their mediation here succeed ?
The Canaanitish woman, well I know,
Prayed not to James or Peter in her need :
She had recourse to only Thee ; and so,
Alone with Thee alone, I hope and plead.
Thou know'st my weal and woe ; make plain the way,
Thou, Lord, for to none other dare I pray.

' Nor will I wander with the common kind,
Who, clogged with falsehood and credulity,
Make vows to Gothard or to Roch, and mind
I know not what Saint Bovo more than Thee ;
Because some friar, as cunning as they 're blind,
Offering to Moloch, his dark deity,
Causes Thy Mother, up in heaven, a Queen,
To load with spoil his sacrifice obscene.

' Beneath the husk of piety these friars
Make a huge harvest for themselves to hold ;
The alms on Mary's altar quench the fires
Of impious greed in priests who burn for gold :
Another of their odious laws requires
That year by year my faults should still be told
To a monk's ears :—I who am young and fair !—
He hears, and straightway flogs his shoulders bare :

'He flogs himself because he feels the sting
My words, impregnate with lasciviousness,
Send to his heart ; so sharp are they, and wring
His lust so nearly, that, in sore distress,
With wiles and wheedling ways, he seeks to bring
Me in his secret will to acquiesce ;
And here confessors oft are shown to be
More learned in pimping than divinity.

'Therefore, O Lord, that know'st the heart of man,
And seest Thy Church in these same friars' grasp,
To Thee with contrite soul, as sinners can,
Who hope their faults forgiven, my hands I clasp ;
And if, my God, from this mad ocean
Thou'lt save me, now, as at my latest gasp,
I vow that never more will I trust any
Who grant indulgences for pound or penny.'

Such prayers, chock-full of rankest heresy,
Prayed Berta ; for she was a German wench :
In those days, you must know, theology
Had changed herself to Roman, Flemish, French ;
But I've my doubts that in the end she'll be
Found squatting *à la* Moor on some Turk's bench,
Because Christ's seamless coat has so been tattered
Its rags have long since to the winds been scattered.

ORLANDINO VIII. 22.

'I do not marvel much,' Rainero cried,
'If the lambs suffer scandals and the fold
Be ruined by these wolves of lust and pride,
Foemen to God beneath God's flag enrolled :
But for the present need I'll soon provide—
Ho ! to my presence drag yon Prior bold !'
Sharp were the words ; the sheriff in a skurry,
He and his serjeants to the convent hurry,

Drag forth that *monstr' horrendum* from his lair,
And lead him straight to Rayner on his throne ;
Folk run together at the brute to stare,
You never saw an ox so overgrown ;

And not a man but stops his nostrils there
From the foul stench of wine, sweat, filth unknown ;
One calls him Bacchus, and Silenus one,
Or hog, or bag of beastliness, or tun.

'Stand forth before my face,' Rainero cries,
'Thou man of God, prophet most reverend !
I know that thou in all the lore art wise,
Of things divine, and what the stars portend ;
With thee the freedom of S. Peter lies,
Great freedom though but little pelf to spend !
Stand forth, I say, before me, Father blest ;
There are some doubts I'd fain have put to rest.

'Truly thou know'st e'en better how much tripe
Must go to stuff the cupboard of thy prog :
'Tis there are stowed more fish, flesh, onions ripe,
Than there be leaves in forest, field, or bog :
Thy scores of partridge, pheasant, woodcock, snipe,
Outnumber the sea sands, thou gorging dog !
Therefore I honour thee no more nor less
Than a beast filled with filth, a stinking cess.

'Bundle of guts, hast thou no shame to show
Thy visage to the eyes of living wight ?
Think'st thou that 'tis for nothing thou dost owe
Thy calling to Christ's sheepfold ?   By this light,
Judas the traitor did no worse, I know,
Than thou what time he sold his Lord at night ;
Caiaphas, Annas, Herod, Pilate, all
Helped Pluto less than thou man's soul to thrall.

'Think'st thou the Benedicts, Pauls, Anthonies,
Gave rules like thine unto their neophytes ?
They fed on lentils, beans, peas, cabbages,
Curbing their own rebellious appetites,
Not merely preaching how the spirit flees
From Satan's fraud and his accursèd rites ;
They slept on sand and marble cold, and sang
Psalms that through night and day unceasing rang.

' Quiet within their cells they stayed, nor dealt
On street or square with idle loitering bands ;
Kindly to wayfarers and meek, they knelt
To wash their feet, and not, like you, their hands ;
And when they left the cloisters where they dwelt,
To traverse hills or plains in foreign lands,
A staff or crutch upon their pilgrimage
Sufficed to prop the faltering steps of age.

' That frugal diet of plain herb and root
You've changed to-day for quails and partridges ;
Some miracle has turned to flesh their fruit,
Their acorns, brambles, and wild strawberries ;
The straw they slept on, hath grown dissolute
With down and cushions ; their lean visages
Are swathed in fat, with double, treble chins,
Red as the sun's face when the day begins.

' Their staves and crutches, O rare miracle
Wrought by these living Saints ! are steeds of price ;
Their reed-built cot, refectory or cell,
Soar into palaces that flout the skies ;
In many an Abbey now lewd strumpets dwell,
Hounds, hawks, the instruments of pride and vice :—
Fools, madmen, idiots, maniacs are ye,
Who've left to priests or friars your wealth in fee !

' What could be worse impiety than thus
To rob your lawful kindred of their own,
And squander it on those obstreperous
Bell-ringing monks, who let one voice alone
Speak in the Church for twenty ?—All that fuss
In praise of poverty is only shown
To bait beneath the shadow of their cowl
Some gudgeon, or birdlime some silly fowl ! '

Such things and others full of angry spite
Said Rayner, contrary to sober reason ;
For if a man should lose his temper quite,
Sense leaves him, he can't speak one word in season :

But when Church rights and wrongs their wrath excite,
I've noticed that your great men often seize on
Some crazy fad ; they fancy, O how silly !
That friars should feed on acorns, willy-nilly.

Then spake the Prior : ' Noble Lord and Sir !
With your forbearance I'll speak with precision.
Ecclesia Dei ne'er was known to err ;
You may have read in Tully this decision :
The Stagyrite, our sole interpreter
Of Gospel text, confirms this definition—
Quod merum Laicus non det judicare
Clericam Preti et Fratris scapulare.

' There is a gloss which lays down, *quod Prelatum*
Non est subjectus legi Constantina,
Affirmans eo quod nullum peccatum
Accidit in persona et re divina.
Et hoc deinceps fuit roboratum
In capite, Ne agro a Clementina.
Et princeps, qui de Ecclesia se impazzabit,
Scomunicatus cito publicabit.

' Saith *Thomas* in a text on which I've pored,
Second distinction of his Chapter *quo,*
Quod unde Spiritus Sanctum hath been stored,
Possibile non est for sin to accrue :
My life hath naught to hide, illustrious Lord,
In visu verbo et opera from you ;
For Christ himself our Saviour teaches that,
Speaking to all, *lux vestra luceat.*

' Behold and see how next my skin I wear
A shirt of wool instead of linen fine !
By hair-cloth of this texture you may swear
I circumspectly walk in duty's line.
Look now a little lower ! '—Free and fair
Laughed Rayner, when the excellent divine
Shows all he's got—an illustration purer
Than e'er occurred to Saint Bonaventura.

ORLANDINO VIII. 73.

I am no heretic, as to my shame
Before the common folk you christen me !
Perchance your lofty Reverence will claim
Me for a cut-throat, come from Saxony,
To wreak my violence on Rome's dread name !
Yet you are wrong : for, look you, Burgundy
Trusts less in German Bishops, or in French,
Or Spanish, than the mighty Roman Bench.

Far more I trust in the high Trinity,
In Father, Son, and eke the Spirit blest ;
In Mary's undefiled virginity,
Since God from her derived his fleshly vest ;
I trust in that inscrutable potency
Granted from God to man, by which behest
He dares, if his enormities be great,
Call himself, not God, but God's delegate.

It is my creed that the good Jesus wrought
All that He came to witness here below ;
I hold that the predicted sword he brought,
Came to bring peace on earth and also woe ;
I hold that a thief's tear, repentance-fraught,
Shuts Hell and opens Heaven ; and this I know
That the firm truth of what the Gospel saith,
Is nought but pure and uncorrupted Faith.

I hold that He was fair without one flaw,
Wore beard and locks around his shoulder sprent ;
I hold the Lamb's blood abrogates the law
And every type of that old Testament ;
Wherefore I hold there differs not a straw
Betwixt the tonsure and the hair unshent ;
But I believe the clergy still were known
For rebels to His work and will alone.

I hold that on the motion of a lewd
Pope of that year, with certain Pharisees,
Pilate did nail Him to the cruel wood
Between two thieves with fierce indignities ;

I hold that thence for men a pledge accrued,
And memory so sweet that still it frees
Us from God's righteous anger, and discloses
The veil that clung before the eyes of Moses.

I speak of His dire passion, and the boon
Most wondrous of His body and His blood,
Eating the which all persons late or soon
May quit those quails and grouse, their desert food ;
I hold that Christ seeks not for eyes that swoon,
Wry necks, and faces set to solemn mood,
But for the heart alone : this is my creed ;
If it be wrong, I waste vain breath indeed.

I hold that Hell exists, and Purgatory,
Beyond this world ; and here I prove it too :
Wherefore, in concert with S. Paul, I glory
In having passed those many trials through,
Not by my might but that great adjutory,
Who calls aloud with ringing voice and true ;
Perils mid hills and robbers, storms and fires,
Perils at sea, and perils from false friars !

My Saviour in the flesh I trust to see,
And hope for ever to enjoy His sight :—
But here the force of faith abandons me ;
Help then, thou Bishop, Great Albertus hight !
Son of Nichomachus, I turn to thee,
Dubbed Doctor of the Church by Thomas wight,
Without whose Metaphysic, as I've read,
The *Verbum Dei* were but ill bestead.

I hold that a lay sinner can repent ;
That Churchmen never are what they pretend—
I speak of bad ones :—d'you mistake my bent,
And in God's house defy me to contend ?—
Pray softly, softly ! It was never meant,
Good servants of our Lord, *your* fame to rend :
Nay, *you* I honour, since you please God duly ;
Places I'd change with *you* really and truly :

Gainst scapular and cord I've nought to tell,
Gainst cowl or tassel, breviary or book ;
That superstition need not choke you, well
I know ; you may be pious as you look :
I swear to all that no man here should smell
Disparagement to monks, from prior to cook ;
I'm aiming at those wolves and hirelings fairly,
Who give large orders and perform them sparely.

ORLANDO INNAMORATO, CANTO XX. THE SUPPRESSED
INDUCTION.

A brand-new story now compels my song,
To make the twentieth canto bright and clear,
Whence all the world shall plainly learn ere long
Some saints are not such saints as they appear ;
For cowls, grey, blue or black, a motley throng,
With dangling breviaries and brows severe,
And often naming on the lips our Lord,
While the heart's cold, no sanctity afford.

A cupping-glass upon your skull, a leech,
A blister, or a tonsure, are all one ;
It will not help you though you gird your breech
With several braces or with one alone ;
Or wear straight vestments, long and lank, that reach
Like coachmen's great-coats to your heels, or drone
Gibberish and Paternosters :—Sainthood needs
More than fair words for foul and filthy deeds.

The hands are where true charity begins ;
Not the mouth, face, or clothes : be mild, humane,
Reticent, sorry for your neighbour's sins,
Pitiful to his suffering and his pain :
Christians need wear no masks ; who wears them, wins
A backway to the fold, and brings it bane,
Scaling the wall by craft—a traitor he,
A thief and knave, who deals in subtlety.

These be that tribe of rogues and rascals whom
Our good Lord hates, the race on whom alone
In wrath he uttered that tremendous doom,
Though every other fault he could condone :
Ye whited sepulchres, ye living tomb,
Fire on the surface, in the soul a stone !
Why will ye wash the outside of the platter ?
First cleanse your heart—that is the graver matter !

'Tis said by some that by-and-by the good
Pope and his Prelates will reform their ways :
I tell you that a turnip has no blood,
Nor sick folk health, nor can you hope to raise
Syrup from vinegar to sauce your food :
The Church will be reformed when summer days
Come without gad-flies, when a butcher's store
Has neither bones nor dogs about the door.

Sanga, this lewd age is an age of lead,
Whence Truth is banished both in deed and word :
You're called a fool, poor-spirited, ill-bred,
If you but name S. Peter and our Lord :
Where'er you walk, where'er you turn your head,
Some rascal hypocrite, with scowl abhorred,
Snarls twixt his teeth ' Freethinker ! Lutheran !'—
And Lutheran means, you know, good Christian.

Those grasping priests have thrown a net full wide :
With bells and anthems, altar-cloth and cope,
They lift their well-decked shrines on every side,
Bent upon life eternal—sorry hope !
This wooden image is the sailor's pride,
That plastered face the soldier's ; piss-pots slope
In rows to Cosmo and S. Damian ;
The pox belongs to stout Sebastian.

Baron S. Anthony hides fire in heart,
Thoughts of the donkey and the swine in head ;
Whence comes it that all monks in every part
Stuff paunch and wallet with flesh, wine, and bread :

Yon Abbot, like Silenus, fills a cart ;
Yon Cardinal's a Bacchus overfed ;
The Pope through Europe sells, a second Mars,
Bulls and indulgences to feed his wars.

The Word of God, aroused from its long trance,
Runs like live fire abroad through Germany ;
The work continues, as the days advance,
Unmasking that close-cloaked iniquity,
Which with a false and fraudulent countenance
So long imposed on France, Spain, Italy :
Now by the grace of God we've learned in sooth
What mean the words Church, Charity, Hope, Truth.

O the great goodness of our heavenly Sire !
Behold, his Son once more appears on high,
Treads under foot the proud rebellious ire
Of faithless Churchmen, who by threat and lie
Strove to conceal the Love that did inspire
The mighty Maker of earth, sea, and sky,
What time he served, and bore our flesh, and trod
With blood the path that leads man back to God.

None speaks in this lost land of his pure blood,
That sinless blood of Christ, both God and man,
Which quelled the serpent's stiff and venomous brood,
The powers malign that reigned where Lethe ran !
In his fair bleeding limbs he slew the lewd
Old Adam from whose sin our woes began,
Appeased his Father's wrath, and on the door
Of impious Hell set bars for evermore.

This is that seed thrice holy and thrice blest,
Promised to our first parents, which doth bring
Unto the stairs of heaven our hope oppressed !
This is that puissant and victorious king,
Whose foot treads man's misjudgment on the crest !
This is that calm clear light, whose sunbeams fling
Shade on the souls and darkness o'er the eyes
Of fools in this world's knowledge vainly wise !

O Christians, with the hearts of Hebrews ! Ye
Who make a mortal man your chief and head,
Of these new Pharisees first Pharisee !
Your soaring and immortal pinions spread
For that starred shrine, where, through eternity,
The Lamb of God is Pope, whose heart once bled
That men, blind men, from yon pure fount on high
Might seek indulgence full and free for aye !

Yet that cooked crayfish hath the face to pray,
Kneeling in chapel opposite that crow,
That Antichrist, upon some holy day—
'Thou art our sail, our rudder !'—when we know
The simple truth requires that he should say
'Thou art the God of ruin and of woe,
Father of infinite hypocrisies,
Of evil customs and all heresies ! '—

O Sanga, for our lord Verona's sake,
Put by your Virgil, lay Lucretius down,
Ovid, and him in whom such joy you take,
Tully, of Latin eloquence the crown !
With arms out-spread, our heart's arms, let us make
To Him petition, who, without our own
Merit or diligence or works, can place
Our souls in heaven, made worthy by his grace !

And prithee see that Molza is aware,
And Navagero, and Flaminio too,
That here far other things should be our care
Than Janus, Flora, Thetis, and the crew
Of Homer's gods, who paint their page so fair !
Here we experience the false and true ;
Here find that Sun, which shows, without, within,
That man by nature is compact of sin.

O good Fregoso, who hast shut thine ear
To all those siren songs of Poesy,
Abiding by the mirror keen and clear,
In joyance of divine Philosophy,

Both Testaments, Old, New, to thee are dear!
Thou hast outworn that ancient phantasy
Which led thee once with Fondulo to call
Plato the link twixt Peter and S. Paul!—

But now Gradasso calls me; I am bid
Back to the follies of my Paladins—
        &c. &c.

APPENDIX III.

On Palmieri's ' Città di Vita.'   (*To illustrate Part I. p.* 171.)

IN the first part of this sketch of Italian literary history (*Renaissance in Italy*, vol. iv. p. 171, note 2) I promised, if possible, to give some further notice of Palmieri's poem entitled the *Città di Vita*. This promise I was unable to fulfil in the proper place. But while my book was going through the press, I obtained the necessary materials for such a study of Palmieri's work through the courtesy of a Florentine scholar, Signor A. Gherardi, who sent me extracts from a MS. existing in the Laurentian Library. This MS., which is an illuminated parchment codex, contains, besides the poem, the commentary of Lionardo Dati, with his Life of the author and two of his letters addressed to Palmieri. Whether or not the codex is an autograph, remains uncertain. But it has this singular interest, that Matteo Palmieri himself presented it to the Art of the Notaries in Florence, sealed and under the express condition that it should not be opened so long as he lived imprisoned in his body—' ut non aperiatur dum in suo religatus corpusculo vivat.' After his death, the Republic decreed a public funeral to their honoured magistrate and servant ; and the MS. in question was placed upon his breast in the church of S. Pier Maggiore, where he was interred in the family chapel of the Palmieri. Alamanno Rinuccini pronounced the panegyrical oration on this occasion ; and in his speech he alluded to 'this bulky volume which lies upon his breast, a poem in *terza rima*, called by him the City of Life.'

It would appear, from the circumstance of the volume having been presented under seal to the Art of the Notaries, that Palmieri, while wishing to secure the safety of his poem, was aware of its liability to censure. What he may have dreaded, happened after his decease ; for his opinions were condemned as heretical, and the picture Botticelli painted for him in illustration of his views, was removed from its place in the Palmieri Chapel of S. Pier Maggiore. This picture is now in the possession of the Duke of Hamilton.

The MS. of the *Città di Vita* passed from the Art of the Notaries into the Laurentian Library. Since the biographical notices from the pen of Palmieri's friend, Lionardo Dati, which this MS. contains, form our most trustworthy source of information about the poet's life, it may be well to preface the account of his poem with an abstract of their contents. Matteo Palmieri was a member of an honourable Florentine family. Born in 1405, he received his first education in grammar from Sozomeno of Pistoja. Afterwards he studied Greek and Latin letters in the schools of Carlo Aretino and Ambrogio Traversari. In early manhood he entered public life, and passed through the various Florentine magistracies to the dignity of Gonfalonier of Justice. The Signory employed him upon embassies to Calixtus III., Frederick III., Alfonso the Magnanimous and Paul II. Matteo devoted his leisure to study and composition. The treatise *Della Vita Civile*, which he wrote in Italian, was a work of his adolescence. Then followed, in Latin, a Life of Niccolò Acciaiolo, a narrative of the successful war with Pisa, and a Universal History, which was subsequently continued by Mattia Palmieri—a Pisan, who, though he bore the same name, was in no wise related to our author. The *Città di Vita* was a work of his mature age. He died probably in 1478.

Matteo told Lionardo Dati that on the first of August 1451, while he was living at Pescia as Governor of the Val di Nievole, he dreamed that his dead friend Cipriano Rucellai appeared to him, and invited him to the yearly festival which was celebrated on that day in a monastery, called Il Paradiso, near Florence. In his dream, Matteo accompanied the ghost of Cipriano, conversing on the way about the state of spirits after death—where they dwell, and how they are permitted to revisit their living friends. Cipriano, moreover, revealed to him weighty matters concerning the nature of the human soul. He told him how God first made angels in innumerable hosts. These angels separated into three companies.

The one band followed Lucifer, when he rebelled. The second held with Michael and abode firm in their allegiance. The third decided neither for God nor for the Devil. After Lucifer's defeat, these angels of the third class were relegated to the Elysian fields, which extend at all points over the extreme periphery of the highest sphere ; and God, wishing to give them a final chance of determining for good or evil, ordained that they should, one by one, be sent to dwell in human bodies. There, attended by a good and a bad spirit, they have the choice of lives, and after their death in the body, are drafted into the trains of Lucifer or Michael according to their conduct. Having communicated this doctrine, Cipriano vanished from his friend's sight with these words upon his lips :

> Misero ad noi quanto mal segno
> Rizoron quelli che si fer ribelli
> Per porre in aquilon loco più degno.

Palmieri forgot or neglected the import of his dream until the year 1455, when he was at Alfonso's Court in Naples. There Cipriano appeared to him again, rebuked him for his careless-ness, and bade him write a poem in *terza rima*, after Dante's method, on the subject of their former discourse. He also recommended him three books, which would assist him in the labour. When Palmieri returned to Florence, he obtained these helps and set about the composition of his poem. It must have been completed in 1464 ; for in this year Dati received a copy, which he styled *opus pæne divinum*, and began to annotate. In 1466 Dati wrote again to Palmieri, thanking him for an emended copy of the work, which the author had sent him from Florence to Rome. Palmieri's own letter accompanying the gift, refers to the poem as already published. This proves (as would, indeed, appear from the title given him by Ficino of *Poeta Theologicus*) that, whatever may have been his dread of a prosecution for heresy, he had at least divulged the *Città di Vita* to the learned.

The poem consists of three books, divided, like Dante's *Commedia*, into one hundred Cantos ; but the extra Canto has by Palmieri been assigned to the last instead of the first Cantica. The title *Città di Vita* was given to it, because Palmieri designed to bring the universe into consideration under the aspect of spiritual existence. The universe, as he conceived it, is the burgh in which all souls live. His object was to show how free-will is innate in men, who have the choice of good and evil, of salvation or perdition, in this life. The origin of evil he relegates to that prehistoric moment of Lucifer's revolt, when the third class of angels refused to side with either God or Devil. In the first book, then, he describes how these angels are transmitted from the Elysian fields to earth, in order that they may become men, and in their mortal body be forced to exercise their faculty of election. In the second book he treats of the way of perdition. In the third book he deals with the way of salvation. Following Dante's precedent in the choice of Virgil, he takes the Sibyl for his guide upon the beginning of this visionary journey.

The heretical portions of the *Città di Vita* are Cantos v. ix. x. xi. of the first Cantica. These deal with the original creation of angelic essences, and with the transit of the indeterminate angels to our earth. Regarding the universe from the Ptolemaic point of view, Palmieri conceives that these angels, who inhabit the Elysian fields beyond the utmost verge of the stellar spheres, proceed on their earthward journey through the several planets, till they reach our globe, which is the centre of the whole. On their way, they gradually submit to animal impressions and prepare themselves for incarnation, according to that conception which made the human soul itself in a certain sense corporeal. It is here that Palmieri adjusts the theory of planetary influences to his theory of free-will. For he supposes that the angels assimilate the qualities of the planetary spheres as they pass through them, being attracted by curiosity to one planet rather than another. At the same time they undergo the action of the three superior elements, which fits them for their final reception into an earthy habitation. After this wise he ingeniously combined his theories of the Creation, the Fall, and Free will, with Averroistic doctrines of intermediate intelligences and speculations collected from Platonistic writings.

The path of the descending angels is, to quote the words of Dati, 'in a straight line beneath the first point of Cancer to the cave of earth, in which line there are ten gates, for each of the planets to wit, and for the three super-terrestrial elements each his gate. The whole of this vast body of the universe is by our poet called the City of Life, forasmuch as in this universe all creatures live. And this journey of the souls from Elysium to their bodies is performed in one year.' It will be observed that Palmieri affected the precision of his master Dante. Having thus conducted the soul to earth, he is no less definite in his description of the two ways, which severally lead to damnation and salvation. In the second Cantica, he employs the space of a whole year compressed into one night, in passing through the eighteen mansions of the passions of the flesh, fortune and the mind. For this journey he has the guidance of an evil spirit. Afterwards, in the third Cantica, he employs the same space of one year compressed into a single day, in traversing the twelve mansions of civil virtue and purgation, through which the soul arrives at beatific life. In this voyage he is guided by a good angel. It is not necessary to enter further into the calculations whereby Palmieri adjusts the chronology and cosmography of his vision to the Ptolemaic theory of the universe.

Though the material of the poem is thus curious, and the structure thus ingenious, it does not rise in style above the level of the works of Frezzi and Uberti (see above, vol. iv. chap. 3). In order to give the reader a specimen of its composition, I will extract a passage from Cantica I. Canto v., which concerns the Divine Being and the Creation of Angels:

> Sopra ogn' altro potere è questo tale,
>   che come e' vuole in tutto può giovare,
>   sanza potenza di voler far male.
> Tal carità volendo ad altri dare
>   la gloria in sè, (?) di se stesso godeva,
>   degnò co' cieli ancor la terra fare.
> Et perche cosa far non si poteva
>   che eterno bene in ciel sempre godesse,
>   se sempre quel goder non intendeva ;
> Intelligenza bisognò facesse
>   con lume di ragione et immortale,
>   ad chi l' eterno ben tutto si desse.

Creatura fè per questo rationale,
  l' angelo et l' huomo acciò che 'l sommo bene
  godessono intendendo quel che e' vale.
Da 'ntenderlo et amar di ragion vene
  volerlo possedere, et con letitia
  per sempre usar sanza timor di pene.
Ad questo Idio creò la gran militia
  del celestiale exercitio et felice,
  che 'n parte cadde per la sua malitia.

INDEX.

TRANSLATIONS IN VERSE BY AUTHOR.

Errata.

LONDON : PRINTED BY
SPOTTISWOODE AND CO., NEW-STREET SQUARE
AND PARLIAMENT STREET